Climate Change, Policy and Security

This book examines the multiple strategies proposed by the international community for addressing global climate change (GCC) from both human and state-security perspectives.

It examines what is needed from major states working within the UN framework to engage with the multiple dimensions of a strategy that addresses GCC and its impacts, where such engagement promotes both human and state security. Two broad frameworks for approaching these issues provide the basis of discussion for the individual chapters, which discuss the strategies being undertaken by major state powers (the US, the EU, China, India, Japan, and Russia). The first framework considers the multiple strategies, mitigation, adaptation, and capacity-building required of the international community to address the effects of GCC. The second framework considers the differentiation of GCC policies in terms of security and how the efficacy of these strategies could be impacted by whether priority is given to state security over human security concerns.

This book will be of much interest to students of human security, climate change, foreign policy, and International Relations.

Don Wallace is Professor Emeritus of Criminal Justice at the University of Central Missouri, USA.

Daniel Silander is Associate Professor in Political Science at the Department of Political Science, Linnaeus University, Sweden.

Series: Routledge Studies in Human Security
Series Editors: Mary Martin
London School of Economics
and
Taylor Owen
University of Oxford

The aim of this series is to provide a coherent body of academic and practitioner insight that is capable of stimulating further consideration of the concept of human security, its impact on security scholarship and on the development of new security practices.

The European Union and Human Security
External Interventions and Missions
Edited by Mary Martin and Mary Kaldor

National, European and Human Security
From Co-Existence to Convergence
Edited by Mary Martin, Mary Kaldor and Narcís Serra

State Responses to Human Security
At Home and Abroad
Edited by Courtney Hillebrecht, Tyler White and Patrice McMahon

Human Security, Changing States and Global Responses
Institutions and Practices
Edited by Sangmin Bae and Makoto Maruyama

Gendering Human Security in Afghanistan
In a Time of Western Intervention
Ben Walter

EU Global Strategy and Human Security
Rethinking Approaches to Conflict
Edited by Mary Kaldor, Iavor Rangelov and Sabine Selchow

Climate Change, Policy and Security
State and Human Impacts
Edited by Donald Wallace and Daniel Silander

For more information about this series, please visit: www.routledge.com/Routledge-Studies-in-Human-Security/book-series/HSS

Climate Change, Policy and Security

State and Human Impacts

Edited by Donald Wallace and
Daniel Silander

LONDON AND NEW YORK

First published 2018
by Routledge
2 Park Square, Milton Park, Abingdon, Oxon OX14 4RN

and by Routledge
711 Third Avenue, New York, NY 10017

Routledge is an imprint of the Taylor & Francis Group, an informa business

© 2018 selection and editorial matter, Donald Wallace and Daniel
Silander; individual chapters, the contributors

The right of Donald Wallace and Daniel Silander to be identified as the
authors of the editorial matter, and of the authors for their individual
chapters, has been asserted in accordance with sections 77 and 78 of the
Copyright, Designs and Patents Act 1988.

All rights reserved. No part of this book may be reprinted or reproduced or
utilized in any form or by any electronic, mechanical, or other means, now
known or hereafter invented, including photocopying and recording, or in
any information storage or retrieval system, without permission in writing
from the publishers.

Trademark notice: Product or corporate names may be trademarks or
registered trademarks, and are used only for identification and explanation
without intent to infringe.

British Library Cataloguing-in-Publication Data
A catalogue record for this book is available from the British Library

Library of Congress Cataloging-in-Publication Data
Names: Wallace, Donald (Donald H.), editor. | Silander, Daniel, 1972– editor.
Title: Climate change, policy, and security : state and human impacts /
edited by Donald Wallace and Daniel Silander.
Description: Abingdon, Oxon : Routledge, 2018. | Series: Routledge studies
in human security | Includes bibliographical references and index.
Identifiers: LCCN 2017059156| ISBN 9781138481336 (hardback) |
ISBN 9781351060479 (e-book)
Subjects: LCSH: Climatic changes–Political aspects. | Climatic changes–
International cooperation. | National security. | Natural disasters–Prevention.
Classification: LCC QC903 .C56327 2018 | DDC 363.738/7456–dc23
LC record available at https://lccn.loc.gov/2017059156

ISBN: 978-1-138-48133-6 (hbk)
ISBN: 978-1-351-06047-9 (ebk)

Typeset in Times New Roman
by Wearset Ltd, Boldon, Tyne and Wear

Contents

List of contributors — vii

1 **Introduction: security and global climate change** — 1
DON WALLACE

2 **The UN regime on global climate change** — 41
DON WALLACE

3 **Geography of GCC: Asia-Pacific—human and state security** — 67
PATRICK D. NUNN AND CAROLA BETZOLD

4 **Geography of GCC: the climate-security nexus in Africa** — 86
DANIEL SILANDER

5 **The United States and global climate change** — 106
NIALL MICHELSEN

6 **The European Union and global climate change** — 131
MARTIN NILSSON

7 **China and global climate change** — 150
DANIEL SILANDER AND MARTIN NILSSON

8 **India and global climate change** — 169
JOHN JANZEKOVIC

9 **Japan and global climate change** — 192
DARLENE BUDD

vi *Contents*

10 Russia and global climate change   216

ANA KARAMAN

11 Conclusion: state powers on global climate change—lessons learned   235

DANIEL SILANDER AND DON WALLACE

Index   251

Contributors

Carola Betzold is a Lecturer of Political Science at the University of Göttingen and Research Fellow at the University of Antwerp's Institute for Development Policy and Management. Her research centers on environmental and in particular climate change politics, with a focus on small island developing states. Carola obtained her PhD from ETH Zurich.

Darlene Budd is a Professor of Political Science and the Director of the International Studies program at the University of Central Missouri, USA. She teaches classes and has conducted research on Asian politics, women and politics, globalization and international studies. She received her PhD in Political Science from the University of Wisconsin-Milwaukee.

John Janzekovic is a Lecturer of Politics and International Relations at the University of the Sunshine Coast, Australia. He is also a Non-resident Teaching and Research Fellow at Linnaeus University in Vaxjo, Sweden. John's research interests include international and humanitarian law, interventionist politics, peace and conflict studies, human rights, terrorism and military ethics. He received his PhD in Political Science from the University of the Sunshine Coast.

Ana Karaman is Vice President and Chief Financial Officer (CFO) of Webster University, USA. She holds a PhD in political science from the University of Wisconsin-Milwaukee. She has served two National Science Foundation Fellowships; the first at Harvard University and the second at Princeton University. She also graduated with a degree in jurisprudence from the Far-Eastern State University in Vladivostok, Russia

Niall Michelsen is an Associate Professor of Political Science and Public Affairs at Western Carolina University, USA. He earned a PhD in Political Science at the University of North Carolina, Chapel Hill. He has published on strategic issues, politics of international organizations, and on the scholarship of teaching and learning.

Martin Nilsson is a Senior Lecturer of Political Science at Linnaeus University, Sweden. He earned his PhD in Political Science from the School of Social

Sciences at Växjö University, Sweden, and has conducted research on European organizations, democratization, and politics in Latin America and Europe.

Patrick D. Nunn is a Professor of Geography at the University of the Sunshine Coast in Australia. He earned a PhD on Quaternary landscape evolution at University College London. Patrick's main research interests for the past 30 years have focused on the Pacific Basin, particularly in the area of climate change; he was a Lead Author of the chapter on 'Sea Level Change' in the most recent IPCC assessment report (AR5).

Daniel Silander is an Associate Professor of Political Science at Linnaeus University, Sweden. He received his PhD at the School of Social Sciences at Växjö University, Sweden, and has conducted research on international politics, democracy and democratization, human security, and humanitarian interventions.

Don Wallace is a Professor of Criminal Justice at the University of Central Missouri, USA, where he teaches and has published on counter-terrorism and civil liberties, the death penalty, and international human rights. He holds an LLM in International Law from the University of Missouri-Kansas City and a JD from the University of Nebraska.

1   Introduction
Security and global climate change

Don Wallace

In the nineteenth century Swedish physical chemist Svante Arrhenius was the first to quantify a connection between human industrialization and the warming of the planet. His 1896 paper observed that the reflective property of atmospheric carbon dioxide could raise global temperatures. Yet, there was no distress in this prediction. Instead, Arrhenius foresaw considerable benefit from increased anthropogenic carbon discharges that might result in a warmer climate preventing another ice age and increasing food production (Nagel, 2010).

This sanguine view stands in complete contrast to the present-day alarm that has arisen from the seeming existential challenges presented by the impacts of global climate change (GCC). Yet, despite this recent recognition of the potential for disaster posed by GCC, the international community is only slowly developing strategies to address this phenomenon. The limited promise of the 2015 Paris Climate Agreement in which nations agreed merely to make voluntary pledges to reduce carbon emissions was placed in turmoil in 2017 by the United States (US) opting to withdraw from the agreement. With the growing global recognition of the challenges posed by the changes to the Earth's atmosphere there has been an expanding discourse of the concept of national and international security that some observers argue should include the impacts of GCC and, consequentially, there has been a call for political actors to include such environmental issues in national and international security agendas. The international community and major power nations variously conceptualize the effects of GCC as a major environmental concern that challenges human security or as leading to violent conflicts that pose threats to state security. The choice of perspectives on the consequences of GCC, either as a threat to human security or to state security, can impact the likelihood of success for the strategies needed to address GCC. Various national military institutions have been issuing statements regarding the emerging threat to state security due to the increasing potential of conflicts over basic resources, whereas an earlier recognition of GCC was viewed in the context of a growing risk to human security due to a shortfall of basic resources.

Among the many crises presently confronting the international community, the impacts of GCC reside on a unique plane in their comprehensiveness, raising challenges for all human society. As such, they necessitate both international and

2 Don Wallace

national responses for solutions (Snyder & Binder, 2009). The challenge for the international community is finding a means to respond to this complex environmental challenge through a coordinated and comprehensive framework (de Chazournes, 2014). No one country can prevent, let alone adequately address, the impacts of climate change. As observed by the United Nations Development Programme (UNDP), collective action is not an option but an imperative (UNDP, 2008, p. 12). However, the international community remains dominated by powerful states and the overriding concern for protection of their sovereignty and security.

This book examines the multiple strategies proposed by the international community for addressing GCC from the human and state security perspectives of major states. The examination will discuss the challenges for these states for addressing broad and possibly conflicting concerns of human and state security as they implement GCC strategies of mitigation, adaptation, and capacity building. Serving as an introduction to the project of this book, this first chapter considers whether concerns for state security may be counterproductive to the interests of human security in the context of these GCC strategies. In this examination, the first part of this chapter considers the developments in the recognition of GCC by the international community in addition to an overview of the identified threats to the environment. This part of the chapter examines the progress that has been made and remains to be accomplished by the international community for addressing GCC. The first part of this chapter outlines the development of GCC as a security issue and its securitization. The second part provides an overview of the concerns of state and human security in the context of GCC. The third part then delineates the strategies of mitigation, adaptation, and capacity-building that the international community is proposing to address GCC. The next part discusses how varying conceptions of security could impact these strategies for addressing the challenges of GCC. This part also discusses the role of major powers in implementing these GCC strategies and the potential of frustration for the success of these strategies when values of human security confront securitization processes for concerns of state security. An overview of the project of this book is presented to conclude this chapter.

The international recognition of GCC and its threats

In 1972 Sweden again provided a role in the recognition of the impact of human activity on the climate by organizing the United Nations Conference on the Human Environment with the United Nations General Assembly (UNGA). This was the first international conference to systematically evaluate global environmental issues and led to the Stockholm Declaration and the subsequent formation of the United Nations Environment Programme (UNEP). This was a seminal event in the history of international environmental politics (Conca & Dabelko, 2014), raising popular and political awareness of environmental change and the causal role of humans (Linnér & Selin, 2003). In 1988 the UNEP and the World Meteorological Organization furthered the internationalization of GCC as an environmental issue by establishing the Intergovernmental Panel on Climate Change (IPCC). The UNGA endorsed the IPCC in late 1988 to provide internationally coordinated scientific assessments on the impact of climate change and realistic response strategies. These activities culminated in the 1992 Earth Summit in Rio de Janeiro, which yielded the Convention on Biological Diversity, the action plan of Agenda 21, and the United Nations Framework Convention on Climate Change (UNFCCC). The UNFCCC is the principal UN convention addressing GCC and epitomizes a global understanding "that change in the Earth's climate and its adverse effects are a common concern of humankind" (UNFCCC, 1992, Preamble). The negotiations undertaken within the UNFCCC framework have eventually resulted in a recent international instrument for the global community to deal with GHG emissions, the 2015 Paris Climate Agreement. This instrument focuses on efforts starting in the year 2020 for mitigation of GHG emissions, adaptation measures, and financial support of nations addressing the effects of GCC. The 2015 Paris Agreement articulates a goal for holding the increase in the global average temperature to "well below 2°C above pre-industrial levels and pursuing efforts to limit the temperature increase to 1.5°C" (UNFCCC, 2015a).

The IPCC has compiled extensive, highly scrutinized data and through its periodic reports has become the source of the internationally accepted science on climate change that is relied on by governments around the world. In 2007, the IPCC (2007) reached the conclusion that "warming of the climate system is unequivocal." In the fourth assessment review, the IPCC presented an immense scientific consensus that GCC is not only real, but also human caused (UNDP, 2008, p. 12). In 2014, the IPCC issued its most recent synthesis report concerning GCC, where it provided an estimate that average global temperature increases are on course to range from 3.2° to 7.2°F (1.8° to 4.0°C) during the twenty-first century, and that GHG atmospheric concentration levels will reach 550 ppm by 2050 (IPCC, 2014a). It will be necessary to achieve stabilization of concentrations at a level below 400 ppm to allow for some certainty that global temperature increases will not exceed the Paris Agreement's less ambitious goal of an increase of 2°C. In April 2016, at its 43rd Session, the IPCC agreed that its next Synthesis Report would be finalized in time for the first UNFCCC global stocktake when nations examine their progress towards the Paris Agreement climate goals (IPCC, 2016). The steady flow of compelling and too visible evidence underscores the large base of scientific certainty on the issue (Wallace, 2009; for a contrary perspective see Hertzberg & Schreuder, 2016).

In its 2014 report, the IPCC observed that climatic heat waves will very likely occur more frequently for longer durations. As the oceans get warmer, the global mean sea level will continue to rise. According to one of the IPCC prediction models, sustained substantial warming could result in the near-complete loss of the Greenland ice sheet and over a millennium could contribute to a global mean sea level rise of up to seven meters (IPCC, 2014a). The IPCC projected that GCC will intensify existing risks and create new ones for biological systems. Marine organisms will face progressively lower oxygen levels and higher magnitudes of ocean acidification with associated risks exacerbated by rising ocean temperature extremes, and with coral reefs and polar ecosystems being highly vulnerable. Many surface plant and many animal species cannot naturally shift their geographical ranges sufficiently fast to keep up with current and projected rates of climate change and will face increased risk of extinction (IPCC, 2014a).

The IPCC observed that, at present, increases in the frequency and intensity of ecosystem disturbances, such as extreme weather events, droughts, windstorms, cyclones, wildfires, retreating glaciers, and pestilence outbreaks, have been detected in many parts of the world (IPCC, 2014a, p. 51). In addition, global warming is acknowledged by scientists to exacerbate vector-borne and water-borne diseases (Beard & Eisen, 2016; Trtanj & Jantarasami, 2016; Physicians for Social Responsibility, n.d.). The earliest and most direct of the various negative consequences arising from GCC will be those that impact fresh water systems around the world (Eckstein, 2009). With the great variability in weather patterns across the globe, the impacts will not be uniform, as some areas of the Earth will have substantially more precipitation and others much less.

Despite these predictions concerning the environmental impacts of GCC, compromises appear to have been made within that part of the international community that has consistently agreed on the validity of GCC and the urgent need to address it. Flowers (2011) observed that although the IPCC is posited as the international body providing the critically needed scientific findings on GCC, it too, has been accused of some capitulation to pressure from major countries whose economic policies are greatly influenced by the fossil fuels industry; thus, the grim findings of the IPCC might be actually minimizing the impacts of GCC. Even if the pledges made by the parties under the Paris Agreement are fulfilled, global temperatures will continue to rise until at least the year 2030 (Kohona, 2016). The pledges made by the Parties as of early 2017 are not sufficient for the reductions that are needed to keep average global temperature from rising above 2°C, and certainly not for the more aspirational goal of 1.5°C (Mathai & Narayan, 2017; Höhne et al., 2016; Bodle et al., 2016). These pledges, as of November 1, 2016, are estimated to "limit warming to about 3.16°C above pre-industrial levels, or in probabilistic terms ... below 3.5°C" (Climate Action Tracker, 2017). In its annual Emission Gap Report (Vega, 2016), the UNEP urged the world, in order to meet the targets set under the Paris Agreement, to 'dramatically' step up efforts to cut greenhouse gas emissions—by some 25% more than already pledged (UN News Centre, 2016).

GCC, security, and securitization

The above section alluded to the detrimental impacts of GCC on the environment and the struggle of the international community to achieve the political momentum to adequately addressing the phenomenon. This section of the chapter considers the consequences of GCC for international state and human security. Security as an international ideal was once defined exclusively in terms of state security, where regard was for the protection of the sovereignty of the affected state from organized violence. With the recognition of the challenges presented by environmental degradation scholars have seen an enlarged scope to the discussion in security studies that includes GCC (Barnett, 2003). Today, there is a greater discussion asserting a position that state security is incomplete without including a goal of human security. This discussion has stressed how state sovereignty embeds human security and how state sovereignty is dependent on human security (Pumphrey, 2008).

State-centric security

The traditional understanding of state security, limited to protecting the state from organized violence, would not have included GCC as a matter of concern. Yet, there was some recognition dating to the 1970s that environmental degradation could constitute threats that were not limited to the well-being of humans, but also to national security (Conca & Dabelko, 2014). There are those who continue to oppose any broadening of the traditional understanding of security for fear that the very term will become devoid of meaning (e.g., Deudney, 1990).

There has been a move for modification to the traditional perspectives of state-oriented constructs of security to place GCC issues on the security agendas of nations and international organizations. Buzan's innovative work, *People, States and Fear* (1983) asserted that the traditional concept of security is too narrowly focused on threats to states and does not comport to a post-Cold War reality. The traditional understanding of state-centric security, based in terms of military aspects, could not adequately account for emerging present-day threats. Several observers (Ullman, 1983; Trombetta, 2008; Floyd, 2010; Detraz & Betsill, 2009; Diez et al., 2016) have argued for expanding from a narrow perspective limited to a military conception of security, to one that would include challenges to environmental quality. States have progressively placed more issues under a security rubric to include matters of economic distress, and natural disasters, in addition to terrorism and civil disturbances. As such it has become increasingly difficult to delineate the outer contours of the concept (Agamben, 2005). Security, then, can serve government leaders by expanding to include political, economic, social, and, importantly, environmental concerns (Spring, 2008; Hassan, 1991). GCC has become a multifaceted issue presenting a state security threat for all nations (Çolakoğlu, 2017).

Despite the conceptual dilemmas, the broadening of the concept of security to include environmental challenges, according to Trombetta (2008) and Diez et al. (2016), has supporters from a strategic perspective who promote the efforts to address these concerns on the political agendas of national and international political authorities. With GCC, a challenging consideration stems from the recognition that there is no external adversary, as is necessitated by the traditional perspective of security. Rather, humans are not just the object of the threat but also the cause of the threat (Diez et al., 2016). As Brauch (2008b, p. 3) observed:

6 *Don Wallace*

[The e]nemy is us, not 'they', it is 'us' 'our consumptive behaviour' and 'our use of fossil fuels' (coal, oil, gas) and that of previous generations since the outset of the Industrial Revolution (*c.*1750) that has been accumulated in the atmosphere and has become the cause of a rapid anthropogenic climate change.

Securitization

The traditional perspective on security is limited to threats from organized violence confronting a state. In a post-Cold War context, it becomes less obvious how non-immediate threats and their concomitant political issues become aspects of security under this older perspective. To this an active discourse has developed on examining the process through which a political issue, such as developing the strategies for confronting GCC, would become considered a security threat.

The origination of the term "securitization" is associated with the Copenhagen School of Security Studies, led by Buzan (1983), Waever (1995) and de Wilde (Buzan et al., 1998). This term is used to denote the process by which a political issue becomes represented as an existential threat. This process consists of some manipulation of the relevant audience into accepting that an issue should be treated as a significant security matter. The relevant audience need not necessarily be the general public, but could be a relevant political leadership. For example, Melley (2012) observed in his assessment of the growth of clandestine institutions in the US since World War II that the manipulation can have an audience within the political leadership as a consequence of the covert institutional infrastructure of a state.

In the process of securitization, once the issue becomes securitized, the emergency measures of the governmental organization become enabled (McDonald, 2008), thus permitting the political leaders to employ exceptional or extraordinary measures, not typically allowed during normal democratic processes. Under the original formulation of securitization by the Copenhagen school there is a strict distinction between normal politics and exceptional or extraordinary measures, which are to be used to address the threat (Diez et al., 2016). This element of exceptionalism becomes frequently present in routinized politics of security concerns (Agamben, 2002). Pease (2009) documented this phenomenon for US society where the manipulation of various threatening concerns over the decades have convinced Americans that they should surrender some civil liberties in exchange for an illusion of security.

Many researchers, according to Diez et al. (2016), have criticized the narrowness of traditional definition of the term, "securitizing." This term is seen to have been modeled on the logic of military security and the traditional perspective provides imprecise definitions of extraordinary measures and of the audience; and it neglects routine measures that, nonetheless, amount to security policies. Typically, the government of the state would be the lead agent in the securitization process, where the government fulfills its national responsibility of promoting security for the state against organized conflict. There has been a framing of the consequences of GCC as a broad threat to both human and state security, thus including domestic and international order (Scott, 2012). Thus, the understanding of the perspectives of major powers for engaging the security challenges posed by GCC become of paramount importance. The concerns over the impacts of GCC have led to international organizations becoming securitizing actors. As will be discussed in Chapter 2, the UN Security Council (UNSC) in 2007 for the first time addressed the impact of GCC as a security danger; in this regard, though with no formal resolution being made, the UNSC securitized the GCC issue (Scott, 2012). Additionally, Brauch (2008b) observed that the IPCC became a securitizing actor, where in its 2007 Fourth Assessment Report it urged that global society take on exceptional policy measures ensuring state security.

GCC and threats to security

This section examines the consequences of GCC in terms of the environmental impact on security, both state and human. The discussion recognizes the divergent directions for national and international policy regarding GCC where one form of security becomes prioritized over the other. In this section, there is consideration of the process of securitization of political issues as it relates to GCC. The various vulnerabilities to GCC are not limited to specific regions in the world. GCC has already had a great impact on human security around the world; "Nothing and nobody is immune from its reach" (Eaton, 2008, p. 789). In 2007, the *Bulletin of the Atomic Scientists* found the dangers posed by GCC to be nearly as dire as those presented by nuclear weapons. The *Bulletin* observed that though the short-term dangers posed by GCC are less dramatic than the destruction by nuclear devices, over the next three to four decades the harm caused by GCC could threaten the survival of human society (Donohue, 2011). For the year 2016, the *Bulletin* found that the international community has so far failed to meet the challenges effectively with these two most pressing existential threats confronting humanity; the Doomsday Clock was reset 30 seconds closer to midnight, the closest to the end of its proverbial day that the clock has been in decades (Mecklin, 2017).

In the first cost-benefit analysis of GCC to be issued with the imprimatur of a major government (Cole, 2008b) the Stern Review on the Economics of Climate Change (Stern, 2006) examined the impact of GCC on, *inter alia*, water resources, food production, and human health and concluded that the benefits of forceful, prompt, and collective action on GCC greatly outweigh the costs of not acting. This widely discussed report observed that much depends on international collective action for there to be an effective response to GCC. Its assumptions, arguments, and recommendations were criticized (e.g., Campbell, 2007), yet in an exacting review though Weitzman (2007) found shortcomings in the Stern Review's analysis, he suggested that its conclusions might be sound on other grounds (Cole, 2008b; see also Helm, 2008). The Stern Review analysis has been the basis for subsequent economic studies (e.g., Ackerman & Stanton, 2008, finding the cost of GCC will reach 3.6% of US GDP by 2100 if emissions are allowed to continue unchanged).

State security and GCC

Apart from the threats to economic security for developed countries, the parts of the world most vulnerable to the challenges wrought by GCC will be those that are least able to address them. The detrimental impacts of climate-related extremes include disruption of food production and water supply and damage to infrastructure and human settlements (IPCC, 2014a, p. 53). The study of the impacts of climate change on national and international security has grown as a research field, particularly in the last decade. Within this broad field, academic scholarship has concentrated primarily on whether climate change is, or may become, a driver of violent conflict (Atapattu, 2009).

Observers note, that as the lack of adequate resources worsens, the security of developing countries and their populations will be at ever-increasing risk from conflict. In this view, GCC, by compromising already weak states, will lead to regional and global insecurity (Reveron & Mahoney-Norris, 2012; Flowers, 2011). In light of the resultant struggle due to GCC over basic necessities, it was bluntly declared by Ismail Serageldin in 1995, former vice president of the World Bank and first chair of the Global Water Partnership, that "If the wars of this century were fought over oil, the wars of the next century will be fought over water" (Jaitly, 2009, p. 21). GCC and its resultant impacts on climatic patterns and precipitation rates will lead to challenges for individuals and states that may be "unprecedented" in human history (Eckstein, 2009, p. 461). Several observers see that the consequences of GCC can imperil the very survival of humanity (Biello, 2009; Wilson, 1983; Brown, 1989; Dalby, 1994; Edwards, 1999; Page, 2000; Barnett, 2001; Welzer, 2012).

> All of the ways in which human beings have dealt with natural disasters in the past, ... could come together in one conflagration: rage at government's inability to deal with the abrupt and unpredictable crises; religious fervor, perhaps even a dramatic rise in millennial end-of-days cults; hostility and violence toward migrants and minority groups, at a time of demographic change and increased global migration; and intra- and interstate conflict over resources, particularly food and fresh water.
>
> (Campbell et al., 2007, p. 85)

The range of threats from GCC begins with anthropogenic climatic disasters, such as more extreme weather events. The range then extends to intensified conflicts within and between states, as dwindling resources stemming from weather-related disasters threaten the means of securing the necessities of life, and, as populations will slip further into extremism, the likelihood of terrorist threats and insurgencies is heightened (Flowers, 2011). In presently fragile nations it is possible that there will be increasing adherence to extremist ideologies and a likelihood of consequent insurgencies (King, 2016).

Campbell et al. (2007) observed that even a relatively small climatic shift in the developing world could precipitate or exacerbate food shortages, water scarcity, spread of diseases, human migration, and natural resource competition. Historically, when a society has become unsustainable at a specific locale, there is the likelihood of migration with unprecedented levels of human displacement (Warren, 2016). The IPCC reported its strong concurrence in the view of the large probability of an increase in displacement over the course of the twenty-first century due to GCC (IPCC, 2014a). Observers charge that this itself can give rise to conflict (e.g., Pumphrey, 2008). Such migration can hinder development by aggravating demands on urban infrastructure and services, undermining economic growth, and increasing the risk of conflicts and social unrest (Mohamoud et al., 2014). These crises become self-perpetuating where conflicts continue over remaining resources, driving human migration, which in turn triggers new food and resource shortages in migration destinations. The first impacts at these new locations would come from the incoming displaced people and their malnutrition and disease that "could aggravate or spark displacement and border security issues" (Brauch, 2008b).

The response in some affected localities to these risks is precipitated not only by shortages of resources for basic needs, but also by rising sea levels (Reveron & Mahoney-Norris, 2012). Of the regions of the world that stand out as being particularly vulnerable to GCC are the low-lying island nations of the Pacific and Indian Oceans (see Chapter 3). The predicted rise in sea level will place at serious risk the lives of some 600 million people living throughout this region (Macabrey, 2009).

The issue of conflict arising from the consequences of GCC has been much studied and debated (Gilley & Kinsella, 2015); much research has examined how GCC may affect conflict (Gleditsch, 2012). In a comprehensive synthesis of the literature on climate and human conflict, one research team examined various types of human conflict, ranging from interpersonal crime to intergroup violence and political instability and extending to institutional breakdown and then to the collapse of civilizations. In this study Hsiang et al. (2013) found that deviations from normal precipitation and mild temperatures systematically increase the risk of conflict, often substantially.

Of the recent armed conflicts in the countries in the region from Syria to Nigeria, there are reports by UN observers that crimes of mass atrocity, if not genocide, have been occurring (English, 2016; Adano & Daudi, 2012). Before the Syrian uprising had begun in 2011, the region was experiencing the most severe drought on record, the effects of which have possibly contributed to political unrest in Syria, a country marked by poor governance and unsustainable agricultural and environmental policies (Fischetti, 2015). Tracing the drought to climate change, Kelley et al. (2015) concluded that human-influenced GCC is implicated in the current Syrian conflict. Though Rothe (2016) noted an absence of clear empirical evidence to link GCC to the conflict, other observers have relied upon the Kelley et al. study to make generalized conclusions (e.g., Mac-Kenzie, 2015 (GCC "triggered the crisis in Syria;") and Erdem, 2017 (concluding that environmental insecurity arising from GCC has the potential of leading to conflicts such as Syria and Darfur)). Though it cannot be said definitively, that climate change led to the crisis in Syria, it is likely this was a contributive factor leading to radicalism and conflict (Hermwille, 2016).

International and national security strategies have evolved to encompass a concept of total security that includes non-military threats such as GCC (Boeno & Ferrão, 2016). National security policies have been considering the likelihood of the threat of insurgencies and conflict arising from the impacts of GCC. Holland and Vagg (2013) observe that a majority of countries identify climate change as a threat to their security with many integrating this concern into their defense and national security planning documents. Military leaders have been highlighting the breadth of the security threats facing the international community arising from GCC (Burleson, 2011). In 2004, the Chief Scientific Advisor of the United Kingdom, Sir David King, suggested that "climate change is a far greater threat to the world's stability than international terrorism" (BBC News, 2004). The European Council (2003) in its European Security Strategy observed that GCC will in future decades aggravate the competition for natural resources and thereby create further unrest and human displacement in affected areas. This view was renewed in its 2015 security strategy review, where it is noted that GCC will contribute to international conflicts (Diez et al., 2016).

There are two sets of risk assessments that the US military and national security communities have undertaken. The first stems from the concerns for the infrastructure of the military, such as sea-level military bases. The second involves GCC serving as an aggravator of existing threats presently situated in fragile states (Femia, 2016). US military and security analyses have proclaimed repeatedly that GCC is a growing state security threat (Regan, 2015; Schwartz & Randall, 2003). In 2015, the US National Security Strategy identified GCC as a major security threat (The White House, 2015), and the US Department of Defense observed that GCC "*will* aggravate existing problems such as poverty, social tensions, environmental degradation, ineffectual leadership, and weak political institutions that threaten domestic stability in a number of countries" (US Department of Defense, 2015, July 23b, emphasis added). The US Defense Department's 2014 Quadrennial Defense Review noted that the stress caused by climate change will exacerbate resource competition for food, water, and other basics, while acting as a "threat multiplier" by aggravating social and environmental conditions that will lead to political instability, and threaten human and state security (Toscano, 2015; Flowers, 2011).

By presuming an inevitable relationship between GCC and organized conflict, there can, however, be a loss of opportunity for reframing the challenges away from a perspective that leads to a presumption of a threat to state security due to GCC. Further, some observers advise that it is too simplistic to view GCC as inevitably leading to conflict (Vidal, 2011; Diez et al., 2016). In his examination of the historical record, the late Kader Asmal (2001), former Chair of World

Commission on Dams, found that rather than leading to conflict and violence, water scarcity has instead led to instances of cooperation and negotiation. Diez et al. (2016) in their study noted that a reflexive linkage between GCC and conflict underestimates the human capacity to deal with resource scarcity cooperatively, or to adjust to changing environmental conditions. Additionally, some observers, noting that a decision to migrate depends on a complex of socioeconomic factors, would argue against a presumption that GCC is a primary cause of forced displacement (Naser, 2012).

Further, imputing civil conflicts to environmental events can prevent a broader examination of causal factors (Vidal, 2011). Such an example is Darfur, where the proliferation of arms and the absence of a democratic Sudanese government have also been primary factors in the conflict (Vidal, 2011). Specifically, the conflict in Sudan can be seen to be based on historical demands for equitable power sharing among various groups, for redistribution of economic resources and benefits, for improved access to and control over increasingly scarce natural resources and for halting the militarization of society, among other governance issues (IRIN, 2007).

In some contrast to the perspective of GCC as an inevitable and direct cause of conflict, is the view of GCC as only a contributing factor. Observers such as Gleditsch (2012) and Floyd (2012) noted methodological issues in the conflict research from the 1990s purporting to demonstrate a direct link between environmental degradation and violent conflict. Additionally, Regan (2015) observed that the above-mentioned Hsiang et al. (2013) study seems to stand alone in the precision of its predictions. Thus, it should not be confidently concluded that conflict is inevitably directly related to GCC. Rather, the consequences of GCC contribute to other factors that could lead to discord and violence (Buhaug, 2016). In his examination for the US Institute of Peace, Sayne (2011) estimated that 40% of all intrastate conflicts in the last 60 years have involved disputes over limited natural resources. Since 1990, two-dozen such conflicts have occurred; not all had links to GCC. But when resource disputes are a factor, this generally doubles the average length as well as the rates of relapse of conflict (Sayne, 2011).

In a seminal critique, at a conceptual level Deudney (1990) further argued for a traditional definition of national security that is limited to organized violence and would exclude the possibility that environmental change could precipitate organized interstate conflict; thus, the effects of GCC would not satisfy a constrained construct that supports a direct causal link to conflict. Instead, GCC only serves to aggravate the indirect instigators of systematic conflict. According to Diez et al. (2016) and Scott and Khan (2016) scholars have been and remain divided on the question of whether it is possible to prove a causal relationship between GCC and conflict.

In this regard, under a view that the effects of GCC work at most as a contributing factor, dependent on context, and that conflict is not necessarily an inevitable result of GCC, there should be some hesitation to advance the simplifying label of "threat multiplier." The discussion on the effects of GCC as the primary source of violent conflict focuses on the presumed inevitability of the causal linkage between the two. In this perspective, even as one of several contributing factors, human reactions to extreme environmental effects of GCC are seen as interacting with more direct causes of conflict that can aggravate and prolong ongoing conflicts. The sense of inevitability that the impacts of GCC lead to conflict is framed in national military assessments that view GCC as a "threat multiplier." The relationship between GCC and conflict is not so preordained as this label implies. Further, the very use of this label denotes its own strategy that is attenuated from the contextual factors in which the risks might become such threats. Using language that was somewhat less suggestive of a causal relationship, the US Department of Defense, in its 2010 Quadrennial Defense Review, observed the probability of GCC as being an "accelerant of instability" (p. 85).

As delineated by Gunter (2016), the underlying connotation should be a recognition that GCC presents the likelihood that nonlinear events are triggered through dangerous feedback mechanisms. In this discourse, substituting the label of "risk exacerbator" (Hauer, 2014) might avoid the almost tautological perspective connoted by the label of "threat multiplier," which seems limited contextually to concerns of state security. Diez et al. (2016) proposed a distinction between facts that involve increasing risk (which "poses a rather long-term potential threat that is characterized by a radical uncertainty and leads to a more diffuse sense of unease," p. 9) as opposed to those increasing security threats (which are "existential, direct and urgent," p. 9).

> Security threats tend to be identifiable or even personifiable…, whereas risk is often a lot more diffuse, with a diffuse referent object…. It is immediately evident that risk may be an appropriate way of framing the threat posed by climate change.
>
> (p. 9)

Human security and GCC

If the concept of state security has been expanded from threats of organized violence that stem from other states, the notion of security itself has been enlarged beyond the concerns limited to the security of the state. The UNDP first introduced the concept of "human security" when it included the term in its 1994 UNDP Human Development Report. This report observed that the "world can never be at peace unless people have security in their daily lives" (UNDP, 1994, p. 22), and asserted:

> The concept of security has for too long been interpreted narrowly: as security of territory from external aggression, or as protection of national interests in foreign policy.
>
> (UNDP, 1994, p. 22)

Thus, the basic idea of promoting human security was to articulate a counter response to the longstanding perspective in the international community that state security is its paramount, if not exclusive, goal (Gasper & Gómez, 2014). The interdependence of state with human security is such that when the security of a people is endangered anywhere in the world, all nations are or will be implicated at some level (UNDP, 1994, p. 22).

The UN created a definition of human security by encompassing two factors: freedom from fear and freedom from want (UNDP, 1994, p. 24). Threats to human security are many, and of these the UNDP recognized over two decades ago, "[e]nvironmental threats are one of the clearest examples [of global challenges to human security]: land degradation, deforestation and the emission of greenhouse gases affect climatic conditions around the globe" (UNDP, 1994, p. 34). Brauch (2008a) observed that the former UN Secretary-General Kofi Annan's insistence (2005 UN Secretary-General's Report) on a human-centered approach to security, which cannot be limited to military terms or to a mere absence of violent conflict, encompasses, *inter alia*, environmental protection and economic development. In 2007, UN Secretary-General Ban Ki-moon reinforced this connection between GCC and human security:

> The adverse effects of changing weather patterns, such as floods and droughts, and related economic costs, including compensation for lost land, could risk polarizing society and marginalizing communities. This, in turn, could weaken the institutional capacity of the State to resolve conflict through peaceful and democratic means, to ensure social cohesion, and to safeguard human rights.
>
> (Ki-moon, 2007)

In this, human security rests on the development and protection of basic resources for poorer countries. In October 2011, UN Secretary-General, Ban Ki-moon, called upon the UN to:

> Focus on sustainable development as the No. 1 priority, to address all these issues. Climate change, food-security issues, energy shortages, water scarcities, disease, health issues and gender empowerment: all these are interconnected. We have to address these issues in an integrated way.
>
> (See Walsh, 2011)

Related to human security, Conca and Dabelko (2014, p. 237) see the paradigm of "environmental security" as a means to "grapple with" the "intensely political themes" related to strategies at addressing GCC. The concept of "environmental security" is consonant with

> human security, in that both identify the individual as the referent object of the security threat and the concern is about the direct impact of GCC on the livelihood of people rather than on the impact of violent conflict on state security
>
> (Diez et al., 2016)

Yet, the relevant international organizations have not created a definition of the term, "environmental security," that could be used to guide policy (Millennium Project, n.d.). The UNDP referred to it only briefly in its 1994 report on human development:

> Environmental threats countries are facing are a combination of the degradation of local ecosystems and that of the global system. These comprise threats to environmental security.
>
> (UNDP, 1994, p. 24)

Despite a lack of an internationally recognized instrumental definition, Conca and Dabelko (2014) find that the paradigm of environmental security is based on several assertions:

> That environmental challenge is an important source of social conflict, that many societies face graver dangers from environmental change than from traditional military threats, and that both environmental and security policies must be redefined to take account of these new realities.
>
> (p. 237)

When situated in security and GCC agendas this redefinition of environmental and security policies can serve to ensure that the challenges of GCC are not narrowly viewed as encompassing only those leading to organized conflict. These policies must be broadly conceived as engaging these new realities of the needs of societies by addressing the range of "environment, development, and security linkages" (Dabelko, 2014, p. 251). A limited focus on state security in the efforts to confront the challenges of GCC will discount the underlying issues that lead to human insecurity, which become factors leading to conflict.

There is an expansion of these agendas when considerations of human security are considered. Similarly, by making the referent point the individual, the expanded notion of human security magnifies the number of areas for considerations of security concerns. Furthermore, a concept of human security, in this environmental context, was also seen to lessen consideration of values that are associated with sovereignty and that come within the remit of the traditional notion of state security. There can be a broadened discourse of possible proactive measures where the focus on the environment is placed in the context of peace and human rights (Conca, 2014). Thus, values of universality, solidarity, and international governance are more prominent in this primacy of environmental security over state security. As such this form of:

> [E]nvironmental security is more than just an effort to reconceptualize threats or to document empirical patterns of environmental degradation and violence. It is also a political agenda aimed at mobilizing the state and society toward a new set of goals and at redirecting resources and energies away from traditional, narrowly military concerns.
>
> (Conca & Dabelko, 2014, p. 238)

Considering the degradation of the environment as a threat to both human and state security has in turn expanded the agenda in the discourse of security studies. The increasing scope of international security now readily includes environmental deterioration, global warming, and climate change. Biswas (2011) observed that these issues have extended human understanding of environmental change, conflict, and vulnerability and explored the roles of conservation and sustainable development in promoting peace, stability, and human security.

International strategies to counter GCC

The consequences of GCC are multi-dimensional, requiring a commensurate set of strategies. As observed by Stern (2006), "Climate change is an externality that is global in both its causes and consequences. The incremental impact of a tonne of GHG on climate change is independent of where in the world it is emitted" (see Livermore, 2017). In the first major global instrument, the 1997 Kyoto Protocol initiated the basic international strategies for addressing GCC and its effects, which could jeopardize both human and state security. The Kyoto strategies include: mitigating climate change, adapting to adverse consequences of GCC, and assisting countries in facilitating the capacities that will increase resilience to the impacts of GCC (UNFCCC, 2014). These strategies were reaffirmed in the 2015 Paris Agreement. This section of the chapter delineates these three basic strategies that the international community has identified for addressing GCC and then considers whether and how they are furthered by the manner in which the security dimensions of GCC are conceptualized.

First strategy: mitigation

In order to slow down the rate of climate change, mitigation efforts consist of processes that address the causes of GHG emissions. Thus, as a first strategy, international efforts must confront the central problem, that of reducing the factors leading to GCC. A focus on efforts of mitigation has long been a central feature of discussions on GCC by the international community. Signatories to the UNFCCC committed themselves to "adopt national policies and take corresponding measures on the mitigation of climate change, by limiting anthropogenic emissions of greenhouse gases and protecting and enhancing its greenhouse gas sinks and reservoirs" (UNFCCC, 2009, Article 4(2a)).

The UNFCCC recognizes differentiated responsibilities observing that "developed countries should take the lead in combating climate change" (UNFCCC, Article 3, 2009). In its 2013 overview the UNFCCC Secretariat observed that the UNFCCC provides a forum for incentivizing and enhancing action on mitigation by all Parties informed by scientific information (UNFCCC Secretariat, 2013). Under the 1997 Kyoto Protocol, binding emissions reductions applied only to developed nations. This structural emphasis on developed nations' obligations in the Kyoto Protocol proved too politically divisive for the

16 *Don Wallace*

US and this country ultimately declined to ratify it (Outka, 2016); Canada became the first signatory-country to repudiate the Kyoto Accord (CBC News, 2011).

In the discussions leading up to the Paris meeting in 2015, the parties to the UNFCCC were asked to publish their planned reductions in GHG emissions or their Intended Nationally Determined Contributions (INDCs). With this, the 2015 Paris Agreement purports to provide tools for states to commit to climate mitigation goals, to collectively accelerate their activities, and to oversee the implementation of these tools (Burleson, 2016; Byrne & Zyla, 2016; UNFCCC, 2015b). However, the Paris 2015 Agreement did not include a call for curbing fossil-fuel extraction (Burleson, 2016). It is estimated that 80% of known fossil fuel reserves must remain unextracted if the increase in warming of the climate is to remain below 2°C, the less-demanding target of the Paris 2015 Agreement (Adler, 2015; McGlade & Ekins, 2015).

Throughout the developed world various mitigation proposals focus on limiting GHG emissions from power plants, converting to renewable sources of energy, or increasing fuel efficiency of motor vehicles (Flatt, 2012). Furthermore, countries are anticipating a significant contribution from efforts in land use and in forest sectors for meeting their INDC mitigation targets (Forsell et al., 2016). Additional mitigation strategies include creating trading-system schemes in carbon emissions, such as the cap-and-trade model.

Second strategy: adaptation

A second GCC strategy involves efforts to allow for impacted societies to adapt to the insufficiently mitigated consequences of GCC. Adaptation is defined by the IPCC as "the adjustment in natural or human systems in response to actual or expected climatic stimuli or their effects" (IPCC, 2007). Considering the lag in time required (likely taking multiple decades) for mitigative changes to take discernable effect in the global climate system, implementation of adaptation measures will be required for at least these multiple decades (Flatt, 2012). Adaptation is an inevitable prospect for humanity, with the strategy being based on basic needs for its survival (Eckstein, 2009). The IPCCC (2014a, p. 19) observed that at the national level:

> National governments can coordinate adaptation efforts of local and sub-national governments, for example by protecting vulnerable groups, by supporting economic diversification and by providing information, policy and legal frameworks and financial support....

In the 1990s, the perceived urgency of attention to mitigation strategies in international climate change policy discussion displaced extensive dialogue on the formulation of adaptation strategies designed to respond to the impacts of GCC. In the last decade this balance has shifted so that adaptation policies have become a focus in international policy formulations (Flatt, 2012; Ruhl, 2000).

The UNFCCC Secretariat, in its 2013 overview, noted that the UNFCCC called upon all Parties to cooperate in preparing for adaptation to the impacts of GCC.

Current projections for the adverse effects of GCC are that they will more likely fall upon those nations least able to adapt to the consequences of GCC over which they had little role in creating (Hall & Weiss, 2012) and that can ill-afford the expenditures (Flatt, 2012). Adaptation measures can include advance-warning devices to allow for evacuation of populations to places of safety in the face of advancing extreme weather events (Kohona, 2016). Other examples of adaptation measures can be seen in the rather acerbic observation where the UNDP (2008) contrasted the adaptation capacities of developed nations with those of their developing counterparts:

> The United Kingdom is spending US$1.2 billion annually on flood defenses. In the Netherlands, people are investing in homes that can float on water. The Swiss alpine ski industry is investing in artificial snow-making machines.... [By contrast in] the Horn of Africa, 'adaptation' means that women and young girls walk further to collect water. In the Ganges Delta, people are erecting bamboo flood shelters on stilts. And in the Mekong Delta people are planting mangroves to protect themselves against storm surges, and women and children are being taught to swim.
>
> (UNDP, 2008)

For many developing countries to succeed at a strategy of adaptation, assistance from developed nations will be necessitated. To this goal, the UNFCCC calls upon developed countries to provide adaptation assistance to their developing counterparts. Further, the parties adopted the Green Climate Fund to oversee some of the US$100 billion, for cutting GHG emissions and adaptation efforts, that developed countries have promised to make available by 2020 (Hall & Weiss, 2012). There will likely be significant costs involved in specific reactive adaptation measures (Murdoch, 2009). However, in the struggle of nations to agree on who should bear the burden of financing the required actions (Scott, 2012), there will likely be significant hurdles to adaptation assistance.

Oxfam estimated that in the developing world, adapting to climate change will cost between US$50–80 billion on a yearly basis (Stillings, 2014). The World Bank (2012) had identified a range of US$70–100 billion a year between 2010 and 2050 as the estimated cost. A more recent estimate from the UN Environmental Programme 2016 Adaptation Gap report indicates that the annual cost of adapting to climate change could rise by the year 2050 to US$280 to 500 billion. The report cautions that though funding for GCC adaptation has increased in the five years leading up to 2014, that unless substantial new funding is found, there will be a significant funding gap by the year 2050 (UNEP, 2016). This more recent estimate will alter the argument that had been made to support expenditures of lower estimated costs of over US$80 billion, which would have represented about 0.2% of developed country GDP, or around 10% of what is currently allocated to military expenditures. Thus, if measured in terms of returns for overall state security, adaptation financing had been seen to be a relatively cost-effective investment (UNDP, 2008). With this more recent UNEP estimate of the costs of adaptation rising to over 50% of military expenditures, that argument will be harder to make. While a concrete number was not included in the legally binding part of the Paris Agreement, reference was made to the joint goal to mobilize $100 billion annually by 2020 and to the need to scale up support to allow for a low carbon, climate resilient transition (Day et al., 2015).

The challenge for successful adaptation policies is problematic largely due to the uncertainty at the localized level of the variety of impacts of GCC. In the methodology, developed for its approach to planning and implementation of climate change plans, the International Centre for Environmental Management (ICEM, 2011) calls for recognition of the cyclical and iterative nature of both mitigation and adaptation, observing that adaptation responses need to be adjusted regularly as experience and new information is obtained. The impacts of GCC are multi-faceted, affecting various political and economic systems in a country with no likely single solution to climate vulnerability.

Third strategy: capacity building

While financial assistance will be needed to facilitate the mitigation and adaptation measures of developing states, there are needs for a wide range of assistance for developing countries. In its 2013 overview, the UNFCC Secretariat noted that the UNFCCC and its Kyoto Protocol contain provisions to ensure that the implementation of the UNFCCC by developing countries is supported and enabled through the provision of resources by developed country Parties. The UNFCCC-related institutions are complemented by arrangements providing means of implementation through capacity building of developing countries with a view to supporting their adaptation efforts (UNFCCC Secretariat, 2013). In this, the Secretariat has identified three underlying aspects for capacity-building as a GCC strategy: the alleviation of poverty, the establishment good governance processes, and the facilitation of the transfer of technology.

Alleviation of poverty

The assistance envisioned by observers goes beyond that of just the immediate needs for mitigation and adaptation efforts. Here "[p]roviding assistance to vulnerable nations," will be needed to facilitate efforts of "suitable international institutions to help create economic prosperity" (Pumphrey, 2008). Thus, the assistance in this context would consist of aid for the overall improvement in the economies of developing countries. For this strategy, the fight against poverty and the fight against the effects of climate change must be viewed as interrelated efforts. They must reinforce each other and success must be achieved jointly on both fronts (UNDP, 2008).

The Nobel Prize winning economist, Thomas C. Schelling, argued that the best adaptation strategy would be to develop the economies of the developing states, because the wealthier they become, the greater their capacity to adapt to climate change (Cole, 2008a). However, there is no single formula for increasing per capita income and inculcating adaptively efficient institutions in developing states. For many, if not most, of these countries, the process will require substantial international assistance, which so far has not been forthcoming for capacity building. Referring to a strategy of "building human resilience," the UNDP observed that investments in social protection and wider human development strategies are needed to "strengthen the capacity of vulnerable people to cope with risk." The estimate of the UNDP was that at least US$40 billion was needed to "strengthen national strategies for poverty reduction in the face of climate change risks" (UNDP, 2008, p. 15). Underlying conditions of technology and resource management and governance abilities will influence the impact of assistance with such resources.

Transferring technologies

The recent developments in the 2015 Paris Agreement on the concept of INDCs showed that developing countries require assistance in monitoring their emissions and for facilitating technological options in the context of their specific development objectives (Day et al., 2015). Thus, another way the developed world can help reduce GCC costs in lesser-developed countries is by innovating and then transferring new mitigation and adaptation technologies (Cole, 2008a). To ensure a willingness to transfer various clean technologies, the concern is for the protection of intellectual property rights with multilateral technology agreements among industrialized and non-industrialized nations (Burleson, 2008).

The Technology Mechanism of the UNFCCC supports developing countries to create or to transfer climate technologies and accelerate sustainable development (UNFCCC, 1992). Under the 2015 Paris Agreement, submissions by countries relating to both finance and technology are to be reviewed by technical experts who will seek to improve clarity and suggest opportunities to share best practices. With the iterative reviews detailing effectiveness and scale of support to the Technology Mechanism and then linking the Technology Mechanism and the UNFCCC financial bodies, this could raise the funds needed with which to accelerate the development and use of renewables and other innovations (Burleson, 2016).

Good governance

For mitigation efforts, where GHG emissions cross international borders, there is a need to engage the efforts of international and regional entities. By contrast, adaptation policies will implicate localities and will have significant localized human impact. The integration of adaptation planning into wider poverty reduction strategies is a priority. Yet, adaptation policies will not be successful if merely attached to systems that are failing to address underlying causes of poverty, vulnerability, and wide social disparities (UNDP, 2008). Additionally,

20   *Don Wallace*

good governance and transparency in decision-making regarding the distribution and use of adaptation funding will be essential to ensure some success in GCC policies (Hall & Weiss, 2012, pp. 357–358).

As a critical aspect for success in these efforts, a program that addresses GCC must be perceived to be legitimate, in that there must be an inclusive, transparent process that incorporates all stakeholders into the decision process (Pumphrey, 2008). Further, the quantity and quality of this cooperation must include the international community, NGOs, and relevant domestic policymakers as well (Burleson, 2011, p. 185). Implementing GCC measures must involve equitable allocation, which can be addressed through provisions for public participation. Installing good governance processes will, in turn, benefit efforts directed at GCC. In this regard, "[f]ostering legitimate states is a key element of [GCC] strategy" (Pumphrey, 2008, p. 14). Accordingly, the effectiveness of this funding depends on how they address programmatic issues, build upon national investment plans, react to recent issues in the financial landscape, and then respond to emerging opportunities (Lattanzio, 2012). In turn, account must be taken of the political and institutional constraints to the adaptive capacity of the affected nations (Ayers, 2009). History has demonstrated that, generally, foreign assistance will be no easy response, with the likelihood of inefficient distribution and use of resources. With properly administered funding there is the likelihood of garnering a modest number of such nations, where the resulting improved economies can better withstand the impacts of GCC (Cole, 2008a).

Implementation of GCC strategies

The prospective success of these three strategies of mitigation, adaptation, and capacity building for addressing GCC will hinge on the framing of the challenges of climate change in terms of security. This section presents an overview of the directions for GCC strategies that could differ due to which security paradigm, human vs. state, is prioritized by the international community. Further, there is discussion concerning these strategies and possible intervention–militarization policies that could arise from major power nations as challenges in the implementation of GCC strategies.

Impact of securitization GCC strategies

Should human security be prioritized in the framing of GCC, the strategies of mitigation, adaptation, and capacity building are enhanced. By contrast, prioritizing state security will direct policy focus to the armed conflicts that are exacerbated by the impact of GCC, likely neglecting the strategies needed to address climate change. Thus, a distinction should be drawn when framing environmental concerns as challenges to human security rather than to state security.

As environmental security has been conceptualized by Brauch (2008a), the underlying factors of human security are served by efforts at mitigation and adaptation directed at GCC as an environmental issue. These factors include certain requirements and objects that both enhance and become enhanced by effective programs of mitigation and adaptation. The factor of "freedom of fear" is underscored by efforts of good governance, rule of law, universal humanitarian standards, and conflict prevention and resolution. "Freedom from want" has as a goal reducing individual and societal vulnerabilities in various spheres including the environment. Additionally, Brauch (2008a) identified an underlying factor of human security as "freedom from hazard impacts," wherein the goal is to reduce vulnerabilities and enhance capacities for societies confronted with natural hazards.

With the strategy of capacity building the distinctions between measures of state security and those of human security become likewise apparent. In a discussion on the causal relationship between GCC and conflict, Biswas (2011) cautioned that the impacts of the weather-related natural disasters, which will be increased by impacts of GCC, differentiate between the nations that are better prepared for the resultant emergency and those countries lacking the resources and infrastructure to better prevent, prepare, and respond to the circumstances of these catastrophes (see also Buhaug, 2016; Kohona, 2016). Thus, a state security perspective that discounts the importance of a broader examination of causal factors of conflicts will likely discount the critical need of ensuring factors necessary for capacity-building: the alleviation of poverty, the establishment of good governance processes, and the transfer of technology. As advocated by Brauch (2008a) the discourse on these GCC strategies is linked to notions of human security where the protection of human welfare is the focus (see Detraz & Betseill, 2009).

The three strategies to address the effects of GCC, described in the previous section that considers mitigation, adaptation, and capacity-building, are linked to norms of global justice and should not be viewed as being outside of normal democratic processes under the rubric of securitization (Herring, 2013; Rachels & Rachels, 2012). Thus, the continuing calls made by the IPCC for more sustainable and equal development do not denote extraordinary responses in this context (Herring, 2013; Rachels & Rachels, 2012), and the process of "securitization" should be confined to those effects of GCC that have been portrayed as threats to state security. From the UNFCCC to the 2015 Paris Agreement, the various international instruments have developed the global response to the effects of GCC and have institutionalized the three described strategies. Arguably, as noted by Ole Wæver, the originator of the securitization theory based upon the logic of exceptional state power, these human security aspects of the international environmental regime constitute a part of normal politics, and should not be considered as extraordinary measures (Floyd, 2008).

The securitization of GCC can depend on geography, where the challenges of GCC are differentiated by location. Low-lying island states are challenged by the threat of termination of their territory, thus an existential threat to the viability of an entire society. Additionally, the negotiations at the various COPs reveal that environmental issues are caught in the political oppositions within the

22 *Don Wallace*

North/South divide (Maertens, 2013). The developed states of the North view GCC as portending the scarcity of resources, the forced migration of masses of humans, and large-scale weather-related disasters (Talkin, 2012).The state-centric framing of security used by the North promotes policies of protection of states against the threats of GCC and de-emphasizes the need for dealing with mitigation and taking responsibility for contributing to GCC (Talkin, 2012; Haley, 2011) and for ultimately changing the status quo that has led to the environmental problems (Mendelsohn et al., 2006). While developed states more readily accept an imperative to frame GCC as a state-security issue, developing countries can see the effects of this securitization as having the likelihood of leading to challenges of their sovereignty (Boeno et al., 2015). This difference in framing between North and South can be observed in the 2007 UNSC debates on GCC where less than 30% of the Southern states agreed that the UNSC was the correct forum to deal with GCC as compared with 70% of Northern states (Detraz & Betsil, 2009, Trombetta, 2008; Holland & Vagg, 2013; see Thwaites, 2014, observing the same for the 2011 UNSC discussions).

Developing states are not as readily accepting of GCC as a state security issue, but rather as a human security issue where continued development, as seen in the earlier discussion on the three strategies, holds some solution. The requirements of the factors of human security are fulfilled by these GCC strategies that address the impacts of a challenging climate as an environmental issue. To respond adequately to these threats to human security, the proactive policies and measures of these internationally recognized strategies of mitigation, adaptation, and capacity-building are needed. All three GCC strategies can achieve a reduction of such vulnerability to human security.

GCC strategies and the major powers

In its assessment of the likelihood for success in confronting the challenges of GCC, the UNDP observed the need for collective action by the international community that relies on comprehensive global strategies carried out by the agendas of individual states:

> Avoiding the unprecedented threats posed by dangerous climate change will require an unparalleled collective exercise in international cooperation.... However, a sustainable global emissions pathway will only be meaningful if it is translated into practical national strategies.
>
> (UNDP, 2008, pp. 19–20)

The impacts from GCC will be disparately experienced among the states, with developing states suffering the most. Each year between 2000 and 2004, approximately 262 million people were affected by climate change disasters, with over 98% of these being located in the developing world (UNDP, 2008, p. 10). In the countries that make up the Organization for Economic Co-operation and Development (OECD) only one in 1,500 people has been affected by climate disaster, whereas for developing countries the comparable figure is one in 19 (UNDP, 2008). The countries that will suffer the most will be those that presently experience:

> Low average per capita income, low rates of literacy, low health status, low life expectancies, limited infrastructure, fragility of economic progress, high vulnerability to economic setbacks, lack of capital, large agricultural sectors, and reliance on export of primary products.
>
> (Anand, 2004, p. 3)

Because the accumulated atmospheric concentrations and their impacts will continue for decades, if not centuries, (IPCC, 2014a), this timeframe itself presents challenges for policymakers and governing institutions. The current generation of political leaders cannot solve the climate change problem because a policy framework for addressing the impacts of GCC has to accommodate the lengthy duration of carbon dioxide emitted into the atmosphere. Manifestations of climate change, including increasing temperature and sea level, may continue for many centuries, or millennia, beyond the point of emissions stabilization (Burns, 2016; Moran, 2011). Further, though the complications arising from GCC are not present or even will be manifest in the lifetimes of today's political leaders, there is presently a needed urgency for implementing a policy to address these issues. Delays in agreeing and implementing GCC policies only add to the accumulation of GHG emissions, increasing the cost of successfully addressing the challenges as the future gets locked into increasingly higher temperatures (UNDP, 2008, p. 11). These higher temperatures likely mean greater devastation and a world where any international cooperation becomes increasingly difficult when nations come to see that their own survival is at risk.

Thus, fundamental to the development of an international strategy to confront GCC is the recognition that the magnitude of the issues involved in the threatening aspects of GCC demand a need for a multi-generational commitment from developed nations, particularly the major powers, to work within an international community. The World Bank (2017) is predicting that if action is insufficient to reduce vulnerability, provide access to basic services, and build resilience, climate change impacts could push an additional 100 million people into poverty by 2030. The UNDP (2008) has observed that the developed nations of the world lack neither the financial resources nor the technological capabilities to act. Most developed governments also accept that solutions to climate change are affordable, certainly more affordable than the costs of inaction. The failure to prevent the devastating effects of GCC will be because the major powers were unable to garner the political will to cooperate and succeed in a strategy for confronting GCC (UNDP, 2008). Developed countries certainly have the capability at reasonably low cost to both mitigate a significant portion of their GHG emissions and to assist developing countries in adjusting to GCC conditions by funding discrete adaptation projects and with capacity building (Cole, 2008a).

24 Don Wallace

Issues of securitization and exceptional measures—mitigation/adaptation

Despite non-state actors, such as IGOs, participating in the securitizing process, the traditional approach to security maintains a focus on the concerns of the state. This approach positions the state as both the provider and beneficiary of security measures and can unintentionally lead to preservation of the status quo of anthropogenic causes of atmospheric carbon in setting strategies to confront GCC. Such influence on strategies is seen in various national defense statements, where the concern for national security encourages political responses that exclude mitigation strategies (Feeney, 2015; Brauch 2008b; Scott, 2012). Feeney (2015) noted that the GCC strategies of developed countries for responding to the effects of GCC prioritize adaptation over mitigation measures.

In the aftermath of the 2016 presidential election, there might be some effort at continuing US strategies at adaptation. Though these will come at the exclusion of mitigation efforts, should the new Secretary of State, former Exxon Mobil chief executive, Rex Tillerson, follow through on his 2012 public statements noting that the challenge of GCC is merely "an engineering problem and it has engineering solutions" (Daily, 2012). Though Tillerson did not delineate these engineering solutions beyond that of "mov[ing] crop production areas around," conceivably they could include geo-engineering (Daily, 2012). The search for a geo-engineering solution was given support in the 2015 National Research Council recommendation for US federal funding for research into technologies to counter the effects of GCC. A reviewer of the NRC report, Clive Hamilton (2015), expressed concern that its warnings about the environmental risks and uncertainties will be overlooked by political leaders who want a solution to GCC that does not involve mitigation efforts. "A fleet of planes daily delivering sulfate particles into the upper atmosphere would be a grim monument to the ultimate failure of unbridled techno-industrialism and our unwillingness to change the way we live" (Hamilton, 2015). As such, the offer of a geo-engineering approach would constitute a technological intervention that entrenches the behaviors that created the problem, and, instead of serving as a solution, would likely delay the manifestation of the consequences of GCC to a time when they could be irreversibly ruinous. Thus, the exclusive embrace of engineering solutions to GCC, whatever they might be, by this US Secretary of State, constitutes, in the language of securitization, exceptional or extraordinary technological measures, which are focused on adaptation efforts.

One could postulate that this privileging of adaptation responses over mitigation strategies reflects the political difficulties of burdening powerful fossil fuel industries with the economic challenges involved in broad efforts that could mean drastically reducing the extraction of fossil fuels. The political will of countries such as the US to dramatically introduce changes to the substantial fossil-fuel sectors of their economies will remain a critical question; furthermore, the expanding economies of China and India have resulted largely from increased consumption of fossil fuels (see Kohona, 2016). Any failure to impose such changes is not because nations lack the capability; Mayer and Rajavuori (2016) noted that a substantial share of fossil fuel reserves are owned by governments and this public sector controls a substantial portion of the means of production. Yet, any burdens placed on the fossil-fuel industry will need to overcome the effects of its long-term efforts to undermine climate science information and impede the emergence of public awareness of GCC (Adams, 2016; Carnwath, 2016).

There will likely be increasing recognition at the international level of adaptation serving merely as an aspect of conflict prevention (Scott & Khan, 2016). In this regard, political leaders in developed states seek adaptation measures in the form of constructing physical barriers and enlarging the immigration enforcement capacities of neighboring countries as relatively inexpensive steps that address the effects of GCC that result in an influx of migrants. These measures impose large costs on human security and conceal the need for wealthier countries both to mitigate their emissions of GHG and to assist in the adaptation programs in developing countries (White, 2011).

For an effective GCC strategy, all states will need to be united in their decisions for taking measures that mitigate these GHG emissions. However, environmental justice would demand that the benefits and burdens should be distributed equitably across communities and populations for both mitigation efforts and adaptation measures (Stillings, 2014). Ultimately, with major powers primarily responsible for the atmospheric concentrations of GHG, assessing legal obligations will be problematic in a current international culture that seeks to preserve the autonomy of States and especially the prerogatives of major powers. The effectiveness of a GCC strategy that must involve the entire international community will only be diminished by a political solution that ensures the autonomous capacity of the sovereignty of the major states.

Issues of securitization and exceptional measures—militarization

The focus on national security will legitimize another GCC strategy beyond those three GCC strategies of mitigation, adaptation, and capacity building. The securitization of environmental issues as state-security issues could ultimately lend support to government officials wanting to legitimize coercive action to protect the state (Biswas, 2011). At one level, the threats from the effects of GCC might be used as justification for measures, such as economic and other non-military sanctions. Where there is a large-scale failure by a state to curb excessive emissions to an extent that threatens a state's survival, there could arise an obligation for the international community to reverse the climate change effects of its own or even of another state. These measures might need to be taken, even by non-injured parties, as obligations *erga omnes* (Gilley & Kinsella, 2015).

Lee (2009) identified three arguments that could be invoked by advocates of national security to justify coercive measures that could even involve military intervention: (1) to halt harmful environmental actions that impact another country; (2) to prevent a country from depriving another from an equitable sharing of environmental resources, such as water; and (3) to acquire necessary resources, such as food, when state survival or a humanitarian crisis is likely. The first of these might be unlikely, as Gilley and Kinsella (2015) have written (citing Deudney, 1990) that any state sufficiently industrialized so that it is a major emitter of GHG will likely be sufficiently advanced to deter an effort at military coercion. Deudney (1990) would likely find the second of these arguments unlikely, since there is a greater likelihood of compensation or other forms of interactions that could redress such issues. Though Trombetta (2008) noted that only a few appeals to state-security have mobilized exceptional military measures or ascribed adversaries in the context of environmental concerns, this reticence may change as the effects of GCC become more extreme. The negative implications favoring a policy centered on state security have been observed in the research by Rothe (2016) where international governance engaged in GCC has proceeded in a piecemeal, technocratic, and disorganized manner.

An emphasis on state security in the securitization of GCC has led to a broadened perspective for nontraditional responses from militaries (Brauch, 2008b). The use of military operations is increasingly seen as necessary and legitimate for disaster relief (Boeno et al., 2015). For example, the CNA Military Advisory Board (2007) observed that an increasing number of calamitous GCC-induced weather events will precipitate increasing demand for the positioning of American troops in different parts of the world. Additionally, Brown et al. (2007) and White (2011) noted that nations will use forceful responses in order to secure resources or construct barriers to restrict migration of refugees. Marzec (2015) has observed that with the effects of GCC becoming more apparent, military institutions throughout the world are taking on a prominent role in the managing of environmental security concerns (see also Scott & Khan, 2016).

A significant amount of military planning now includes the provision of disaster relief. Brzoska (2015) observed that with an expansion of traditional military roles; the securitization of GCC issues has contributed to the transformation of some security practices (see also De Brito, 2011). Present-day military organizations have developed significant capacities to manage disasters and carry out recovery programs (Biswas, 2011). Almost all nations that have official military planning have stated that their governments consider missions, such as human assistance and disaster relief, to be critical responsibilities of their armed forces (Holland & DeGarmo, 2014).

Some observers have found some consolation where the securitization of GCC as a state security issue can be seen as having created a sense of urgency among political leaders to do something about mitigation and adaptation measures (Brown et al., 2007; De Brito, 2011). De Brito (2012) observed that measures taken by the European Union (EU) upon securitization of GCC have resulted in the urgency to undertake environmental measures rather than to implement traditional security measures. Trombetta (2008) noted that this process of transformation for GCC is part of a broader re-articulation of an agenda where security-based notions of emergency are legitimized. Thus, new roles with alternative means are being opened for security providing states. There is likely a need for such a form of emergency assistance, where the military could be the only entity that can provide the level of necessary response to the "natural disasters rendered more frequent by climate change and to instigate postconflict development that is environmentally sustainable" (Scott & Khan, 2016, p. 91).

Other observers do not see this increased role in disaster relief as entirely benign and raise concerns about military solutions to security concerns raised by GCC. This framing of GCC would imply its militarization to policymakers, potentially excluding non-military environmental solutions that will be shorn of resources, with attention paid to military responses (De Brito, 2011). By contrast, in a much earlier time, Lester Brown in a 1977 Worldwatch Institute report expressed optimism that national defense outlays could be redirected from traditional conceptions of combat toward environmental challenges (Brown, 1977).

There is a likelihood that in perceiving GCC as a national-security issue this will lead to a self-fulfilling prophecy where the militarization itself aggravates the challenges and perceived threats of climate change (Feitleson, Tamimi, & Rosenthal, 2012). Needed cooperative efforts to implement the three GCC strategies discussed above could be inhibited by a militarized emphasis on state security (Floyd, 2008; Trombetta, 2008; Gilley & Kinsella, 2015). This lack of cooperative action can lead to different framings of the threats posed by GCC and thus reinforce differences and conflicts within and between states (Talkin, 2012). Ultimately, under a paradigm of the militarization of GCC challenges, there could be a loss of a sense of mutual dependency among nations that is needed in the efforts to address GCC (Deudney, 1999, 1990).

Feeney (2015) noted that a broadened role for addressing GCC of the state military apparatus continues to maintain the nation-state as a key actor in the security discourse. To counter this broadened role, the invocation of human security responses is a necessary though insufficient factor in redirecting GCC strategies, since, to some extent, the language of human security gets co-opted into a relabeling of preferred policy practices without substantive changes. For example, while extolling the expanded GCC-induced mission of the US military Reveron and Mahoney-Norris (2012, p. 61) collapsed the efforts to provide humanitarian assistance, with the longer list of operations having more to do with fostering state security, such as "training foreign militaries, and building security, justice, and law enforcement institutions to strengthen state governance and sovereignty."

GCC and the return to state security

How the impact of GCC is framed, either as a threat to state security or as one to human security, can be more important than the reality of this threat. The Copenhagen School does not advocate for any particular issue to be considered a matter of state security, rather it has identified the process by which problems are transformed into security issues. Thus, the effects of GCC could be considered under the rubric of securitization, where climate security is introduced in the discourse of policy-making and the effects of GCC as a threat to the security of the state or the international community are accepted (Scott, 2012). Regarding this transformation Peoples and Vaughan-Williams (2010) write, that what is important is how the political leadership presents the threat not the reality of the nature of the threat. Thus, there need be no objective security threat (Waever, 1995) from GCC for its securitization.

Where there might be only limited support for viewing GCC as an important factor leading to armed conflict, in a survey of the pertinent research Gleditsch (2012) noted that framing the climate issue as a state security problem could influence the perceptions of the political actors and contribute to a self-fulfilling prophecy. The response may be directed at the violence rather than at the underlying causes that are exacerbated by GCC. Thus, how the concept of security is prioritized in terms of state and human security, where the latter includes concerns of environmental security, can have profound effects on the conceptualization by political institutions of security needs.

To the extent that the concepts of state security compete with those of human security and the impacts of GCC operate at the center of this competition, a status quo is maintained that favors the economic interests of strong nation-states over the necessary international cooperation that will ensure the success of mitigation, adaptation, and capacity building efforts. The state security perspective for addressing the effects of GCC fits well with a strategy of preserving the strategic interests of nation-states. The securitization of GCC under the rubric of state security, allows for an avoidance of determining responsibility, prioritizes state security adaptation over mitigation strategies, and engenders exceptionalist security policies at the expense of measures that enhance human security.

Aim and structure of this study

There is the large potential of an existential threat from the impact of GCC to human society that can only be addressed on a global scale over a period of time spanning multiple generations of national and international political leaders. This threat to human society encompasses both human and state security. This book seeks to understand various national strategies of major countries for addressing the challenges of GCC in the contending contexts of human and state security. In Annex I to the report of the 21st COP held in 2015 in Paris there is provided a list of countries and their global greenhouse gas emissions. From this, it can be determined that as a group the major power nations of the US, China, India, Russia, and Japan, along with the member states of the EU, are responsible for over 65% of current global carbon emissions (UNFCCC, 2016). The debates on GCC policies in these various nations and in the EU have evolved in divergent ways along the concerns of human and state and have important consequence for climate strategies. A coherent concept of GCC policy will necessarily require an integrated strategic cooperation among these different powerful nations considering their influence in international organizations and, for several, their wealth. To this there are substantial barriers to such international cooperation, which include:

> Uncertainty, mistrust, conflicting interests, different views of causality, complex linkages to other issues, and the myriad problems of coordinating the behavior of large numbers of actors.
>
> (Conca & Dabelko, 2014, p. 133)

This book will examine the multiple GCC strategies that encompass both human and state security. The examination will discuss what is needed from major states to confront broad security concerns that encompass the themes of human security that compete with the status quo of state and international security. Whether state security is privileged over human security in efforts to address GCC can depend on the "exact ways in which the securitization of climate change unfolds" (Diez et al., 2016, p. 3). This first chapter has provided the introduction to the topic and an overview of the issues under examination for this book. Here, there has been a discussion of the international recognition of the GCC phenomenon and its consequences. Additionally, the chapter examined how GCC has become perceived as both a state and human security threat. Two frameworks were presented in this chapter that can yield questions on how major nations approach the challenges of GCC. In an overview, the first framework considered the multiple strategies, mitigation, adaptation, and capacity building, for the international community to address the effects of GCC. A second framework considers the differentiation of GCC policies in terms of security and how the efficacy of these strategies could be impacted by whether state security is prioritized over human security.

In providing answers to these questions, this book presents chapters that focus on the specific major state powers of the US, China, India, Russia, and Japan, plus one chapter on the European Union (EU). The US (see Chapter 5) with its Trump Administration has in place as top officials of the Environmental Protection Agency and the Department of Interior individuals who have taken public stands contradicting the science of human-caused climate change (Milman, 2016), further there has been a shift from a general interest in poverty reduction and economic development, apart from any linkage of these issues to GCC, to the paramount issue of state security (Porter, 2017). The focus on the EU (its members producing 12.08% of GHG emissions) is due to its self-recognition as a normative environmental authority for a union of democratically, economically, and technologically developed countries (see Chapter 6). China has recently overtaken the US in the percentage of global GHG emissions (20.09% vs. 17.89%) and continues its economic expansion, particularly its emphasis on renewable energy technologies, and has expressed the view that GCC should be addressed in terms of development issues (see Chapter 7). India sits at the threshold of significant economic expansion and population increase, and with its continuing dependence on coal unless there is significant development assistance provided, its percentage share of GHG emissions will likely increase from its present 4.10% (see Chapter 8). As seen in Chapter 9, Japan with 3.79% of global GHG emissions has a long history of industrialization and development and an intriguing record of environmental concern in light of its history of a paucity of natural resources. Russia with 7.53% of global GHG emissions has considerable concerns regarding state security and a permanent position on the UN Security Council (see Chapter 10), and sees economic opportunities unfolding in some of the consequences of GCC.

Each of the respective chapters will consider the theme of a national agenda (or as in its chapter, an EU agenda) on GCC as it impacts human and state security. These countries are identified for this study because of their responsibility in contributing to the concentration of GHG emissions, and, for several, their resources to facilitate the needs of other countries as they undertake the necessary efforts for increasing mitigation, adaptation, and capacity building. Additionally, there is consideration of the nation's defense policies that recognize the threats posed by the effects of GCC to state and human security. For each chapter on these major powers the discussion includes consideration of the following prominent concerns:

a   How is the problem perceived by the state and the extent of the awareness of the threat of GCC that itself is incremental, yet global, in nature?
b   How does the national government approach the threat domestically in terms of the GCC strategies, delineated in this introductory chapter?
c   How does the government approach the threat within the efforts of the UN in its attempts to address GCC?
d   Based on the notion that these states have the capacities to further the strategies that addresses GCC, what factors might be limiting the capacities (i.e. sufficient abilities: willingness and readiness) to deal with GCC from a security perspective.

Prior to these six chapters, which focus on the policies of major nations, three chapters provide context both to international policy on GCC and to geographical areas that are presently grievously impacted by GCC. Chapter 2 addresses the efforts of the UN in its attempt to address through an international effort the challenges presented by GCC. Following this discussion are Chapters 3 and 4, which examine, the Asia-Pacific region and Africa, and the security challenges that arise from some specific consequences of GCC for these parts of the world. For all the countries and regions identified in these chapters there are varying relationships with the international community in the goal of establishing an international structure that seeks to address the concerns associated with GCC. There is a decided unequal sharing of political power between developed and developing countries that will be in the background of a critical approach considered in several of these chapters. Following the six chapters on the examination of specific major states there is a concluding chapter that examines the lessons that have been, or are yet to be, learned.

Introduction   31

In its assessment of the likelihood for success in confronting GCC, the UNDP observed the need for collective action by the international community that relies on strategies carried out by states:

> Avoiding the unprecedented threats posed by dangerous climate change will require an unparalleled collective exercise in international cooperation.... However, a sustainable global emissions pathway will only be meaningful if it is translated into practical national strategies.
>
> (UNDP, 2008, pp. 19–20)

Ultimately, the goal of this book is to provide some means for assessing how concerns of state and human security impact the practicality of these national strategies regarding the challenges presented by climate change.

References

Ackerman, Frank & Stanton, Elizabeth A. (2008, May). *The cost of climate change: What we'll pay if global warming continues unchecked.* National Resources Defense Council. Accessed June 1, 2017: www.nrdc.org/sites/default/files/cost.pdf

Adams, Kenneth Alan (2016). The psychohistory of climate change: A clear and present danger. *The Journal of Psychohistory*, 44(2), 114–135.

Adano, Wario R. & Daudi, Fatuma (2012, May). *Links between climate change, conflict and governance in Africa.* Institute for Security Studies Paper No. 234. Accessed June 15, 2016: www.issafrica.org/uploads/Paper_234.pdf

Adler, Ben (2015, December 9). The Paris climate agreement won't call for keeping fossil fuels in the ground. *Grist.* Accessed July 1, 2016: https://grist.org/climate-energy/the-paris-climate-agreement-wont-call-for-keeping-fossil-fuels-in-the-ground/

Agamben, Giorgio (2002). Security and terror (transl. Carolin Emcke). *Theory and Event*, 5(4), 24.

Agamben, Giorgio (2005). *State of exception* (transl. Kevin Attell), Chicago, IL: University of Chicago Press.

Anand, Ruchi (2004). *International environmental justice: A North–South dimension.* London: Routledge.

Asmal, Kader (2001). Water is a catalyst for peace. *International Journal of Water*, 1(2), 200–209.

Atapattu, Sumudu (2009). Climate change, human rights, and forced migration: Implications for international law. *Wisconsin International Law Journal*, 27, 607–636.

Ayers, Jessica (2009). International funding to support urban adaptation to climate change. *Environment & Urbanization*, 21(1), 225–240.

Barnett, J. (2001). Adapting to climate change in Pacific Island countries: The problem of uncertainty. *World Development*, 29(6): 977–993

Barnett, J. (2003). Security and climate change. *Global Environmental Change*, 13(1), 7–17.

BBC News (2004, January 9). *Global warming "biggest threat."* Accessed January 1, 2017: http://news.bbc.co.uk/2/hi/science/nature/3381425.stm

Beard, Charles B. & Eisen, Rebecca J. (2016). *Vector-borne diseases. The impacts of climate change on human health in the United States: A scientific assessment.* U.S.

32 Don Wallace

Global Change Research Program. Accessed December 29, 2016: https://health2016.globalchange.gov/vectorborne-diseases.

Biello, David (2009, November 23). Can climate change cause conflict? Recent history suggests so. *Scientific American*. Accessed June 1, 2017: www.scientificamerican.com/article/can-climate-change-cause-conflict/

Biswas, Niloy Ranjan (2011, winter). Is the environment a security threat? Environmental security beyond securitization. *International Affairs Review*, vol. 20. Accessed: www.iar-gwu.org/node/300

Bodle, Ralph, Donat, Lena, & Duwe, Matthias (2016). The Paris Agreement: Analysis, assessment and outlook. CCLR, *Carbon & Climate Law Review*, 10(1), 5–22.

Boeno, R., Boeno, R., & Soromenho-Marques (2015, December). Climate change and securitization: The construction of climate deterrence. *Coleç. Meira Mattos*, 9(36), 607–617.

Boeno, R. & Ferrão, J. (2016). Climate change and land use planning in security strategies. *Social Analysis*, 221(4), 802–821.

Brauch, Hans Günter (2008a). Conceptualising the environmental dimension of human security in the UN. *International Social Science Journal*, 59(193), 19–48.

Brauch, Hans Günter (2008b). Securitizing climate change. Paper presented at the 50th ISA Annual Convention, New York, February 15–18, 2008.

Brown, Lester. 1977. *Worldwatch Paper 14: Redefining national security*. Washington, DC: Worldwatch Institute.

Brown, N. (1989). Climate, ecology and international security. *Survival*, 31(6), 519–532.

Brown, O., Hammill, A. and McLeman, R. (2007). Climate change as the "new" security threat: Implications for Africa. *International Affairs*, 83(6), 1141–1154.

Brzoska, Michael (2015). Climate change and military planning. *International Journal of Climate Change Strategies and Management*, 7(2), 172–190.

Buhaug, Halvard (2016). Climate change and conflict: Taking stock. *Peace Economics, Peace Science and Public Policy*, 22(4), 331–338.

Burleson, Elizabeth (2008). A climate of extremes: Transboundary conflict resolution. *Vermont Law Review*, 32, 477–523.

Burleson, Elizabeth (2011). Energy revolution and disaster response in the face of climate change. *Villanova Environmental Law Journal*, 22, 169–188.

Burleson, Elizabeth (2016, March 29). Paris Agreement and consensus to address climate challenge. *Insights*, 20(8), American Society of International Law. Accessed July 1, 2016: www.asil.org/insights/volume/20/issue/8/paris-agreement-and-consensus-address-climate-challenge

Burns, Wil (2016) Loss and damage and the 21st conference of the parties to the United Nations Framework Convention on Climate Change. *ILSA Journal of International & Comparative Law*, 22, 415–433.

Buzan, Barry (1983). *People, states and fear*. Chapel Hill, NC: University of North Carolina Press.

Buzan, Barry, Wæver, Ole & de Wilde, Jaap (1998). *Security—A new framework for analysis*. London: Lynne Rienner.

Byrne, J. Peter & Zyla, Kathryn A. (2016). Climate exactions. *Maryland Law Review*, 75, 758–786.

Campbell, Kurt M., Gulledge, Jay, McNeill, J.R., Podesta, John, Ogden, Peter, Fuerth, Leon, Woolsey, R. James, Alexander, T.J., Lennon, Smith, Julianne, Weitz, Richard, & Mix, Derek (2007, November). *The age of consequences: The foreign policy and national security implications of global climate change*. Accessed May 26, 2016:

https://csis-prod.s3.amazonaws.com/s3fs-public/legacy_files/files/media/csis/pubs/071105_ageofconsequences.pdf

Carnwath, Lord (2016). Climate change adjudication after Paris: A reflection. *Journal of Environmental Law*, 28, 5–9.

CBC News (2011, December 12). *Canada and Kyoto: A history of the country's involvement and its greenhouse gas emissions*. Accessed January 3, 2017: www.cbc.ca/news2/interactives/canada-kyoto/

Climate Action Tracker (2017). *Effect of current pledges and policies on global temperature*. Accessed January 20, 2018: http://climateactiontracker.org/global.html

CNA (2007). *National security and the threat of climate change*. Accessed January 20, 2018: www.cna.org/CNA_files/pdf/National%20Security%20and%20the%20Threat%20of%20Climate%20Change.pdf

Çolakoğlu, Elif (2017). The climate change and energy security nexus. *Ataturk University Faculty of Economics and Administrative Sciences Journal*, 31, 71–84.

Cole, Daniel H. (2008a). Climate change, adaptation, and development, *UCLA Journal of Environmental Law & Policy*, 26, 1–20.

Cole, Daniel H. (2008b). The Stern Review and its critics: Implications for the theory and practice of benefit-cost analysis. *Natural Resources Journal*, 48, 53–90.

Conca, Ken & Dabelko, Geoffrey (2014). *Green planet blues: Critical perspectives on global environmental politics* (5th ed.). Boulder, CO: Westview Press.

Dabelko, Geoffrey (2014). An uncommon peace: Environment, development, and the global security agenda. In Ken Conca & Geoffrey Dabelko (Eds.), *Green planet blues: Critical perspectives on global environmental politics* (pp. 244–257). Boulder, CO: Westview Press.

Daily, Matt (2012, June 27). *Exxon CEO calls climate change engineering problem. Reuters*. Accessed December 28, 2016: www.reuters.com/article/us-exxon-climate-id USBRE85Q1C820120627

Dalby, S. (1994). The politics of environmental security, in Jyrki Kakronen (Ed.), Green *security or militarized environment?* (pp. 25–53). Dartmouth: Aldershot.

Day, Thomas, Röser, Frauke Tewari, Ritika, Takeshi, Carsten Warnecke, Kuramochi, Hagemann, Markus, Fekete, Hanna, Sterl, Sebastian, Kurdziel, Marie, Gonzales, Sofia, & Höhne, Niklas (2015, December 14). *What the Paris Agreement means for global climate change mitigation*. New Climate Institute. Accessed July 1, 2016: https://newclimate.org/2015/12/14/what-the-paris-agreement-means-for-global-climate-change-mitigation/

De Brito, Rafaela Rodrigues (2011). A climate for conflict or cooperation? Addressing the securitisation of climate change. Paper presented at Third Global International Studies Conference, 17–20 August 2011, University of Porto, Portugal.

De Brito, Rafaela Rodrigues (2012). The securitisation of climate change in the European Union. In *Global security risks and West Africa: Development challenges* (pp. 120–134). Paris: OECD Publishing.

de Chazournes, Laurence Boisson (2014). The climate change regime—Between a rock and a hard place? *Fordham Environmental Law Review*, 25, 625–651.

Detraz, Nicole & Betsill, Michele M. (2009). Climate change and environmental security: For whom the discourse shifts. *International Studies Perspectives*, 10(3), 303–320.

Deudney, D. (1990) The case against linking environmental degradation and national security. *Millennium*, 19 (3): 461–476

Deudney, D. (1999) Environmental security: A critique. In D. Deudney & R. Matthew (Eds.), *Contested grounds: Security and conflict in the new environmental politics* (pp. 187–219). Albany, NY: SUNY Press.

Diez, Thomas; von Lucke, Franziskus; & Wellmann, Zehra (2016). *The securitisation of climate change: Actors, processes and consequences*. New York: Routledge.

Donohue, Laura K. (2011). The limits of national security. *American Criminal Law Review*, 48, 1573–1756.

Eaton, Seth W. (2008). Winter is frigid, so I say bring on the greenhouse effect! A legal and policy discussion of the strategies the United States must employ to combat global warming. *Pepperdine Law Review*, 35, 787–834.

Eckstein, Gabriel (2009). Water scarcity, conflict, and security in a climate change world: Challenges and opportunities for international law and policy. *Wisconsin International Law Journal*, 27, 409–461.

Edwards, M. J. (1999) Security implications of a worst-case scenario of climate change in the South-west Pacific. *Australian Geographer*, 30(3), 311–330.

English, Robert, (2016, February 19). Foreign-policy realist of 2016. *Nation Magazine*.

Erdem, Engin (2017). Environmental security in the context of human security concept. *Journal of Gazi Academic View*, 10(19), 255–281.

European Council (2003, December 12). *A secure Europe in a better world: European security strategy*. Accessed January 20, 2018: a_secure_europe_in_a_better_world-1. pdf

Feeney, Elizabeth (2015, February 6). Adaptation, mitigation and the securitization of climate change. *E-International Relations*. Accessed December 10, 2016: www. academia.edu/11026509/Adaptation_Mitigation_and_the_Securitization_of_Climate_ Change

Feitelson, E. Tamimi, A., & Rosenthal, G. (2012). Climate change and security in the Israeli-Palestinian context. *Journal of Peace Research*, 49, 241–257.

Femia, Francesco (2016). (2016, January/February). *Dangerous intersection: Climate change and national security*. The Environmental Forum. Accessed June 5, 2017: https://elliott.gwu.edu/sites/elliott.gwu.edu/files/The%20Debate_Forum_2016_Jan%20 %281%29.pdf

Fischetti, Mark (2015, March 2). *Climate change hastened Syria's civil war*. Accessed June 1, 2017: www.scientificamerican.com/article/climate-change-hastened-the-syrian-war/

Flatt, Victor B. (2012). Adapting laws for a changing world: A systemic approach to climate change. *Florida Law Review*, 64, 269–293. Accessed May 19, 2016: http:// scholarship.law.ufl.edu/flr/vol. 64/iss1/6

Flowers, Arija (2011). National security in the 21st century: How the National Security Council can solve the president's climate change problem. *Sustainable Development Law & Policy*, 11, 50–55.

Floyd, Rita (2008). The environmental security debate and its significance for climate change. *The International Spectator*, 43(3), 51–65.

Floyd, Rita (2010). *Security and the environment. Securitisation theory and US environmental security policy*. New York: Cambridge University Press.

Floyd, Rita (2012, January 20). Climate change, environmental security studies and the morality of climate security. *E-International Relations*. Accessed December 10, 2016: www.e-ir.info/2012/01/20/climate-change-environmental-security-studies-and-the-morality-of-climate-security/

Forsell, Nicklas, Turkovska, Olga, Gusti, Mykola, Obersteiner, Micahel, den Elzen, Michel, & Havlik, Petr (2016). Assessing the INDC's land use, land use change, and forest emission projections. *Carbon Balance and Management*, 11; 26–43.

Introduction 35

Gasper, Des & Gómez, Oscar A. (2014, December 16). *Human security—Twenty years on*. UN Development Programme, Human Development Reports. Accessed May 19, 2016: http://hdr.undp.org/en/content/human-security-%E2%80%93-twenty-years

Gilley, Bruce, & Kinsella, David (2015, April-May). Coercing climate action. *Survival*, 57(3), 7–28.

Gleditsch, Nils Petter (2012). Whither the weather? Climate change and conflict. *Journal of Peace Research*, 49(1), 3–9.

Gunter, Jr., Mike (2016). Book review: Climate change and European security. *Review of Policy Research*, 33(3), 338–340.

Haley, Lucy (2011). Book note: Human security and non-citizens: Law, policy and international affairs. *Stanford Journal of International Law*, 47, 265–269.

Hall, Margaux J. & Weiss, David C. (2012). Avoiding adaptation apartheid: Climate change adaptation and human rights. *Yale Journal of International Law*, 37, 309–366.

Hamilton, Clive (2015, March 10). Geoengineering is not a solution to climate change. *Scientific American*. Accessed December 28, 2016: www.scientificamerican.com/article/geoengineering-is-not-a-solution-to-climate-change/

Hassan, Shaukat (1991). *Environmental issues and security in South Asia*. Adelphi Paper (no. 262), International Institute for Strategic Studies.

Hauer, Moritz (2014). *Climate change complexity broadening the horizon from Copenhagen to Paris*. Thesis, Faculty of Culture and Society. Malmo University.

Helm, D. (2008). Climate-change policy: Why has so little been achieved? (PDF). *Oxford Review of Economic Policy*, 24(2), 211–238. doi:10.1093/oxrep/grn014. Retrieved 2 September 2009.

Hermwille, Lukas (2016). Climate change as a transformation challenge—A new climate policy paradigm? *Gaia: Okologische Perspektiven in Natur-, Geistes- und Wirtschaftswissenschaften*, 25(1), 19–22.

Herring, Eric (2013). Historical materialism. In Alan Collins (Ed.), *Contemporary security studies* (3rd ed.) (pp. 42–53). Oxford: Oxford University Press.

Hertzberg, Martin & Schreuder, Hans (2016). Role of atmospheric carbon dioxide in climate change. *Energy & Environment*, 27(6–7), 785–797.

Höhne, Niklas H., Kuramochi, Takeshi, Warnecke, Carsten, öser, Frauke R., Fekete, Hanna, Hagemann, Markus, Day, Thomas, Tewari, Ritika, Kurdziel, Marie, Sterl, Sebastian & Gonzales, Sofia (2016): *The Paris Agreement: Resolving the inconsistency between global goals and national contributions*. Accessed June 5, 2017: www.researchgate.net/publication/309653866_The_Paris_Agreement_resolving_the_inconsistency_between_global_goals_and_national_contributions

Holland, Andrew & DeGarmo, Albert James (2014). *Military perspectives on climate change from around the world*. The Global Security Defense Index on Climate Change. American Security Project. Accessed December 11, 2016: www.americansecurityproject.org/climate-energy-and-security/climate-change/gsdicc/

Holland, Andrew & Vagg, Xander (2013, March 21). *Global Security Defense Index on climate change: Preliminary results*. American Security Project. Accessed December 11, 2016: www.americansecurityproject.org/ASP%20Reports/Ref%200121%20-%20Global%20Security%20Defense%20Index%20P-Results.pdf

Hsiang, S.M., Burke, M., & Miquel, E. (2013). Quantifying the influence of climate on human conflict. *Science* 341(6152), 1235367, doi:10.1126/science.1235367

ICEM (2011). *ICEM CAM brief climate change adaptation and mitigation methodology (CAM)*. Accessed January 20, 2018: www.icem.com.au/documents/climatechange/cam/CAM%20brief.pdf

IPCC (2007). *Climate Change 2007: Working Group II: Impacts, Adaptation and Vulnerability.* [Glossary A–D.] Accessed March 19, 2016: www.ipcc.ch/publications_and_data/ar4/wg2/en/annexessglossary-a-d.html

IPCC (2014a). *Climate Change 2014: Synthesis report.* Contribution of Working Groups I, II and III to the Fifth Assessment Report of the Intergovernmental Panel on Climate Change [Core Writing Team, R.K. Pachauri and L.A. Meyer (Eds.). IPCC, Geneva, Switzerland. Accessed March 19, 2016: www.ipcc.ch/pdf/assessment-report/ar5/syr/SYR_AR5_FINAL_full_wcover.pdf

IPCC (2014b). *Climate Change 2014: Impacts, adaptation, and vulnerability.* Accessed June 5, 2017: www.ipcc.ch/report/ar5/wg2/

IPCC (2016). *Strategic planning schedule AR6.* Intergovernmental Panel on Climate Change. Accessed May 29, 2017: http://ipcc.ch/

IRIN (2007, June 28). *Climate change—only one cause among many for Darfur conflict.* Accessed May 26, 2016: www.irinnews.org/news/2007/06/28-0

Jaitly, Ashok (2009). South Asian perspective on climate change and water policy. In David Michel & Amit Pandya (Eds.), *Troubled waters: Climate change, hydropolitics, and transboundary resources* (pp. 17–31). Stimson Center, accessed May 19, 2016: www.stimson.org/rvproto/partner.cfm?SN=RV200902021934

Kelley, Colin P., Mohtadi, Shahrzad Cane, Mark A., Seager, Richard, & Kushnir, Yochanan (2015). *Climate change in the Fertile Crescent and implications of the recent Syrian drought. Proceedings of the National Academy of Sciences.* Accessed May 26, 2016: www.pnas.org/content/112/11/3241.full

Ki-moon, Ban (2007, April 17) *U.N. Sec. General, Statement at the Security Council debate on energy, security and climate.* Accessed May 19, 2016: www.un.org/apps/news/infocus/sgspeeches/search_full.asp?statID=79#

King, Marcus (2016, January/February). *Dangerous intersection: Climate change and national security.* The Environmental Forum. Accessed June 5, 2017: https://elliott.gwu.edu/sites/elliott.gwu.edu/files/The%20Debate_Forum_2016_Jan%20%281%29.pdf

Kohona, Palitha (2016). Climate change—are we really confronting this challenge? *Environmental Policy and Law*, 46(2), 109–111.

Lattanzio, Richard K. (2012). International climate change financing: The climate investment funds. *Environmental Research Journal*, 6(6), 503–520.

Lee, James R. (2009). *Climate change and armed conflict.* New York: Routledge.

Linnér, Björn-Ola & Selin, Henrik (2003). *The thirty year quest for sustainability: The legacy of the 1972 UN conference on the human environment.* Paper presented at Annual Convention of International Studies Association, Portland, Oregon, USA, February 25—March 1, 2003, as part of the panel "Institutions and the Production of Knowledge for Environmental Governance."

Livermore, Michael A. (2017). The perils of experimentation. *Yale Law Journal*, 126, 636–694.

Macabrey, Jean-Marie (2009, March 11). Researchers: Sea levels may rise faster than expected, *New York Times.* Accessed May 26, 2016: www.nytimes.com/cwire/2009/03/11/11climatewire-researchers-warn-that-sea-levels-will-rise-m-10080.html

MacKenzie, Debora (2015, September 9). Why welcoming refugees makes economic sense for Europe. *New Scientist.* Accessed June 4, 2017: www.newscientist.com/article/mg22730383-800-why-welcoming-more-refugees-makes-economic-sense-for-europe/

Maertens, Lucile (2013). *A depoliticized securitization? The case of environmental securitization within the United Nations.* Paper presented at 8th Pan-European Conference on International Relations, Krakow, Poland, September 18–21, 2013.

Marzec, Robert P. (2015). *Militarizing the environment: Climate change and the security state.* Minneapolis, MN: University of Minnesota Press.

Mathai, Manu, & Narayan, P.S. (2017, March 25). The Paris Agreement and after. *Current Science,* 112(6), 1099–1100.

Mayer, Benoit & Rajavuori, Mikko (2016). National fossil fuel companies and climate change mitigations under international law. *Syracuse Journal of International Law & Commerce,* 44, 55–120.

McDonald, M. (2008). Securitization and the construction of security. *European Journal of International Relations* 14(4), 563–587.

McGlade, Christophe & Ekins, Paul (2015). The geographical distribution of fossil fuels unused when limiting global warming to 2°C. *Nature.* 517, 187–190. Accessed December 29, 2016: www.nature.com/nature/journal/v517/n7533/full/nature14016.html

Mecklin, John (2017). It is two and a half minutes to midnight—2017 Doomsday Clock Statement. *Bulletin of the Atomic Scientists.* Science and Security Board. Accessed January 29, 2017: http://thebulletin.org/sites/default/files/Final%202017%20Clock%20Statement.pdf

Melley, Timothy (2012). *The covert sphere secrecy, fiction, and the national security state.* Ithaca, NY: Cornell Press.

Mendelsohn, Robert, Dinar, Ariel, & Williams, Larry (2006). The distributional impact of climate change on rich and poor countries. *Environment & Development Studies,* 159–178 (2006).

Millennium Project (n.d.). Accessed: http://millennium-project.org/millennium/es-2def.html

Milman, Oliver (2016, December 12). Trump's transition: Sceptics guide every agency dealing with climate change. *Guardian.* Accessed December 30, 2016: www.theguardian.com/us-news/2016/dec/12/donald-trump-environment-climate-change-skeptics

Mohamoud, Awil, Kaloga, Alpha, & Kreft, Sonke (2014) *Climate change, development, and migration: an African diaspora perspective.* Germanwatch. Accessed May 26, 2016: http://germanwatch.org/en/download/9112.pdf

Moran, Daniel (2011). *Climate change and national security: A country-level analysis.* Washington, DC: Georgetown University Press.

Murdoch, Gillian (2009, April 28). *Q + A: How does climate change hit GDP?,* Reuters. Accessed May 26, 2016: www.reuters.com/article/2009/04/27/us-climate-adb-sb-idUSTRE53Q0K720090427

Nagel, John Copeland (2010). Climate exceptionalism. *Environmental Law,* 40, 53–88.

Naser, Mostafa Mahmud (2012). Climate change, environmental degradation, and migration: A complex nexus. *William & Mary Environmental Law & Policy Review,* 36, 713–768.

Outka, Uma (2016). The Obama Administration's Clean Air Act legacy and the UNFCCC, *Case Western Reserve Journal of International Law,* 48, 109–125.

Page, E. (2000). Theorizing the link between environmental change and security. *Review of European Community & International Environmental Law* 9(1): 33–43

Peoples, Columba & Vaughan-Williams, Nick (2010). *Critical security studies. An introduction.* Abingdon: Routledge.

38   Don Wallace

Physicians for Social Responsibility (n.d.). *Health implications of global warming: Vector-borne and water-borne diseases.* Accessed June 28, 2016: www.psr.org/assets/pdfs/vector-borne-and-water-borne.pdf

Porter, Eduardo (2017, July 11). Is a more prosperous world more secure? Not as Trump sees it. *New York Times.* Accessed July 13, 2017: www.nytimes.com/2017/07/11/business/economy/trumps-security-vision-leaves-little-room-for-plowshares.html?_r=0

Pumphrey, Carolyn (2008). *Global climate change: National security implications.* Strategic Studies Institute: US Army War College, Carlisle, PA.

Rachels, James & Rachels, Stuart (2012). *The elements of moral philosophy.* New York: McGraw-Hill.

Regan, Patrick M. (2015). *The politics of global climate change.* London: Paradigm Publishers.

Reveron, Derek S. & Mahoney-Norris, Kathleen A. (2012). Issue spotlight: Incorporating human security into national strategy. *The Georgetown Public Policy Review*, 17, 61–77.

Rothe, Delf (2016). *Securitizing global warming.* New York: Routledge.

Ruhl, J.B. (2000). Working both (positivist) ends toward a new (pragmatist) middle in environmental law, 68 *Geo. Wash. L. Rev.* 522, 523.

Sayne, Aaron (2011, June). *Climate change adaptation and conflict in Nigeria. United States Institute of Peace. Special Report 274.* Accessed May 26: www.usip.org/sites/default/files/Climate_Change_Nigeria.pdf

Schwartz, Peter & Randall, Doug (2003). An abrupt climate change scenario and its implications for United States National Security. Accessed May 19, 2016: http://eesc.columbia.edu/courses/v1003/readings/Pentagon.pdf

Scott, Shirley (2012). The securitization of climate change in world politics: How close have we come and would full securitization enhance the efficacy of global climate change? *Review of European, Comparative, and International Environmental Law*, 21, 220–230.

Scott, Shirley & Khan, Shahedul (2016). The implications of climate change for the military and for conflict prevention including through peace missions. *Air & Space Power Journal Africa & Francophonie*, 7(3), 82–94. Accessed June 6, 2017: www.au.af.mil/au/afri/aspj/apjinternational/aspj_f/article.asp?id=189

Shear, Michael (2017, June 1). Trump will withdraw U.S. from Paris Climate Agreement. *New York Times.* Accessed June 2, 2017:www.nytimes.com/2017/06/01/climate/trump-paris-climate-agreement.html

Snyder, Jared, & Binder, Jonathan (2009). The changing climate of cooperative federalism: The dynamic role of the states in a national strategy to combat climate change. *UCLA Journal of Environmental Law & Policy*, 27, 231–260.

Sowers Spring, Ursula Oswald & Hans Gunter Brauch, (2008) Reconceptualizing security in the 21st century: Conclusions for research and policy-making. In Hans Gunter Brauch et al. (Eds.), Globalization and environmental challenges: Reconceptualizing security in the 21st century (pp. 941–952). Berlin: Springer.

Stern, Nicholas (2006). *Stern Review Report on the economics of climate change.* Accessed June 1, 2017: http://webarchive.nationalarchives.gov.uk/20100407172811/www.hm-treasury.gov.uk/stern_review_report.htm

Stillings, Zackary (2014). Human rights and the new reality of climate change: Adaptation's limitations in achieving climate justice. *Michigan Journal of International Law*, 35, 637–671.

Talkin, Jared (2012, May 17). The securitization approach: A desirable option for future climate change policies?, *Consilience: The Journal of Sustainable Development.*

Accessed: 12 December, 2016: www.consiliencejournal.org/blog/2012/05/17/the-securitization-approach-a-desirable-option-for-future-climate-change-policies/

The White House (2015). *National security strategy*. Accessed June 6, 2017: https:// obamawhitehouse.archives.gov/sites/default/files/docs/2015_national_security_ strategy_2.pdf

Thwaites, Joe (2014). Climate change at the UN Security Council: Conceptual and procedural controversies. In Ken Conca & Geoffrey Dabelko (Eds.). *Green planet blues: Critical perspectives on global environmental politics* (pp. 300–310). Boulder, CO: Westview Press.

Toscano, Julia (2015). Climate change displacement and forced migration: An international crisis. *Arizona Journal of Environmental Law & Policy*, 6, 457–490.

Trombetta, Maria Julia (2008). Environmental security and climate change: Analysing the discourse. *Cambridge Review of International Affairs*, 21(4), 585–602.

Trtanj, Juli M. & Jantarasami, Lesley (2016). *Water-related illness. The impacts of climate change on human health in the United States: A scientific assessment.* U.S. Global Change Research Program. Accessed: December 29, 2016: https://health2016. globalchange.gov/water-related-illness#figure-167.

Ullman, Richard (1983). Redefining security. *International Security*, 8(1), 129–153.

UN News Centre, 2016). *"Dramatic" action needed to cut emissions, slow rise in global temperature—UN Environment report*. United Nations. Accessed: December 31, 2016: www.un.org/apps/news/story.asp?NewsID=55464#.WgeveSMrLZv

UNDP (1994). *Human development report 1994*. Accessed May 19, 2016: http://hdr. undp.org/sites/default/files/reports/255/hdr_1994_en_complete_nostats.pdf

UNDP (2008). *Human development report 2007/2008: Fighting climate change: Human Solidarity in a divided world*. Accessed May 26, 2016: http://hdr.undp.org/en/content/ human-development-report-20078

UNEP (2016, May). *Adaptation finance gap report*. UN Environmental Programme. Accessed June 1, 2017: www.unep.org/climatechange/adaptation/gapreport2016/

UNFCCC (1992). *United Nations framework convention on climate change: FCC/ INFORMAL/84/Rev.1 GE.14-20481 (E)*. Accessed January 20, 2018: http://unfccc.int/ files/essential_background/convention/background/application/pdf/convention_text_ with_annexes_english_for_posting.pdf

UNFCCC (2009, May 9). *S. Treaty Doc No. 102–38, 1771 U.N.T.S. 107*. Accessed May 19, 2016: https://unfccc.int/resource/docs/convkp/conveng.pdf

UNFCCC (2014). *Kyoto Protocol*. Accessed June 28, 2016: http://unfccc.int/kyoto_ protocol/items/2830.php.

UNFCCC (2015a). *Adoption of the Paris Agreement. FCCC/CP/2015/L.9/Rev.1*. Accessed July 1, 2016: http://unfccc.int/resource/docs/2015/cop21/eng/l09r01.pdf

UNFCCC (2015b). *Negotiation updates COP 21/CMP 11*. Accessed May 19, 2016: http://unfccc.int/meetings/paris_nov_2015/in-session/items/9320.php

UNFCCC (2016, January 29). *Report of the Conference of the Parties on its twenty-first session, held in Paris from 30 November to 13 December 2015. FCCC/CP/2015/10*. Accessed December 31, 2016: http://unfccc.int/resource/docs/2015/cop21/eng/10. pdf#page=30

UNFCCC Secretariat (2013). *An overview of the mandates, as well as the progress of work under institutions, mechanisms and arrangements under the convention. FCCC/ ADP/2013/INF.2*. Accessed June 28, 2016: http://unfccc.int/resource/docs/2013/adp2/ eng/inf02.pdf

40 *Don Wallace*

UNGA (United Nations General Assembly) (2005, March 21). *In larger freedom: towards development, security and human rights for all. Report of the Secretary-General.* UN Doc A/59/2005.

UN Security Council (2007). *Security Council holds first-ever debate on impact of climate change on peace, security, hearing over 50 speakers.* Meetings coverage and press releases. Accessed March, 2013: www.un.org/News/Press/docs/2007/sc9000.doc. htm.

US Dept of Defense (2010, February) *Quadrennial defense review report.* Accessed January 20, 2018: www.defense.gov/Portals/1/features/defenseReviews/QDR/QDR_as_of_29JAN10_1600.pdf

US Dept of Defense (July 29, 2015) DOD releases report on security implications of climate change. Accessed: www.defense.gov/News/News-Releases/News-Release-View/Article/612812/dod-releases-report-on-security-implications-of-climate-change.

US Dept of Defense (July 23b, 2015). *National security implications of climate-related risks and a changing climate.* Accessed May 19, 2016: www.globalsecurity.org/military/library/report/2015/national-implications-of-climate-change_150724.pdf.

Vega, Joyce (2016, November 5). United Nations admits carbon emission goals fall short, Paris Agreement to solve problem. *News Every Day.* Accessed December 31, 2016: www.newseveryday.com/articles/52088/20161105/united-nations-admits-carbon-emission-goals-fall-short-paris-agreement-to-solve-problem.htm

Vidal, John (2011, November 21) Sudan—battling the twin forces of civil war and climate change. *Guardian.* Accessed May 26, www.theguardian.com/environment/2011/nov/21/sudan-civil-war-climate-change

Waever, Ole (1995) Securitization and desecuritization. In Ronnie Lipschutz (Ed.) *On security* (pp. 46–86), New York: Columbia University Press.

Wallace, Perry E. (2009). Climate change, corporate strategy, and corporate law duties. *Wake Forest Law Review,* 44, 757–776.

Walsh, Bryan (2011, October 26). Q&A with U.N. Secretary-General Ban Ki-Moon, *Time magazine.* Accessed May 19, 2016: http://content.time.com/time/specials/packages/article/0,28804,2097720_2097779_2097780,00.html

Warren, Phillip Dane (2016). Forced migration after Paris COP21: Evaluating the "climate change displacement coordination facilities." *Columbia Law Review,* 116, 2103–2144.

Weitzman, M.L. (2007). A review of the Stern Review on the economics of climate change (PDF). *Journal of Economic Literature,* 45 (3): 703–724. doi:10.1257/jel.45.3.703.

Welzer, Harald (2012). *Climate wars: What people will be killed in the 21st century.* New York: Polity.

White, Gregory (2011). *Climate change and migration: Security and borders in a warming world.* Oxford: Oxford University Press.

Wilson, T. (1983). Global climate, world politics and national security. In V. Nanda (Ed.). *The world of climate change: The role of international law and institutions.* Boulder, CO: Westview Press.

World Bank (2012). *Economics of adaptation to climate change: Global cost estimate.* Accessed May 19, 2016: http://climatechange.worldbank.org/content/adaptation-costs-global-estimate.

World Bank (2017). *Climate finance: Overview.* Accessed June 24, 2017: www.worldbank.org/en/topic/climatefinance/overview.

2 The UN regime on global climate change

Don Wallace

With a prodigious concern for the environment the United Nations (UN) has facilitated major international summits on the subject, such as those beginning in 1972 in Stockholm and continuing with the 1992 and 2012 Earth Summits in Rio de Janeiro. The 1992 Rio Conference was formative in its accomplishments, which promoted an agenda focusing on environmental and developmental concerns. Several instruments resulting from this 1992 Earth Summit have become some of the most important international documents for the environment and for sustainable development. These include the Rio Declaration on Environment and Development, Agenda 21, Forest Principles, the Convention to Combat Desertification, and the UN Framework Convention on Climate Change (UNFCCC). The UN Commission on Sustainable Development was established by the United Nations General Assembly (UNGA) in December 1992 to ensure effective follow-up of the Rio Earth Summit including the achievement of the goals of Agenda 21, an action plan covering sustainable development. The texts of these instruments contain clearly stated goals for environmental protection (Mair, 2014).

Several UN bodies have been created to coordinate and foster activities of environmental protection (Conca, 2015). Some of these UN agencies have come to emphasize the challenges of global climate change (GCC) for their endeavors in countries that have been impacted by conflict (Mason, 2014). Many of the UN system's activities on climate change are coordinated through the Working Group on Climate Change, which facilitates system-wide participation of some 40 UN specialized agencies, funds, programs and other bodies to facilitate a coherent approach and joint action of the UN system (UNSCEB, 2014). Its members include *inter alia*: The World Meteorological Organization, World Health Organization, World Bank Group, International Monetary Fund, UN Development Programme, UN Environment Programme, Office of the UN High Commissioner for Refugees, and the UNFCCC. Through this Working Group, its members exchange information, collaborate on joint programming and operational activities, and coordinate their contributions to various system-wide climate change priorities (UNSCEB, 2016). Additionally, the UNGA has consistently included environmental issues on its agenda and various UN Secretary-Generals have identified environmental matters as important challenges for the international community (Conca, 2015). Of the two principal councils of the UN, the Economic and Social Council and the Security Council (UNSC), the former has made the environment in general a major focus of its mandate by initiating various programs and entities including the Commission on Sustainable Development, as well as providing consultative status to numerous environmental NGOs (Conca, 2015).

With this book examining concerns with human and state security challenges impacted by GCC, this chapter considers two primary entities that facilitate the UN role in directly addressing the challenges of GCC for human and state security: (1) the UNFCCC regime and (2) the efforts regarding GCC that have been made by the UNSC. The first of these entities has become the foundation by which GCC has been addressed at the international level. This is the multilateral process embodied in the several formal treaties, the UNFCCC, the Kyoto Protocol, and the 2015 Paris Agreement, and in decisions taken by the Parties under these instruments (Scott, 2015). Through the UNFCCC process, the international community has negotiated various treaties, accords, and protocols that have led to a regime devoted to the human security challenges being engendered by GCC and have established the basic strategies of mitigation, adaptation, and capacity building. This regime coordinates the UN's most important efforts into the domain of interstate negotiations through its annual meetings of the Conference of the Parties.

The UNSC will be examined in light of its authority to address threats to international peace and security. The UNSC's authority, to address threats to international peace and security, could arguably apply to the challenges presented by GCC, such as climate migration, spread of disease, or violent conflict produced or exacerbated by GCC. In contrast to what is seen with the UNFCCC process, the UNSC as an institution has been a reluctant participant in concerns of the environment, particularly those of GCC. In the few explicit discussions on GCC, the UNSC has encountered strong objections from developing countries and from some of its permanent members for considering GCC in terms of state security concerns. However, there is an expanding indirect role of the UNSC that could involve specific, discrete security challenges arising from GCC.

The UNFCCC regime on security and GCC

At the center of the cooperative effort by states is the international regime on climate change that consists of the various agreements developed through the auspices of the UNFCCC (Gilley & Kinsella, 2015). In 2015, the Paris Agreement joined the 1992 UNFCCC and the 1997 Kyoto Protocol as the major agreements that form the central foundation of international climate governance. It was in 1992 that, in order to provide broad principles of the international climate change regime at both the normative and institutional levels, the UNFCCC was adopted at the Earth Summit in Rio de Janeiro (Bodansky, 2000). GCC was originally viewed as a distinct environmental concern, thus the initial policies proposed under the UNFCCC were based on this premise, only later did GCC take on development concerns (Hermwille, 2016). The UNFCCC entered into force in 1994. As of the beginning of 2017, with near universal participation, this treaty is acceded to by 197 parties (196 States and the European Union) (UN Climate Change Newsroom, 2017).

Individualization of objectives and obligations

The basic objective of the UNFCCC is not to reverse greenhouse gas emissions, but to stabilize them (Freestone, 2013) "at a level that would prevent dangerous anthropogenic interference with the climate system" (UNFCCC, Article 2). To accomplish this relatively more modest objective, the UNFCCC established a number of institutions, primarily the Conference of the Parties (COP) and subsidiary bodies on scientific advice and implementation. Additionally, the UNFCCC initiated procedures for reporting and reviewing efforts to achieve stabilization of the atmospheric level of greenhouse gas (GHG) emissions (Dessai, 1999).

There is no universally applicable best set of policies under the UNFCCC, rather, the decision of what constitutes "dangerous anthropogenic interference" requires value judgments, which will vary among different regions of the world (IPCC, 2001). Factors that might affect this assessment of dangerous anthropogenic interference with the climate include the local nature and consequences of climate change impacts, the adaptive capacity of a particular region (the ability to adjust to climate change, and its mitigative capacity (the ability of a country or region to reduce GHG emissions) (IPCC, 2001).

This level of malleability in obligations under the UNFCCC can be identified in additional provisions. Under Article 3(1) of the UNFCCC, Parties are called upon to act "to protect the climate system," though on the basis of "common but differentiated responsibilities and respective capabilities." The most vulnerable countries to adverse impacts of GCC are developing countries with their lower capacity for adaptation as compared to industrialized countries (Mason, 2011; see Chapter 4). Recognizing the differences in capability (as well as perhaps, implicitly, culpability) between developing and developed countries, the UNFCCC calls upon the latter group to take the lead in combating climate change, including its undefined "adverse effects." The conflicting interpretations between the two groups of states over the scope of the obligation of developed states for providing assistance to developing states indicate that more specification in the language of this treaty is needed (Mason, 2011).

In addition to the pliable general obligation in Article 3(1), an additional constraint to the goal of protecting the climate is seen in the preambular language that recalls the principle that States have a "sovereign right to exploit their own resources pursuant to their own environmental and developmental policies." As Scott (2015, p. 74) observed, this sovereign right of exploitation conflicts with the goal of preventing "dangerous anthropogenic interference with the climate." It appears that the parties needed reassurance that efforts identified in the UNFCCC to address climate change would be accomplished without negatively affecting the pursuit of economic growth (Scott, 2015), while preserving the privilege of each state to reap its natural resource supply, even under deteriorating environmental conditions (Skillington, 2012; see Campbell, 2017, explicitly identifying the major industrializing countries of China and India as benefiting from this arrangement).

Mitigation, adaptation, and capacity building

Because of objections from the United States (US), there are no binding commitments in the UNFCCC for mitigation of emissions (Falkner et al., 2011). The core of the UNFCCC lies in Article 4, which identifies the actions to which all parties to the UNFCCC are committed to undertake the "commitments" of the convention (Winebarger, 2012). Under Article 4(1), which invokes the similar language of Article 3, Parties make pledges to address climate change and states are allowed to take into account their common, but differentiated responsibilities and consider "their specific national and regional development priorities, objectives and circumstances." The most demanding requirement of the UNFCCC is for the developed states to adopt national policies to mitigate climate change, with the goal to return to the emissions levels of 1990 by the year 2000 (Winebarger, 2012). Whether or not the developed states adopted these policies, there is no enforcement mechanism for redressing violations of the specific Article 4 commitments. Thus, in this regard, the UNFCCC is a non-binding treaty (Winebarger, 2012) and these provisions are "generally hortatory obligations" (Freestone, 2013, p. 676).

Additionally, Article 4 binds the Parties to develop inventories, adopt policies for adaptation and mitigation, and coordinate with other Parties to meet the goals of the convention. For the developed nations, there are obligations under Article 4(3) to provide new and additional financial resources to developing countries. Article 11(1) of the UNFCCC defines the institution, which will mobilize the new financial resources required by the treaty, as the Financial Mechanism. Here, assistance will be provided as either a grant or on a concessional basis.

Security: human and state

A context of concern for state security is not explicitly recognized in the UNFCCC. The adverse impacts from GCC, which are to be considered in the Article 4 commitments, are better construed as relating to challenges to human security. These include the "adverse effects on the economy, on public health and on the quality of the environment" (UNFCCC, Article 4(1)(f)). Article 3(1) also frames the imperative for addressing GCC at the human level, with the invocation of the normative ideal that "[t]he Parties should protect the climate system for the benefit of present and future generations of humankind" (UNFCCC, Article 3(1)). Additionally, the preambular language to the UNFCCC observes, without specifying, that increased GHG emissions "adversely affect natural ecosystems and humankind," though these adverse effects are not further specified and do not identify an existential concern for humankind being implicated by GCC. Further, the UNFCCC does not make an explicit connection between GCC and the challenges to state security or national sovereignty, let alone make reference to the possibility of GCC leading to conflict either within a society or between states.

The 1992 Earth Summit Rio de Janiero Conference, which adopted the UNFCCC treaty, predates the 1994 report of the UN Development Programme (UNDP) that first introduced the concept of "human security." The 1994 UNDP Human Development Report observed that the "world can never be at peace unless people have security in their daily lives" (UNDP, 1994, p. 1), making the connection of human security to state security at an international level. Though it could not have made reference to the UNDP report, the 1992 UNFCCC does voice concerns for the adverse effects on aspects of what is now known as human security. Further, the UNFCCC did not identify any challenges to international or state security emanating from concerns over the challenges presented by GCC.

Subsequent developments

As a framework providing for objectives, basic principles, various procedures, and some institutions, few obligations are demanded of the Parties by the 1992 UNFCCC. For the parties, the agreement provides minimal immediate political or economic consequences for not upholding its minimal obligations (Scott, 2015). The UNFCCC regime has so far been ineffective in reducing GHG emissions (Held & Hervey, 2011). Importantly, the UNFCCC contemplated further treaties to specify the means for reducing emissions (Scott, 2015).

Kyoto

With a view of strengthening the UNFCCC, the first Conference of Parties created the Ad hoc Group on the Berlin Mandate to develop a process of appropriate action by providing legally binding targets to be taken by the Parties to the UNFCCC (Dessai, 1999). These negotiations culminated in the 1997 Kyoto Protocol and its requirement for developed countries to reduce GHG emissions by accomplishing obligatory results by the years 2008–2012 using a 1990 baseline. The main goal of the Kyoto Protocol was to mitigate GHG emissions in ways that reflected underlying differences in wealth and capacity among the parties. The principle of common obligations that are differentiated for developed and developing countries was continued from the UNFCCC to the Kyoto Protocol as a central component for responding to GCC (Moomaw, 2015), thus developing countries were exempted from these targets (McGee, 2011). For developing countries, because there are no requirements for them to take steps of mitigation or adaptation, the Kyoto Protocol provided only an aspirational goal of engaging in economic development with lower rates of GHG emissions (Moomaw, 2015).

46 *Don Wallace*

Implementation of the Kyoto agreement proceeded with a variety of challenges emerging from the lack of full participation by developed nations and from its exclusion of developing nations from binding obligations (Peterson et al., 2016). Though hailed at the time as a major milestone in the fight against GCC, the US did not formally ratify the Kyoto Protocol and Canada subsequently withdrew its accession from the agreement. Only after much effort to attain the requisite number of accessions did the Kyoto Protocol enter into force in February 2005 (Falkner et al., 2011).

Both the UNFCCC and Kyoto Protocol are structured on a recognition of the responsibility of the developed countries for producing the majority of accumulated GHGs. However, much has changed for this perspective since 1997, particularly with the annual emissions from developing nations now exceeding those of developed countries (Moomaw, 2015; den Eizen et al., 2013). The volume of GHG emissions has steadily increased for China (which was placed in Kyoto's list of developing nations), and in 2005 it surpassed the US as the world's largest carbon emitter (Li, 2016).

The Kyoto Protocol obligated developed countries during the First Commitment Period of 2008 to 2012 to an overall target of an average of a 5.2% reduction below 1990 levels (Winebarger, 2012). For the Second Commitment Period, known as the 2012 Doha Amendment to the Kyoto Protocol, extending to 2020, several countries indicated their unwillingness to participate in this subsequent phase of emissions reduction (Moomaw, 2015). These countries included Russia, Canada, and Japan, which rejected the obligation of setting new targets on emission reductions when emerging nations, such as China and India, have none (Doherty & Lewis, 2012). While entry into force requires the acceptances of 144 states, as of April 2017, only 77 states had ratified the Doha Amendment (UNFCCC, 2017a).

Copenhagen to Paris

The unenthusiastic response to Doha's second round of commitments and the contentious negotiations, which preceded the failed attempt to achieve a post-Kyoto agreement in Copenhagen in 2009, indicated the need for a new approach that could avoid the shared argument from both developing and developed countries that addressing climate change means interference with economic development (Moomaw, 2015). Whether to include the developing countries that were becoming major sources of GHG emissions became a stumbling block in the prelude to the Copenhagen COP (Falkner et al., 2011). By the time of the Copenhagen COP in 2009, the focus of international efforts on confronting GCC had shifted from attempting to achieve jointly planned action toward a decentralized effort that instead stressed the imperative of economic growth (Brookes, 2010). Thus, in 2009 the major powers at the Copenhagen COP, by avoiding a commitment to mitigation efforts or to provide funding for adaptation efforts of developing countries, focused on securing their national interests, rather than promote a global response to GCC (Falkner et al., 2011).

Although the 2012 Doha Amendment did not gain broad acceptance, the Doha COP meeting extended until 2020 the Kyoto Protocol, which had been due to expire by the end of 2012. Additionally, there was a consensus at Doha for setting a date in 2015 for the development of a new international document. This new agreement would be more than a mere amendment to the Kyoto Protocol, rather it would succeed this Protocol in 2020, and would itself be a separate instrument under the UNFCCC (Scott & Andrade, 2012). This new document would become the 2015 Paris Climate Change Agreement.

The international community came to see the obligations of the Kyoto Protocol, being premised on specific emission reduction requirements, as problematic for the success of the efforts at addressing GCC. With neither the US nor China being bound by the emissions reduction targets of Kyoto this also became a major reason for the reduced likelihood of any possible achievements for the Kyoto arrangement (Scott, 2015). Additionally, the divergent perspectives among the Parties regarding who is responsible for GCC and who is most vulnerable, and whether anyone has the abilities to ameliorate the situation, had made reaching a consensus on either mitigation or adaptation policies increasingly difficult. The UNFCCC process had aggravated the divide between those states that have the technology and financial ability to address GCC, and those states that require the support of others (DePledge & Feakin, 2012). Thus, GCC negotiations are largely impacted by the politics of global inequality in light of the economic challenges for addressing the reduction of GHGs (Wong, 2015).

2015 and Paris

Despite the challenges for reaching a consensus on a new document at the 21st COP meeting of 195 nations agreed upon a new instrument, the 2015 Paris Climate Change Agreement. Consensus was reached among these countries for taking measures within the UNFCCC framework that involve GHG mitigation, adaptation to the impacts of climate change, and capacity-building of developing nations.

A newly introduced approach of the Paris Agreement places great reliance on the intended nationally determined contributions (INDCs) of countries' efforts under a framework of transparency that includes a regular evaluative process of these efforts (Peterson et al., 2016). The INDCs are not formally part of the Paris Agreement, although it refers to them. Their content is also not binding (Bodle et al., 2016), in that parties are only obliged under Article 4(2) of the Paris Agreement to "pursue" measures "with the aim of achieving the objectives" of their INDCs. The non-binding nature of these targets resulted from the resistance by some of the industrialized countries to the requirements being placed solely on developed countries under the Kyoto Protocol during the first commitment period (Mathai & Narayan, 2017). The global "stocktake" under Article 14 provides for periodic five-year assessments of the efforts of parties. Article 3 requires the INDCs to be "ambitious," "represent a progression over time," and be established "with the view to achieving the purpose of this Agreement." Each

48 *Don Wallace*

further five-year assessment, under a principle of "progression," should establish a more ambitious target than the previous one (Paris Agreement, Article 3). Parties are required to consider the best methods of controlling GHG emissions and for mitigating the impacts of climate change (Warner, 2016). In this respect, unlike the Kyoto Protocol, the Paris Agreement is not a hierarchical international agreement, but rather provides for voluntary, state-party driven pledges regarding the INDCs (Fry & Amesheva, 2016).

Parties are not bound by the language of the Paris Agreement to comply with their INDCs to curtail emissions, though they are required to review their progress every five years. Thus, there is a reliance on establishing necessary details of compliance measures by future COPs. Details will entail the transparent and serious processes that will be needed to develop the metrics for assessing comparability of efforts by parties, reporting the results of the assessments, along with some policy-surveillance mechanisms (Aldy & Pizer, 2015). Bodansky (2016) suggested that the use of a "soft" instrument as opposed to legally binding obligations might alleviate the concerns of the various actors at the international level. However, as Milman (2015) observed, the lack of obligation beyond a submission and review of volunteered individual targets is not without its controversy; James Hansen, a pioneer on the present-day scientific knowledge of GCC declared the Paris Agreement a "fraud," finding "no action, just promises" (Pengelly, 2015).

Mitigation, adaptation, loss and damage, and capacity building

The Paris Agreement continues the UNFCCC's call for GCC strategies of mitigation, adaptation, and capacity building (Bodle et al., 2016). In the Paris Agreement, the concern for mitigation is to hold, with some modest specificity, the "increase in the global average temperature to well below 2°C above pre-industrial levels and to pursue efforts to limit the temperature increase to 1.5°C above pre-industrial levels" (Paris Agreement, Article 2). To achieve this, the Parties agreed "to undertake and communicate ambitious efforts" through domestic policy, while recognizing the need to support developing country Parties to allow for effective implementation of the Agreement (Paris Agreement, Article 3; see Outka, 2016).

For adaptation, the Paris Agreement expressed a goal to increase the "ability to adapt to the adverse impacts" of GCC and to "foster climate resilience" (Paris Agreement, Article 2). This emphasis on adaptation culminates a recognition, which had been developing in the decade prior to the Paris Agreement, that the efforts of the world community to mitigate emissions had been ineffective and that a shift in policy emphasis to a substantive commitment to adaptation was necessary (Burns, 2016). Additionally, the Paris Agreement provides recognition that adaptation policies, if perceived as efforts to moderate potential damages from climate change, are themselves insufficient in light of the probable negative effects of GCC for developing countries. Over the past decade support has developed for a concept known as "loss and damage" (Paris Agreement, Article

8). This concept arises from the recognition that the impacts of GCC will not be adapted to, but will involve impacts to ecosystems and human institutions for which there could be "irrecoverable negative impacts, such as loss of freshwater resources or culture or heritage" (Burns, 2016, p. 417). This provision on loss and damage in the Paris Agreement was included to serve as a continuation of the Warsaw International Mechanism for Loss and Damage Associated with Climate Change Impacts established at the COP 19 meeting in Warsaw (UN Climate Change Newsroom, 2016); this continuation however, does not entail a commitment to a principle of liability for states (Sands, 2016).

A further strategy was the underscoring of the need to provide "finance flows" (Paris Agreement, Article 2(1)). There is an explicit recognition in the Paris Agreement of the need to support developing countries to effect the implementation of its provisions (Paris Agreement, Article 3). Prior to 2025 the Conference of the Parties, serving as the meeting of the Parties to the Paris Agreement, is required to set a new collectively quantified goal from a floor of US$100 billion per year (COP-21, 2015, para. 54), taking into account the needs and priorities of developing countries (Paris Agreement, Article 9(3)). Much remains to be seen (Kohona, 2016), as attempts at achieving similar goals set in previous COPS on finance mechanisms have been viewed by developing nations with disappointment (Ferrey, 2013).

Security and accession

Also in 2015, the UN led the effort to establish the Sustainable Development Goals (SDGs) that replaced the earlier Millennium Development Goals (MDGs). These earlier MDGs were adopted at the Millennium Summit of the UN in 2000 to set the world's targets, including environmental sustainability, for addressing extreme poverty in its many forms. While the MDGs were supposed to be achieved by 2015, an extended process was needed to continue development goals for the years 2015–2030. In addition to a recognition in the new agenda of the SDGs for the need to foster "personal security" (UNGA, 2015, Article 34), the SDGs recognize the reciprocal relationship between sustainable development and state and human security:

> We are determined to foster peaceful, just and inclusive societies which are free from fear and violence. There can be no sustainable development without peace and no peace without sustainable development.... Sustainable development cannot be realized without peace and security; and peace and security will be at risk without sustainable development.
> (UNGA, 2015, Preamble & Article 35)

In Goal 13 of the SDGs there is an explicit overture to take urgent action to combat climate change and its impacts (UNGA, 2015, Article 59). Goal 13 makes specific acknowledgement that the UNFCCC is the primary international, intergovernmental forum for negotiating the global response to climate change.

The adoption of the SDGs by the UN General Assembly preceded, by a few weeks, the unanimous acceptance of the Paris Agreement on climate change. In this the Paris Agreement gets incorporated into the SDGs allowing for a convergence of the two processes fostered by the UN that reach the objective of sustainable development (Fry & Amesheva, 2016). In this regard, there is reference to the Parties' human rights obligations in the preamble of the Paris Agreement, the first multilateral environmental agreement to do so (Savaresi, 2016).

The Paris Agreement expresses a level of urgency, not seen in the UNFCCC or the Kyoto Protocol. The preambular section of the 2015 Paris Agreement recognizes an existential level of concern for human security in

> that climate change represents an urgent and potentially irreversible threat to human societies and the planet and thus requires the widest possible cooperation by all countries, and their participation in an effective and appropriate international response, with a view to accelerating the reduction of global greenhouse gas emissions.
>
> (Paris Agreement, 2015, Preamble)

This recognition stands in marked contrast to the more tepid expression of concern noted in the 1992 UNFCCC agreement, which merely recognized that GCC "*may* adversely affect natural ecosystems and humankind" (UNFCCC, 1992, Preamble, emphasis added). Yet, the overt concern for human security of the Paris Agreement seems somewhat undermined by the lack of a hierarchical authority legislating and enforcing explicit targets for GHG reduction. The voluntary more practicable approach to target setting stems from the experience of the intransigence of major GHG-emitting powers refusing to relinquish their sovereign authority to an outside entity.

This sense of urgency for the fate of human societies has carried over to the accession phase for the agreement. The agreement was opened for signature in an Earth Day ceremony in New York City, on April 22, 2016. Though only 26 parties had ratified the document by August 2016, as of April 2017, 149 UNFCCC members have ratified the treaty. By its terms the Paris Agreement entered into force 30 days after 55 countries that produce 55% of the world's GHGs acceded to the agreement (Paris Agreement, Article 21). These requisites were met on November 4, 2016.

Consensus before and after Paris

The achievements of the Paris Agreement were constrained by the need for compromise (Osofsky et al., 2016), particularly where the multilateral climate regime of the UNFCCC, involving 197 Parties, adopts decisions by consensus. This process of inclusion allows a country or a group of countries to hinder progress (van Asselt & Bößner, 2016). Prior to the Paris Agreement smaller coalitions of states had arisen in the mid-2000s to provide an action-oriented alternative to the Kyoto process. The most prominent example, the Asia-Pacific Partnership on

Clean Development and Climate (APP) from 2006 to 2011, included Australia, Canada, China, India, Japan, South Korea, and the US, and purported to work with industry partners on development and transfer of climate technologies (Scott & Andrade, 2012). Arguably, this coalition constituted a diversion from the broader multilateral efforts of the UN climate regime and was seen as being self-serving (Eckersley, 2010). The APP during the Obama presidency was shifted to other initiatives (van Asselt & Bößner, 2016). In the early 2000s there was the same perception of hindrance in a broad multilateral approach to GCC that prompted activity at regional, national, and sub-national institutions. These efforts included individual state governments in the US developing GHG initiatives to address mitigation and, with the EU, initiating an emission-trading regime (Scott & Andrade, 2012; see Chapter 6).

Though with the Paris Agreement there has been a reinvigoration of the multilateral international approach to address GCC, this will not entirely supplant the efforts of smaller coalitions of states or the activities at national and sub-national levels. The details of the broad strokes of the Paris Agreement will need to be further developed at subsequent COP meetings and at national, sub-national, and non-governmental levels (Osofsky et al., 2016). Over 19,000 government officials and 6,000 representatives of NGOs and businesses attended the Paris COP. Not only did the event culminate in the international agreement, but it provided the setting for numerous pledges by a variety of entities at all levels from nations to IGOs, NGOs, and businesses. Observers have noted that it is the breadth of this consensus, and its continuation, that will be required to ensure the success of the implementation of this formal instrument (Bodansky, 2016; van Asselt & Bößner, 2016; Savaresi, 2016). Developing an approach for best utilizing this seemingly fragmented structure of diverse and heterogeneous global governance will present a challenge (Pattberg & Zelli, 2016). Of concern is the observation by Widerberg (2016) that the spreading of authority and of function across various state and non-state entities, can lead to ambiguity of legitimacy, willingness, and responsibility for addressing GCC challenges.

The 22nd session of the Conference of the Parties (COP-22), convened in November 2016 in Marrakech, with a focus of furthering the details that will enable the Paris Agreement when it comes into effect in 2020. One of the tasks of COP-22 was to demonstrate that the UNFCCC process would continue the momentum created with the Paris COP-21 by the actions of non-state actors and by other international agreements such as the 2016 Kigali Amendment to the Montreal Protocol and the 2016 provision to International Civil Aviation Organization (ENB-b, 2016). COP-22 coincided with the 2016 US Presidential elections and it was speculated that much of its efforts were accelerated in an unstated effort to "Trump-proof" the Paris Agreement, which allows for withdrawal three years after its effective date and then requires a full year before a withdrawal by a party can take effect. Outgoing US Secretary of State John Kerry observed, at COP-22, in remarks that did not explicitly reference the new US President: "It's within our power to put the planet back on a better track. ... Doing that requires holding ourselves ... accountable to facts, not opinion; to

52   *Don Wallace*

science, ... and certainly not to political bromides and slogans" (Hirji, 2016). Under the requirements of Article 28 of the Paris Agreement, the intended US withdrawal, announced June 1, 2017 (Shear, 2017), will not be effective until November 4, 2020, at the earliest (UNFCCC, 2017a). This will be one day after the next US Presidential election, but two months prior to the start of the victor's term of office. Before the effective date of the withdrawal, the Trump Administration will likely reject a view that it is required to be actively engaged in the implementation of the Paris Agreement (see Chapter 5) (ENB-b, 2016).

The Marrakech Action Proclamation (UNFCCC, 2016) continued the sense of exigency for the need to adequately address GCC, "our climate is warming at an alarming and unprecedented rate and we have an urgent duty to respond." There was a call for efforts at adaptation and for building capacity where the Parties agreed to "underscore the need to support efforts aimed to enhance their adaptive capacity, strengthen resilience and reduce vulnerability," and "to strengthen and support efforts to eradicate poverty, ensure food security and take stringent action to deal with climate change challenges in agriculture." Contrary to the earlier stated perception in the UNFCCC treaty that there is a trade-off between economic growth and environmental protection, the Marrakech Action Proclamation envisions that the "transition in our economies required to meet the objectives of the Paris Agreement provides a substantial positive opportunity for increased prosperity and sustainable development" (UNFCCC, 2016). This assertion at least suggests some temporizing of the UNFCCC's recognition of a privilege of sovereign states to reap their natural resources at the expense of the environment and a rejection of a zero-sum perspective regarding economic development and environmental protection.

The many hard-learned lessons achieved by the UNFCCC regime in the attempts to further the international efforts for addressing GCC may yet provide significant results as it progresses to the year 2020, when the Paris Agreement supplants the Kyoto Protocol. However, there are challenges that remain at all levels of strategies for mitigation, adaptation, and capacity building. Further, the advent of the Trump Administration in the US signifies a renewed lack of unanimity in the international community, arising at a time when UNFCCC regime saw with the 2015 Paris Agreement a formal recognition of the existential nature of the threat and of the pressing need for renewed, concerted effort to address the issue of GCC.

The UNSC on GCC and security

In addition to the developments of the UNFCCC regime in its fluctuating efforts to ensure aspects of human security, UN institutions have been the locus of intense international discussion regarding GCC in terms of its role for exacerbating, if not causing, violent disorder (DePledge & Feakin, 2012) that could threaten state security through extreme weather events, scarce resources, or migration crises (Nevitt, 2015). Among the first international instruments making an explicit connection between GCC and peace and security was that

The UN regime on global climate change   53

passed by the UNGA in 2009 in response to the campaign by a coalition of Pacific island nations (Gray, 2012). This resolution was made in the context of the primary responsibility of the UN for the maintenance of international peace and security (UNGA, 2009, Resolution 63/281). Distinct from this limited recognition by the UNGA, this section of this chapter focuses on the efforts of the UN Security Council (UNSC), and its authority over international peace and security that consider discrete GCC-related issues.

UNSC Charter authority

The UNSC has the legal mandate under the UN Charter to maintain international peace and security. Under Chapters VI and VII, the UNSC can assess a situation to determine whether there is a threat to international peace (Article 39) and then, under Articles 41 and 42, its Chapter VII authority can justify the authorization of either non-military measures or the military use of force to address this identified threat. Arguably, both the need to act and the response to be taken to confront the threat will depend on the nature of the event or condition that is threatening international peace and security.

The Charter does not stipulate what constitutes a qualifying threat, allowing the UNSC considerable latitude for this determination. A threat to human security was traditionally insufficient to justify UNSC authority under Chapter VII (Gray, 2012). A threat to peace under early historical practice was limited to the existence of armed conflict (Hood, 2015; see Chapter 4 on Africa for a discussion on GCC and armed conflicts). Yet, despite the historical practice, the scope of this authority has been in flux along the two underlying issues under Chapter VII of what constitutes a threat to peace and what measures the UNSC may take to maintain or restore international peace and security (Cogan, 2015). Since the end of the Cold War, the UNSC has indicated an expanding view that includes non-traditional security challenges (Nevitt, 2015). To invoke the UNSC's Chapter VII power in the context of climate change, the precondition of a threat to international peace and security must be one that encompasses a challenge posed by GCC. Under an expanding conception of a threat to international security there has also been an enlargement of the measures that will be considered for addressing the identified challenge.

Various observers see that an expanding Chapter VII authority arguably covers both the causes and consequences of GCC (DePledge & Feakin, 2012; Gilley & Kinsella, 2015). Scott and Andrade (2012) observed that the UNSC used its Chapter VII authority, in light of the 2001 September 11 terrorist attacks and the subsequent concerns on the proliferation of weapons of mass destruction, to impose a series of binding obligations on all states, where these resolutions were not directed at any specific country and did not provide for an explicit termination date. UNSC Resolution 1373 required all Member States under Chapter VII to adjust their national laws so that they could ratify existing international conventions relating to terrorism. UNSC Resolution 1540, concerning weapons of mass destruction, established similar obligations under Chapter

VII for all States, such as a requirement to modify domestic legislation. Thus, both resolutions identified international threats without linking them to specific states or armed conflicts, then obligated member states to provide preventative and remedial domestic measures to confront them (Gilley & Kinsella, 2015). This non-traditional use of Chapter VII authority could likewise similarly apply to the disruptive consequences of GCC where there is no single responsible state, yet the consequences can be catastrophic for undetermined victims. In this vein, observers (DePledge & Feakin, 2012; Gilley & Kinsella, 2015; Scott & Andrade, 2012) have argued that Chapter VII authority encompasses dynamic responses for addressing GCC that can be required of nations by the UNSC to deal with underlying causes and consequences of GCC. Under Chapter VII there is authority for the UNSC to compel states to address the causes and consequences of threats to international security (Nevitt, 2015).

> [A UNSC] resolution on climate change mitigation or adaptation could require all states to ratify specific climate change treaties, impose additional obligations on all states, and establish a committee to monitor compliance. As with Security Council Resolution 1540, this could include an emphasis on capacity building. A committee could be established to provide the [UNSC] with the necessary scientific and other expertise, as well as progress reporting.
>
> (Scott & Andrade, 2012)

The UNFCCC, the Kyoto Protocol, and the Paris Agreement involve mitigation, adaptation, and capacity building goals if not obligations. Importantly, broadening the authority of the UNSC under Chapter VII to cover a range of obligations that includes mitigation would erase any arguable legal basis in the difference between acting on the consequences of climate change as opposed to addressing GCC itself. Eliminating this difference would completely reject any remnant of restriction on UNSC authority under a fading traditional perspective that limits Chapter VII concerns to ongoing armed conflict and excludes situations of threats to human security (Scott 2012).

The UNSC has formally considered the explicit impact of GCC on international security on only four occasions, and without passing any formal resolutions (Scott & Khan, 2016). In 2007, the United Kingdom (UK) as chair organized the Council's first open debate on the relationship between GCC and security issues. In 2011, Germany arranged the second similar debate on GCC and security. In 2013 and 2015, there were confidential Arria-Formula meetings of the UNSC on GCC and security. With these debates, the UNSC found itself divided, with the US, the UK, and France supporting an expanded UNSC role for addressing GCC issues in a security context, and with Russia and China, supported by much of the developing world, opposing such measures (Warren, 2016). During the 2007 discussion China's representative, Liu Zhenmin, asserted that though GCC may have certain security implications, China found it more an issue of sustainable development, and voiced support for pragmatic discussions on such issues within the context of the UNFCCC regime. The Russian UNSC representative, Vitaly Churkin, expressed similar support for the role of the UNFCCC for addressing GCC and noted that the UNSC should only deal with the consideration of questions that directly relate to its mandate (UNSC, 2007). The concern was voiced that just the decision by the UNSC to hold the debate would itself undermine the mandate of the relevant processes of the UNFCCC that were already addressing these issues (UNSC, 2007). Member states (notably India and Russia) questioned the evidentiary basis for a causal link between climate change and security (Conca et al., 2017). Gilley and Kinsella (2016) observed that China and Russia would probably veto any UNSC resolutions that called for the use of coercive measures to address GCC threats.

In 2011, the UNSC did unanimously pass a Presidential Statement recognizing the adverse effects of GCC for security, though reaffirming that the UNFCCC is the primary body for addressing climate change (Warren, 2016; Warren & Utterback, 2015). The Statement identified concern both "over the possible adverse effects of climate change that may, in the long run, aggravate certain existing threats to international peace and security" and for "possible security implications of the loss of territory of some States caused by sea-level-rise" (UNSC, 2011b). Observers (see Warren, 2016; Scott & Andrade, 2012) have noted that this finding could provide a basis to justify invoking UNSC security measures in the future, should the different views among the P-5 members be resolved.

With the emergence of the concept of "human security" in international discussions in the early 1990s, the perspective of protection of the state from armed conflicts was supplemented with concerns for the protection of individuals (Hood, 2015). In recent developments, the UNSC has assumed greater authority under its Chapter VII powers to maintain international peace where it has increasingly taken the view that the underlying causes of failing and failed states serve as threats to world order, and that it may need to take nontraditional measures to restore fragile states (Agnew, 2016). Dating back to 1992 the President of the UNSC declared, "non-military sources of instability in the economic, social, humanitarian and ecological fields have become threats to peace and security" (UNSC President, 1992). Making this connection between the "ecological" field and security provided an earlier basis for invoking UNSC security measures for discrete GCC challenges that present humanitarian crises.

UN Security Council: GCC and R2P principles

In its 2005 Resolution 1625, the UNSC affirmed its broad determination to strengthen its conflict prevention capacities (UNSC, 2005), allowing it to better address the intrinsic causes of humanitarian crises. With these required measures, the UNSC took a proactive approach that enlarges its role in conflict prevention to the extent of taking measures concerning the origins of conflict (Gilley & Kinsella, 2015). To this Scott and Khan (2016) observed that the language of UNSC Resolution 1625 requested the UN Secretary-General to assist countries at "risk of armed conflict ... in addressing the root causes of armed conflict" (UNSC Resolution 1625, para. 3(b). This greater willingness to address the factors underlying humanitarian crises has been amplified by the adoption of the principles of the responsibility to protect (R2P), which have enhanced the UNSC authority under Chapter VII (Silander & Wallace, 2015). These principles enshrine the concept of humanitarian intervention and provide a further justification for international intervention into the domestic remit of a nation-state, which could be analogous to GCC-related strategies of mitigation, adaptation, and capacity building (Conca et al., 2017).

In 2009, the UN Secretary-General outlined three key elements for conceptualizing an international responsibility to protect (Silander & Wallace, 2015). As a first element, Ban Ki-moon noted that states have the primary responsibility to protect their populations against mass atrocity crimes. Second, the international community should provide assistance to states in building a capacity to protect their populations from such catastrophes, doing so by addressing underlying conditions that lead to such disastrous results. As a third element, the international community should take measures, including intervention, when states fail to protect their populations from mass atrocity crimes. Under the 2005 UN World Summit Report, military intervention under the auspices of R2P should be authorized only by the UNSC (Miller, 2015) and premised on a finding of a threat to international peace. As the 2009 UN Secretary-General's Report on implementing R2P noted, R2P "strategy stresses the value of prevention, and, when it fails, of early and flexible response tailored to the specific circumstances of each case" (UNGA, 2009). Under the principles of R2P, the emphasis of a duty to act could be satisfied by prevention through development and improvement of human security needs. Clearly, "waiting until war breaks out or until masses of people become internally displaced or refugees is too late and unacceptable to the international community" (Reveron & Mahoney-Norris, 2012, p. 70).

First two R2P principles and GCC strategies

R2P was developed as a means to advise nations and the international community of their obligations to address both human and state security. Yet, the three obligations of R2P do not neatly conform to the necessary strategies for addressing GCC of mitigation, adaptation, and capacity building, though Conca (2015) observed that under a responsibility to prevent, which underlies R2P, proactive measures for both mitigation and adaptation would be necessitated. For example, where states have a first obligation to address the needs of their citizens under the first principle of R2P, most developing states afflicted by the effects of GCC have no control over the global production of GHG emissions, considering their marginal GHG contributions. Thus, obligations to mitigate the root problem must be left to developed and major developing states, which have contributed the most to the problem of carbon emissions.

However, the second principle of R2P does resonate in the scenario of GCC. Under R2P, the international community has an obligation to assist afflicted

The UN regime on global climate change   57

states in building a capacity to protect their populations from the effects of GCC. Here, strategies at adaptation could benefit from support from the international community where efforts are needed to ameliorate the aggravating conditions that result from GCC. Further, the GCC strategy of building capacity fits within this second principle of R2P considering its goal of providing resources for the afflicted society to facilitate the technologies and the poverty reduction reforms that are needed to increase resilience to the effects of GCC.

Third R2P principle of response

Finally, the international community may be required to provide an emergency response to intervene with military assistance should a GCC precipitated disaster strike and the afflicted nation is unprepared and overwhelmed by the calamity. There might be some distinguishing characteristics between the contemplated risks to populations that precipitate R2P responses with those risks that arise from GCC challenges. Outside the GCC context as noted above for R2P there seems to be a consensus that a response of international military intervention, which must be approved by the UNSC, is justified only where a local population is being threatened by or is suffering the effects of mass atrocity crimes. Whereas for GCC disasters that are likely weather-related catastrophic events, the harm inflicted on the population is not as purposeful or as acute as with the infliction of mass atrocity crimes being considered in the R2P context. The harms resulting from GCC events will likely be due to a lack of resources and inadequate management ability for addressing emergencies that arise from weather-related disasters, such as flooding or drought.

The suspicions held by lesser-developed countries of the altruistic nature of the intervention made under the guise of R2P are likely also to be continued in the GCC context (Wong, 2009). In this, the international community has experienced scenarios where countries, following large-scale natural disasters, have rejected outside assistance for its distressed population (e.g. the Myanmar government refused to accept foreign aid after Cyclone Nargis swept over the country, see Frattaroli, 2014). This rejection of outside assistance prompted France to make a futile attempt to have the UNSC invoke R2P principles (Conca, 2015).

There are challenges to the applicability of R2P principles to GCC as a formal matter. In 2005 the UNGA excluded natural disasters from the scope of the R2P doctrine, intending to address only instances of international crimes of mass atrocity (Frattaroli, 2014). The UN Secretary-General also sounded a discouraging note that validated the UNSC's refusal to invoke R2P for the crisis caused by Myanmar's refusal to permit international aid operations (Conca, 2015) and specifically excluded R2P principles from applying to climate change (Malone, 2015). This position of the UN Secretary-General has found endorsement by work of the International Law Commission (ILC, 2012). The doctrinal refusal by the UN to recognize the applicability of R2P to GCC engendered humanitarian crises displays "blindness to environmental realities" (Malone, 2015, p. 1460).

58   *Don Wallace*

Further, the mass atrocity crimes that permit the invocation of R2P principles (Silander et al., 2016) are analogous to the same concerns that underscore the challenges of GCC (Malone, 2009):

> For a crime against humanity, the environmental destruction must be sufficiently widespread or systematic to be considered "inhumane acts of a similar character" to the specified atrocities "intentionally causing great suffering, or serious injury to body or to mental or physical health." ... The Rome Statute specifically incorporates and addresses the norms of the Protocols to the Geneva Convention and the Environmental Modification Convention, and ... at least raises the possibility that war crimes necessarily entail consideration of environmental destruction by incumbent governments or their challengers.
>
> (p. 24)

Thus, the principles of R2P while functionally apposite are not sufficiently formally recognized to include GCC in principle to the extent it would justify military intervention. But, cooperation of states can be required under the Chapter VII authority of the UNSC to use measures that fall short of military intervention in a range of challenges, which are ultimately linked to the consequences of GCC-related events, that would further R2P principles.

From opposition to increased UNSC Authority: GCC and pandemics

The recent practices of the UNSC under its Chapter VII authority suggest that the limitations of R2P to an identifiable risk of mass atrocity crimes may be attenuating. Thus, an identifiable threat to peace from either armed conflict or mass atrocity crimes will not be needed. The Chapter VII authority of the UNSC has in practice developed to encompass natural disasters, pandemics, and the destructive impacts of environmental crises. The UNSC has issued resolutions concerning the discrete effects of climate events at least as an indirect threat to international security. In 1992, UNSC Resolution 794 authorized the use of force under Chapter VII to protect aid and food deliveries in Somalia. Although not explicitly recognized as such, this was a response to an extreme weather event—drought in that country—of which GCC will likely produce more (Scott & Andrade, 2012; Scott, 2012).

Among the many threats to human security that could jeopardize state security would be the consequences of environmental hazards, such as the dramatic environmental changes that are leading to a greater likelihood of global pandemics (Giorgetti, 2013). While the spread of disease that has currently become a matter of international concern may be the product more of globalization processes and not necessarily of GCC, the effects of GCC will be to make possible the increased geographical reach of many diseases once thought to be restricted to the poorer, developing regions of the globe and their specific climates. Furthermore, GCC is literally uncovering threats of pandemics, such as where Russian researchers in 2016, investigating an outbreak of anthrax found, in the Yakutia region in Siberia, 120-year-old corpses, originally buried during a major smallpox epidemic. In the corpses, exposed by the melting permafrost, the researchers found fragments of the virus' DNA (Johnston, 2016). A less sanguine result could have been an exposure to the smallpox virus itself.

Related to the need to address a possible GCC-induced pandemic, is the precedent for expanding UNSC authority to confront threats to international peace. Such a precedent does not involve ongoing armed conflict or mass atrocity crimes resulting from GCC-related challenges. Though not connected to GCC, the UNSC in 2000 resolved that the HIV/AIDS pandemic could pose a risk to stability and security (UNSC, 2000, Resolution 1308). This was the first time that the UNSC has dealt directly with a public health concern. Then, for the only subsequent time of dealing with such a problem, in September of 2014, the UNSC unanimously passed Resolution 2177 to address the Ebola outbreak in West Africa. This time the disease epidemic was declared to be a present threat to international peace and security under Chapter VII. In this the UNSC encouraged states to take steps to bring the disease under control. The UNSC unequivocally "determined" that a pandemic "constitute[d] a threat to international peace and security." This resolution passed with the greatest number of states ever cosponsoring a UNSC resolution, despite the lack of indication that Ebola was likely to generate armed conflict in the short or even medium term (Hood, 2015). With its Resolution 2177, there is now some precedent for action by the UNSC to confront the increased prospect of epidemics of water- and vector-borne diseases, as well as other specific threats that result from GCC (Hood, 2015). Conceivably, the UNSC could similarly identify the risk of long-buried deadly viruses recently exposed by the effects of GCC. The means used to address this form of GCC-generated threat to international peace, could take the form of military assistance from the international community, where such was deemed to have been crucial in controlling the spread of the Ebola virus (Scott & Khan, 2016).

In the few UNSC discussions on linking GCC directly to international and state security, as noted above, there was strong opposition to an extension of UNSC authority over maintenance of international peace and security matters involving GCC (Kanetake, 2016). However, the chronological sequence of these events, the strong opposition in 2007 to an expanded UNSC role in dealing with GCC explicitly as a security matter and then the 2014 overwhelming endorsement of such a role in the threatened pandemic of Ebola, suggests some role in the future for the UNSC for addressing specific challenges related to GCC. With this increasing securitizing involvement of the UNSC in discrete events that can be related to GCC, there is seen a gradual transfer of emergency power to the international level, that will lead to challenges to the legitimacy of traditional leading institutions in public health (Heath, 2016). The UNSC accreted to itself such power in establishing binding policies on dealing with the Ebola crisis.

The UN Secretary-General has underscored the securitization process of health concerns, which will arise as the effects of GCC become more pronounced. In his 2005 report, *In Larger Freedom*, the UN Secretary-General pronounced his readiness to use his powers to call to the attention of the UNSC those instances of overwhelming outbreaks of infectious diseases that threaten international peace and security (UNGA, 2005). Further, the Secretary-General at a 2011 meeting of the UNSC identified pandemics (in addition to GCC and transnational organized crime) as a defining challenge to international peace and security (UNSC, 2011a). The status of the World Health Organization as the leading institution in public health is now challenged by the potentially competitive efforts of other international bodies, such as the UNSC as well as the World Bank (Heath, 2016). The desperate need for resources by developing countries in order to take adaptive measures for confronting GCC and to staunch the loss and damage from its effects will effectively endow significant power to the mechanisms that control the financing of these resources and could lead to bureaucracies that challenge the expertise of these traditional leaders in areas, such as public health, that foster human security (Heath, 2016).

Addressing the specific effects of a GCC-induced threat will allow for an indirect process by these institutions of securitization. The UNSC resolution on the outbreak of Ebola represents the emergence of an acceptable discourse on specific non-traditional threats to international peace and security (Burci & Quirin, 2014). This discourse contributes to the significance for climate event challenges observed for the 1992 UNSC Resolution 794 that authorized Chapter VII protection for aid and food deliveries in drought-stricken Somalia. A securitization process could evolve out of the recognition that discrete events resulting from GCC will precipitate specific challenges in various forms to human security particularly in failed or failing states that can become threats to state security (Giorgetti, 2013). This approach is limited in its focus to the consequences of GCC as opposed to its causes.

By comparison, the use of UNSC authority to require countries to address, through the UNFCCC regime, the broad causes of GCC presents a much more profound challenge to the sovereignty of major power nations. Furthermore, because of the less democratic process of decision-making by the UNSC in comparison with that of multilateral treaty regimes, and because of the enforcement powers the UNSC can employ under its Chapter VII authority, Scott (2012) observed that in the context of securitization, decisions by the UNSC would constitute the invocation of extraordinary measures beyond normal politics.

Conclusion

The UNFCCC regime constitutes a call for both developed and emerging nations to take action and has provided at least an organizational arrangement for a collective effort (Moomaw, 2015). An explicit plan may yet become delineated for achieving the goals of the 2015 Paris Agreement. Importantly, the initial assertion of a needed trade-off between development and climate protection, is temporized with a contrary assertion in the 2016 Marrakech Action Proclamation. Still, not all developed nations are convinced of the necessity for a broad international effort for confronting the challenges of GCC. Developing nations

The UN regime on global climate change   61

will need assurance of the genuineness of the promise of assistance from their developed counterparts.

As generalized concerns for security from GCC challenges increase beyond potential armed conflict and mass atrocity crimes scenarios, there will be a growing moment for the UNSC to enlarge upon the precedents that have seen increased UNSC authority for requiring actions from member states in expanded definitions of discrete threats to security. Yet, central to the concept of the protection of human security was its comprehensive approach in addressing structural causes of human insecurity; this presumes that action becomes necessary well before security issues reach acute crisis points (Hood, 2015) and that the action that is taken must do more than merely restore a state of peace but also address causal factors. The negative impacts of GCC could represent the results of long-developing disasters; success in confronting these challenges will depend on timely resolving structural factors and on addressing the deleterious effects on a society.

Security motivations are powerful political tools, and the developing threats from GCC will be providing more such inducements. The challenge for major powers that have considerable control over the institutions of global governance will be to wield these instruments for the common good of humanity (Carlarne, 2009). A broadly perceived comprehensive environmental role for the UNSC may still find complete fulfillment (Conca, 2015). The measures taken thus far that identify specific results of events relatable to GCC as threats to international peace and security, which will only increase in number and magnitude as climate change ensues, suggest that the UNSC has taken at least some significant strides to that fulfillment. However, the likelihood of coherent action is diminished by the nature of the UNSC for being reactive, hierarchical, poorly informed, and weak in monitoring capabilities (Conca et al., 2017).

Permitting many of these GCC-induced discrete situations to be viewed by the UNSC as a threat to the peace will dramatically broaden its mandate (Hood, 2015). Yet, an even more dynamic, preventive strategy may need to be imposed by the UNSC that would compel UN member states to adopt as binding the measures that have been presented by the UNFCCC as being voluntary in nature. Here, at some level, an inter-generational neglect of adequately establishing GCC-related mitigation and adaptation efforts will need to substitute as a presumption for a finding of the requisite threat to security. This substitution would greatly expand upon a showing of a specific crisis that traditionally has been required under the UN Charter for a finding of a threat to the international security and peace that has enabled UNSC action.

References

Agnew, Alison (2016). A combative disease: The ebola epidemic in international law. *Boston College International and Comparative Law Review*, 39, 97–128.

Aldy, Joseph E. & Pizer, William A. (2015). Alternative metrics for comparing domestic climate change mitigation efforts and the emerging international climate policy architecture. *Review of Environmental Economics and Policy*, 10, 3–24.

Bodansky, Daniel (2000). The United Nations framework convention on climate change: A commentary on a commentary. *Yale Journal of International Law*, 25, 315–317.

Bodansky, Daniel (2016). The Paris climate change agreement: A new hope? *American Journal of International Law*, 110, 288–319.

Bodle, Ralph, Donat, Lena, & Duwe, Matthias (2016). The Paris Agreement: Analysis, assessment and outlook. *Carbon & Climate Law Review*, 1, 5–22.

Brookes, Tom (2010). From a global burden to an engine of growth: Reframing climate policy after Copenhagen. *The Fletcher Forum of World Affairs Journal*, 34, 125–129.

Burci, Gian Luca & Quirin, Jakob (2014, November 14). Ebola, WHO, and the United Nations: Convergence of global public health and international peace and security. *ASIL Insights*. Accessed February 21, 2017: www.asil.org/insights/volume/18/issue/25/ebola-who-and-united-nations-convergence-global-public-health-and

Burns, Wil (2016). Loss and damage and the 21st Conference of the Parties to the United Nations framework convention on climate change. *ILSA Journal of International & Comparative Law*, 22, 415–433.

Campbell, David (2017). The sense in Coase's criticism of Pigou: The ceteris paribus case for intervention. *Journal of Law, Economics & Policy*, 13, 39–54.

Carlarne, Cinnamon (2009). Risky business: The ups and downs of mixing economics, security and climate change. *Melbourne Journal of International Law*, 10, 439–469.

Cogan, Jacob Katz (2015). Stabilization and the expanding scope of the security council's work. *American Journal of International Law*, 109, 324–339.

Conca, Ken (2015). *An unfinished foundation: The United Nations and global environmental governance*. Oxford University Press: New York.

Conca, Ken, Thwaites, Joe, & Lee, Goueun (2017, May). Climate change and the UN Security Council: Bully pulpit or bull in a china shop? *Global Environmental Politics*, 17, 1–20.

COP-21 (2015). *Adoption of the Paris Agreement-Draft decision -/CP.21. Conference of the Parties Twenty-first Session. FCCC/CP/2015/L.9/Rev.1*. Accessed December 10, 2016: http://unfccc.int/resource/docs/2015/cop21/eng/l09r01.pdf

den Eizen, Michel, Olivier, Jos, Höhne, Niklas, Janssens-Maenhout, Greet (2013). Countries' contributions to climate change: Effect of accounting for all greenhouse gases, recent trends, basic needs and technological progress. *Climatic Change*, 121, 397–412.

Dessai, Suraje (1999). The Fifth Conference of the Parties to the United Nations Framework Convention on Climate Change: An advancement or derailment of the process? *Colorado Journal of International Environmental Law and Policy*, 1999, 192–207.

Doherty, Regan & Lewis, Barbara (2012, December 8). Doha climate talks throw lifeline to Kyoto Protocol. *Reuters World News*. Accessed January 29, 2017: www.reuters.com/article/us-climate-talks-idUSBRE8B60QU20121208

DePledge, Duncan, and Feakin, Tobias (2012). Climate change and international institutions: Implications for security. *Climate Policy*, 12 (2012) S73–S84.

Eckersley, Robyn (2012). Moving forward in the climate negotiations: Multilateralism or minilateralism? *Global Environmental Politics*, 12(2), 24–42.

ENB-b (Earth Negotiations Bulletin, 2016, November 21). A brief analysis of the Marrakech Climate Change Conference. 12(9), 36–38. Accessed January 2, 2017: www.iisd.ca/climate/cop22/enb/.

Falkner, Robert, Stephan, Hannes, & Vogler, John (2011). International climate policy after Copenhagen: Toward a "building blocks" approach. In David Held, Angus Hervey, Marika Theros (Eds.), *The governance of climate change* (pp. 202–222). Cambridge: Polity Press.

Ferrey, Steven 2013). Corporate energy responsibility: International and domestic perspectives on supply and demand in the new millennium. *Fordham Environmental Law Review*, 25, 84–140.

Frattaroli, Jessica Lucia (2014). A state's duty to prepare, warn, and mitigate natural disaster damages. *Boston College International & Comparative Law Review*, 37, 173–208.

Freestone, David (2013). Change and sea level rise (panel 3): Can the UN climate regime respond to the challenges of sea level rise? *University of Hawai'i Law Review*, 35, 671–685.

Fry, James D. & Amesheva, Inna (2016). Cleaved international law: Exploring the dynamic relationship between international climate change law and international health law. *The Fletcher Forum of World Affairs Journal*, 40, 73–92.

Gilley, Bruce, & Kinsella, David (2015, April-May). Coercing climate action. *Survival*, 57(3), 7–28.

Giorgetti, Chiara (2013). International health emergencies in failed and failing states. *Georgetown Journal of International Law*, 44, 1347–1386.

Gray, Christine (2012). Climate change and the law on the use of force. In R. Rayfuse & S. Scott (Eds.), *International Law in the Era of Climate Change* (pp. 219–240). Northampton, MA: Edward Elgar Publishing.

Heath, J. Benton (2016). Global emergency power in the age of ebola. *Harvard International Law Journal*, 57, 1–47.

Held, David, & Hervey, Angus (2011). Democracy, climate change and global governance: Democratic agency and the policy menu ahead. In David Held, Angus Hervey, Marika Theros (Eds.), *The governance of climate change* (pp. 89–110). Cambridge Polity Press: UK.

Hermwille, Lukas (2016). Climate change as a transformation challenge—A new climate policy paradigm? *Gaia: Okologische Perspektiven in Natur-, Geistes- und Wirtschaftswissenschaften*, 25(1): 19–22.

Hirji, Zahra (2016, November 21). Marrakech climate talks end on positive note despite Trump threat. *Inside Climate News*. Accessed: February 2, 2017: https://inside climatenews.org/news/21112016/paris-climate-change-agreement-cop-22-marrakech-donald-trump

Hood, Anna (2015). Ebola: A threat to the parameters of a threat to the peace? *Melbourne Journal of International Law*, 16, 29–51.

ILC (2012, April 9). *Fifth report on the protection of persons in the event of disasters*, International Law Commission. UN Document A/CN.4/652.

IPCC (2001). *Climate Change 2001: Synthesis report*. Intergovernmental Panel on Climate Change. Accessed August 4, 2016. www.grida.no/publications/other/ipcc_tar/?src=/climate/ipcc_tar/vol. 4/english/017.htm

Johnston, Ian (2016, August 16). Smallpox could return as Siberia's melting permafrost exposes ancient graves. *Independent*. Accessed August 25, 2016: www.independent. co.uk/environment/smallpox-siberia-return-climate-change-global-warming-permafrost-melt-a7194466.html

Kanetake, Machiko (2016). Subsidiarity in global governance: Subsidiarity in the maintenance of international peace and security. *Law and Contemporary Problems*, 79, 165–187.

Kohona, Palitha (2016). Climate change—Are we really confronting this challenge? *Environmental Policy and Law*, 46(2), 109–111.

Li, Anthony (2016). Hopes of limiting global warming? China and the Paris Agreement on climate change. *China Perspectives*, 1, 49–54.

Mair, Caroline (2014). Climate change: The greatest challenge for the future and a major cross-sectoral area of intervention. *International Community Law Review*, 16, 177–213.

Malone, Linda A. (2009). Green helmets: Eco-intervention in the twenty-first century, American Society of International Law. *Proceedings of the Annual Meeting*, 103, 19–38.

Malone, Linda A. (2015). Environmental justice reimagined through human security and postmodern ecological feminism: A neglected perspective on climate change. *Fordham International Law Journal*, 38, 1445–1471.

Mason, Michael (2011). The ends of justice: Climate vulnerability beyond the pale. In David Held, Angus Hervey, Marika Theros (Eds.), *The Governance of Climate Change* (pp. 162–182). Cambridge: Polity Press.

Mason, Michael (2014). Climate insecurity in (post)conflict areas: The biopolitics of United Nations vulnerability assessments. *Geopolitics*, 19, 806–828.

Mathai, Manu, & Narayan, P.S. (2017, March 25). The Paris Agreement and after. *Current Science*, 112(6), 1099–1100.

McGee, Jeffrey Scott (2011). Exclusive minilateralism: An emerging discourse within, international climate change governance? *Journal of Multidisciplinary International Studies*, 8(3), 1–29.

Miller, Nathan J. (2015). International civil disobedience: Unauthorized intervention and the conscience of the international community, *Maryland Law Review*, 74, 315–375.

Milman, Oliver (2015, December 12). James Hansen, father of climate change awareness, calls paris "a fraud." *Guardian*. Accessed January 2, 2017: www.theguardian.com/environment/2015/dec/12/james-hansen-climate-change-paris-talks-fraud

Moomaw, William (2015). Will the Paris Climate accord and future climate treaties be a vision or a roadmap? *The Fletcher Forum of World Affairs Journal*, 39, 41–48.

Nevitt, Mark P. (2015). The commander in chief's authority to combat climate change. *Cardozo Law Review*, 37, 437–502.

Osofsky, Hari, Benjamin, Lisa, Gerrard, Michael, Peel, Jacqueline, & Titley, David (2016). The 2015 Paris Agreement on climate change: Significance and implications for the future. *Environmental Law Reporter*, 46, 10267–10281.

Paris Agreement (2015). *United Nations framework on climate change.* Accessed August 4, 2016: http://unfccc.int/files/essential_background/convention/application/pdf/english_paris_agreement.pdf

Pattberg, Philipp & Zelli, Fariborz (2016). Global environmental governance in the anthropocene: An introduction. In Philipp Pattberg & Fariborz Zelli (Eds.), *Environmental politics and governance in the anthropocene* (pp. 1–12), Routledge: New York.

Pengelly, Martin (2015, December 12). Obama praises Paris climate deal as tribute to American leadership. *Guardian*. Accessed January 21, 2018: www.theguardian.com/us-news/2015/dec/12/obama-speech-paris-climate-change-talks-deal-american-leadership

Peterson, Thomas, Chester, Steven, & McKinstry, Robert (2016). Unlocking willpower and ambition to meet the goals of the Paris Climate Change Agreement (part one): Shifting needs of law, policy, and economics. *Environmental Law Reporter*, 46, 11024–11033.

Reveron, Derek S. & Mahoney-Norris, Kathleen A. (2012). Incorporating human security into national strategy. *Georgetown Public Policy Review*, 17, 61–77.

Sands, Philippe (2016). Climate change and the rule of law: Adjudicating the future in international law. *Journal of Environmental Law*, 18, 19–35.

Savaresi, Annalisa (2016). The Paris Agreement: An early assessment. *Environmental Policy and Law*, 46(1), 14–18.

Scott, Shirley (2012). The securitization of climate change in world politics: How close have we come and would full securitization enhance the efficacy of global climate change policy? *Review of European Community & International Environmental Law*, 21, 220–230.

Scott, Shirley (2015). Does the UNFCCC fulfil the functions required of a framework convention? Why abandoning the united nations framework convention on climate change might constitute a long overdue step forward. *Journal of Environmental Law*, 27, 69–89.

Scott, Shirley, & Andrade, Roberta (2012). The global response to climate change: can the security council assume a lead role? *Brown Journal of World Affairs*, 18, 215–226.

Scott, Shirley & Khan, Shahedul (2016). The implications of climate change for the military and for conflict prevention including through peace missions. *Air & Space Power Journal Africa & Francophonie*, 7(3), 82–94. Accessed June 6, 2017:

Shear, Michael (2017, June 1). Trump will withdraw U.S. from Paris Climate Agreement. *New York Times*. Accessed June 6, 2017: www.nytimes.com/2017/06/01/climate/trump-paris-climate-agreement.html

Silander, Daniel & Wallace, Don (2015). The United Nations, international organizations and responsibility to protect. In Daniel Silander & Don Wallace (Eds.), *International organizations and the implementation of the responsibility to protect: The humanitarian crisis in Syria* (pp. 9–36). Routledge: London.

Skillington, Tracey (2012). Cosmopolitan justice and global climate change: Toward perpetual peace or war in a resource-challenged world? *Irish Journal of Sociology*, 20, 132–152.

UN Climate Change Newsroom (2016). *Warsaw international mechanism for loss and damage associated with climate change impacts*. Accessed August 4, 2016: http://unfccc.int/adaptation/workstreams/loss_and_damage/items/8134.php.

UN Climate Change Newsroom (2017). *Status of ratification of the convention*. Accessed January 4, 2017, http://unfccc.int/essential_background/convention/status_of_ratification/items/2631.php

UNDP (1994). *Human development report 1994*. Accessed May 19, 2016: http://hdr.undp.org/sites/default/files/reports/255/hdr_1994_en_complete_nostats.pdf

UNSCEB (2014). *How the United Nations system supports ambitious action on climate change*. UN System Chief Executives Board for Coordination. Accessed June 1, 2017: www.unsceb.org/CEBPublicFiles/CEB%202014%20How%20the%20UN%20System%20Supports%20Ambitious%20Action%20on%20Climate%20Change_en.pdf

UNSCEB (2016). *Working group on climate change*. UN System Chief Executives Board for Coordination. Accessed June 1, 2017: www.unsceb.org/content/hlcp-working-group-climate-change

UNFCCC (1992). *United Nations framework on climate change*. Accessed August 4, 2016: http://unfccc.int/files/essential_background/background_publications_htmlpdf/application/pdf/conveng.pdf

UNFCCC (2016). *Marrakech action proclamation for our climate and sustainable development*. Accessed January 2, 2017: http://unfccc.int/files/meetings/marrakech_nov_2016/application/pdf/marrakech_action_proclamation.pdf

UNFCCC (2017). *Status of the Doha Amendment*. Accessed June 20, 2017: http://unfccc.int/kyoto_protocol/doha_amendment/items/7362.php

UNGA (2005, March 21). *In larger freedom: Towards development, security and human rights for all Report of the Secretary-General.* A/59/2005. Accessed February 21, 2017: www.un.org/en/ga/search/view_doc.asp?symbol=A/59/2005

UNGA (2009, June 3). *Climate change and its possible security implications.* A/RES/63/281 Accessed January 4, 2017: www.un.org/en/ga/search/view_doc.asp?symbol=A/RES/63/281

UNGA (2015). *Resolution adopted on 25 September 2015, A/70/1. Transforming our world: the 2030 Agenda for Sustainable Development.* A/RES/70/1.

UNSC (2000, July 17). *Resolution 1308. S/RES/1308 (2000).* Accessed January 4, 2017: https://documents-dds-ny.un.org/doc/UNDOC/GEN/N00/536/02/PDF/N0053602.pdf?OpenElement.

UNSC (2005, September 14). *Resolution 1625. S/RES/1625 (2005).* Accessed January 4, 2017: www.un.org/en/ga/search/view_doc.asp?symbol=S/RES/1625(2005)

UNSC (2007, April 17). *UN Security Council 5663rd meeting, Climate Change. S/PV.5663.* Accessed July 12, 2016, www.un.org/en/ga/search/view_doc.asp?symbol=S/PV.5663

UNSC (2011a, November 23). *6668th Meeting: Maintenance of international peace and security. S/PV.6668.* Accessed February 21, 2017: www.un.org/en/ga/search/view_doc.asp?symbol=S/PV.6668

UNSC (2011b, July 20). *Security Council, in statement, says 'contextual information' on possible security implications of climate change important when climate impacts drive conflict.* Meetings Coverage and Press Releases, 6587th meeting. Accessed February 2, 2017: www.un.org/press/en/2011/sc10332.doc.htm

UNSC President (1992). Press Release, Note by the President of the Security Council, U.N. Press Release S/23500 (January 31, 1992).

van Asselt, Harro and Bößner, Stefan (2016). The shape of things to come: Global climate governance after Paris. *Carbon & Climate Law Review*, 1, 46–61.

Warner, Elizabeth Ann Kronk (2016). Looking to the third sovereign: Tribal environmental ethics as an alternative paradigm. *Pace Environmental Law Review*, 33, 397–436.

Warren, Phillip Dane (2016). Forced migration after Paris Cop21: Evaluating the "climate change displacement coordination facility." *Columbia Law Review*, 116, 2103–2144.

Warren, Dane & Utterback, Nathan (2015, July 7). *Special meeting on climate change.* Climate law blog. Columbia Law School. Accessed: January 4: https://perma.cc/2MSW-RRVD.

Winebarger, Lisa (2012). Standing behind beastly emissions: The U.S. subsidization of animal agriculture violates the united nations framework convention on climate change. *American University International Law Review*, 27, 991–1035.

Widerberg, Oscar (2016). Mapping institutional complexity in the anthropocene: A network approach. In Philipp Pattberg & Fariborz Zelli (Eds.), *Environmental politics and governance in the anthropocene* (pp. 81–102), Routledge: New York.

Wong, Jared (2009). Reconstructing the responsibility to protect in the wake of cyclones and separatism. *Tulane Law Review*, 84, 219–263.

Wong, Penny (2015). From Copenhagen to Paris: Climate change and the limits of rationality, multilateralism, and leadership. *The Brown Journal of World Affairs*, 21, 268–283.

3 Geography of GCC

Asia-Pacific—human and state security

Patrick D. Nunn and Carola Betzold

Covering around one quarter of the Earth's surface, the Asia-Pacific region[1] is geographically diverse yet exhibits commonalities that justify its treatment as a whole. It comprises the southeast corner of the Asian continent and associated island groups (including Japan, Indonesia, and the Philippines) as well as larger ocean-bounded landmasses (principally Australia, New Guinea, and New Zealand) and, farther east, innumerable smaller islands scattered across the vast Pacific Ocean.

Over the past 30 years, the Asia-Pacific region has exhibited unprecedented economic and population growth; average per capita gross domestic product (GDP) more than doubled from US$1,704 in 1984 to US$3,894 in 2014, while the region's population increased from 2.5 billion to 3.8 billion in the same period—growth trajectories that are expected to continue over the next few decades.[2]

The region has the largest proportion of people living in the Low Elevation Coastal Zone (LECZ)—contiguous coasts less than 10m above sea level—compared with total coastal population (living within 100km of the shoreline) than anywhere else; 40.2% in East Asia and the Pacific, 35% in South Asia compared with an average 16% elsewhere; ten of the 15 countries with the largest poor rural LECZ populations are in the Asia-Pacific region (Barbier, 2015). The region also has the world's highest concentration of coastal megacities—those with more than ten million inhabitants[3]—and comparatively high rates of (coastal) urbanization (Gross, Ye, & Legates, 2014). While population growth rates have been slowing (UNESCAP, 2016) and there are signs that both population and economic growth are higher in non-coastal areas than coastal areas (Kummu et al., 2016), it nevertheless seems certain that there will be more rather than fewer people living in the Asia-Pacific LECZ in 15 years' time (UNESCAP, 2016).[4]

Of the 41 countries in the Asia-Pacific region, nine are classified as Least Developed Countries (LDCs), 18 as Developing Countries and 11 as Developed Countries;[5] categories that can be crudely linked to the capacity (human and economic) of each country to respond effectively to disaster and climate change (Gursky, Burkle, Hamon, Walker, & Benjamin, 2014; Manton & Stevenson, 2014). Less easily measured is the ability and will of particular governments to

68 *Patrick D. Nunn and Carola Betzold*

respond appropriately to climate change. The Notre Dame Global Adaptation Index includes both vulnerability to climate change and adaptation "readiness" (Chen et al., 2015). According to this measure, the Asia-Pacific[6] is on average more vulnerable and less prepared than the rest of the world, although there are important cross-country differences. For example, Papua New Guinea and Myanmar receive the lowest scores, while more developed countries like New Zealand fare considerably better (Chen et al., 2015).

Global climate change is expected to have massive impacts on the people and environments of the Asia-Pacific region in myriad ways that have been comprehensively explained, particularly in the relevant chapters of the most recent IPCC assessment (Hijioka et al., 2014; Nurse et al., 2014). In places, lands may "disappear," coastal squeeze will become more pronounced and coastal geographies thereby involuntarily reconfigured. There will be issues around food and water security that will affect millions of people, driving many to migrate in ways that will challenge state security and inter-state relations. And then there will be the underlying non-climatic stressors such as population growth and urbanization that in many places will exacerbate the situation.

This chapter explains the recent and projected (future) impacts of global climate change on the Asia-Pacific region before considering how these may alter both its human (individual) and state security profiles There is a focus on the current preparedness of Asia-Pacific countries and groupings by considering their awareness of global climate change and their understanding of its security implications This chapter concludes with a discussion about how the region's actors can be made more aware of the probable effects of global climate change on human and state security.

GCC in the Asia-Pacific: recent and future human impacts

Manifestations of recent climate change in the Asia-Pacific include temperature rise, increasingly variable precipitation, and sea-level rise. For more than 50 years, temperature in Southeast Asia has been increasing decadally with more hot days (and warm nights). Precipitation does not show a consistent regional trend but in most parts wet-season rainfall has decreased while the number of extreme rainfall events has increased, often in association with a reduction in frequency of lighter rainfall events. In different ways, the combination of changing temperature and precipitation has impacted food production and potable-water availability in most parts of the region over the last few decades and is an underlying cause of increasing disease outbreaks and diminishing public health in some parts.[7]

Sea level has generally been rising faster than the global average (3.2 mm/year) in the western Pacific with rates in the Sea of Japan averaging 5.4 mm/year (1993–2001) and island groups like Solomon Islands and those in Micronesia experiencing rates averaging more than 10 mm/year (1993–2009) (Becker et al., 2012; Hijioka et al., 2014). Sea-level rise is likely the main driver of shoreline retreat and increased frequencies and magnitudes of lowland flooding in the

Asia-Pacific—human and state security   69

region over the past few decades. Catastrophic floods, particularly in Asian mega-deltas, have had greater impacts because of rising sea level (Karim & Mimura, 2008; Smith, Thomsen, Gould, Schmitt, & Schlegel, 2013). Groundwater salinization, a related impact, currently poses a greater threat to livelihoods (Lata & Nunn, 2012), especially for people living in river deltas (Hoque et al., 2016) and on low-lying coasts and atoll islands (Chattopadhyay & Singh, 2013; Ketabchi, Mahmoodzadeh, Ataie-Ashtiani, Werner, & Simmons, 2014). Ocean acidification, a consequence of increasing carbon dioxide (CO_2) uptake by oceans from the atmosphere (where supply is increasing because of increasing combustion of fossil fuels), is increasingly impacting marine food-producing ecosystems in the region (Heenan et al., 2015).[8]

Finally, given that the Asia-Pacific region is "the most disaster-prone area of the world" (Hashim & Hashim, 2016: 85), it is important to comprehend the influence of climate change on hydrometeorological hazards here, including floods, droughts, and tropical cyclones (hurricanes or typhoons). Throughout the region, climate change is exacerbating the effects of these hazards (Thomas, Albert, & Hepburn, 2014).

Turning now to possible future impacts in the Asia-Pacific, temperatures in much of the Asia-Pacific are projected to rise >3°C (above the late twentieth-century baseline) by 2100 depending on global emissions of greenhouse gases. Under the (presently more likely) RCP8.5 emissions scenario, precipitation increases are projected, especially as stronger tropical cyclones become more common and the intensity of the Indian summer monsoon increases—although projections are comparatively crude and inevitably disguise much regional variability (Hijioka et al., 2014). While global efforts are underway to mitigate the causes of accelerated climate change, adaptation is required in the shorter term—and probably for a century or more. Given the climatic diversity of the Asia-Pacific region, the production of more site-specific projections of future climate is needed to allow more realistic local-area adaptation.

Higher temperatures will impact food production, particularly rice, which is being grown close to its heat-stress limit in many parts of the region (Lassa, Lai, & Goh, 2016), although future increased CO_2 and precipitation may help offset this in places.[9] Water scarcity is expected to become a major issue, especially in the more densely populated and more-exposed parts of the region, an issue that is clearly linked to population growth rates (increasing demand) and sea-level rise among other factors (Gosling & Arnell, 2016). Switching to new (e.g., more salt-resistant) or genetically modified food crops may prove an important part of the solution to food security in the region, although climate change is likely to force a spatial reconfiguration of the map of food production, requiring that some growers will need to learn how to grow novel crops and that trade networks are themselves reorganized.

Given the concentration of Asia-Pacific people occupying the LECZ, sea-level rise is inevitably a major concern for the future. Whether this permanently inundates places where people currently live (including places from which they subsist) or whether it simply renders them unproductive, perhaps because of increased flood frequency and salinization, it is likely to result in the large-scale movement of people out of the present coastal zone, crowding into places (like cities) that are perhaps already densely populated, or competing with established rural populations for land and the right to food production (Dasgupta, Laplante, Murray, & Wheeler, 2011). This situation will be magnified by storm surges affecting cyclone-vulnerable coastal cities with Manila, Karachi, and Jakarta likely to experience disproportionately high impacts (Brecht, Dasgupta, Laplante, Murray, & Wheeler, 2012). Population growth reduction is a core solution to these challenges, although the inevitability of population relocation should motivate Asia-Pacific governments to take charge of the process within their borders and contribute to regional initiatives in order to minimize associated problems.

The dependence of Asia-Pacific coastal peoples on marine (-associated) waters for routine sustenance is also threatened by rising (sea-surface) temperatures causing coral bleaching, ocean acidification impacting marine-carbonate faunas, and sea-level rise that will reconfigure nearshore marine ecosystems, many of which are already stressed from decades of unsustainable human interactions and pollution (Hoegh-Guldberg & Bruno, 2010).[10] For most nearshore-dependent coastal communities, anticipating a gradual decline in wild-food productivity, a shift to farmed marine foods is likely to offset the threat of food insecurity to some degree. Fisheries management, including the establishment of (locally managed) marine protected areas in which key food species can be conserved, is a viable solution for Pacific Island countries in particular (McLeod, Salm, Green, & Almany, 2008; Olds, Albert, Maxwell, Pitt, & Connolly, 2013). Aquaculture is also potentially a subsistence solution for dependent coastal peoples and can present them with an income source (Cleasby et al., 2014; Okuzawa et al., 2008).

Finally, warmer temperatures will exacerbate human health issues already of concern owing to growing populations and urbanization in the region. Situations in which increased lowland flooding prevails, leaving *in-situ* populations without drinking water for prolonged periods, are likely to become more common. For example, the spread of chikungunya and dengue fever, "the most important mosquito-borne viral disease in the world" (Benitez, 2009: 1070), throughout the Asia-Pacific over the past few decades is likely to have been accelerated by rising temperature and sea level. Adaptation to insufficient drinking water should focus on water conservation and increasing water productivity (including reuse) that will also address many health issues as well as genetic modification of disease-carrying organisms that will reduce their ability to spread disease, especially in the aftermath of natural disasters when people are at their most vulnerable.

Linking GCC to security in the Asia-Pacific

Together with non-climatic factors like population growth and urbanization, especially in the LECZ, the longer-term climatic drivers of security risk in the

Asia-Pacific described in the previous section explain why background (underlying) risk is increasing and will increase in this region. Yet, for planning purposes, it is the shorter-onset types of climatic risk that will have the most immediate impacts on security, not least because these risks will be superimposed on a changing background risk environment. For example, while (background) sea-level rise is projected to accelerate over the rest of the twenty-first century (Church et al., 2013), the most visible effects on inhabited river deltas and other low-lying coasts will be from wave extremes, such as storm surges, that may have enduring effects on security even dealing "knock-out" blows to some coastal communities by forcing their relocation. One example from Asia refers to the people—perhaps half the world population (especially in China and India)—who depend on water, much of it from seasonal melt of snow, deriving from the Himalaya-Hindu Kush (HKH) region (Barnett, Adam, & Lettenmaier, 2005). Warming is causing the accelerated melting of (HKH) glaciers and is maintaining a 'normal' short-term (dry-season) water supply but will inevitably lead to sustained shortages "with water systems going from plenty to want in perhaps a few decades or less" (op. cit.: 306).

That said, it is important to note that acute human (and state) insecurity always emerges from a combination of factors and, as many authors have noted, it is exceedingly difficult to attribute any particular situation to climate change. Indeed, climate change may be used as a scapegoat in some situations, enabling key players (even states) to escape responsibility. For example, Bangladeshis living in the Ganges–Brahmaputra–Meghna delta are periodically affected by storm surges, the increasingly severe effects of which have been attributed to sea-level rise[11] (allowing extreme waves to reach farther inland) and monsoon intensification. Yet, the estimated 180 million people living in this region have few options for migration, often something also shunned for cultural reasons, so remain in an increasingly exposed location. The decreasing acreage of protective mangrove forest in the Sundarbans exacerbates this exposure. In addition, the construction of cross-border dams (in India) on the Ganges is, by reducing the amount of alluvium reaching the delta, also rendering the area more vulnerable. In short, there is a plethora of human factors that explain the periodic and tragic impacts of storm surges on this delta, many of which could be ameliorated if appropriate action were taken at national and regional levels (Ayeb-Karlsson, van der Geest, Ahmed, Huq, & Warner, 2016; Karim & Mimura, 2008; Mallick & Vogt, 2012).

Human security

Human security—"a condition that exists when the vital core of human lives is protected, and when people have the freedom and capacity to live with dignity" (Adger et al., 2014: 759)—is threatened most by short-onset changes ("disasters") that punctuate longer-term trends which also have considerable disruptive potential. Following the most recent IPCC report (Adger et al., 2014), the effects of climate change on human security were here discussed under two headings: deprivation of immediate basic needs (livelihoods, water, housing) and erosion of livelihood assets (agriculture and food security, human capital [health, education, loss of life]). Both short-onset events and longer-onset climate-linked changes impact these aspects of human security.

At Lataw Village (Tegua Island, Vanuatu), relative sea level rose by 150 mm between 1997 and 2009, causing houses to be routinely flooded and subsistence food gardens to become regularly inundated with seawater. While this is likely to be an effect of both sea-level rise and tectonic subsidence (Ballu et al., 2011), it manifests a situation expected to become more frequent in the next few decades in the region. The impacts on housing and livelihoods were profound, so the community was helped to move to higher ground and to establish a new settlement and food gardens. A concern that this new site is still within reach of the tsunami waves that periodically affect Vanuatu sparked a discussion about insufficient adaptation (Siméoni & Ballu, 2012).

The densely populated Ganges Valley (plain) of India receives perhaps 70% of its summer inflow from (seasonally) melting glaciers, something that will inevitably decline in the future as increased temperatures continue, increasingly causing shrinkage and loss of HKH glaciers and ice cover (Barnett et al., 2005). The inherent vulnerability of the area's population to flooding is illustrated by that which occurred on August 18, 2008 when embankments failed along the Kosi River, a major left-bank tributary of the Ganges that originates in eastern Nepal and receives most of its flow from HKH glacier melt, causing the abrupt displacement of 3.5 million people in India and 60,000 in Nepal (Moench, 2010). What is key is that this event occurred when the Kosi was at below-average (August) levels, its massive human impact attributable to "a failure of interlinked physical and institutional infrastructure systems in an area characterized by complex social, political, and environmental relationships" (Hijioka et al., 2014: 1347). The example isolates the human vulnerability in such places that will amplify the effects of future extreme events, such as the floods that are likely to increase over the next few decades as landslide dams in the HKH are periodically breached (Sud, Mishra, Varma, & Bhadwal, 2015). Understanding of the innate vulnerability of Ganges populations presents an opportunity for adaptation to future extremes.

In many parts of the Asia-Pacific region, but especially along its coasts, the removal of natural protection against extreme events has increased the exposure of nearby populations to these. Good examples include mangrove forests that still line many tropical coasts, both continental and island, but were once formerly far more extensive. A neat example from Ovalau Island (Fiji) showed that 14 of the 16 coastal villages had cleared their coastal mangrove fringes several decades ago, largely at the behest of the colonial government, and are now experiencing concerning shoreline erosion and coastal flooding; the two villages where cultural taboos forbade mangrove clearing are having no such problems (Nunn, 2000). A clear demonstration of the value of mangroves in protecting vulnerable coastal populations came from studies of the 1999 super cyclone that struck Orissa (India), which found that damage to property, agriculture (including livestock) and other assets was significantly lessened because of mangroves; losses per household in a mangrove-protected village were US$33 per household compared to $154 per household in villages protected by an embankment but no mangroves (Das & Vincent, 2009).

Adaptation may seem self-evident as a means of reducing threats to human security but this is not always so. For example, the effects of climate change (especially shoreline erosion, groundwater salinization, ocean acidification) on nearshore (marine and coastal) food resources are in places driving people away from traditional subsistence-based livelihoods towards wage employment. Yet, as this response proves unsatisfactory or unsustainable, so they often return to using marine and coastal resources, placing more pressure on these, and thereby contributing to further (climate-driven) degradation. This has been characterized as the "poverty-environment trap" and is suggested to be a common situation for poor households in rural coastal areas (Barbier, 2015). An example has been documented for rural Kahua Village (Solomon Islands) where an increased emphasis on cash cropping and commercial fishing is driving social changes that will make cooperative (unpaid) adaptive responses to future climate change—once the norm in such communities—far more difficult (Fazey, Pettorelli, Kenter, Wagatora, & Schuett, 2011).

State security

There are three main ways in which climate-forced deterioration of human security in the Asia-Pacific region will impact state security: loss of livelihoods and/or water scarcity and/or disease outbreak/s requiring state intervention; displacement of people leading to migration, both internal and cross-border; and, concentration of people in areas with insufficient resources to sustain them leading to civil unrest. Each of these is discussed separately below, although it is recognized that they are not discrete challenges but ones that may overlap in both time and space.

Loss of livelihoods, water scarcity, disease

For countries where many inhabitants are currently unable to feed themselves adequately, climate change poses an additional source of stress to livelihoods as well as aggravating water scarcity and disease outbreaks and spread. Statistics for entire countries allow the direct implications of climate change for state security to be estimated. For example, Asia-Pacific countries exposed to coastal flooding are likely to be severely impacted by future sea-level rise. In the next few decades, nearly half the coastal GDP of Myanmar and the Philippines may be lost as a result of flooding (Barbier, 2015). Coastal wetlands, often key to coastal people's livelihoods, are also predicted to be similarly impacted; losses in the Asia-Pacific region are predicted to be far greater than other parts of the world[12] (Blankespoor et al., 2014). In the event of a one-meter sea-level rise, China is expected to lose 76% ($9,810\,km^2$) of its coastal wetlands and Myanmar 56% ($1,922\,km^2$).

The next few decades are therefore likely to see the inhabitants of many of the parts of the region most exposed to climate change less able than now to subsist from locally sourced foods leading to growing in-country demands for government assistance with basic needs (water, food, and shelter). Disasters are likely to spark the greatest such demands but these will have increased because of the increasing background climate changes, especially sea-level rise and lowland flooding. Understanding and mapping the challenge helps with future planning. For example, the detailed mapping of vulnerability to sea-level rise of communities in the Mekong Delta (Vietnam), which plays a key role in regional food security, allows identification of "hotspots" as well as places where community livelihoods could be adequately sustained for decades (Nguyen & Woodroffe, 2016).

The key issue with growing demands for basic needs from climate-affected populations is the ability and will of national governments to respond, or at least facilitate an effective response. While government ability to respond is relatively easy to measure, the issue of "will" is more troublesome. For example, for three weeks after Cyclone Nargis devastated livelihoods of people living in the Irrawaddy Delta (Myanmar), the government—possibly fearful for its own survival—rejected foreign humanitarian aid until persuaded otherwise by ASEAN (Association of Southeast Asian Nations) (Paik, 2016).

Displacement and migration

Often, when cries for help are not effectively answered or indeed when *in-situ* conditions appear unable to be restored (sufficiently soon) to tolerable levels, affected people will often move elsewhere in search of a place where they expect to survive. These are among the multifarious triggers of migration in the Asia-Pacific region that (in 2010) was estimated to contain 27.5 million international migrants, around 13% of the global figure (IOM, 2011).[13] Within a single country, migrants often move from rural to urban (or peri-urban) areas in the expectation of finding paid employment and being closer to national sources of assistance.[14] Migration between countries, particularly to escape hardship, discrimination or conflict, is becoming increasingly common and is placing a strain on the economic and human resources of host countries, particularly when there are health issues associated with migrant influxes.[15]

Out-migration across international borders involves (potential) loss of human resources and, by extension productive capacity that may be of concern. In-migration puts increased pressure on resources as a result of which migrants may be confined to refugee camps where their welfare may be largely the responsibility of international agencies, especially the UNHCR (the UN Refugee Agency). Yet, in stark contrast to the many negative assessments of migration and the ways it will inevitably increase as a result of climate change is the view that migration is a valid adaptation response to this, as much in the future as it has been in the past; and that "if properly managed, and efforts made to protect the rights of migrants, migration can provide substantial benefits to both origin and destination areas, as well as to the migrants themselves" (ADB, 2012: viii).

The effects of future climate change on migration in the Pacific Islands, where this has not been such a feature of recent decades as elsewhere in the region (Connell, 2010), have been much discussed (Connell, 2016; Dreher & Voyer, 2015). It seems almost certain that within the next few decades, many coastal communities throughout the Pacific Islands will be involuntarily displaced by a rising sea level, especially in the western island groups where it is rising fastest. Since there is little land in public or state ownership in most island countries, this situation will raise tensions between land-holding and land-claiming groups that has already reached boiling point in some countries.[16]

Climate-driven conflict

Throughout history, the climate-driven diminishment of resources for subsistence populations has invariably produced conflict (Hsiang & Burke, 2014) and there is no reason to suppose that the modern globalized world has somehow succeeded in insulating itself from that outcome in the future. That said, identifying "hotspots" of future climate-driven conflict presents an opportunity for forward planning to inhibit its development.

Perhaps the most probable driver of future climate-linked conflict is competition for land, a proxy for resources, when this is rendered in insufficient supply following either short-onset changes (natural disasters) or longer-term depletion of a particular resource base. This was noted above for the Pacific Islands region but is also illustrated for the wider region by Bangladesh where accelerating land loss (Sarwar & Woodroffe, 2013) and developments intended to relieve the situation are stimulating out-migration and urban drift as well as also fuelling conflict (Burke, 2015; Nayak, 2015).

Within the Asia-Pacific region, increasing water scarcity as a result of future climate change is likeliest to lead to conflict in India, Pakistan, and Northeast China, although this is not inevitable (Link, Scheffran, & Ide, 2016). The issue is illustrated by the current dependence of around one-tenth of the global population depending on water in the Ganges-Brahmaputra-Meghna system that empties into the Bay of Bengal. To allow effective water distribution and reduce the risks of future conflict, there needs to be a shift from engineering interventions (mostly around dam-building and irrigation) to eco-management and hydro-diplomacy (Bandyopadhyay & Ghosh, 2009). A similar situation obtains in the Lower Mekong (Vietnam) (Givental & Meredith, 2016).

By the middle of this century, two-thirds of people will live in cities; most future urbanization will take place in developing countries and much will be climate-linked. In terms of spawning urban violence, studies have shown that it is not rural-urban migration per se that is key, but rather the socioeconomic marginalization of (recent) migrants (Ostby, 2016). Schemes aimed at reducing this, like Thailand's slum upgrade program (*Baan Mankong*), have been shown to be effective in reducing urban violence.

Increasing conflict attributable to climate change requires adaptive action at both national and regional levels, not least because most such conflicts have the

Regional and national awareness of GCC impacts on security

Climate change acts as a threat multiplier. Socio-economic challenges such as poverty, low education levels or reliance on specific economic sectors are made worse by climate change. In the Asia-Pacific, high levels of poverty and the prevalence of smallholder and subsistence agriculture (Thapa & Gaiha, 2011) translate into comparatively low adaptive capacity and a high exposure and sensitivity to climate change risks (Salamanca & Nguyen, 2016). While all countries of the Asia-Pacific recognize that they are vulnerable to climate change, the extent to which they are prepared and have the capacity and political will to cope with and adapt to climate change differs.

The University of Notre Dame Global Adaptation Index (ND-GAIN) seeks to quantify the level of countries' vulnerability—including their exposure, sensitivity, and adaptive capacity—as well as adaptation preparedness (Chen et al., 2015).[17] According to the ND-GAIN data, the Asia-Pacific is overall slightly more vulnerable but also slightly more prepared than the rest of the world. There are clear differences in the region. Developed countries fare notably better with regard to the readiness and adaptive capacity scores. Accordingly, New Zealand, Singapore, Japan, and Australia are the best prepared and have the greatest adaptive capacity. In contrast, Least Developed Countries such as Myanmar or Bangladesh but also Papua New Guinea have both low readiness and adaptive capacity. Yet, when adjusting scores for GDP *per capita*, Myanmar considerably improves its ranking; in other words, Myanmar is much more prepared than its level of GDP *per capita* might suggest, something that also applies to Kiribati.

As well as the Maldives and Timor-Leste, Pacific Island countries fare worse than continental countries in terms of exposure and sensitivity. In terms of adaptive capacity and preparedness, the islands are more mixed; for example, Palau scores fairly high while Papua New Guinea and Solomon Islands score quite low for adaptive capacity and preparedness.

Vulnerability seems to be directly related to preparedness and the political will to respond to climate change. From their review of adaptation plans and policies in six ASEAN countries, Salamanca and Nguyen (2016) conclude that climate-change readiness stems largely from governments' perceptions of vulnerability. Disasters in particular serve as "focusing events." Within ASEAN, Vietnam and the Philippines are thus adaptation pioneers while countries less exposed to disasters—like Malaysia or Laos—instead generally adopt a wait-and-see approach. This classification of countries based on exposure to disasters and other climate impacts also helps identify the different security understandings of Asia-Pacific countries.

Pacific island countries have been very vocal about climate change and have framed it in security terms more than most Asian countries. Globally, climate change has increasingly become securitized—that is, understood as a security issue (Boas, 2015). Small island states, especially those of the Pacific, favor this take on climate change and have repeatedly described it as a threat to human and international security. In the 2007 United Nations Security Council debate on climate change, Papua New Guinea's representative Robert Aisi, speaking on behalf of the Pacific Islands Forum, explained that "the dangers that small islands and their populations face are no less serious than those faced by nations and peoples threatened by guns and bombs" (in UN Security Council, 2007). In the second UN Security Council debate on climate change in 2011, Marcus Stephens, then President of Nauru, speaking on behalf of many small island states, similarly described climate change as "the single greatest security challenge of all":

> Because of climate change, our islands face dangerous and potentially catastrophic impacts that threaten to destabilize our societies and political institutions. Our food security, water security and public safety are already being undermined.
>
> (In UN Security Council, 2011)

In contrast to the Pacific (and Asian) island nations, Asian countries, notably the emerging economies of China and India, have generally been less vocal about climate change and more reluctant to interpret climate change as a security threat. They rejected debating climate change in the UN Security Council and instead see climate change mainly as a development issue, as the Chinese statement in the 2007 UN Security Council debate illustrates:

> Climate change may have certain security implications, but generally speaking it is in essence an issue of sustainable development.
>
> (Liu Zhenmin in UN Security Council, 2007)

The ASEAN countries have similarly subordinated climate change concerns to economic development for a long time. If they link climate change to security, it is mainly through concerns about energy security. Climate change impacts on human security are relevant to these states insofar as threats to economic development may undermine state legitimacy and therefore threaten national security (Gerstl, 2010). This is slowly changing as ASEAN and neighboring states increasingly acknowledge the security implications of climate change (Gerstl, 2010; Salamanca & Nguyen, 2016). For example, the intended nationally determined contribution of China submitted ahead of the 2015 Paris Summit thus explained that:

> [T]o act on climate change in terms of mitigating greenhouse gas emissions and enhancing climate resilience, is not only driven by China's domestic needs for sustainable development in ensuring its *economic security, energy security, ecological security, food security as well as the safety of people's*

life and property and to achieve sustainable development, but also driven by its sense of responsibility to fully engage in global governance, to forge a community of shared destiny for humankind and to promote common development for all human beings.

(People's Republic of China, 2015, emphasis added)

Conclusion

The Asia-Pacific is clearly vulnerable to climate change. The region is already experiencing adverse effects of climate change, including—but not limited to—sea-level rise, ocean acidification, increased frequency and intensity of meteorological hazard events like floods and tropical storms, and temperature increase. These short-onset and longer-onset impacts have serious consequences for human and state security in the Asia-Pacific. With a high share of the population living in the LECZ—and an expected increase in coastal populations, particularly in urban areas—sea-level rise, for instance, threatens infrastructure as well as livelihoods since many agricultural and industrial activities are also concentrated in the LECZ. Relocation, where possible, is likely to exacerbate existing or create new conflicts over land and water.

Some of the climate change impacts described in this chapter are no longer avoidable, some already manifest. Even if the world stopped emitting greenhouse gases immediately, adaptation is necessary. This concession should not hinder mitigation, including by the countries of the Asia-Pacific. Given the large and growing populations and economies in the region, in particular the emerging economies of Asia as well as the region's developed countries (especially Australia, New Zealand, Japan, and Singapore) should seek to reduce their fast-growing emissions. Pacific Island countries are leaders in this respect, pursuing ambitious renewable energy targets: for example, Cook Islands, Niue, and Tuvalu all aspire to becoming 100% renewable-energy powered by 2020 (Betzold, 2016).

At the same time, all countries of the Asia-Pacific need to cope with and adapt to changing climatic conditions. This chapter has already cited some examples of adaptation measures, such as relocating to areas that are on higher grounds and further inland as happened in Vanuatu (Siméoni & Ballu, 2012) or maintaining or replanting mangrove forests along the coast (Nunn, 2000). Given that adaptation preparedness and adaptive capacity are closely related to socio-economic development, adaptation measures that seek to build capacity and focus on socio-economic drivers of vulnerability, such as education or poverty, are no-regrets-measures (Muttarak & Lutz, 2014).

Although the more vulnerable countries in the region, notably the Pacific Island countries, seem to be most aware of the dangers of climate change and understand climate change primarily as a security issue, all countries of the region have recognized their vulnerability to climate change and seem—to a greater or lesser extent—willing to address the problem. It may be taken as an encouraging sign that all but three of the 31 independent countries in the

Asia-Pacific have ratified the 2015 Paris Agreement,[18] and all but four have submitted their intended nationally determined contribution, specifying their plans for mitigation and/or adaptation.[19]

Notes

1 For this chapter, the region includes the following nations: in Asia—Bangladesh, Brunei Darussalam, Cambodia, China, Hong Kong, India, Indonesia, Japan, Lao People's Democratic Republic, Macao, Malaysia, Maldives, Myanmar, Pakistan, Philippines, Singapore, Sri Lanka, Thailand, Timor-Leste, and Viet Nam; and in the Pacific—American Samoa, Australia, Cook Islands, Fiji, French Polynesia, Guam, Kiribati, Marshall Islands, Micronesia (Federated States of), Nauru, New Caledonia, New Zealand, Niue, Northern Marianas Islands, Palau, Papua New Guinea, Samoa, Solomon Islands, Tonga, Tuvalu, and Vanuatu.

2 Population and GDP data are from the (United Nations Statistics Division, 2016). For the US territories, population data are from the (United States Census Bureau, 2016) and GDP data from the (Bureau of Economic Analysis, 2016). Note that Niue is excluded, and that no GDP data was available for US territories for 1974.

3 There are 28 megacities worldwide (UNDESA, 2014); the 15 in the Asia-Pacific region are (in decreasing size order), Tokyo, Delhi, Shanghai, Mumbai, Osaka, Beijing, Dhaka, Karachi, Kolkata, Chongqing, Manila, Guangzhou, Tianjin, Shenzhen, and Jakarta.

4 For Southeast Asia, population growth rates dropped from 1.9% in 1990 to 1.1% in 2015 and are projected to be at 0.7% in 2030; the equivalent figures for the Pacific are 1.6%, 1.5%, and 1.1% (UNESCAP, 2016).

5 Categorization is based on income groups provided by the (World Bank, 2016), whereby we refer to high income countries as developed and to all others as developing countries. Further, we ranked Niue and the Cook Islands as developed, Nauru as developing. The list of LDCs is taken from the United Nations Committee for Development Policy (2016).

6 Note that the ND-GAIN is available only for the larger independent countries in the region.

7 A study of rising dengue incidence in Singapore attributed 14% causation to rising temperature, the remainder to urbanization (Struchiner, Rocklov, Wilder-Smith, & Massad, 2015).

8 A study of the South China Sea showed "anomalous and unprecedented acidification during the 20th century, pacing the observed increase in atmospheric CO_2" (Liu et al., 2014: 1).

9 A study of rice production in Cambodia found that it might decrease by 45% by the 2080s (Chun et al., 2016). Climate change has already forced adaptation to rice production methods in Taiwan where the alternate wetting and drying technique has proved able to sustain former production levels (Kima, Chung, Wang, & Traore, 2015).

10 Even in the relatively pristine coastal waters of Solomon Islands, total fish demand is likely to exceed production by 2050 (Dey, Gosh, Valmonte-Santos, Rosegrant, & Chen, 2016).

11 The rate of sea-level rise in the Bay of Bengal is 4.0–7.8 mm/year (Singh, 2002), higher than the global average of 3.2 mm/year.

12 An economic loss of US$736,600 million, some 44% of global economic loss (Blankespoor, Dasgupta, & Laplante, 2014).

13 An estimated 10.7 million people were displaced in Asia by short-onset climate-related and extreme weather events in 2011, a figure that includes 3.4 million in Southeast Asia (ADB, 2012).

80 *Patrick D. Nunn and Carola Betzold*

14 A study of Ho Chi Minh City (Vietnam) found that environmental factors are an important driver of inward migration (quoted in ADB, 2012: 31).
15 An example is provided by the Muslim Rohingya, long marginalized in Buddhist Myanmar, who have migrated to Malaysia, Thailand, and Bangladesh where many are either now long-term refugee-camp residents or unable to work legally (Ullah, 2016).
16 Public demonstrations and riots, ostensibly pro-democracy, in Tonga in 2006 had at their root the dependency of most Tongans on the beneficence of the land-owning nobility for access to farming land (Campbell, 2008). Similar concerns about land rights underpinned violent clashes in Solomon Islands in the late 1990s (Kabutaulaka, 1999).
17 ND-GAIN scores are available only for the 32 independent countries of the Asia Pacific.
18 Only Myanmar, Philippines and Timor-Leste have, as of February 2017, not ratified the Paris Agreement. See status of ratification on the UNFCCC website (UNFCCC, 2017b).
19 Only Brunei Darussalam, Myanmar, Philippines, and Timor-Leste have, as of February 2017, not submitted their (intended) nationally determined contribution. See the interim registry of the UNFCCC (UNFCCC, 2017a).

References

ADB, A. D. B. (2012). *Addressing climate change and migration in Asia and the Pacific.* Retrieved from: www.adb.org/sites/default/files/publication/29662/addressing-climate-change-migration.pdf

Adger, W. N., Pulhin, J. M., Barnett, J., Dabelko, G. D., Hovelsrud, G. K., Levy, M., Oswald Spring, Ú., & Vogel, C. H. (2014). Human security. In C. B. Field, V. R. Barros, D. J. Dokken, K. J. Mach, M. D. Mastrandrea, T. E. Bilir, M. Chatterjee, K. L. Ebi, Y. O. Estrada, R. C. Genova, B. Girma, E. S. Kissel, A. N. Levy, S. MacCracken, P. R. Mastrandrea, & L. L. White (Eds.), *Climate Change 2014: Impacts, adaptation, and vulnerability. Part A: Global and sectoral aspects. Contribution of Working Group II to the Fifth Assessment Report of the intergovernmental panel on climate change* (pp. 755–791). Cambridge: Cambridge University Press.

Ayeb-Karlsson, S., van der Geest, K., Ahmed, I., Huq, S., & Warner, K. (2016). A people-centred perspective on climate change, environmental stress, and livelihood resilience in Bangladesh. *Sustainability Science*, 11(4), 679–694. doi:10.1007/s11625-016-0379-z

Ballu, V., Bouin, M. N., Simeoni, P., Crawford, W. C., Calmant, S., Bore, J. M., Kanas, T., & Pelletier, B. (2011). Comparing the role of absolute sea-level rise and vertical tectonic motions in coastal flooding, Torres Islands (Vanuatu). *Proceedings of the National Academy of Sciences of the United States of America*, 108(32), 13019–13022. doi:10.1073/pnas.1102842108

Bandyopadhyay, J., & Ghosh, N. (2009). Holistic engineering and hydro-diplomacy in the Ganges-Brahmaputra-Meghna Basin. *Economic and Political Weekly*, 44, 40–50.

Barbier, E. B. (2015). Climate change impacts on rural poverty in low-elevation coastal zones. *Estuarine Coastal and Shelf Science*, 165, A1–A13. doi:10.1016/j.ecss.2015.05.035

Barnett, T. P., Adam, J. C., & Lettenmaier, D. P. (2005). Potential impacts of a warming climate on water availability in snow-dominated regions. *Nature*, 438(7066), 303–309. doi:10.1038/nature04141

Becker, M., Meyssignac, B., Letetrel, C., Llovel, W., Cazenave, A., & Delcroix, T. (2012). Sea level variations at tropical Pacific islands since 1950. *Global and Planetary Change*, 80–81(1), 85–98. doi:10.1016/j.gloplacha.2011.09.004

Benitez, M. A. (2009). Climate change could affect mosquito-borne diseases in Asia. *Lancet*, 373(9669), 1070–1070.

Betzold, C. (2016). Fuelling the Pacific: Aid for renewable energy across Pacific Island countries. *Renewable and Sustainable Energy Reviews*, 58, 311–318.

Blankespoor, B., Dasgupta, S., & Laplante, B. (2014). Sea-level rise and coastal wetlands. *Ambio*, 43(8), 996–1005. doi:10.1007/s13280-014-0500-4

Boas, I. (2015). *Climate migration and security. Securitisation as a strategy in climate change politics*. New York: Routledge.

Brecht, H., Dasgupta, S., Laplante, B., Murray, S., & Wheeler, D. (2012). Sea-level rise and storm surges: High stakes for a small number of developing countries. *The Journal of Environment & Development*, 21(1), 120–138. doi:10.1177/1070496511433601

Bureau of Economic Analysis. (2016). Gross domestic product (GDP) for the U.S. territories. Retrieved from www.bea.gov/national/gdp_territory.htm

Burke, J. (November 8, 2015). Progress fans flames of militant unrest in changing Bangladesh. *Guardian*.

Campbell, I. C. (2008). Across the threshold: Regime change and uncertainty in Tonga 2005–2007. *Journal of Pacific History*, 43(1), 95–109. doi:10.1080/0022334080 2054719

Chattopadhyay, P. B., & Singh, V. S. (2013). Hydrochemical evidences: Vulnerability of atoll aquifers in Western Indian Ocean to climate change. *Global and Planetary Change*, 106, 123–140. doi:10.1016/j.gloplacha.2013.03.008

Chen, C., Noble, I., Hellmann, J., Coffee, J., Murillo, M., & Chawla, N. (2015). *University of Notre Dame global adaptation index country index technical report*. Retrieved from index.gain.org/about/methodology

Chun, J. A., Li, S., Wang, Q. G., Lee, W. S., Lee, E. J., Horstmann, N., Park, H., Veasna, T., Vanndy, L., Pros, K., & Vang, S. (2016). Assessing rice productivity and adaptation strategies for Southeast Asia under climate change through multi-scale crop modeling. *Agricultural Systems*, 143, 14–21. doi:10.1016/j.agsy.2015.12.001

Church, J. A., Clark, P. U., Cazenave, A., Gregory, J. M., Jevrejeva, S., Levermann, A., Merrifield, M. A., Milne, G. A., Nerem, R. S., Nunn, P. D., Payne, A. J., Pfeffer, W. T., Stammer, D., & Unnikrishnan, A. S. (2013). Sea level change. In T. F. Stocker, D. Qin, G.-K. Plattner, M. Tignor, S. K. Allen, J. Boschung, A. Nauels, Y. Xia, V. Bex, & P. M. Midgley (Eds.), *Climate Change 2013: The physical science basis. Working Group I contribution to the Fifth Assessment Report of the intergovernmental panel on climate change* (pp. 1137–1308). Cambridge: Cambridge University Press.

Cleasby, N., Schwarz, A. M., Phillips, M., Paul, C., Pant, J., Oeta, J., Pickering, T., Meloty, A., Laumani, M., & Kori, M. (2014). The socio-economic context for improving food security through land based aquaculture in Solomon Islands: A pen-urban case study. *Marine Policy*, 45, 89–97. doi:10.1016/j.marpol.2013.11.015

Connell, J. (2010). Pacific islands in the global economy: Paradoxes of migration and culture. *Singap J Trop Geogr*, 31. doi:10.1111/j.1467-9493.2010.00387.x

Connell, J. (2016). Last days in the Carteret Islands? Climate change, livelihoods and migration on coral atolls. *Asia Pacific Viewpoint*, 57(1), 3–15. doi:10.1111/apv.12118

Das, S., & Vincent, J. R. (2009). Mangroves protected villages and reduced death toll during Indian super cyclone. *Proceedings of the National Academy of Sciences of the United States of America*, 106(18), 7357–7360. doi:10.1073/pnas.0810440106

Dasgupta, S., Laplante, B., Murray, S., & Wheeler, D. (2011). Exposure of developing countries to sea-level rise and storm surges. *Climatic Change*, 106(4), 567–579. doi:10.1007/s10584-010-9959-6

Dey, M. M., Gosh, K., Valmonte-Santos, R., Rosegrant, M. W., & Chen, O. L. (2016). Economic impact of climate change and climate change adaptation strategies for fisheries sector in Solomon Islands: Implication for food security. *Marine Policy*, 67, 171–178. doi:10.1016/j.marpol.2016.01.004

Dreher, T., & Voyer, M. (2015). Climate refugees or migrants? Contesting media frames on climate justice in the pacific. *Environmental Communication—a Journal of Nature and Culture*, 9(1), 58–76. doi:10.1080/17524032.2014.932818

Fazey, I., Pettorelli, N., Kenter, J., Wagatora, D., & Schuett, D. (2011). Maladaptive trajectories of change in Makira, Solomon Islands. *Global Environmental Change-Human and Policy Dimensions*, 21(4), 1275–1289. doi:10.1016/j.gloenvcha.2011.07.006

Gerstl, A. (2010). *The depoliticization and "ASEANization" of human security in Southeast Asia: ASEAN's counter-terrorism and climate change policies*. Paper presented at the 7th Pan European International Relations Conference, Stockholm.

Givental, E., & Meredith, D. (2016). Environmental and political implications of Vietnam's water vulnerabilities: A multiscale assessment. *Singapore Journal of Tropical Geography*, 37(1), 59–75. doi:10.1111/sjtg.12135

Gosling, S. N., & Arnell, N. W. (2016). A global assessment of the impact of climate change on water scarcity. *Climatic Change*, 134(3), 371–385. doi:10.1007/s10584-013-0853-x

Gross, J. S., Ye, L., & Legates, R. (2014). Asia and the Pacific Rim: The new peri-urbanization and urban theory. *Journal of Urban Affairs*, 36, 309–314. doi:10.1111/juaf.12109

Gursky, E. A., Burkle, F. M., Hamon, D. W., Walker, P., & Benjamin, G. C. (2014). The changing face of crises and aid in the Asia-Pacific. *Biosecurity and Bioterrorism-Biodefense Strategy Practice and Science*, 12(6), 310–317. doi:10.1089/bsp. 2014.0025

Hashim, J. H., & Hashim, Z. (2016). Climate change, extreme weather events, and human health implications in the Asia Pacific Region. *Asia-Pacific Journal of Public Health*, 28, 8S–14S. doi:10.1177/1010539515599030

Heenan, A., Pomeroy, R., Bell, J., Munday, P. L., Cheung, W., Logan, C., Brainard, R., Amri, A. Y., Aliño, P., Armada, N., David, L., Rivera-Guieb, R., Green, S., Jompa, J., Leonardo, T., Mamauag, S., Parker, B., Shackeroff, J., & Yasin, Z. (2015). A climate-informed, ecosystem approach to fisheries management. *Marine Policy*, 57, 182–192. doi:10.1016/j.marpol.2015.03.018

Hijioka, Y., Lin, E., Pereira, J. J., Corlett, R. T., Cui, X., Insarov, G. E., Lasco, R. D., Lindgren, E., & Surjan, A. (2014). Asia. In V. R. Barros, C. B. Field, D. J. Dokken, M. D. Mastrandrea, K. J. Mach, T. E. Bilir, M. Chatterjee, K. L. Ebi, Y. O. Estrada, R. C. Genova, B. Girma, E. S. Kissel, A. N. Levy, S. MacCracken, P. R. Mastrandrea, & L. L. White (Eds.), *Climate Change 2014: Impacts, adaptation, and vulnerability. Part B: Regional aspects. Contribution of Working Group II to the Fifth Assessment Report of the intergovernmental panel on climate change* (pp. 1327–1370). Cambridge: Cambridge University Press.

Hoegh-Guldberg, O., & Bruno, J. F. (2010). The impact of climate change on the world's marine ecosystems. *Science*, 328(5985), 1523–1528. doi:10.1126/science.1189930

Hoque, M. A., Scheelbeek, P. F. D., Vineis, P., Khan, A. E., Ahmed, K. M., & Butler, A. P. (2016). Drinking water vulnerability to climate change and alternatives for adaptation in coastal South and South East Asia. *Climatic Change*, 136(2), 247–263. doi:10.1007/s10584-016-1617-1

Hsiang, S. M., & Burke, M. (2014). Climate, conflict, and social stability: What does the evidence say? *Climatic Change*, 123(1), 39–55. doi:10.1007/s10584-013-0868-3

IOM (International Organization for Migration). (2011). *Regional strategy for Asia and the Pacific 2012–2015*. Bangkok: International Organization for Migration.

Kabutaulaka, T. T. (1999). Solomon Islands. *Contemporary Pacific*, 11(2), 443–449.

Karim, M. F., & Mimura, N. (2008). Impacts of climate change and sea-level rise on cyclonic storm surge floods in Bangladesh. *Global Environmental Change*, 18(3), 490–500. doi:10.1016/j.gloenvcha.2008.05.002

Ketabchi, H., Mahmoodzadeh, D., Ataie-Ashtiani, B., Werner, A. D., & Simmons, C. T. (2014). Sea-level rise impact on fresh groundwater lenses in two-layer small islands. *Hydrological Processes*, 28(24), 5938–5953. doi:10.1002/hyp.10059

Kima, A. S., Chung, W. G., Wang, Y. M., & Traore, S. (2015). Evaluating water depths for high water productivity in irrigated lowland rice field by employing alternate wetting and drying technique under tropical climate conditions, Southern Taiwan. *Paddy and Water Environment*, 13(4), 379–389. doi:10.1007/s10333-014-0458-7

Kummu, M., de Moel, H., Salvucci, G., Viviroli, D., Ward, P. J., & Varis, O. (2016). Over the hills and further away from coast: Global geospatial patterns of human and environment over the 20th–21st centuries. *Environmental Research Letters,* 11(3). doi:10.1088/1748-9326/11/3/034010

Lassa, J. A., Lai, A. Y. H., & Goh, T. (2016). Climate extremes: An observation and projection of its impacts on food production in ASEAN. *Natural Hazards*, 84, S19–S33. doi:10.1007/s11069-015-2081-3

Lata, S., & Nunn, P. (2012). Misperceptions of climate-change risk as barriers to climate-change adaptation: A case study from the Rewa Delta, Fiji. *Climatic Change*, 110(1–2), 169–186. doi:10.1007/s10584-011-0062-4

Link, P. M., Scheffran, J., & Ide, T. (2016). Conflict and cooperation in the water-security nexus: A global comparative analysis of river basins under climate change. *Wiley Interdisciplinary Reviews-Water*, 3(4), 495–515. doi:10.1002/wat2.1151

Liu, Y., Peng, Z. C., Zhou, R. J., Song, S. H., Liu, W. G., You, C. F., Lin, Y., Yu, K., Wu, C., Wei, G., Xie, L., Burr, G., & Shen, C. C. (2014). Acceleration of modern acidification in the South China Sea driven by anthropogenic CO2. *Scientific Reports*, 4. doi:10.1038/srep05148

Mallick, B., & Vogt, J. (2012). Cyclone, coastal society and migration: Empirical evidence from Bangladesh. *International Development Planning Review*, 34(3), 217–240. doi:10.3828/idpr.2012.16

Manton, M. J., & Stevenson, L. A. (Eds.). (2014). *Climate in Asia and the Pacific: Security, society and sustainability* (Vol. 56). Dordrecht: Springer.

McLeod, E., Salm, R., Green, A., & Almany, J. (2008). Designing marine protected area networks to address the impacts of climate change. *Frontiers in Ecology and the Environment*, 7(7), 362–370. doi:10.1890/070211

Moench, M. (2010). Responding to climate and other change processes in complex contexts: Challenges facing development of adaptive policy frameworks in the Ganga Basin. *Technological Forecasting and Social Change*, 77(6), 975–986. doi:10.1016/j.techfore.2009.11.006

Muttarak, R., & Lutz, W. (2014). Is education a key to reducing vulnerability to natural disasters and hence unavoidable climate change? *Ecology and Society*, 19(1). doi:10.5751/es-06476-190142

Nayak, A. K. (2015). Development induced displacement and arms conflicts in Bangladesh. *Conflict Studies Quarterly*, (11), 3–23.

Nguyen, T. T. X., & Woodroffe, C. D. (2016). Assessing relative vulnerability to sea-level rise in the western part of the Mekong River Delta in Vietnam. *Sustainability Science*, 11(4), 645–659. doi:10.1007/s11625-015-0336-2

Nunn, P. D. (2000). Coastal changes over the past 200 years around Ovalau and Moturiki Islands, Fiji: Implications for coastal zone management. *Australian Geographer*, 31(1), 21–39. doi:10.1080/00049180093510

Nurse, L., McLean, R., Agard, J., Briguglio, L. P., Duvat, V., Pelesikoti, N., Tompkins, E., & Webb, A. (2014). Small islands. In V. R. Barros, C. B. Field, D. J. Dokken, M. D. Mastrandrea, K. J. Mach, T. E. Bilir, M. Chatterjee, K. L. Ebi, Y. O. Estrada, R. C. Genova, B. Girma, E. S. Kissel, A. N. Levy, S. MacCracken, P. R. Mastrandrea, & L. L. White (Eds.), *Climate Change 2014: Impacts, adaptation, and vulnerability. Part B: Regional aspects. Contribution of Working Group II to the Fifth Assessment Report of the intergovernmental panel on climate change.* Cambridge: Cambridge University Press.

Okuzawa, K., Maliao, R. J., Quinitio, E. T., Buen-Ursua, S. M. A., Lebata, M., Gallardo, W. G., Garcia, L. M. B., Jurgenne, H., & Primavera, J. H. (2008). Stock enhancement of threatened species in Southeast Asia. *Reviews in Fisheries Science*, 16(1–3), 394–402. doi:10.1080/10641260701678496

Olds, A. D., Albert, S., Maxwell, P. S., Pitt, K. A., & Connolly, R. M. (2013). Mangrove-reef connectivity promotes the effectiveness of marine reserves across the western Pacific. *Global Ecology and Biogeography*, 22(9), 1040–1049. doi:10.1111/geb.12072

Ostby, G. (2016). Rural–urban migration, inequality and urban social disorder: Evidence from African and Asian cities. *Conflict Management and Peace Science*, 33(5), 491–515. doi:10.1177/0738894215581315

Paik, W. (2016). Domestic politics, regional integration, and human rights: Interactions among Myanmar, ASEAN, and EU. *Asia Europe Journal*, 14(4), 417–434. doi:10.1007/s10308-016-0458-x

People's Republic of China. (2015). China's Intended nationally determined contribution: Enhanced actions on climate change. Retrieved from www4.unfccc.int/ndcregistry/Pages/All.aspx

Salamanca, A., & Nguyen, H. (2016). *Climate change adaptation readiness in the ASEAN countries.* Stockholm: Stockholm Environment Institute Discussion Brief.

Sarwar, M. G. M., & Woodroffe, C. D. (2013). Rates of shoreline change along the coast of Bangladesh. *Journal of Coastal Conservation*, 17(3), 515–526. doi:10.1007/s11852-013-0251-6

Siméoni, P., & Ballu, V. (2012). Le mythe des premiers réfugiés climatiques: mouvements de populations et changements environnementaux aux îles Torrès (Vanouatou, Mélanésie). *Annales de Géographie*, 3, No 685. doi:10.3917/ag.685.0219

Singh, O. P. (2002). Spatial variation of sea level trend along the Bangladesh coast. *Marine Geodesy*, 25(3), 205–212. doi:10.1080/01490410290051536

Smith, T. F., Thomsen, D. C., Gould, S., Schmitt, K., & Schlegel, B. (2013). Cumulative pressures on sustainable livelihoods: Coastal adaptation in the Mekong delta. *Sustainability*, 5(1), 228–241. doi:10.3390/su5010228

Struchiner, C. J., Rocklov, J., Wilder-Smith, A., & Massad, E. (2015). Increasing dengue incidence in Singapore over the past 40 years: Population growth, climate and mobility. *PloS one*, 10(8). doi:10.1371/journal.pone.0136286

Sud, R., Mishra, A., Varma, N., & Bhadwal, S. (2015). Adaptation policy and practice in densely populated glacier-fed river basins of South Asia: A systematic review. *Regional Environmental Change*, 15(5), 825–836. doi:10.1007/s10113-014-0711-z

Thapa, G., & Gaiha, R. (2011). *Smallholder farming in Asia and the Pacific: Challenges and opportunities.* Paper presented at the New Directions for Smallholder Agriculture, Rome.

Thomas, V., Albert, J. R. G., & Hepburn, C. (2014). Contributors to the frequency of intense climate disasters in Asia-Pacific countries. *Climatic Change*, 126(3–4), 381–398. doi:10.1007/s10584-014-1232-y

Ullah, A. (2016). Rohingya crisis in Myanmar: Seeking justice for the "stateless." *Journal of Contemporary Criminal Justice*, 32(3), 285–301. doi:10.1177/1043986216660811

UNDESA. (2014). *World urbanization prospects: The 2014 revision, highlights (ST/ESA/ SER.A/352).* Retrieved January 22, 2018 from: https://esa.un.org/unpd/wup/publications/files/wup2014-highlights.pdf

UNESCAP. (2016). *Statistical Yearbook for Asia and the Pacific 2015.* Retrieved January 22, 2018 from: www.unescap.org/sites/default/files/SYB2015_Full_Publication.pdf

UN Security Council. (2007). 5663rd meeting, Tuesday, 17 April 2007, 10 a.m. New York: UN Document Number S/PV/5663.

UN Security Council. (2011). 6587th meeting, Wednesday, 20 July 2011, 10 a.m. New York: UN Document Number S/PV.6587.

UNFCCC. (2017a). *NDC Registry (interim).* Retrieved from www4.unfccc.int/ndcregistry/ Pages/All.aspx.

UNFCCC. (2017b). *Paris Agreement—Status of Ratification.* Retrieved from http:// unfccc.int/paris_agreement/items/9444.php.

United Nations Committee for Development Policy. (2016). *List of least developed countries (as of May 2016).* Retrieved from www.un.org/en/development/desa/policy/cdp/ ldc/ldc_list.pdf

United Nations Statistics Division. (2016). *National accounts main aggregates database.* Retrieved from http://unstats.un.org/unsd/snaama/dnlList.asp

United States Census Bureau. (2016). *International data base.* Retrieved from www. census.gov/population/international/data/idb/informationGateway.php

World Bank. (2016). *World Bank country and lending groups.* Retrieved from https:// datahelpdesk.worldbank.org/knowledgebase/articles/906519

4 Geography of GCC

The climate-security nexus in Africa

Daniel Silander

Global climate change (GCC) consequences have not been equally experienced around the world and the future will show great variations of climate impact from one region to another. GCC is real, leading to security challenges and calls for mitigation and adaptation strategies (Mazo, 2009a, 2009b). This chapter is not focusing on a particular state, but rather has a regional scope on discussing climate change consequences in Africa. Africa is the lowest carbon emitter in the world (The World Bank, 2016; Magrath 2010; Hope, 2010), but the continent is extremely vulnerable to climate change. Despite the fact that less than 3% of the worldwide emissions of greenhouse gases come from African states (Hope, 2010, p. 451), many African states are placed among the top ten of states most affected by GCC. Climate change will have the most negative impact in societies, such as those in Africa, where social and economic despair presently exist and where communities are heavily dependent on natural resources. Climate change has led to an overall rise of temperature, escalation of droughts, storms, rising sea levels, and floods across the continent, with climate hot spots in the desertification of the Sahara and Sahel regions and the massive melting of snow on Mt. Kenya and Mt. Kilimanjaro. It is also responsible for social tensions over natural resources in Kenya, the northern parts of Nigeria, and Sudan, among many other places. It is likely that GCC may cause further stress on many African societies that have very limited capacities to mitigate the impact on state and human security. When state leaders and world organizations address climate change and search for measures to be taken to adapt to climate change, the less-developed regions and most impoverished countries have limited economic and political capacities and are weak, unstable states (Mohamoud et al., 2014; Hausler & McCorquodale, 2011; Helm & Hepburn, 2009; Podesta & Ogden, 2008; Brown et al., 2007; Intergovernmental Panel on Climate Change, 2001).

For decades, political tension, conflicts, and wars have had fatal consequences for African state and human security. In previous decades, research has pointed out explanations for war-torn African societies: colonial legacies, lack of economic development and good governance, social injustice, corruption, ethnic tension and poverty, among other factors. In more recent decades, a growing number of studies point out global climate change as a driver or triggering factor for conflicts and wars. Although research continues to be divided on the causal links between GCC and armed conflicts, there is much scholarly agreement that GCC leads to scarcity of vital human resources and jeopardizes state and human security in Sub-Saharan Africa. Although there is very limited evidence, which suggests that climate change directly causes conflict and war, GCC may be seen as one factor adding stress to societies and state governments (Scheffran et al., 2012; Scheffran & Battaglini, 2011; pp. 27–39; Mazo, 2009b, pp. 38–39; Mazo, 2009c, pp. 87–88, Freedom in the World, 2014; Salehyan, 2008).

Based on the descriptions in the introductory chapter on challenges of GCC, and the urgent need of a viable international response to safeguard global society, this chapter aims to discuss the climate–security nexus in the most challenged African states. This chapter is divided into four sections following this introduction. The next section presents an overview of some elements of climate change that impact African societies and addresses the limited common African efforts to find regional strategies and policies on GCC. It is followed by a discussion on how climate change is a driver for conflict and war in fragile states with malfunctioning political institutions. GCC and political fragility is a dangerous combination for state and human security in sub-Saharan Africa and is highlighted by a case-study analysis on the developments in Darfur. A fourth section concludes this chapter.

GCC in Africa: changes and challenges

Over the last decade or so, there has been a growing global political concern over climate change with a growing amount of scholarly work based on environmental, economic, social, and political perspectives (Canter, 2016; Birnbacher & Thorseth, 2015; Dessler & Parson, 2010; Messer, 2010; Harrison & Sundstrom, 2010; Brown & Crawford, 2008; Aldy & Stavins, 2007). Over time, there has developed an agreement among most state leaders and international-, transnational-, and non-governmental organizations that GCC is aggravating conditions for life and safety around the world, although there has been disagreement between the developed and less developed states on how to mitigate and adjust to climate change (Hickmann, 2016; Urry, 2015; Scott, 2012, 2008; Doyle, 2009; Brown & Crawford, 2008; McMichael et al., 2006; Nevell, 2006; Betsill & Bulkeley, 2006; Karl & Trenberth, 2003; Barnett, 2003).

The consequences of GCC are not evenly distributed. On the contrary, different geographical regions around the world have different vulnerabilities to climate change, and state governments around the world pursue different levels of capabilities to mitigate these challenges to state and human security. Africa is a continent with much vulnerability to climate change. This is due to high exposure to climate change and low capacities to efficiently mitigate climate challenges (Kumssa & Jones, 2010, p. 453). Africa is a vast continent with a breadth of geographical attributes and vulnerabilities to climate change, and Africa also consists of over 50 state governments with varying capacities to handle contemporary challenges to security (Roessler, 2016; Busby et al., 2014; Ubelejit, 2014).

88   *Daniel Silander*

Although many African societies have seen substantial development over recent decades, some African states are facing socioeconomic and political challenges. In recent years, economic growth has stalled due to political as well as economic factors (Rodrik, 2016). The recent economic downturn could be explained in terms primarily of lower prices on export commodities such as gas, oil, metals, and minerals (The World Bank, 2016). The political factors include the continual lack of good governance, rule of law, counter-corruption measures, democratic legacy, democratic oversight of the military and ethnic and political unity (see Freedom House, 2016; Houngnikpo, 2016; Eizenstat et al., 2005). Africa is lagging behind the economic and social developments seen in many Asian states over the last few decades. The urgent call for continued economic growth in Africa is compounded by the increasing population throughout the continent. This has led to a greater need for resources such as food, water, energy, and infrastructure as well as policies on poverty reduction, education and health care. With urgent calls for development and politically initiated policies to promote prosperity and wealth in African societies comes further pressure on the environment. At the same time, developing African states are increasing energy consumption, based on mostly fossil fuels, to promote the economies, which will have increasing negative effects on the change. On the other hand, a political halt to energy consumption and effort to limit carbon emissions could perhaps lead to limited economic development, growing social tension, social despair, and poverty, and may trigger political instability. The alternative path, initiating a transition from fossil resources to environmentally friendly, low-carbon energy sources, would come with some short-termed transitional costs for many African economies (Adano & Daudi, 2012, p. 1).

Although most African states have acknowledged climate change and politically argued for mitigation and adaption policies and strategies to protect state and human security, there has arisen a very late and an unstructured African position on climate change within international organizations and forums. This has had a further negative impact on GCC change challenges. Most of the institutionalized work on climate change has occurred within the Group of 77 and China (G77/China), the Alliance of Small Island States (AOSIS), the Organization of Petroleum Exporting Countries (OPEC), and the Least Developed Countries (LDC-Group), among others (Roger & Belliethathan, 2016, pp. 91–92; OPEC, 2016; LDC, 2013; Kasa et al., 2008).

A first crucial step for African cooperation on climate change happened in July 1991, at the First Regional African Ministerial Preparatory Conference of the United Nations Conference on Environment and Development (UNCED) in Cairo. The many talks resulted in a shared African position on development and environmental issues stressing the importance of, *inter alia*, economic development, quality of life, poverty reduction, and environmental protection. A second important step for African diplomacy on the climate challenge was the preparatory talks for the Earth Summit in 1992. These negotiations addressed the importance of speaking with one African voice on environmental challenges and seeking a common platform of principles and values on climate change (Roger

& Belliethathan, 2016, p. 94). A third symbol of a common African reaction to global climate change can be dated to the eighth African Union (AU) Summit meeting in 2007. AU specifically addressed concerns over climate change in Africa and acted to use the AU as a platform for approaching climate change challenges in the international debate. At the Summit, there seemed to be a growing agreement among most African leaders that climate change was particularly a problem for African societies and how the international community, including the G77/China, had to approach climate change in a coordinated way and speak with one voice. Since then, the AU Commission has played the role of harmonizing and coordinating member states' policies to seek a common strengthened position internationally. The AU Commission has highlighted the importance of discussing and developing suitable strategies of mitigation and adaption to limit the consequences of climate change and for determining measures on capacity building, research, and expertise as well as financing.

However, a common African stand for addressing GCC has continued to be hampered by traditional notions of state sovereignty and national economic and political interests, as embedded in the AU Commission institutionally as a body consisting of state representatives. Here some states such as Ghana, Kenya, and South Africa have declared a national climate change policy, while for instance, Nigeria, Botswana, and Zimbabwe among others have not. For example, South Africa pushed for economic development leading to high levels of greenhouse gas production; less developed states have protested against such development by demanding more industrialized African states commit more firmly to the mitigation of climate change. As part of the BASIC group of states (Brazil, South Africa, India, and China), South Africa has met furious political accusations from AU member states over its continued dependence on fossil fuels and thereby undermining a common stand on climate change (Chin-Yee, 2016; CAP, May 26, 2015; Hurell & Sengupta, 2012; Masters, 2011, pp. 257–264).

Some important progress, however, has been seen by the African Group of Negotiators (AGN). The AGN was established in the early 1990s as a regional body concerned about climate change consequences. Although the AGN met similar challenges as faced by the AU, in state sovereignty preferences over regional shared policies and limited resources and expertise for addressing climate change, the AGN has become more proactive over recent years based on a greater political and economic commitment to speak with one voice in climate change negotiations (Roger & Belliethathan, 2016, pp. 92–93). A strategy of "One Continent, One Voice" (see Chin-Yee, 2016, p. 360) has turned out to be quite successful based on a moral legitimacy for addressing the significant concerns over climate changes in Africa, but also based on improved diplomatic skills by African leaders, increased technological capacities, and improved expertise among the negotiating staff at international conferences. The AGN seemed to have identified that a common position, proactive presence at negotiations, and political and economic support were essential ingredients for speaking internationally with one African voice. From 2005 onward, the AGN had successfully received more political and economic power to represent African interests at the Conference of Parties (COP)-12 in Nairobi throughout the COP22 in Marrakesh (Roger & Belliethathan, 2016, pp. 103–104). This progress is an important step taken and the common African stance, to speak with one voice, must continue to protect state and human security in the region (UN News Centre, June 15, 2014).

How, then, has climate change impacted African societies? What are the consequences of an increased average global temperature, droughts, changed rainfall patterns, warmer seas, rising sea levels, melting ice caps on natural resource-based African societies and late regional reactions? *A first impact of climate change is food and water scarcity.* Volatile weather conditions, including major changes in rainfall and temperature, have led to great pressure on the productive landscape in many African societies (Hope, 2017; Wheeler & von Braum, 2013; Perkins, 2013; Brown & Crawford, 2008). A study identified five African states suffering from water stress/scarcity in 1990, compared with a projection of 20 states in 2025 (see Mazo, 2009c, p. 96). The majority of African people make their living through agriculture and fisheries, which is about 40% of all exports and 34% of the GDP in sub-Saharan Africa (Hope, 2010, p. 455). Agriculture and fisheries are extremely vulnerable to climate change. Food shortages are a major insecurity for the people in many African societies, where there is food poverty and malnutrition in many households (Nagothu, 2015). It has been estimated that in a decade or so, the agricultural output will decrease by 50% in the poorest countries in eastern and southern Africa (Mazo, 2009, p. 99).

Scarcity of water includes both the lack of water for drinking water and for hygiene and sanitation. About 33% of the African population faces a severe scarcity of clean water, leaving many African societies under water-stress (Institute of Security Studies, 2012; see also Reig et al., December 12, 2013; Rijsberman, 2006). Scarcity of water also includes desertification and land degradation with a negative impact on the production of food. Most African societies continue to be dependent on rain-fed agriculture. Countries such as Cameroon, Chad, Ethiopia, Nigeria, Sudan, South Africa, and Zimbabwe have all faced major challenges due to reduced production of cereal and crops, (Hope, 2010, pp. 455–456). Scholars have predicted an increase in the average temperature in Africa by 2050 of about 1.5 to 3°C, leaving some regions on the continent with a decrease of 10% in annual rainfall (IPCC, 2007). Studies have pointed out that southern Africa has faced more concentrated rainfall over fewer days than previously, that western Africa has seen a dramatic reduction in rainfall since the 1960s and that eastern Africa has seen an increase of rainfall in the northern sector, but a decline in the southern sector, leaving some areas with too much water during too few days and other areas with almost no water at all (Hope, 2010, p. 452). For example, both Malawi and Uganda have been challenged by less rain over time, jeopardizing small farmers' abilities to survive, resulting in increased levels of malnutrition, poverty, and diseases (Magrath, 2010, pp. 892–894). In the Sahel region, the rainy conditions of the 1950s and 1960 changed to dry conditions and desertification of additional areas from the 1970s to the 1990s (Oba, 2014; Hope, 2010). This negative trend is also related to the increase in population that many African societies are facing, resulting in further scarcity of food and water. For example, Burkina-Faso (2–8%/year) and Ghana (1.9%/year) have rapidly growing populations and are heavily dependent on agriculture. Overall, it has been estimated that the continent's population of 1.1 billion in 2013 will increase to 2.4 billion in 2050 (Population Reference Bureau, 2013, 2014; Mohamoud et al., 2014, p. 10). Rapid population growth presents substantial obstacles for addressing extreme poverty in Sub-Saharan Africa (Brown & Crawford, 2008, pp. 45, 50).

The consequences of climate change, including land degradation, desertification, rainstorms, or limited rainfalls pose serious challenges to the labor force in the agricultural sector and to food security. With increasing population growth there is greater need to cultivate less arable land. An estimate stresses that about 65% of the agricultural land in Africa has faced soil degradation since the 1950s, about two-thirds of the African continent is today arid or desert and that about 35 to 40% of African land is becoming useless for cultivation because of climate change (Mohamoud et al., 2014, pp. 7–8, 16; see also UN Convention to Combat Desertification, June 17, 2017; Thompsell, February 4, 2017). The UN has stated that by 2030, the need for food, energy, and water will increase about 30–50% over 2012 levels) (UNCCD, 2013; see also Kumssa & Jones, 2010; Raleigh & Urdal, 2007).

> The economy of Sub-Saharan Africa is heavily dependent on agricultural production and this has generated immense interest in the impact of climate change on agriculture. The region also has the highest percentage of malnourished inhabitants in the world, with nearly 70 per cent of people living in a state of chronic hunger. This situation is expected to worsen under climate change, which could push crops, livestock and farmers out of their livelihood niches, and increase the frequency and severity of floods and droughts.
>
> (Adano & Daudi, 2012, p. 1)

A second challenge of climate change is forced migration and displaced people. The main reason behind migration and displaced people is said to be desertification and deforestation due to warmer weather and droughts that are degrading farmland (Manou et al., 2017). The scarcity of farmland has resulted in the migration of farmers, due to socioeconomic despair as well as political instability from increased populations in cities competing for limited infrastructure, which has caused social tension (Mohamoud et al., 2014, pp. 7–9). The increasing number of climate change refugees or migrants has led to intensified competition over land and resources, leading to growing tension between urban and rural areas within African societies (Messer, 2010, p. 51; Brown & Crawford, 2008, p. 43; see also McAdam, 2012; Martin, 2010; Brown, 2008).

It is most likely that ongoing climate change will result in population movements becoming a further factor within and across African societies (Intergovernmental Panel on Climate Change, 2014; Martin, 2010; Mazo, 2009a). The political dimension of migration becomes apparent, as migration will impact integration, urbanization, food and water supply, infrastructure capacities, and public health and safety. African government and public authorities on regional and local levels must address migration in terms of urbanization; poverty in the countryside pushes people into urban areas, but marginalization in rural areas is also a factor when poverty and sickness in the countryside causes people to be unable to move away from a life in despair (Mohamoud et al., 2014, p. 10). In recent decades, urban poverty has grown significantly in Africa. While poverty before was mostly a rural phenomenon, urban poverty is today an increasing problem in countries such as Gambia, Kenya, Madagascar, Malawi, Mozambique, Sierra Leone, and Zambia, among other states, with the poverty rate at 50% or higher (Hope, 2010, p. 454). Farmers migrating from rural areas into cities too often have very limited education and practical skills for existing job offerings in companies and factories, leading to despair and a lack of livelihood in slums outside city centers (Kumssa & Jones, 2010, p. 457).

In some ways, migration is, from an individual perspective, an act of adaption to climate change. It is a way for people to adjust to the consequences of climate change and attempt to secure a livelihood and a level of safety (Mazo, 2009a). In many coastal areas in Africa, rising sea levels are another growing concern as migration into inland areas provides further social tension. In inland areas, migration flows may add to already existing challenges for people who are in competition for food, water, and farmland. This is especially true when migration crosses borders and a rising number of people contribute to preexisting social and political tensions based on ethnic and political divisions. Migration has, for example, led to growing political tension in various inter-state conflicts that include Chad–Sudan, Uganda–Sudan–DRC–Central African Republic, Rwanda–Burundi and Rwanda–DRC. In these cases, migration has caused overcrowded areas where an already existing division of people, based on ethnicity, has caused further political tension and led fragile states to become even more weakened. In some cases, migrants also come from war-torn societies and bring memories of violence and strife into new territories, causing insecurity and instability as displaced persons (Messer, 2010: 61; Mazo, 2009a, p. 129; see also Fukui & Markakis, 2005).

In sum, GCC for Africa has many negative consequences on human security. It challenges people's livelihood in terms of scarcity of water and food, increases migration and social tension and puts severe stress on state functions. Climate change is a challenge to economic growth and development and may cause political destabilization in those African societies that are already suffering from fragile institutions, political disintegration and turmoil (see Adger et al., 2014, p. 758; Scheffran & Battaglini, 2011, pp. 29–30). We will now discuss the climate–security nexus.

Climate change in poorly functional states

There has been much scholarly interest in the climate–security nexus (see Bretthauer, 2016; Livingstone, 2015; Hentz, 2014; Dalby, 2008; Salehyan, 2008;

Grover, 2007; Kahl, 2006; Klare, 2001). The debate over climate change and securitization began in early 2000, according to the report by the IPCC published in 2007. The report addressed major human security concerns with ongoing climate change. In 2007, the UN Security Council (UNSC) also addressed the climate–security nexus, and the Secretary-General Ban Ki-moon stated that climate change may become a serious risk comparable to war (see Scheffran & Battaglini, 2011, p. 27). Since then, the bulk of academic work on the potential climate security nexus has grown significantly. Research has, for some decades, stated that GCC is a triggering factor for armed conflicts. Some research has claimed a direct link between years with higher temperatures to increased numbers of internal deadly civil conflicts. One example would be the severe negative consequences drier weather has on agricultural economies in Sub-Saharan African societies. It has been argued that rising temperatures cause higher risks for civil war,

> … with a 1°C increase in temperature in our preferred specification leading to a 4.5 percent increase in civil war in the same year and a 0.9 percent increase in conflict incidence in the next year…, such a 1°C warming represents a remarkable 49 percent relative increase in the incidence of civil war.
>
> (Burke et al., 2009, p. 1)

Since many African states' economies are based on agriculture, and about 95% of Africa's farming is rain-fed, climate change is an alarming driver toward conflict. It may cause groups of people to feel deprived and therefore rise against other groups of people that are in control of key resources (Institute of Security Studies, 2012, p. 4). For example, the Institute of Security Studies has shed light on social tension and conflicts between pastoralists and farmers in southern Ethiopia, in northern Nigeria and in southern Sudan. These conflicts have been based on droughts and competition over water and pasture. The Institute has also identified Algeria as an illustrative case of limited arable land (about 3%), growing desertification, and water and food scarcity leading to social tension and political conflicts. Social tension and escalating conflicts have also been seen in Chad and Mali due to rising temperatures and drought having a negative influence on food production and human security (Institute of Security Studies, 2012, p. 3). The overall message is that climate change triggers scarcity of resources, and in the long run potentially triggers social tension and political instability. Climate change, in terms of increasing heat, drought, rising sea levels, glacial melt, storms, desertification, shrinking water supply, competition for farmland and food scarcity are all potential triggering factors for social and political unrest (Brown et al., 2007; Moritz, 2006; Carius et al., 2004).

However, it is important to understand that global climate change does not always necessarily cause conflicts and wars, but should be seen as a driver of armed conflict in Africa due to the negative impact climate change has on the living conditions for people. Much more research is needed to understand exactly when and where climate change may cause an increase in conflict and war and jeopardize state and human security in sub-Saharan Africa (Hentz, 2014; Burke et al. 2009; Theisen, 2008; Salehyan, 2008; Urdal, 2005). For example, although research identifies an increase in temperature over the coming decades, there is limited research on how such an increase may impact sub-Saharan state and human security (see Bretthauer, 2016).

To understand the risk of conflict, how the effects of climate change are addressed by governments is a crucial issue for further research. Scarcity of resources, migration, and intensified competition for basic needs in food, water, shelter, and health may lead to social tension and armed conflict, but perhaps also, according to some scholars, constructive cooperation. While most literature on GCC and conflict have stated a link between climate change and security, scholars have also, however, argued that competition over scarcity of resources may lead to cooperation to meet common security challenges (see Bretthauer, 2016; Carius et al., 2004). Such cooperation may be initiated by state institutions seeking technological innovations, financial instruments, and social policies to adapt to climate change impact. Such cooperation may also come from the bottom-up initiatives taken by local authorities or civil society organizations finding common solutions to common dire situations.

> All agree that climate change is always associated with conflict. The more constructive question is how political context shapes conflict and its transformations. In fact, many experts attest that it is inaccurate to conclude that water scarcity, drought, desertification, or climate change cause political instability and rebellions; in their opinion, it is the political context that shapes such conflicts and natural resource degradation.
>
> (Messer, 2010: 7–8)

There has been a growing interest in focusing on the importance of governance to deal with global climate change and conflicts (Bulkeley & Newell, 2015; Azim, 2013; Messer, 2010; Adger et al., 2009). Badly governed societies are often associated with a scarcity of resources and measures to be used to mitigate climate change. The literature on failing states has addressed states with poor governance and inadequate state capacities to provide for societal functions vital to wealth, health, and development (Scheffran & Battaglini, 2011, p. 30). While some scholars would perhaps argue that climate change is a root cause of violent conflicts, most scholars would instead argue that climate change might be a driver, depending on the functionality of the state. Climate change and poor governance may both be explanatory factors to armed conflicts, and the combination of the two is often seen in developing states in Africa. "Conflict and state failure make adaption to and mitigation of climate change more difficult, as state institutions become less able to implement adaption measures ..." (Mazo, 2009c, p. 104).

Many African states are politically fragile with limited resources. Annual measurements provided by Freedom House[1] on political rights and civil liberties in states worldwide have shown a poor record on rights and liberties in many African states. It has been stated that about 40% of the African states are not free regarding fundamental political rights and civil liberties, about 40% are partly free and only 20% free. This has left many African societies and populations with very weak political institutions and poor relations between those who govern and those who are governed. Corruption, lack of transparency, concentration of power, limited freedom of expression and association, deficient civil society, and military influence are some of the major challenges in many African states (Freedom in the World 2016, 2014; The Fund for Peace, 2016; McClure, 2015; Kumssa & Jones, 2010, p. 455).

Many African states have also had problems in functioning as robust political entities (Harbeson & Rothchild, 2016; Roessler, 2016; see also Fukuyama, 2004; Rotberg, 2003; Clapham, 2002). This has created even more pressure on African societies as governments have had very limited capacities to protect populations from humanitarian catastrophes. While scholars on climate change have come to stress the importance of governance in Africa to mitigate climate change consequences on state and human security, scholars on security studies have identified numerous fragile states in Africa that are deeply vulnerable to climate change (Hehir & Robinson, 2007). The main focus in these studies has been on political institutions and performance for securing state and human security. A functional state governs the people by providing for both state security and human security. However, many African states have inadequately performed when providing these duties (Harbeson & Rothchild, 2016; see also Lund, 2006; Rotberg, 2003; Jackson, 2003; Clapham 2002). As argued by the World Bank:

> Ultimately, better governance is the outcome of a long-term political and social process, conditioned by a country's and region's history, embedded in its institutions, and driven by its social movements. It is the citizens of a country and their leaders who reform governance.
>
> (World Bank, 2007, p. 248)

Based on the Fragile State Index (The Fund for Peace, 2016),[2] consisting of annual measurements on the level of weakness among states in the world, previous measurements of state and human security have identified numerous weakened and failing states in Africa. Based on existing fault lines within some African societies in terms of caste, class, ethnicity, language, or race; and challenges in terms of scarcity of resources, climate change, corruption and authoritarianism have led to social tension, political turmoil, and violence. One of the mostly challenged states is Nigeria. Political turmoil after the election of 2015, a worsened economy due to lower oil prices, and military insurgencies in the northern regions of the country have challenged Nigerian statehood. Additionally, neighboring Cameroon has seen weakened state performances due to internal military insurgencies and pressures from displaced people from Nigeria putting extreme demand on food, water, and medical supplies in the country. Both Chad and Niger have also been challenged by political violence, refugee flows, and scarcity of resources, resulting in overall growing regional insecurity. While the Fragile State Index identifies many African states among the most

96 Daniel Silander

worsening and worsened states, such as Djibouti, Gambia, Ghana, Guinea Bissau, Libya, Mali, Mozambique, and Senegal, it also acknowledges warning signs in the otherwise economically progressive South Africa including political divisions, corruption, and social unrest (The Fund for Peace, 2016; see also Freedom House, 2016).

African societies are, to a great extent, characterized by a combination of climate change challenges, poor governance, and existing domestic fault lines between people. This has too many times led to social tension, political instability, and even war resulting in humanitarian catastrophes involving genocide and mass atrocities (Hentz, 2014; Messer, 2010). The combination of malfunctioning governance and climate change challenges is a contemporary and highly dangerous reality in many African societies. As stated previously, Africa is challenged by climate change consequences and has limited resources to be used for adaptation.

> African societies cannot meet, and should not be expected to meet, all adaptation costs on their own; that would be both an impossibility and a gross injustice: African countries are poor and being asked to adapt to a problem they had little or no responsibility for causing, whose impacts they are bearing the brunt of. But, African governments can start to prioritize their resources better to meet the triple threats of climate variability, climate change and environmental degradation. For African governments to implement the rights policies, African public opinion has to be more aware of and concerned about the threat of climate change and press politicians to act and hold them to their promises.
>
> (Magrath, 2010, p. 896)

Darfur: the first climate change conflict?

Sub-Saharan Africa, and especially the Sahel region, has the dangerous combination of fragile states and high vulnerability to climate change (Mazo, 2009c, pp. 108–109; see also Mazo, 2010; Barltrop, 2010; Faris, 2009). Sudan has been identified as one of the most fragile states in the world (Barltrop, 2010; see also Mazo, 2009c: 90). In 2007, the current UN Secretary-General, Ban Ki-moon, declared the civil war in the Darfur region of Sudan to be the first climate change conflict in the world (Notaras, 2009; Mazo, 2009a). On June 16, 2007, Ki-moon stated: "Amid the diverse social and political causes, the Darfur conflict began as an ecological crisis, arising at least in part from climate change" (Ki-moon, 2007). Statements based on the data presented by the United Nations Environment Programme (UNEP) show how decreasing rainfalls for decades had led to desertification and an expanded Sahara, resulting in growing tensions between farmers and herders (UNEP, 2007).

Sudan constituted one of the largest African states in the area, located in northeastern Africa. Darfur is a region of about six million people in western Sudan. The civil war in Darfur began in February 2003. Para-military groups in

The climate-security nexus in Africa 97

the Sudan Liberation Movement (SLM) and the Justice and Equality Movement (JEM), mostly based on non-Arab Muslim Fur, Zaghawa, and Masalit ethnic groups, accused the government of politically and economically oppressing non-Arabs in Darfur and launched attacks against Sudanese authorities. In a short period of time, government forces launched a systematic ethnic cleansing of non-Arabs in the region, resulting in several hundreds of thousands of civilians killed, including casualties in combat and by war-related starvation and diseases. In addition, the war in Darfur led to a massive forced migration of over two million people within and across Sudanese borders living in humanitarian despair. The aggressiveness from the government forces supported by militias, primarily against three ethnic tribes, resulted in a humanitarian catastrophe classified by some governments as genocide (Barltrop, 2010; Mazo, 2010; Ki-moon, 2007; Mazo, 2009d, pp. 73–74).

In late 2003, the Sudanese government and rebel forces signed a peace agreement after several diplomatic mediated talks with representatives from Norway, Italy, the UK, and the US. However, international interference in Sudan and Darfur over oil resources undermined the objectives set out in the peace agreement and resulted in further violence, now between rebel forces from the western Darfur against government forces. In the summer of 2004, the UNSC supported the African Union (AU) in its effort to monitor the new ceasefire and to protect civilians from further harm. In 2006, a new peace agreement was concluded, with further UNSC resolutions for monitoring the peace accord, allowing peace-keeping forces, and using the International Criminal Court (ICC) to prosecute war crimes. The Darfur Peace Agreement was the result of numerous diplomatic talks in Nigeria, but was soon challenged when only one rebel group was willing to sign the agreement. The remaining rebel groups questioned how the proposed agreement could lead to any progress for Darfur regarding compensation for victims, protection of displaced people, and political representation. The Sudanese government, on the other hand, was willing to approve the agreement, but had a historical record of agreeing to peace agreements but not taking supportive action. During the ongoing conflict, the Sudanese government had signed agreements, but did not follow up on their implementation (Dagne, 2010; Mohamed, 2009; Sikainga, 2009).

Since 2006, the situation in Darfur has become even more complex with armed conflicts between the central government and rebel forces, but also between different opposition factions and between the government and Arab groups dissatisfied with the central authority's inadequate actions for protecting their safety and wealth. In October 2008, President Omar Hassan Al-Bashir initiated peace talks, but was rejected by rebel factions due to the ongoing violence against civilians. In 2010, the Sudan government signed different agreements with different opposition forces, but without resulting in any increased stability or a halt to the violence and in 2011, the Doha Document for Peace in Darfur was signed between the government and the umbrella organization, the Liberation and Justice Movement (LJM), although many rebel forces once again refused to participate (Thomson Reuters Foundation, July 31, 2014). In addition, in January 2011, South Sudan voted in a referendum for its independence from Sudan resulting in the Republic of South Sudan becoming a sovereign state in mid-July, 2011. However, in 2013–2015, another civil war began leading to about 2.2 million displaced people destabilizing the state and region to such an extent that Sudan and South Sudan were both under threat of state collapse (BBC, February 24, 2017).

While the conflict has faded from the spotlight, ongoing violence continues to displace, injure, and kill people today. The security situation continues to deteriorate, with millions displaced, hundreds of thousands living as refugees, and millions in need of food and other vital aid. The discovery of gold in Darfur has further fueled violence and displacement throughout the region, and the dynamics of the conflict have since escalated from the initial outbreak of violence in 2003. Diplomatic negotiations have continued to fail the civilians in Darfur at the same time as the international attention has focused on other security challenges in the world. Insecurity and violence remain in Darfur despite the existence of UN/AU (UNAMID) peacekeeping forces in the region. Human rights organizations continue to address ongoing war crimes, such as the suspected use of chemical weapons against civilians. Although the International Criminal Court (ICC) issued an arrest warrant in 2009 and 2010 for President Omar Hassan Al-Bashir in Sudan on crimes against humanity and war crimes and genocide, nothing has happened despite his many international travels (Shetty, 2016).

Many scholarly studies have discussed the main causes behind the conflict, and scholars have not fully agreed on how to explain why the war in Darfur broke out as it did (Akasha, 2014; Johnson, 2011). Some studies have also questioned Ban Ki-Moon's statement on a climate change conflict. However, most scholars have argued that poor and brutal governance, ethnic tension, climate change, and competition for land and water between agriculturalists and pastoralists are core factors behind the long-term tensions in the region (Mazo, 2009d, p. 76). One of the root causes of the Darfur war has been the decades of declining rainfall in southern Sudan. Ki-moon stated correctly that the overall challenge of the lack of water, including the situation in the southern parts of Sudan, as one explanation, which is anthropogenic global warming. The drier weather in Darfur put severe stress on settled farmers in the region and resulted in growing social tension between local farmers and Arab nomadic herders over farmland and water (Ki-moon, 2007; Mazo, 2009d). Darfur's economy is based on agriculture with crop farming as the dominant activity in the region. Due to droughts, farming has, over the last two or three decades, become much more problematic, creating a situation where there is a scarcity of food and water as well as competition over fertile land and land ownership between pastoralists and sedentary farmers. Pastoral nomadism has, by tradition, invoked customary rights to use the land on which the pastoralists have migrated. However, with the change of climate continuing from the late 1970s, many local farmers changed their activities from harvesting crops to raising animals, creating a situation of social tension over access to grazing land between pastoralists and farmers.

The climate-security nexus in Africa   99

A second and important factor in the armed conflicts was the policy of the Sudanese authorities in Khartoum, for supporting Arab networks and an Arab identity in Darfur by arming paramilitary groups (Barltrop, 2010; Sikainga, 2009; Strauss, 2005). With an Arab-dominated government since the late 1980s, non-Arab farmers began to feel more and more marginalized from the political and economic resources. The government policies in Darfur were perceived as supporting Arabs and segregating non-Arabs from Arabs and other non-Arab tribes. As a consequence, in the early 2000s, both the Fur and Zaghawa tribes started to arm and then formed the JEM and the SLA, leading to the ensuing civil war in Darfur (The International Coalition for the Responsibility to Protect, 2016; Mazo, 2009d). Poor governance has also led to conflicts and war, not only between Arabs and non-Arab tribes in Darfur, but more lately between former government-supported paramilitary groups and the government. Poor governance in Sudan and continued competition over resources such as farmland, as well as oil reserves where international interests have been involved, have continued to destabilize Sudan and Darfur, leaving Sudan as one of the most fragile states in Africa (Sikainga, 2009; Messer, 2010).

In sum, there have been many drivers behind this conflict; poor governance, militarization, ethnic tension and climate change are some of the most important ones. Climate change has been a threat multiplier in Darfur as an exacerbating factor that put severe stress on a society already in jeopardy due to political, economic, and social factors. As argued by Sikainga (2009),

> The current Darfur conflict is a product of an explosive combination of environmental, political, and economic factors. It is well known that environmental degradation and competition over shrinking resources have played, and continue to play, a critical role in communal conflicts in the Sahelian countries such as Mali, Niger, and Chad. In this regard, Darfur is no exception.

Conclusions

Research on global climate change and conflicts has provided mixed results on root causes to violence in African societies. Scholars have argued that climate change has at times been the explanatory factor for war, while other scholars have argued that political and economic challenges are primary reasons for political instability and conflicts. An intermediate perspective views climate change and poor governance as drivers to conflicts in Sub-Saharan Africa. This chapter has argued that global climate change provides profound state and human security challenges to African governments and people. It has led to scarcity of vital resources in food, water, sanitation, and health and has challenged political and economic structures, infrastructure, and integration. Scarcity of food and water has forced people to migrate to seek a better life, but has also left groups of people further marginalized without resources to survive. In addition, GCC challenges have been met with very limited efforts in many African societies.

100 *Daniel Silander*

This has been due to poorly governed states with major challenges in authoritarianism, corruption, ethnic divisions, and fragile, dysfunctional institutions. Undemocratic governments are a major challenge for Africa to efficiently deal with state and human security challenges; poor and fragile governments on the verge of collapse are another. There is a great danger of future climate change consequences for state and human security. Today, Africa is the most vulnerable geographical area in the world due to climate change consequences and limited state capacities to address the effects. The more recent African efforts to come together internationally and address climate change are very important for the possibilities for adapting to climate change consequences.

Notes

1 Freedom House is a non-profit organization, which was established in 1941 and has provided evaluations of political rights and civil liberties in the world.
2 The Fund for Peace is a non-profit organization, which was established in 1957, has provided analysis of violent conflict and security in the world.

References

Adano, Wario R. & Daudi, Fatuma (2012). Links between climate change, conflict and governance in Africa. *Institute for Security Studies*, May, No. 234: 1–20.

Adger, Neil, Lorenzone, Irene & O'Brien, Karen L. (Eds.) (2009). *Adapting to climate change—Thresholds, values and governance*. Cambridge: Cambridge University Press.

Adger, Neil W., Pulhin, Juan M., Barnett, J., Dabelko, G.D., Hovelsrud, Grete K., Levy, Marc, Oswald Spring, Ürsula & Vogel, Coleen H. (2014). Human security, in V.R. Barros, D.J. Dokken, K.J. Mach, M.D. Mastrandrea, T.E. Bilir, M. Chatterjee, K.L. Ebi, Y.O. Estrada, R.C. Genova, B. Girma, E.S. Kissel, A.N. Levy, S. MacCracken, P.R. Mastrandrea, & L.L. White (Eds.) *Climate change 2014: Impacts, adaptation, and vulnerability. Part A: Global and sectoral aspects.* Cambridge: Cambridge University Press.

Akasha, Mohamed Osman (2014). *Darfur—A tragedy of climate change*. Hamburg: Anchor Academic Publishing.

Aldy, Joseph & Stavins, Robert (2007). *Architectures for agreement*. Cambridge: Cambridge University Press.

Azim, Zia (2013). *Post-Kyoto climate governance—Confronting the politics of scale ideology and knowledge*. New York/London: Routledge.

Barltrop, Richard (2010). *Darfur and the international community—The challenges of conflict resolution in Sudan*. London/New York: I.B. Tauris.

Barnett, Jon (2003). Security and climate change. *Global Environmental Change*, 13(1): 7–17.

BBC (2017, February 24). *South Sudan country profile*. Accessed March 4, 2017: www.bbc.com/news/world-africa-14069082

Betsill, Michele M. & Bulkeley, Harriet (2006). Cities and the multilevel governance of global climate change. *Global Governance: A Review of Multilateralism and International Organizations*. 12(2): 141–159.

Birnbacher, Dieter & May Thorseth (Eds.) (2015). *The politics of sustainability—philosophical perspectives*. New York: Routledge.

The climate-security nexus in Africa   101

Bretthauer, Judith (2016). *Climate change and resource conflict—The role of scarcity.* London & Alexander: Routledge.

Brown, Oli (2008). *Climate change and forced migration: Observations, projections and implications. Human Development Report 2007/2008, Fighting climate change: Human solidarity in a divided world.* Geneva: Human Development Report.

Brown, Oli & Crawford, Alec (2008). Climate change: A new threat to stability in West Africa? Evidence from Ghana and Burkina Faso. *African Security Review*, 17(3): 39–57.

Brown, Oli, Hammill, Anne & Mcleman, Robert (2007). Climate change as the "new" security threat: Implications for Africa. *International Affairs*, 83(6): 1141–1154.

Bulkeley, Harriet & Newell, Peter (2015). *Governing climate change.* New York/London: Routledge.

Burke, Marshall B., Miguel, Edward, Satyanathd, Shanker, Dykemae, John A., & Lobell, David B. (2009). Warming increases the risk of civil war in Africa. *Current Issue.* 106(49): 20670–20674. Accessed September 5, 2016: www.pnas.org/content/106/49/20670.full.

Busby, Joshua W., Smith, Todd G. & Krishnan, Nisha (2014). Climate security vulnerability in Africa mapping 3.0. *Political Geography, Climate Security Vulnerability in Africa Mapping 3.0.* 43: 51–67.

Canter, David (Ed.) (2016). *Social science perspectives on climate change.* New York: Routledge.

CAP (Common African Position) (2015, May 26). Draft African Union strategy on climate change. Accessed July 23, 2017: http://cap.africa-platform.org/resources/draft-african-union-strategy-climate-change

Carius, Alexander, Dabelko, Geoffrey D. & Wolf, Aaron T. (2004). Water, conflict and cooperation. *POLICY BRIEF • The United Nations and Environmental Security.* ECSP Report, Issue 10. Accessed July 15, 2017: http://s3.amazonaws.com/academia.edu.documents/34260756/ecspr10_unf-caribelko.pdf?AWSAccessKeyId=AKIAIWOWYYGZ2Y53UL3A&Expires=1500877368&Signature=iicO85irUQ92HlOgs%2FfYFljJ5%2Bs%3D&response-content-disposition=inline%3B%20filename%3DECSP_REPORT_at_BULLET_ISSUE_10_at_BULLET.pdf

Chin-Yee, Simon (2016). African and the Paris Climate Change Agreement. *African Affairs*, 115(459): 359–368.

Clapham, Christopher (2002). The challenge to the state in a globalized world. *Development and Change*, 33(5): 775–795.

Dagne, Ted (2010). *Sudan—The crisis in Darfur and the status of the North–South agreement.* Washington: CRS Report for Congress.

Dalby, Simon (2008). Environmental change. In Paul, D. (Ed.) *Williams security studies: An introduction* (pp. 311–323). New York: Routledge.

Dessler, Andrew & Parson, Edward A. (2010). *The science and politics of global climate change—A guide to the debate.* Cambridge: Cambridge University Press.

Doyle, Julie (2009). Climate action and environmental activism: The role of environmental NGOs and grassroots movements in the global politics of climate change, in Tammy Boyce & Justin Lewis (Eds.) *Climate change and the media* (pp. 103–116). New York: Peter Lang.

Eizenstat, Stuart, Porter, John Edward & Weinstein, Jeremy (2005). Rebuilding weak states. *Foreign Affairs*, January/February. Accessed July 23, 2017: www.foreignaffairs.com/articles/2005-01-01/rebuilding-weak-states

Faris, Stephan (2009). *Forecast—the surprising—and immediate—consequences of climate change.* New York: Henry Holt and Company.

Freedom House (2016). *Freedom in the world—Sub-Saharan Africa*. Accessed August 24, 2016: https://freedomhouse.org/report/freedom-world/freedom-world-2016

Freedom in the World (2014). *Sub-Saharan Africa*. Washington DC/New York: Freedom House.

Fukui, Katsuyoshi & Markakis, John (2005). *Ethnicity and conflict in the Horn of Africa*. Oxford: James Currey Oxford.

Fukuyama, Francis (2004). The imperative of state-building. *Journal of Democracy*, 15(2): 17–31.

Grover, Velma (Ed.) (2007). *Water: A source of conflict or cooperation?* Enfield, New Hampshire: Science Publishers.

Harbeson, John W. & Rothchild, Donald (Eds.) (2016). *Africa in world politics— Constructing political and economic order*. Bouldon: Wrestview Press.

Harrison, Kathryn & McIntosh Sundstrom, Lisa (Eds.) (2010). *Global Commons, Domestic Decisions—The Comparative Politics of Climate Change*. Cambridge & London: The MIT Press.

Hausler, Kristin & McCorquodale, Robert (2011). Climate change and its impact on security and survival. *Commonwealth Law Bulletin*, 37(4): 617–627.

Hehir, Aidan & Robinson, Neil (Eds.) (2007). *State-building: Theory and practice*. London/New York: Routledge.

Helm, Dieter & Hepburn, Cameron (Eds.) (2009). *The economic and politics of climate change*. Oxford: Oxford University Press.

Hentz, James J. (Ed.) (2014). *Routledge handbook of African security*. New York: Routledge.

Hickmann, Thomas (2016). *Rethinking authority in global climate governance—How transnational climate initiatives relate to the international climate regime*. New York: Routledge.

Hope, Sr. Ronald Kempe (2010). Climate change and poverty in Africa. *International Journal of Sustainable Development & World Ecology*, 16(6): 451–461.

Houngnikpo, Mathurin C. (2016). *Guarding the guardians—Civil–military relations and democratic governance in Africa*. New York: Routledge.

Hurrell, Andrew & Sengupta, Sandeep (2012). Emerging powers, North–South relations and global climate politics. *International Affairs*, 88(3), 1 May 2012: 463–484.

Intergovernmental Panel on Climate Change (IPCSS) (2001). *Climate change 2001: Impacts, adaptation and vulnerability*. Cambridge: Cambridge University Press. Accessed September 13: www.grida.no/climate/ipcc_tar/wg2/index.htm

IPCC (2007). *Climate Change 2007, IPCC fourth assessment report: Synthesis report + summary for policy makers*. Intergovernmental Panel on Climate Change, pp. 1–24.

Jackson, Paul (2003). Warlords as alternative forms of governance. *Small Wars & Insurgencies*, 14(2): 131–150.

Johnson, Douglas, H. (2011). *The root causes of the Sudan's civil war—Peace or truce*. Kampala: Fountain Publishers.

Kahl, Colin H. (2006). *States, scarcity, and civil strife in the developing world*. Princeton, NJ: Princeton University Press.

Karl, Thomas R. & Trenberth, Kevin E. (2003). Modern global climate change. *Science*, 302(5651): 1719–1723.

Kasa, Sjur, Gullberg, Anne T. & Heggelund, Gorild (2008). The Group of 77 in the international climate negotiations: Recent developments and future directions. *International Environmental Agreements: Politics, Law and Economics*, 8(2): 113–127.

Ki-moon, Ban (2007, June 16). *A climate culprit in Darfur.* Accessed September 13, 2016: www.washingtonpost.com/wp-dyn/content/article/2007/06/15/AR2007061501857.html

Klare, Michael T. (2001). *Resource wars: The new landscape of global conflict.* New York: Henry Holt and Company, LLC.

Kumssa, Asfaw & Jones, John F. (2010). Climate change and human security in Africa. *International Journal of Sustainable Development & World Ecology,* 17(6): 453–461.

LDC (Least Developed Countries) (2013, November 11). *LDC Group at UN climate change negotiations.* Accessed July 23, 2017 https://ldcclimate.wordpress.com/2013/11/11/developing-countries-unanimously-call-for-loss-and-damage-mechanism-at-warsaw-climate-conference-as-tragedy-of-super-typhoon-haiyan-unfolds/

Livingstone, David N. (2015). Stop saying climate change causes war—The dangerous ethical implications of letting humans off the hook for their conflicts. *Foreign Policy.* Accessed September 2: http://foreignpolicy.com/2015/12/04/stop-saying-climate-change-causes-war-paris-cop-21-bernie-sanders/

Lund, Christian (2006). Twilight institutions: Public authority and local politics in Africa. *Development and Change,* 37(4): 685–705.

Magrath, John (2010). The injustice of climate change: Voices from Africa. *Local Environment,* 15(9): 891–901.

Manou, Dimitra, Baldwin, Andrew, Cubie, Dug, Mihr, Anja, & Thorp, Teresa (Eds.) (2017). *Climate change, migration and human rights—Law and policy perspectives.* New York: Routledge.

Martin, Susan (2010). Climate change, migration, and governance. Global governance: A review of multilateralism and international organizations. *International Migration,* 16(3): 397–414.

Masters, Lesley (2011). Sustaining the African common position on climate change: International organisations, Africa and COP17. *South African Journal of International Affairs,* 18(2): 257–269.

Mazo, Jeffrey (2009a). Chapter Five: Climate change and security. *The Adelphi Papers,* 49(409): 119–136.

Mazo, Jeffrey (2009b). Chapter One: Global warning and climate change. *The Adelphi Papers,* 49(409): 15–42.

Mazo, Jeffrey (2009c). Chapter Four: Conflict, instability and state failure: The climate factor. *The Adelphi Papers,* 49(409): 87–118.

Mazo, Jeffrey (2009d). Chapter Three: Darfur: The first modern climate-change conflict. *The Adelphi Papers,* 49(409): 73–86.

Mazo, Jeffrey (2010). *Climate conflict—How global warming threatens security and what to do about it.* Abingdon: Routledge.

McAdam, Jane (2012). *Climate change, forced migration and international law.* Oxford: Oxford University Press.

McClure, Kellen (2015). *5 Governance challenges for Africa.* Accessed September 5, 2015: https://freedomhouse.org/blog/5-governance-challenges-africa.

McMichael, Anthony J., Woodruff, Rosalie E. & Hales, Simon (2006). Climate change and human health: Present and future risks. *The Lancet,* 367(9513): 859–869.

Messer, Ellen (2010). *Climate change and violent conflict—A critical literature review.* Oxfam America. Accessed September 8, 2016: www.oxfamamerica.org/static/media/files/climate-change-and-violent-conflict.pdf

Mohamed, Adam Azzain (2009). *Evaluating the Darfur peace agreement: a call for an alternative approach to crisis management.* Uppsala: Department of Peace and Conflict Research, Uppsala University.

Mohamoud, Awil, Kaloga, Alpha & Kreft, Sönke (2014). *Climate change, development, and migration: An African diaspora perspective*. African Diaspora Policy Centre. Bonn: Germanwatch.

Moritz, Mark (2006). Changing contexts and dynamics of farmer-herder conflicts across West Africa. *Canadian Journal of African Studies*, 40(1): 1–40.

Nagothu, Udaya Sekhar (Ed.) (2015). *Food security and development—Country case studies*. New York: Routledge.

Nevell, Peter (2006). *Climate for change—Non-state actors and the global politics of the greenhouse*. Cambridge: Cambridge University Press.

Notaras (2009). Does climate change cause conflict? Our World—Brought to you by UN University. Accessed September 12, 2016: https://ourworld.unu.edu/en/does-climate-change-cause-conflict

Oba, Gufu (2014). *Climate change adaptation in Africa—An historical ecology*. New York: Routledge.

OPEC (2016). *OPEC embraces adoption of historic Paris Agreement on climate change*. Accessed July 24, 2017 www.opec.org/opec_web/en/press_room/3432.htm

Perkins, Patricia E. (2013). *Water and climate change in Africa—Challenges and community initiatives in Durban, Maputo and Nairobi*. New York: Routledge.

Podesta, John & Ogden, Peter (2008). The security implications of climate change. *The Washington Quarterly*, 31(1): 115–138.

Population Reference Bureau (2013). *World population data sheet 2013*. Accessed August 27, 2016: www.prb.org/pdf13/2013-population-data-sheet_eng.pdf

Population Reference Bureau (2014). *World population data sheet 2014*. Accessed August 27, 2016: www.prb.org/pdf14/2014-world-population-data-sheet_eng.pdf

Puddington, Arch (Ed.) (2017). *Freedom in the world 2016—the annual survey of political rights and civil liberties*. Lanham/Boulder/New York & London: Rowman & Littlefield.

Raleigh, Clionadh & Urdal, Henrik (2007). Climate change, environmental degradation and armed conflict. *Political Geography* 26(6): 674–694.

Reig, Paul, Maddocks, Andrew & Gassert, Francis (December 12, 2013). *World's 36 most water-stressed countries—World Resources Institute*. Accessed July 24, 2017: www.wri.org/blog/2013/12/world%E2%80%99s-36-most-water-stressed-countries

Rijsberman, Frank R. (2006). Water scarcity: Fact or fiction? *Agricultural Water Management*, 80(1–3): 5–22.

Rodrik, Dani (2016). An African growth miracle? *Journal of African Economy*, 25(4): 1–18.

Roessler, Philip (2016). *Ethnic politics and state power—The logic of the coup—civil war trap*. Cambridge: Cambridge University Press.

Roger, Charles & Belliethathan, Satishkumar (2016). Africa in the global climate change negotiations. *International Environment Agreements*, 16: 91–198.

Rotberg, Robert I. (Ed.) (2003). *When states fail: Causes and consequences*. Princeton, NJ: Princeton University Press.

Salehyan, Idean (2008). From climate change to conflict? No consensus yet. *Journal of Peace Research*, 45(3): 417–434.

Scheffran, Jürgen & Battaglini, Antonella (2011). Climate and conflicts: The security risks of global warming. *Regional Environmental Change*, 11(1): 27–39.

Scheffran, Jürgen, Brzoska, Michael, Günter Brauch, Hans, Michael Link, Peter & Schilling, Janpeter (eds.) (2012). *Climate change, human security and violent conflict—Challenges for societal stability*. London/New York: Springer Verlag.

The climate-security nexus in Africa   105

Scott, Shirley V. (2008). Securitizing climate change: International legal implications and obstacles. *Cambridge Review of International Affairs*, 21(4): 603–619.

Scott, Shirley V. (2012). The securitization of climate change in world politics: How close have we come and would full securitization enhance the efficacy of global climate change policy? *Reciel—Review of European, Comparative & International Environmental Law*, 21(3): 220–230.

Shetty, Salil (2016, September 29). Chemical weapons are being used against the Darfuris. This is a war crime. *Guardian*. Accessed February 14, 2017 at www.theguardian.com/commentisfree/2016/sep/29/chemical-weapons-used-against-darfuris-war-crime

Sikainga, Ahmad (2009). *"The world's worst humanitarian crisis": Understanding the Darfur conflict*. Accessed September 2, 2016: http://origins.osu.edu/article/worlds-worst-humanitarian-crisis-understanding-darfur-conflict

Strauss, Scott (2005). Darfur and the genocide debate. *Foreign Affairs Jan./Feb*. Accessed September 5: www.foreignaffairs.com/articles/sudan/2005-01-01/darfur-and-genocide-debate

Theisen, Ole M. (2008). Other pathways to conflict? Environmental scarcities and domestic conflict. Paper presented at the 47th Annual Convention of the International Studies Association, March 22–25, San Diego, CA.

The Fund for Peace (2016). *Fragile states index 2016*. Accessed September 9: http://fsi.fundforpeace.org/

The International Coalition for the Responsibility to Protect (2016). *The crisis in Darfur*. Accessed September 15, 2016: www.responsibilitytoprotect.org/index.php/crises/crisis-in-darfur

Thompsell, Angela (2017, February 24). *Soil erosion in Africa—Causes and efforts to control*. Accessed July 24, 2017: www.thoughtco.com/soil-erosion-in-africa-43352

Thomson Reuters Foundation (July 31, 2014). *Darfur conflict*. http://news.trust.org//spotlight/Darfur-conflict

Ubelejit, Nte Timothy (2014). The undermining of state capacity by climate change and vulnerabilities. *Global Journal of Political Science and Administration*, 10(3): 1–10.

UN Convention to Combat Desertification (June 17, 2017). *2017 World day to combat desertification—Addressing desertification, land degradation and drought in Africa*. Accessed July 24, 2017: www.unccd.int/en/regional-access/Africa/Pages/alltext.aspx

UNEP (2007). *Sudan: Post-conflict environmental assessment*. Nairobi: UN Environmental Programme.

UN News Centre (2014, June 15). *UN urges G77+China to unite on combating poverty, climate change*. Accessed July 23, 2017: www.un.org/apps/news/story.asp?NewsID=48053#.WXSk9v4Umpo

Urdal, Henrik (2005). People vs. Malthus: Population pressure, environmental degradation, and armed conflict revisited. *Journal of Peace Research* 42(4): 417–434.

Urry, John (2015). Climate change and society. In Jonathan Michie, Cary L. Cooper (Eds.) *Climate change and society* (pp. 45–59). London: Palgrave Macmillan.

Wheeler, Tim & von Braum, Joachim (2013). Climate change impacts on global food security. *Science*, 341(6145): 508–513.

The World Bank (2007). *The World Bank world development report 2008: Agriculture for development*. Washington, DC: The World Bank.

The World Bank (2016). *Overview*. Accessed August 26, 2016: www.worldbank.org/en/region/afr/overview

5 The United States and global climate change

Niall Michelsen

The United States (US) is the second largest emitter of greenhouse gasses (GHG), which automatically places it at the center of discussions of global actions in response to global climate change (GCC). Furthermore, the US far exceeds any other country in its military deployments in locations across the planet. This means that the US perceives its security in global terms, but it does not necessarily follow that the US draws connections between security and climate change in a similarly broad fashion. As an international actor in the climate change issue area, the US is also characterized by a very politically powerful fossil fuel energy sector along with a strong environmentally minded civic society and a regulatory state that has successfully imposed several important restrictions on environmentally harmful activities (e.g., the Clean Air Act; the Montreal Protocol). While the energy industries are not uniformly and unalterably opposed to environmental legislation or regulations, they are a powerful force (Downie, 2017; Kim et al., 2012). The result of these factors is that the US has at times pushed the world community forward on GCC and sometimes tried to slow the process down. Its relationship with the United Nations Framework Convention on Climate Change (UNFCCC) has been uneven and the new Trump Administration rejects the anthropogenic nature of GCC and the accelerating increase in global temperatures (Plumer, 2017b).

This chapter discusses the evolution of US policies towards mitigation, adaptation, and capacity building between 1992 and 2017. Over this period, US climate change policies varied dramatically with the changes in Presidential leadership rather than due to alterations in the scientific evaluations of the issue. The first part provides a brief description of how the presidential administrations during that period viewed climate change in terms of its human origins and specifically in terms of the obligations of rich industrial countries like the US to bear most of the costs associated with it. The second part focuses on the approach to mitigation taken by the George H.W. Bush, Bill Clinton, and George W. Bush Administrations since mitigation was the climate topic around which much of the political debate centered. The third part looks at how the administrations viewed climate change in terms of security. The fourth part provides a more detailed look at the Obama Administration's views and actions on these matters and discusses the transition to the Trump Administration. This transition

United States and global climate change 107

is dramatic because President Obama was a true believer in anthropogenic climate change and President Trump's actions have thus far belied his post-election claim that he has an "open mind" on climate change (Gore, Kiely, & Robertson, 2016). Finally, the chapter concludes with an evaluation of different future paths the US might take in the upcoming years.

Presidential administrations' perceptions on climate change

The issue of climate change has an interesting place in the American political system. Unlike many other countries the human cause of GCC is far from a consensus opinion in the US. For the US, climate change is a partisan issue that ebbs and flows depending on the political tides rather than with either a scientific consensus or the development of international norms. Thus, while the scientific consensus grows year by year, the American public belief in the human causes of climate change has fluctuated over time with a strong correlation with political party identification (Saad & Jones, 2016). Whereas the US Department of Defense clearly accepts without caveats the scientific consensus, there is no unanimity among political elites. Bolsen, Druckman, and Cook (2015) found that ideological polarization around climate change is alive and strong among the public and among policymakers, but that it was not present among scientists.

This is partly due to the high information costs associated with understanding climate change, and the resulting tendency of citizens to base their conclusions on party identification, ideology, and exposure to media (Rugeley & Gerlach, 2012). Recent surveys have identified an increase in concern, with a 2016 Gallup survey showing a marked increase across both political parties in 2015–2016 moving from 55% to 64%. While this was the highest in eight years, it was far below the high-water mark of 2000 in which 72% of Americans worried about GCC (Saad & Jones, 2016).

Instead, issues related to climate change interact with the fundamental ideological divide between the two major political parties. One is much more internationalist, while the other is fond of unilateral actions. One has affinity for working towards cooperative arrangements with the other members of the international community, while the other is happy to have the market and individual choices (at either the national level or the individual level) solve problems that arise. One party fundamentally trusts that compromises that respect the legitimate interests of actors can lead to mutually beneficial outcomes, while the other party sees international negotiations as zero-sum in nature. The national Republican Party has become increasingly hostile to actions on climate change mitigation or spending on adaptation (Saad & Jones, 2016; Bolsen et al., 2015). The implacable Republican rejection may be softening and if so, it is significant that the change emanates from security concerns over low-lying islands connected with US military activities jeopardized by rising sea levels (Allen-Ebrahimian, 2017b).

Not surprisingly, this has generated variations in policies by the US government unlike the international scientific consensus that has moved in a relatively linear fashion. At the 1992 Earth Summit, President George H.W. Bush tacitly accepted the premise that humans, especially those of the world's richest developed nations, bore substantial responsibility (Bush, 1992). The Clinton Administration enthusiastically embraced this position and subsequently negotiated and signed the Kyoto Protocol. This agreement contained an implicit recognition that the developed nations should move first because they have the necessary resources, but more fundamentally, that the developed nations bore the responsibility. Without the developed nations assuming responsibility and mitigating their GHG emissions, no solution would be possible (Royden, 2002).

When the Administration of George W. Bush assumed office in 2001, the new President acknowledged the responsibility that fell onto the US, but immediately and continually pointed to scientific uncertainty surrounding the subject (Bush, 2001). While claiming to seek a policy consistent with sound science, it faced accusations from the scientific community of shaping the scientific findings to fit its political preferences. The Administration supplemented this claim of scientific uncertainty in the face of a growing international consensus by pointing out the projected high economic costs to the US economy of implementing the mitigation and adaptation policies. Since the Kyoto Protocol was never submitted to the Senate for ratification, the Bush Administration did not have to repeal or remove the US signature from the agreement, but ignore it and pursue its own approach (Kahn, 2003).

The Obama Administration moved into alignment with the international consensus on the matter. President Obama entered office in 2009 acknowledging the human causes of GCC and the consequent moral and prudential need for the US to assume a leading role in moving the international community towards effective action (Kincaid & Roberts, 2013; Pugh, 2015). While Obama remained committed to the idea of US leadership on GCC throughout his two terms in office, his rhetoric shifted away from the politically charged terms of climate change and global warming towards championing clean energy (Kincaid & Roberts, 2013).

The new Trump Administration is staffed by climate change skeptics with the President himself giving voice to skepticism during his campaign for office where he famously cast the climate change as a concept created by and for the Chinese (Harrington, 2016). While his initial cabinet appointments contained a mix of deniers and believers, the confirmation of a climate change denier, Scott Pruitt, as Environmental Protection Administrator was of greatest concern (Detrow, 2017; Foran, 2016; Davenport, 2016b). Since assuming office, Pruitt has moved aggressively to repeal environmental regulations. This is consistent with the Administration's view that environmental protections are harmful to economic growth (Davenport, 2017b). One group of environmental scholars titled their report "The EPA Under Siege" based on their analysis of data and interviews of Environmental Protection Agency employees (Lave & Wylie, 2017).

In politics, government officials and supporters of robust climate change policies have advanced several types of arguments. A first type of justification is a global justice argument that maintains that everyone is obligated to help the most

United States and global climate change 109

endangered states, especially since the most endangered states are not the major contributors to the problem (Democratic Party Platform, 2000). A slightly different global justice argument is that since the advanced countries have contributed most to the problem, with the US being historically the foremost emitter of greenhouse gasses (GHG), the US and other developed countries bear an obligation to fund most of the costs (Democratic Party Platform, 1996). Another justification is a positive economic argument that clean technologies of the twenty-first century represent an opportunity for the US to take the lead in a growing economic sector (Democratic Party Platform, 2004; Greenstone & Sunstein, 2016). A final type of justification is a prudential argument that even if the science is wrong or overstated, developing the technologies and other energy-saving innovations will be good for the country in the long term (*The Economist*, 2016a).

Opponents of strong action on climate change offer a variety of arguments. One recurring argument is that the underlying science is not convincing. Much is made of any controversies that open the door to questions (Republican Party Platform, 2016; Jacques, 2012). Economic arguments against strong action set environmental regulations as barriers to economic growth. Thus, strong climate change actions would likely lead to sub-optimal economic outcomes. This would take place at the global and national levels (Republican Party Platform, 2008), and is close to arguments that claim that incentivizing the market is superior to setting mandatory regulations (Republican Party Platform, 2004; McCright & Dunlap, 2003). Finally, opponents reject the connection made between climate change and national security (Republican Party Platform, 2012).

While the US energy sector is powerful and influential especially within certain states and the Republican Party, it is not a monolithic entity as shown by the number of US energy companies pleading with President Trump to remain in the Paris Agreement (Francis, 2017). Research points to another underlying factor that pushes the US away from many international environmental agreements. Goldstein and Hudak (2017) showed that conservative parties in the US endow property rights with extreme significance, and this distinguishes them from their European ideological counterparts. In the US, property rights are associated with individual freedom so that, while industries such as coal lose workers and share of the energy market, they retain potent political influence by tapping into US constitutional protections of property and the defense of US sovereignty.

Even skeptical administrations have maintained the federal agencies tasked with preparing for and managing the effects associated with climate change adaptation. Executive branch agencies have by the nature of their responsibilities eschewed ideology in favor of grappling with rising tides, stronger storms, and drought. When natural disasters hit and cause major damage to lives and property, the US government agency designed to lend assistance is the Federal Emergency Management Agency (FEMA) and its parent organization the Department of Homeland Security (Department of Homeland Security, n.d.). FEMA specifically identified climate change as a source of natural disasters. According to its website:

110 *Niall Michelsen*

The challenges posed by climate change, such as more intense storms, frequent heavy precipitation, heat waves, drought, extreme flooding, and higher sea levels could significantly alter the types and magnitudes of hazards faced by communities and the emergency management professionals serving them. Regardless of why the climate is changing, emergency managers have to be poised to respond to disasters and support preparedness efforts nationwide.

(Federal Emergency Management Agency, n.d.-b)

The EPA identifies a number of actual and predicted negative repercussions of climate change. Among these are heat-related deaths: from 1979 to 2014, 9,000 Americans died with heat during extreme weather events listed as a contributing factor (US Environmental Protection Agency, 2016).[1]

The US on GCC and mitigation

The mitigation debate in the US is illustrated by the two approaches taken by the Clinton and the George W. Bush administrations. US attention to mitigation began with the 1992 Earth Summit and the Clinton Administration wasted little time in announcing its intention to cut back on GHG emissions. In April 1993, President Clinton used Earth Day to announce his administration's plan to cut GHG to 1990 levels by 2000 (Clinton, 1993b). The plan failed because Congress was unwilling to enact a tax for this purpose, forcing the Clinton Administration to fashion an ambitious and far-reaching Climate Change Action Plan involving 44 separate action plans (DeAngelis, 1994). This, too, was thwarted by Congressional resistance to the funding this plan required (Royden, 2002).

By 1997 the international community was ready to establish specific climate change obligations at the Conference of the Parties (COP) in Kyoto, Japan. In order to secure sufficient international support for the Kyoto Protocol, the Clinton Administration accepted inequalities enshrined in the CBDR-RC (common but differentiated responsibilities and respective capabilities) (Vogler, 2016). This meant that the developed countries (including the US) agreed to binding restrictions on their GHG emissions, while the developing countries (including China and India) were exempt from any such restrictions.

However, in a strong rebuke, the US Senate passed the Byrd-Hagel Resolution on a unanimous vote of 95–0 on July 25, 1997 (Vogler, 2016, p. 93). The resolution called upon US negotiators not to sign any agreement that would not hold to any degree the developing nations to mitigation obligations. Since any treaty would require Senate ratification, the resolution was designed to effectively shut down the US positions at the Kyoto meeting. The key sticking point in the domestic American political context was the concept "developed nations go first". This is the basis of the differentiation of Annex I (advanced industrial economies) and non-Annex I (developing economies) countries and their obligations. The resolution also highlighted the perceived economic costs of a climate deal in their reasoning. Although the US economy was healthy at the time, the

Senate was not comfortable with the US willingly conferring an advantage onto two robust economic challengers: China and India (Royden, 2002).

Nonetheless, the Clinton Administration continued pressing its objectives at the Kyoto meeting and achieved some, but not all of its goals. The US Administration sought to have the Kyoto Protocol include obligations for the developing countries, knowing that Congress was upset that the US (along with other developed countries) was voluntarily putting itself at a disadvantage relative to the rapidly developing and export-oriented economies of China, India, and Brazil (Royden, 2002). Furthermore, the Administration pushed for carbon sinks to be included in the Protocol. This would shift the mitigation burden away from totally energy-oriented matters to land management issues. Along with this, the US pushed for implementation that would allow the developed countries to assist other countries (particularly, but not necessarily only developing countries) in mitigating their GHG emissions, or expanding their carbon sinks. Under these plans, the US could count some external activities towards their own mitigation commitments while at the same time claiming that the developing countries were indeed contributing to the mitigation goals of the Kyoto Protocol. When the European Union (EU) proposed the goal of reducing GHG emissions to 15% below 1990 levels by 2010, the Clinton Administration responded that the goal was "unrealistic and unachievable" (cited in Royden, 2002, p. 434). The Kyoto Protocol incorporated binding emissions targets and allowed market-based solutions that the US insisted upon (Royden, 2002).

Having signed the Kyoto Protocol, the Clinton Administration confronted the perplexing issues of securing its ratification by the Senate. It sought to address the two components of the Byrd-Hagel Resolution. First, it specifically targeted Argentina and Kazakhstan, the two G-77 members who split from that group to voluntarily accept emissions limits as a signal that developed countries were not the only ones making sacrifices (Downie, 2013). The second goal was to fashion an analysis showing the economic costs would be manageable, but this ran into the divide between Treasury and the Council of Economic Advisors (CEA). Ultimately, the CEA analysis concluded that the US had effectively negotiated flexibility into the process such that the economic costs to the US would be "relatively modest." Treasury maintained that the economic costs of complying with Kyoto would be substantial (Downie, 2013). This division within the Democratic administration about the economic costs left open an opportunity for the next Republican administration to emphasize the predicted economic costs of implementation as a reason to move slowly on climate change.

In the process of examining domestic factors, including Congress and the electorate, Downie (2013) identified national actors of importance whose roles vary over time contributing to some variance in the US attitude towards the Kyoto negotiations. Specifically, these are the White House; the State Department, the Environmental Protection Agency, the Department of Energy, and the Treasury Department (Downie, 2013, p. 23). Downie found that the early Clinton Administration sought to demonstrate to the world community that it was very different from the Bush Administration. This pushed the administration

112 *Niall Michelsen*

into accepting the bargain at the center of the Kyoto Protocol and culminated in the Clinton Administration's Climate Change Action Plan (Royden, 2002).

When the Clinton Administration signed the Protocol in 1998 in Buenos Aires, Senator Hagel said at the press conference, "(I)n signing the Kyoto Protocol, the President blatantly contradicts the will of the US Senate" (quoted in Royden, 2002, p. 458). Thus, even though it achieved many of its objectives in the negotiations the Administration was unable to change the sentiment within the US Senate and therefore it never sent the Protocol for ratification.

The George W. Bush Administration came into office in 2001 with a rhetorical commitment to the goals of Kyoto but with two crucial caveats. The commitment was based in the President's acknowledgement in June 2001 that:

> Our country, the United States is the world's largest emitter of manmade greenhouse gases. We account for almost 20 percent of the world's manmade greenhouse emissions. We also account for about one-quarter of the world's economic output. We recognize the responsibility to reduce our emissions.... We also recognize the other part of the story—that the rest of the world emits 80 per cent of all greenhouse gases. And many of those emissions come from developing countries.
>
> (Bush, 2001)

Bush was objecting to the division of responsibilities between Annex I and non-Annex I states. Bush's second objection was the purported high economic costs that would be associated with meeting the obligations set forth in the Kyoto Protocol. These two caveats formed a powerful interlocking pair because some of the major economic competitors were China and India, which had no obligations to reduce their GHG emissions since they fell into the non-Annex I countries. Nonetheless, in that June speech he pledged to create the US Climate Change Research Institute (Bush, 2001). This was in keeping with his pledge to have US climate change policy that was "science-based." Subsequently critics claimed that scientific uncertainty was a façade justifying inaction (e.g., Union of Concerned Scientists (n.d.); Clinton, 2007). Senator Hillary Clinton criticized the Bush Administration because "Instead of recognizing the irrefutable evidence, this Administration has launched a war on science itself. Political appointees have censored studies on global warming, silenced climate experts" (Clinton, 2007).

The Bush Administration also came under criticism for claiming that the US's federal system, wherein solutions are left to the individual states, was a superior approach to a centralized top-down organized effort to cut GHG emissions. Critics said that by pointing to the states, the federal government was attempting to conceal that it was doing little (Revkin & Lee, 2003). The Bush Administration commissioned a study of the climate science as soon as it entered office. The report was issued in August 2001, and employed a framework drawn from an earlier 2001 publication by the National Academy of Sciences. It set out a series of research objectives and strategies designed to reduce uncertainties in

United States and global climate change 113

climate change projections, ensure a viable monitoring system, and enhance research into the environment-society interactions. Centering the analysis on scientific uncertainty reinforced the view that climate science was underdeveloped and implications were poorly understood (US Climate Change Research Initiative, 2001).

Thus, prior to 2009, the Clinton Administration had struggled to get a climate change regime that would meet international objectives while also getting Senate support needed for ratification. It had success on the first but failed abysmally on the second (Downie, 2013). The George W. Bush Administration was little concerned about mitigation; it was much more concerned with economic costs. Its dismissive attitude towards international norms that were evolving on climate change fit with its overall unilateral approach to problems (Pugh, 2015). This would change with the Obama Administration.

The US Administrations on GCC and security

State of the Union Addresses by the President (State of the Union Addresses, 2017) given each January can reveal a great deal about their view of climate change and security. These are often laundry lists of administration goals, setting out the agenda for the next year, but they offer insights into Presidential goals and priorities. Bill Clinton in 1993 was not willing to draw the explicit linkage between climate change and security; rather he saw the changing global environment "as challenges to the health of our global environment" (Clinton, 1993a). In 1997 Clinton linked climate change to the need to "also protect our global environment" (Clinton, 1997). However, no specific challenge to state or human security was mentioned. By 1998 Clinton was ready to make the connection between a changing climate that can "put our children and grandchildren at risk" (Clinton, 1998). He based his claim about the threat on the views of the "vast majority of scientists" and maintained that the trade-off between protecting the environment and growing the economy was a false choice. By 2000 in his final State of the Union Address Clinton was even more emphatic: "The greatest environmental challenge of the new century is global warming ... deadly heat waves and droughts will become more frequent, coastal areas will flood, and economies will be disrupted" (Clinton, 2000).

Clinton's successor, President George W. Bush, restricted his State of the Union references to climate change to issues of energy independence until he acknowledged in his 2007 speech that technological breakthroughs would be necessary to "help us confront the serious challenge of global climate change" (Bush, 2007). In 2008 Bush stated that the "United States is committed to strengthening our energy security and confronting global climate change" (Bush, 2008). However, he never made explicit a connection between the military or political security of the country or the world to climate change (Bush, 2008).

President Barack Obama was the most explicit of the presidents in connecting climate change to security. Beginning with his first State of the Union speech in 2009 where he spoke of how "to truly transform our economy, to protect our security, and save our planet from the ravages of climate change, we need to ultimately make clean, renewable energy the profitable kind of energy" (Obama, 2009). In 2010, Obama addressed the climate change issue in a decidedly new way by claiming that US global leadership involves "engagement that advances the common security and prosperity of all people ... we have gone from a bystander to a leader in the fight against climate change" (Obama, 2010). In 2011, he promised to "invest in biomedical research, information technology, and especially clean energy technology and investment that will strengthen our security, protect our planet, and create countless new jobs for our people" (Obama, 2011). In 2012, he announced "the Department of Defense, working with us, the world's largest consumer of energy, will make one of the largest commitments to clean energy in history" (Obama, 2012; Environmental and Energy Study Institute, 2011). In his 2013 State of the Union speech Obama blamed climate change for "heat waves, droughts, wildfires, floods—all are now more frequent and more intense" (Obama, 2013). In 2014 this had escalated to "a changing climate [that] is already harming Western communities struggling with drought and coastal cities dealing with floods" (Obama, 2014). In 2015 Obama declared that "no challenge poses a greater threat to future generations than climate change." He later said

> if we don't act forcefully, we'll continue to see rising oceans, longer, hotter heat waves, dangerous droughts and floods, and massive disruptions that can trigger greater migration and conflict and hunger around the globe. The Pentagon says that climate change poses immediate risks to our national security.
>
> (Obama, 2015)

Climate change was a major portion of Obama's 2016 State of the Union address and he used the opportunity to stress, "climate change is just one of many issues where our security is linked to the rest of the world" (Obama, 2016). He also noted, "When we lead nearly 200 nations to the most ambitious agreement in history to fight climate change, yes, that helps vulnerable countries, but it also protects our kids" (Obama, 2016).

Employing the Copenhagen School model of securitization, Hayes and Knox-Hayes examined the Obama Administration's efforts to securitize climate change (Hayes & Knox-Hayes, 2014). They point out that a President and his executive branch are privileged in their ability to declare (or not) something a security threat. Attaching state security to climate change extracts the issue from normal political processes and moves it to a realm where the executive's security expertise in its several departments gives it the upper hand. Not only does this shift the debate to a different realm, it also can have spillover effects on other issues. For example, if mitigating and adapting to climate change is a security issue, then questions regarding development aid to African countries that are vulnerable to climate-induced problems are also security issues. Furthermore, successful securitization could not only weaken the ability of Congress to challenge the

President on climate, it could also disrupt international cooperation efforts if the US were focused more on traditional state security issues while others are focused more on protecting human security. Another concern is that securitizing the climate change issue brings it into the realm of the military and therefore risks skewing adaptation efforts in a direction that benefits military or state needs more than the civilian populations, "policies may end up being geared towards state security over human security" (Detraz, 2011, p. 115). Utilizing the military for dealing with climate issues entails accepting the typically huge environmental footprints associated with military actions. It is not impossible for military actions to be environmentally benign, but that has not been a priority until recently.

In their analysis of policy documents, Hayes and Knox-Hayes (2014) identified several cases where the new President Obama, Secretary of State Clinton, and Senator John Kerry drew connections between security and climate change. Newly elected President Obama said "Climate change ... if left unaddressed, will continue to weaken our economy and threaten our national security." In 2009, Secretary of State Clinton said, "It is at once an environmental, economic, energy and national security issue with grave implications for America's and the worlds' future." Senator John Kerry in his role on the Senate Foreign Relations Committee in 2009 said "Many today do not see global climate change as a national security threat but it is profoundly so" (Hayes & Hayes-Knox, 2014).

Despite these efforts, the authors concluded that the Obama Administration was "unsuccessful in terms of generating broader public support" (Hayes & Knox-Hayes, 2014, p. 94). But they noted that the effort succeeded in bringing the military into the center of discussions about the severity of the global climate change issue. The US Department of Defense maintains close contact with the non-profit Center for Climate and Security. The Center's website houses documents dating as far back as 2003 that illustrate the long-standing view that there is an important connection between climate change and US national security interests (Center for Climate and Security, 2016). One of the very first research documents focused on the implications of abrupt climate changes, as opposed to gradual climatic changes (Schwartz & Randall, 2003).

The US Department of Defense issued a 2015 report identifying and assessing the nature of the threat posed to the DoD in its various regional commands (National Security Implications of Climate-Related Risks and a Changing Environment, 2015). The report begins with an unequivocal statement:

> DoD recognizes the reality of climate change and the significant risk it poses to U.S. interests globally. The National Security Strategy, issued in February 2015, is clear that climate change is an urgent and growing threat to our national security, contributing to increased natural disasters, refugee flows, and conflicts over basic resources such as food and water. These impacts are already occurring, and the scope, scale and intensity of these impacts are projected to increase over time.

The report identified four types of climate-related security risks: (1) Persistent recurring conditions such as flooding, drought, and higher temperatures; (2) More frequent and/or more severe extreme weather events; (3) Sea level rise and temperature changes; (4) Decreases in Arctic ice cover, type, and thickness. These risks, which the report stated, "impacts human security and, more indirectly, the ability of governments to meet the basic needs of their populations" (National Security Implications of Climate-Related Risks and a Changing Environment, 2015). Affected countries that are unable to handle those strains are susceptible to succumbing to political and social disorder, which can then cause American interests to be harmed or put at risk. While this DoD report emphasized adaptation efforts working in cooperation with our international partners including increased training, providing extra equipment and building infrastructure in areas identified as being susceptible to climate related disasters they also addressed mitigation efforts. Specifically, the DoD has pursued energy efficiency and promoted the use of renewable energy sources, such as solar power (National Security Implications of Climate-Related Risks and a Changing Environment, 2015).

In September 2016, the Center published a work by its Climate and Security Advisory Group made up of 42 "military, national security, homeland security, intelligence and foreign policy experts." Their purpose was to encourage the entire federal government to increase the priority of GCC in their deliberations. Their recommendations were to "assign a cabinet-level official to lead on domestic climate change security issues" and to add a senior climate security position on the National Security Council staff. Their reasoning incorporated the Department of Defense understanding that GCC is real and placing new demands on capabilities and conceptions. The document is completely focused on adaptation actions and represents a bifurcated response to GCC wherein the military emphasizes responding to climate change impacts, while other government agencies can focus on mitigation efforts (Center for Climate and Security, 2016).

The transition from Barack Obama to Donald Trump

In 2009, the Obama Administration entered office clearly acknowledging the reality of GCC but faced internal constraints imposed by Congress and a divided public. The conflicted picture is visible in the fate of the 2009 Waxman–Markey Bill (American Clean Energy and Security Act) with its cap-and-trade GHG mitigation measures, which passed the House of Representatives with strong support from Obama, but was never brought to a vote in the Senate (Goldenberg, 2009). Having failed at the legislative approach the Obama Administration switched to the administrative route in the form of the Clean Power Plan that placed the Environmental Protection Agency in charge of establishing emission standards for new and existing power plants (Downie, 2017).

The nature of the transition from Bush to Obama is evident in the fate of the Asia-Pacific Partnership on Clean Development and Climate (APP). The Bush Administration launched this initiative in 2006 in close cooperation with business interests in the energy field. Critics worried that it was designed to be a replacement for the Kyoto Protocol. The Obama Administration signaled that it was more interested in the Copenhagen COP-17 in December 2009 (Pugh, 2015). The APP was formally closed in 2011.

In funding for climate change projects, the Obama Administration organized its external funding to assist in capacity building internationally through the Global Climate Change Initiative (GCCI) (Lattanzio, 2015). The GCCI had three focal points. The first was adaptation assistance to developing countries most at risk. The second was mitigation action by funding the deployment of clean energy programs in the developing world, working through various multilateral funding organizations. The third is also mitigation in design with a focus on funding sustainable forestry that would reduce GHG associated with deforestation (Lattanzio, 2015). The most current budget information runs from 2010 through a request for 2016 funding. From a beginning total of $945 million allocated in 2010, the request for FY 2016 was $1.289 billion. That represents a growth of 36%. While the growth is impressive, the actual budget numbers pale in comparison to US defense spending against traditional national security threats. Moreover, 2010 to 2012 actually witnessed a decrease in funding of 9%. In the context of the Great Recession, it is not surprising that the US Congress was focused on domestic spending at the expense of externally oriented climate change funding. Moreover, the Republicans had regained control of the House of Representatives in the 2010 elections with many members adamantly opposed to any Administration proposal including the word "climate" (Kincaid & Roberts, 2013).

Funding of the GCCI was routed through three avenues: the first being USAID, the State Department being the second, and the Treasury the third. Roughly speaking the funds were allocated evenly with USAID receiving slightly less than the others. USAID funding concentrated on development assistance and economic support of climate policies designed to "support bilateral and regional climate change activities" (Lattanzio, 2015). State Department funding was dedicated to an Economic Support Fund and went to a variety of regional and global environmental organizations, and through a handful of climate change oriented international programs (Intergovernmental Panel on Climate Change (IPCC); UNFCCC). Treasury funding went towards debt restructuring for Caribbean and South American countries in order to preserve tropical forests, to international programs dedicated to clean technologies, to the Global Environment Facility, to the Green Climate Fund, and to the Strategic Climate Fund. Each of these three environmental funds has overlapping climate related foci, but all support adaptation efforts, and clean energy development. The Global Environmental Facility is a universal international organization with 183 states as members, and dedicates 50% of its budget to climate change. The Green Climate Fund is an international organization that focuses on helping developing countries in their mitigation and adaptation efforts. The Strategic Climate Fund is based in the World Bank system and focuses on providing developing countries with forestry and other climate change technologies (Lattanzio, 2015).

In the Congressional Research Service's (CRS) report on the GCCI, the reasons Congress should support the budget requests included: Natural Disaster Preparedness; National Security; and International Leadership. The CRS case for natural disaster preparedness focused on the situation facing developing countries experiencing climate related disasters. The CRS cited the funding for adaptation activities as a means to prepare developing countries before such climate related humanitarian issues arise. National security was linked, in its analysis, to the threat of growing instability and weakened political institutions resulting from climate induced costs to which local governments are ill-equipped to respond. In terms of leadership, the CRS referred indirectly to the benefits that accrue to the US from having a strong voice that advances US interests and values along an array of global issues that include but go beyond climate change (Lattanzio, 2015).

The Copenhagen COP in 2009 was projected to be a major event in the foreign policy of the new President Barack Obama (Kincaid & Roberts, 2013). In style, in rhetoric, and in what the world hoped would be in substance, Obama seemed likely to provide the impetus to move the process forward. However, the global economic crisis that was striking the developed world at the same time complicated the President's plan. Specifically, the Senate once again (as on the eve of the Kyoto Protocol agreement) threatened to undermine any promises the President could make regarding US climate change actions by his administration. Obama's own Democratic Party was divided while the opposition Republican Party was united against promises that the US would curtail its use (and thus production) of fossil fuels (Broder, 2009).

In the aftermath of the failure of the Copenhagen meeting to set binding climate change commitments, the Obama Administration began negotiating directly with China. The two represent the largest GHG emitters and any agreement between them would go a long way towards bringing everyone else along. This led to a dramatic announcement of a China–US climate change agreement in 2015, which led the way towards the 2016 Paris Agreement. The Paris Agreement addressed US's standard objections (Dimitrov, 2016). Nationally determined commitments are now the norm and all states are obligated to suffer some costs as part of the agreement. Lurking in the background internationally, but often mentioned in domestic contexts, is the economic argument that cutting GHG emissions would assuredly hurt the American economy. The projected harm to the US economy is not largely advanced on the international level because the US is among the richest countries in the world so a complaint from the US is not acceptable those with fewer resources.

With a new administration coming to power in 2017, and one that is highly skeptical of the science and motivations behind climate change, the political landscape has changed considerably. On the eve of the Trump Administration taking office, the outgoing Obama Administration transferred half a billion dollars to the Green Climate Fund (Goodenough, 2017). When justifying its decision to withdraw from the Paris Agreement, the Trump Administration specified its opposition to the Obama Administration's pledge of $3 billion and its intention to stop further payments (Henry, 2017a). This change from Obama to Trump is dramatic but is representative of the split between the American political parties and within the American public (Stokes, Wike, & Carle, 2015).

The Trump Administration's decision to exit from the Paris Climate Agreement indicates that the climate skeptics within the Administration have prevailed over those who, like Secretary of State Rex Tillerson, accepted climate change and the need for international agreements to address the problem (Batchelor, 2017; Shear, 2017; Plumer, 2017a). Because the Paris agreement went into effect in 2016, the US would not be able to formally exit immediately, but the Trump Administration would be free to ignore the voluntary goals set in the agreement (Davenport, 2016a; Henry, 2017b; Shear, 2017). For some, the relative ease with which the Trump Administration was able to remove the US from the Paris Agreement is indicative of the free hand that the American executive typically has on foreign policy issues, when not viewing itself bound by the restrictions on its treaty authority, especially those that do not directly connect with war (Miller & Sokolsky, 2017).

Critics are particularly concerned about the fate of the Obama Administration's Clean Power Plan launched in 2015 but stopped by the federal courts since 2016 (US Environmental Protection Agency, n.d.-a). This Plan was at the center of Obama Administration mitigation efforts, with goals of reducing power plant carbon emissions and therefore overall US GHG contributions to ensure that carbon emissions would be 17% below 2005 amounts by 2020, so completely jettisoning it would be very significant (US Environmental Protection Agency, n.d.-b.; Davenport, 2017b).

While the Trump Administration's steps thus far are troubling, there are at least three sources of reassurance for critics. First, despite the Trump Administration's decision to withdraw the US from climate change efforts, there are forces at work that may limit the damage (Thompson & Bajaj, 2017). One such force is that the environmental regulations on GHG already in place will continue to shape behaviors (Schwartz, 2015). Those regulations have changed the incentive structure of companies that might also wonder what is likely to succeed the Trump Administration. Moreover, several companies including those in the important energy section are worried that American isolation on the climate might affect their ability to act around the globe (Francis, 2017). A number of prominent Republicans have warned that simply walking away from climate change efforts will be very unpopular (Feldstein et al., 2017). Instead, they recommend a set of tax and rebate policies to replace the regulations of the Clean Power Plan while achieving similar environmental benefits.

Second, another source of stability lies in the scientific expertise maintained within the federal bureaucracy that may survive the change of political appointees at the top. The tension between political agendas and scientific understandings date back at least to the early days of the atomic scientists (Buzbee, 2016; Goldman et al., 2017; Union of Concerned Scientists, 2017). Several US government agencies have websites wherein references to climate change are prominent and consistent with anthropogenic GCC reasoning. A review of cabinet level departmental websites in early 2017 indicated that a few have minimal information, mostly Climate Change Adaptation Plans from 2014. Others have much more material including policy positions and scientific data reports. In addition, there was a great deal of linking across departments, with the US Global Change Research Program site as the central source. The point is that even if climate change skeptics fill the upper reaches of government it will still be difficult for them to dismantle the knowledge and programs within the federal government (Editorial Board, 2016). Nonetheless, in the first day in office the Trump Administration ordered the removal of all references to climate change from the whitehouse.gov website (Raymond, 2017). Efforts by universities to save data from the departmental websites of the Obama Administration were undertaken (Varinsky, 2017). Prominent among these efforts include the Environmental Data & Governance Initiative, which since January 2017 has worked with DataRefuge and over 20 leading research universities in "monitoring, documenting, and analyzing change to federal environmental agencies" (Environmental Data & Governance Initiative, 2017).

A third source of optimism comes from the federal nature of the American political system, which allots to the states and cities considerable leeway in some matters. Sometimes, the states have led the way, at one time prompting President Obama to urge the federal government to match California's environmental protection actions (Knox-Hayes 2012, p. 560). The two most populous states in the US, California and New York seem poised to continue to address GCC (Editorial Board, 2016). The Democratic governors of both states have indicated their willingness to resist some of the federal initiatives they expect to come from the Trump Administration (Editorial Board, 2016). Between them, these two large states are committed to reducing GHG 40% below 1990 levels by 2030. Governor Brown of California intends to conduct his own international climate change diplomacy and maintain this state's compliance with the Federal Clean Air Act even if the national government stops enforcement (Nagourney & Fountain, 2016). Due to California's economic size, its impact can have a stabilizing effect on overall US mitigation and adaptation results. California, in particular, has "long been a leader on vehicle emissions" and more than a dozen states have followed (Nagourney & Fountain, 2016). The important role that major US cities can play in mitigating GCC has also been recognized internationally (Tamkin, 2017).

Conclusion

To this point in time, the US has contributed positively to the GCC issue globally. It played constructive roles in the major agreements reached on the issue and has made substantial changes domestically. According to Environmental Protection Agency reporting on US GHG emissions, between 1990 and 2014 total emissions increased by 7%. The EPA noted that since 2005 the emissions have dropped by 7% (US Environmental Protection Agency, n.d.-b). Moreover, the US has great capacity at its disposal to deal with mitigation and adaptation. It still leads the world in research and development and the federal government funded $147 billion for all basic scientific and research purposes and $2.6 billion for the US Global Change Research Program in 2016 (USGCRP) (Historical Trends, 2013; GlobalChange.gov, n.d.). Included in the USGCRP are the National Oceanic and Atmospheric Administration and the Departments of Energy, Agriculture, and Interior.

The US has significant leverage to either accelerate or slow the global progress towards serious climate change cooperation. The US is effectively a veto state due to being historically the largest producer of GHG and, along with China, it still represents one of the largest emitters (Chasek, Downie, & Brown, 2010). This means the US can dilute the impact of any agreement reached by everyone else if it stands outside the agreement. Conversely, when the US accepts its responsibility it represents significant advances for the global effort. In fact, the US has played both those roles within the climate change regime. Significant US interactions with the UNFCCC process include the Earth Summit in 1992, the Kyoto Protocol in 1997, the Copenhagen COP in 2009, the Paris meeting in 2015, finishing with the US–China climate change agreement reached in 2016. Two points are especially important. First, the US signed but could not secure ratification of the Kyoto Protocol. The Obama Administration faced the same domestic political obstacle and sidestepped Congressional oversight of the Paris agreement, claiming it was authorized under the 1992 treaty (Demirjian & Mufson, 2015). Thus, even when Democrats control the White House, US participation in these agreements is tentative.

The future role that the US will play in international efforts to combat GCC is murky at best. The ability of the US to play a consistent role in international efforts on GCC is strongly constrained by its fragmented political system and the lack of consensus between its two main political parties. The ebb and flow of US efforts coincide with the periodic transfer of power at the executive branch level, which does not always correspond to the distribution of power within its two legislative houses. Well-financed lobbying interests, specifically those associated with the energy sector play significant roles constraining the ability of the government to pass domestic legislation or endorse international agreements.

The new Trump Administration, in speech and action, has evolved from early ambivalence to a fundamental rejection of a perspective of climate change being human-caused (*The Economist*, 2016b; Allen-Ebrahimian, 2017a; Davenport, 2017a). Administration budget proposals have projected deep cuts in the Environmental Protection Agency and the Trump Administration seems intent upon eliminating the Obama Administration's key mitigation effort under the Clean Power Act (Davenport, 2017a). In the area of climate, the combination of climate deniers appointed to the cabinet and in other advisory roles is especially troubling. Action taken on the controversial XL Keystone Pipeline displays a view that privileges economics over environmental protection in a zero-sum calculation and their desire to increase fossil fuel production (McKibben, 2017).

Moreover, these actions also directly and indirectly raise doubts about future US commitments to international multilateralism. In these respects, it suggests a fundamental re-orientation of US international policy. The tension between the

America First approach which portrays American interests as paramount and the US as global leader is not yet fully resolved and is likely to be re-negotiated in the future (Allen-Ebrahimian, 2017a; Kupchan, 2017). It is not a new tension but it seems particularly powerful at this particular time. While the isolationist strand in the US is well documented and recognized as being a product of the separation of the US and the other global powers by the Atlantic and Pacific oceans (Hastedt, 2015), the current debate will take place in a time where those oceans are rising and endangering the great American cities located along the coasts. In this particular case, the oceans are no longer what will stop the threats from reaching our shores, but are the threats to the shores themselves. The most recent G-20 meeting (July 20, 2017, in Hamburg, Germany) provided visual and textual clues to the marginalizing of the US in multilateral gatherings. In the opening photo shoot, President Trump was conspicuous by being at the far edge of the participants. This symbolic signal was reinforced with the summit's climate document expressing the consensus among 19 members with a prominent footnote to the Preamble reading "The United States is currently in the process of reviewing many of its policies related to climate change and continues to reserve its position on this document and its contents" (G20, 2017b). The G20's Leaders' Declaration: Shaping an Interconnected World likewise acknowledged that the US was not ready to act in coordination with others:

> We take note of the decision of the United States of America to withdraw from the Paris Agreement. The United States of America announced it will immediately cease the implementation of its current nationally-determined contribution and affirms its strong commitment to an approach that lowers emissions while supporting economic growth and improving energy security needs. The United States of America states it will endeavour to work closely with other countries to help them access and use fossil fuels more cleanly and efficiently and help deploy renewable and other clean energy sources, given the importance of energy access and security in their nationally-determined contributions.
>
> (G20, 2017a)

The G-20 typically issues statements that have received consensus support and this type of acknowledgement of a member not acceding to the document is rare and represents the wide divide between the US and the other leading world powers on GCC (Kirton, 2017; Cooper & Thakur, 2013).

Storms, beachfront erosion, and droughts are problems that have afflicted the US at various times and locations (Federal Emergency Management Agency, n.d.-a). Prioritizing adaptation over mitigation could be in the US national interest if the worst effects of climate change occurred beyond its borders, and if the projected costs of adaptation are lower than the projected costs of mitigation. Economists and the IPCC have challenged many of the estimates of high economic costs of mitigation (Intergovernmental Panel on Climate Change, n.d.; Stern, 2006). For any particular country, the ideal mix of adaptation and mitigation may vary. However, adaptation when focused on the home state is essentially a private response while mitigation actions represent public goods whose benefits cannot be restricted (Kane & Shogren, 2000). Even if the economic costs favor adaptation, adopting such a position would represent an abdication of the US global leadership role.

Optimists maintain that many of the US actions already undertaken would be tough to undo because a new status quo has arisen. For example, *The Economist* argued that despite Trump's desire to promote US fossil fuel production, US producers will not expand production if the market is not profitable. They further observe that companies will make investment decisions based on long-term calculations and will be conservative towards assuming any Trump-era deregulations will be permanent. Ultimately, this view argues that technological advances and regulatory mechanisms implanted since 1992 have reached a point where cleaner energy is cheaper and likely to get cheaper (Obama, 2017).

Another stabilizing force is the slow-moving nature of huge governmental bureaucracies. Developing through decades, the climate change framework is deeply embedded in those organizations. The American federal system also places natural limits on decisions made in Washington. Forces that are more contingent include a recent call from eminent establishment Republicans for market-oriented climate solutions, along with a substantial resistance to the Trump Administration broadly from a wide swath of the civic society (Feldstein et al., 2017). Another optimistic sign was the Republican dominated House of Representatives passing a defense-funding bill containing these words "climate change is a direct threat to the national security of the United States" (quoted in Allen-Ebrahimian, 2017b).

Some US Presidents have cast the climate change issue in terms of threatening human and national security. It is highly unlikely that President Trump will cast climate change issues in security terms. More often, the national security is cast in terms of economic and energy security.

Note

1 This was originally accessed on January 22, 2017 on the EPA website live, but is now accessible only via a January 19, 2017 snapshot. The live EPA website as of July 15, 2017 is www.epa.gov/sites/production/files/signpost/cc.html.

References

Allen-Ebrahimian, B. (2017a, July 7). G-20 Communique may further isolate U.S. on climate change. *Foreign Policy*. Retrieved July 16, 2017 from http://foreignpolicy. com/2017/07/07/g-20-communique-may-further-isolate-u-s-on-climate-change-trump-merkel/

Allen-Ebrahimian, B. (2017b, July 14). In landmark move, GOP Congress calls climate change 'direct threat' to security. *Foreign Policy*. Retrieved July 16, 2017 from http://foreignpolicy.com/2017/07/14/in-landmark-move-gop-congress-calls-climate-change-direct-threat-to-security/?utm_source=Sailthru&utm_medium=email&utm_campaign=Ed%20pix%207-14&utm_term=%2AEditors%20Picks

Batchelor, T. (2017). Trump "will definitely pull out of Paris climate change deal." *Independent*. UK. Retrieved July 16, 2017 from www.independent.co.uk/news/world/americas/donald-trump-paris-climate-change-deal-myron-ebell-us-president-america-pull-out-agreement-a7553676.html/

Bolsen, T., J.N. Druckman, & F.L. Cook. (2015). Citizens' scientists', and policy advisors' beliefs about global warming. *Annals of American Academy of Political and Social Science, 658*, 271–295.

Broder, J.M. (2009, December 12). Senate poses obstacles to Obama's climate pledge. *New York Times*. Retrieved March 10, 2017 from www.nytimes.com/2009/12/13/weekinreview/13broder.html

Bush. G.H.W. ((1992, June 13). The President's news conference in Rio de Janeiro. Retrieved March 10, 2017 from www.presidency.ucsb.edu/ws/?pid=21079

Bush, G.W. (2001, June). Discusses global climate change. Retrieved February 19, 2017 fromhttps://georgewbush-whitehouse.archives.gov/news/releases/2001/06/20010611-2.html

Bush, G.W. (2007, January 23). Address before a joint session of the Congress on the state of the union. Retrieved February 19, 2017 from www.presidency.ucsb.edu/ws/index.php?pid=24446

Bush, G.W. (2008, January 28). Address before a joint session of the Congress on the state of the union. Retrieved February 19, 2017 from www.presidency.ucsb.edu/ws/index.php?pid=76301

Buzbee, W.W. (2016, December 8). Dismantling climate rules isn't so easy. *New York Times*. Retrieved from www.nytimes.com/2016/12/08/opinion/dismantling-climate-rules-isnt-so-easy.html

Center for Climate and Security. (2016, September 14). Climate-and security advisory group briefing book for a new administration. Retrieved March 10, 2017 from https://climateandsecurity.files.wordpress.com/2016/09/climate-and-security-advisory-group_briefing-book-for-a-new-administration_2016_11.pdf

Chasek, P., Downie, D.L., & Brown, J.W. (2010). *Global environmental politics* (5th Ed.). Colorado: Westview.

Clinton, H. (2007). Speech on energy and climate change. Retrieved February 19, 2017, from www.cfr.org/climate-change/hillary-clintons-speech-energy-climate-change/p14715

Clinton, W.J. (1993a, February 17). Address before a joint session of Congress on administration goals. Retrieved February 19, 2017 from www.presidency.ucsb.edu/ws/index.php?pid=47232

Clinton W.J. (1993b, April 21). President's remarks in Earth Day speech. Retrieved February 19, 2017 from https://clinton6.nara.gov/1993/04/1993-04-21-presidents-remarks-in-earth-day-speech.html

Clinton, W.J. (1997, February 4). Address before a joint session of the Congress on the state of the union. Retrieved February 19, 2017 from www.presidency.ucsb.edu/ws/index.php?pid=53358

Clinton, W.J. (1998, January 27). Address before a joint session of the Congress on the state of the union. Retrieved February 19, 2017 from www.presidency.ucsb.edu/ws/index.php?pid=56280

Clinton, W.J. (2000, January 27). Address before a joint session of the Congress on the state of the Union. Retrieved February 19, 2017 from www.presidency.ucsb.edu/ws/index.php?pid=58708

Cooper, A.F. & Thakur, R. (2013). *The group of 20 (G20)*. New York: Routledge.

United States and global climate change 125

Davenport, C. (2016a, November 18). Diplomats confront new threat to Paris Climate pact: Donald Trump. *New York Times*. Retrieved February 18, 2017 from www.nytimes.com/2016/11/19/us/politics/trump-climate-change.html

Davenport, C. (2016b, December 19). Climate change and the incoming Trump government. *New York Times*. Retrieved December 19, 2016, from www.nytimes.com/interactive/2016/12/19/us/politics/climate-change-trump-administration.html

Davenport, C. (2017a, March 9). E.P.A. chief doubts consensus view of climate change. *New York Times* Retrieved March 10, 2017, from www.nytimes.com/2017/03/09/us/politics/epa-scott-pruitt-global-warming.html

Davenport, Coral. (2017b, July 1). Counseled by industry, not staff, E.P.A. chief is off to a blazing start. *New York Times*. Retrieved July 16, 2017 from www.nytimes.com/2017/07/01/us/politics/trump-epa-chief-pruitt-regulations-climate-change.html

DeAngelis, T. (1994). Clinton's climate change action plan. *Environmental Health Perspectives*, 102(5), 448–449.

Demirjian, K., & S. Mufson. (2015, November 30). Trick or treaty? The legal question hanging over the Paris climate change conference. *Washington Post*. Retrieved March 10, 2017 from www.washingtonpost.com/news/powerpost/wp/2015/11/30/trick-or-treaty-the-legal-question-hanging-over-the-paris-climate-change-conference/?utm_term=.715c31ff5164

Democratic Party Platform. (1996, August 26). Retrieved from www.presidency.ucsb.edu/ws/index.php?pid=29611

Democratic Party Platform. (2000, August 14). Retrieved March 10, 2017 from www.presidency.ucsb.edu/ws/index.php?pid=29612

Democratic Party Platform. (2004, July 27). Retrieved March 10, 2017 from www.presidency.ucsb.edu/ws/index.php?pid=29613

Department of Homeland Security. (n.d.) Climate change. Retrieved on March 10, 2017, from www.dhs.gov/keywords/climate-change

Detraz, N. (2011). Threats or vulnerabilities? Assessing the link between climate change and security. *Global Environmental Politics*, 11(3), 104–120.

Detrow, S. (2017, February 17). Scott Pruitt confirmed to lead environmental protection agency. Retrieved February 19, 2017, from www.npr.org/2017/02/17/515802629/scott-pruitt-confirmed-to-lead-environmental-protection-agency

Dimitrov, R.S. (2016). The Paris Agreement on climate change: Behind closed doors. *Global Environmental Politics*, *16(3)*, 1–11.

Downie, C. (2013). Three ways to understand state actors in international negotiations: Climate Change in the Clinton years (1993–2000). *Global Environmental Politics*, *13(4)*, 22–40.

Downie, C. (2017). Fighting for King Coal's crown: Business actors in the US coal and utility industries. *Global Environmental Politics*, 17(1), 21–39.

Editorial Board. (2016, December 26). States will lead on climate change in the Trump era. *New York Times*. Retrieved February 19, 2017 from www.nytimes.com/2016/12/26/opinion/states-will-lead-on-climate-change-in-the-trump-era.html

Environmental and Energy Study Institute (2011, July). Fact sheet: DoD's efficiency and renewable energy initiatives. Retrieved February 19, 2017 from www.eesi.org/files/dod_eere_factsheet_072711.pdf

Environmental Data & Governance Initiative (2017). Retrieved February 19, 2017, from https://envirodatagov.org/

Federal Emergency Management Agency (FEMA). (n.d.-a). *Climate change*. Retrieved February 19, 2017, from www.fema.gov/climate-change

Federal Emergency Management Agency (FEMA) (n.d.-b.). *Overview of Federal disaster assistance*. Retrieved February 20, 2017, from https://training.fema.gov/emiweb/downloads/is7unit_3.pdf

Feldstein, M.S., Halstead T., & Mankiw, N.G. (2017, February 8). *A conservative case for climate action*. Retrieved February 20, 2017, from www.nytimes.com/2017/02/08/opinion/a-conservative-case-for-climate-action.html

Foran, C. (2016, December 25). Donald Trump and the triumph of climate-change denial. *The Atlantic*. Retrieved July 16, 2017 from www.theatlantic.com/politics/archive/2016/12/donald-trump-climate-change-skeptic-denial/510359/

Francis, David. (2017, June 5). Major energy firms plead with Trump to stay in Paris. *Foreign Policy*. Retrieved July 16, 2017 from http://foreignpolicy.com/2017/06/05/major-energy-firms-plead-with-trump-to-stay-in-paris/

G20. (2017a, July 8). G20 Hamburg climate and energy action plan for growth. Retrieved July 16, 2017 from www.g20.utoronto.ca/2017/2017-g20-climate-and-energy-en.pdf

G20. (2017b, July 8). G20 leaders' declaration: Shaping an interconnected world. Retrieved July 16, 2017 from www.g20.utoronto.ca/2017/2017-G20-leaders-declaration.html

GlobalChange.gov. (n.d.). Retrieved February 20, 2017, from www.globalchange.gov/

Goldenberg, S. (2009, June 26). Barack Obama's US climate change bill passes key Congress vote. *Guardian*. Retrieved from www.theguardian.com/environment/2009/jun/27/barack-obama-climate-change-bill

Goldman, G., Reed, G., Halpern, M., Johnson, C., Berman, E., Kothari, Y., & Rosenberg, A. (2017, January). *Preserving scientific integrity in federal policymaking*. Retrieved February 19, 2017, from www.ucsusa.org/center-science-and-democracy/promoting-scientific-integrity/preserving-scientific-integrity

Goldstein, Bernard D., & Hudak, Juliann M. (2017). Comparison of the role of property rights in right wing and left wing American and European environmental policy deliberations. *Environmental Science & Policy*, 68, 28–34.

Goodenough, P. (2017, January 17). *Final days: Obama sends $500M to UN climate fund; Trump vowed to cancel "global warming payments."* Retrieved February 19, 2017, from www.cnsnews.com/news/article/patrick-goodenough/final-days-obama-sends-another-500-million-un-climate-fund-trump-has

Gore, D., Kiely, E., & Robertson L. (2016, November 23). *Trump on climate change*. Retrieved February 19, 2017, from www.factcheck.org/2016/11/trump-on-climate-change/

Greenstone, M., & Sunstein, C.R. (2016, December 15). Donald Trump should know: This is what climate changes costs us. *New York Times*.

Harrington, R. (2016, November 9) President-elect Donald Trump doesn't believe in climate change. Here's his platform on the environment. *Business Insider*. Retrieved February 19, 2017, from www.businessinsider.com/donald-trump-climate-change-global-warming-environment-policies-plans-platforms-2016-10

Hastedt, G.P. (2015). *American foreign policy: Past, present, and future* (10th ed.). Lanham, MD: Rowman & Littlefield.

Hayes, J., & J. Knox-Hayes. (2014). Security in climate change discourse: Analyzing the divergence between EU and US approaches to policy. *Global Environmental Politics*, 14(2), 82–101.

Henry, D. (2017a, January 25). *Trump preparing review of Paris deal, other treaties: Report*. Retrieved February 19, 2017, from http://thehill.com/policy/energy-environment/316150-trump-preparing-review-of-paris-deal-other-us-treaties-report

Henry, D. (2017b, July 14). *Trump aims to use UN climate fund for coal plants: Report.* Retrieved July 16, 2017 from http://thehill.com/policy/energy-environment/342077-trump-aims-to-use-un-climate-fund-for-coal-plants-report

Historical Trends in Federal R&D. (2013, June 11). Retrieved February 19, 2017, from www.aaas.org/page/historical-trends-federal-rd

Intergovernmental Panel on Climate Change. (n.d.) *Fifth assessment report.* Retrieved July 16, 2016. Retrieved from www.ipcc.ch/report/ar5/index.shtml

Jacques, P.J. (2012). A general theory of climate denial. *Global Environmental Politics,* 12(2), 9–17.

Kahn, G. (2003). The fate of the Kyoto Protocol under the Bush Administration. *Berkeley Journal of International Law,* 21(3), 548–571.

Kane, S. & Shogren, J.F. (2000). Linking adaptation and mitigation in climate change policy. *Climatic Change,* 45(1), 75–102.

Kim, S.E., Urpelainen, J., &Yang, J. (2012). Electric utilities and American climate policy: Lobbying by expected winners and losers. *Journal of Public Policy,* 36(2), 251–275.

Kincaid, G., &. Roberts, T. J. (2013). No talk, some walk: Obama Administration first-term rhetoric on climate change and US international climate budget commitments. *Global Environmental Politics,* 13(4), 41–60.

Kirton, J. (2017, July 8). *A summit of solid success at Hamburg in 2017.* Retrieved on July 16, 2017. Retrieved from www.g20.utoronto.ca/analysis/170708-kirton-success.html

Knox-Hayes, J. (2012). Negotiating climate legislation: Policy path dependence and coalition stabilization. *Regulation & Governance,* 6, 545–567. https://doi.org/10.1111/j.1748-5991.2012.01138.x

Kupchan, C. (2017). The West will have to go it alone, without the United States. *Foreign Policy.* Retrieved July 16, 2017 from http://foreignpolicy.com/2017/06/13/the-west-will-have-to-go-it-alone-without-the-united-states-trump/

Lattanzio, R.K. (2015). *Global Climate Change Initiative (GCCI): Budget authority and request,* FY2010-FY2016—R41845.pdf. Retrieved February 19, 2017, from https://fas.org/sgp/crs/misc/R41845.pdf

Lave, R. ed., & Wylie, S. ed. (2017, June). *The EPA under siege: Trump's assault in history and testimony.* Environmental Data & Governance Initiative. Retrieved July 16, 2017 from https://100days.envirodatagov.org/

McCright, A.M. and Dunlap, R.E. (2003). Defeating Kyoto: The conservative movement's impact. *Social Problems. 50(3),* 348–373.

McKibben, B. (2017, January 25). *On pipelines, Donald Trump looks backward.* Retrieved February 19, 2017, from www.nytimes.com/2017/01/25/opinion/on-pipelines-donald-trump-looks-backward.html

Miller, A.D. & Sokolsky, R. (2017, June 20). Why Trump's foreign policy can't be stopped. *Foreign Policy.* Retrieved February 19, 2017 from http://foreignpolicy.com/2017/06/20/why-trumps-foreign-policy-cant-be-stopped/

Nagourney, A. & H. Fountain (2016, December 26). *California, at forefront of climate fight, won't back down to Trump.* Retrieved February 19, 2017 from www.nytimes.com/2016/12/26/us/california-climate-change-jerry-brown-donald-trump.html

National Security Implications of Climate-Related Risks and a Changing Climate (2015, July 23). Retrieved February 19, 2017 from http://archive.defense.gov/pubs/150724-congressional-report-on-national-implications-of-climate-change.pdf?source=gov delivery

Obama, B. (2009, February 24). *Address before a joint session of the Congress*. Retrieved February 19, 2017 from www.presidency.ucsb.edu/ws/index.php?pid=85753

Obama, B. (2010, January 27). *Address before a joint session of the Congress on the state of the union*. Retrieved February 19, 2017, from www.presidency.ucsb.edu/ws/index.php?pid=87433

Obama, B. (2011, January 25). *Address before a joint session of the Congress on the state of the union*. Retrieved February 19, 2017, from www.presidency.ucsb.edu/ws/index.php?pid=88928

Obama, B. (2012, January 24). *Address before a joint session of the Congress on the state of the union*. Retrieved February 19, 2017, from www.presidency.ucsb.edu/ws/index.php?pid=99000

Obama, B. (2013, February 12). *Address before a joint session of Congress on the state of the union*. Retrieved February 19, 2017, from www.presidency.ucsb.edu/ws/index.php?pid=102826

Obama, B. (2014, January 28). *Address before a joint session of the Congress on the state of the union*. Retrieved February 19, 2017, from www.presidency.ucsb.edu/ws/index.php?pid=104596

Obama, B. (2015, January 20). *Address before a joint session of the Congress on the state of the union*. Retrieved February 19, 2017, from www.presidency.ucsb.edu/ws/index.php?pid=108031

Obama, B. (2016, January 12). *Address before a joint session of the Congress on the state of the union*. Retrieved February 19, 2017, from www.presidency.ucsb.edu/ws/index.php?pid=111174

Obama, B. (2017). The irreversible momentum of clean energy. *Science*. Retrieved March 10, 2017, from https://doi.org/10.1126/science.aam6284

Plumer, Brad. (2017a, June 7). The U.S. won't actually leave the Paris Climate deal anytime soon. *New York Times*. Retrieved July 16, 2017, from www.nytimes.com/2017/06/07/climate/trump-paris-climate-timeline.html

Plumer, Brad. (2017b, June 15). Energy department closes office working on climate change abroad. *New York Times*. Retrieved July 16, 2017, from www.nytimes.com/2017/06/15/climate/energy-department-closes-office-working-on-climate-change-abroad.html

Pugh, G. (2015). *Clean energy diplomacy from Bush to Obama. Issues in science and technology*. Retrieved March 10, 2017, from http://issues.org/31-3/clean-energy-diplomacy-from-bush-to-obama/

Raymond, A.K. (2017, January 20). The White House website removes mentions of climate change. *New York Magazine*.

Republican Party Platform. (2004, August 30). Retrieved March 10, 2017, from www.presidency.ucsb.edu/ws/index.php?pid=25850

Republican Party Platform. (2008, September 1). Retrieved March 10, 2017, from www.presidency.ucsb.edu/ws/index.php?pid=78545

Republican Party Platform. (2012, August 27). Retrieved March 10, 2017, from www.presidency.ucsb.edu/ws/index.php?pid=101961

Republican Party Platform. (2016, July 18). Retrieved March 10, 2017, from www.presidency.ucsb.edu/ws/index.php?pid=117718

Revkin, A.C., and Lee, J. 8. (2003, December 11). *White House attacked for letting states lead on climate*. Retrieved February 19, 2017, from www.nytimes.com/2003/12/11/us/white-house-attacked-for-letting-states-lead-on-climate.html

Royden, A. (2002). U.S. climate change policy under President Clinton: A look back. *Golden Gate University Law Review*, 32(4), 415–478.

Rugeley, C.R. & Gerlach, J. (2012). Understanding environmental public opinion by dimension: How heuristic processing mitigates high information costs on complex issues. *Politics & Policy*, 40(3), 444–470.

Saad, L. & Jones, J.M. (2016). *U.S. concern about global warming at eight-year high.* Retrieved March 10, 2017, from www.gallup.com/poll/190010/concern-global-warming-eight-year-high.aspx?version=print

Schwartz, J. (2015, March 3). *The new optimism of Al Gore.* Retrieved February 19, 2017, from www.nytimes.com/2015/03/17/science/the-new-optimism-of-al-gore.html

Schwartz, P., & Randall, D. (2003). *An abrupt climate change scenario and its implications for United States national security.* California Inst of Tech Pasadena Jet Propulsion Lab. Retrieved from http://oai.dtic.mil/oai/oai?verb=getRecord&metadataPrefix=html&identifier=ADA469325

Shear, Michael D. (2017, June 1). Trump will withdraw U.S. from Paris Climate agreement. *New York Times.* Retrieved July 16, 2017, from www.nytimes.com/2017/06/01/climate/trump-paris-climate-agreement.html

State of the Union Addresses (n.d.). *State of the union addresses of the presidents of the United States.* Retrieved February 19, 2017, from www.presidency.ucsb.edu/sou.php

Stern, N. (2006). What is the economics of climate change? *World Economics*, 7(2), 1–10.

Stokes, B., Wike, R., & Carle, J. (2015, November 5). *Global concern about climate change, broad support for limiting emissions.* Retrieved March 10, 2017, from www.pewglobal.org/2015/11/05/global-concern-about-climate-change-broad-support-for-limiting-emissions/

Tamkin, Emily. (2017, June 6). "We'll always have Paris," Countries tell U.S. cities ready to fight climate change. *Foreign Policy.* Retrieved July 16, 2017, from http://foreignpolicy.com/2017/06/05/well-always-have-paris-countries-tell-u-s-cities-ready-to-fight-climate-change/

The Economist. (2016a, November 26). *What will happen if America's president-elect follows through on pledges to tear up environmental laws?* Retrieved February 19, 2017, from www.economist.com/news/international/21710811-rest-world-will-figure-out-way-stay-course-what-will-happen-if-americas

The Economist. (2016b, November 26). *Climate change in the era of Trump.* Retrieved February 19, 2017, from www.economist.com/news/leaders/21710807-or-without-america-self-interest-will-sustain-fight-against-global-warming-climate

Thompson, Stuart A., & Bajaj, Vikas. (2017, June 20). The green energy revolution will happen without Trump. *New York Times.* Retrieved July 16, 2017, from www.nytimes.com/interactive/2017/06/20/opinion/green-energy-revolution-trump.html

Union of Concerned Scientists. (n.d.). *Climate change research distorted and suppressed.* Retrieved Match 10, 2017, from www.ucsusa.org/our-work/center-science-and-democracy/promoting-scientific-integrity/climate-change.html

Union of Concerned Scientists. (2017, January 26). *Resist this: The Trump Administration's Control + Alt + Delete strategy on climate change.* Retrieved Match 10, 2017, from http://blog.ucsusa.org/erika-spanger-siegfried/the-trump-administrations-strategy-on-climate-change

US Climate Change Research Initiative (CCRI). (2001, August). *Survey of Research Strategies to Reduce Scientific Uncertainties—www.hsdl.org/?view&did=469577.* Retrieved February 19, 2017, from www.hsdl.org/?view&did=469577

US Environmental Protection Agency. (EPA). (n.d.-a). *Clean power plan for existing power plants [policies and guidance]*. Retrieved February 19, 2017, from www.epa.gov/cleanpowerplan/clean-power-plan-existing-power-plants

US Environmental Protection Agency. (EPA). (2016, 4th ed.). *Climate change indicators in the United States*. Retrieved July 14, 2017, from https://19january2017snapshot.epa.gov/sites/production/files/2016-08/documents/climate_indicators_2016.pdf

US Environmental Protection Agency. (EPA). (n.d.-b). *Fact sheet: Overview of the clean power plan*. Retrieved February 25, 2017, from www.epa.gov/cleanpowerplan/fact-sheet-overview-clean-power-plan

Varinsky, D. (2017). Scientists across the US are scrambling to save government research in 'Data Rescue" events. *Business Insider*. Retrieved from www.businessinsider.com/data-rescue-government-data-preservation-efforts-2017-2

Vogler, J. (2016). *Climate change in world politics*. London: Palgrave Macmillan.

6 The European Union and global climate change

Martin Nilsson

Most Western European states have a relatively long history of developing different progressive environmental policies, but since the late 1990s, the European Union (EU), presently with 28 pre-Brexit member states across Europe, has been taking the leading global role in the effort to address all sorts of environmental issues, including global climate change (GCC) (Pavese & Torney, 2012; Jordan, van Asselt, Berkhout, & Huitema, 2012; Downie, 2013; Babonneau, Hauri, & Vielle, 2014). While each of the member states still has its own national environmental policy, with domestic regulations and laws, the EU sets certain common obligatory standards as well. In the most recent EU treaty, the Treaty of Lisbon (2007), environmental issues were formally established as a shared competence area between the supranational EU level and the member states' national level. At the supranational level, all EU policies and decisions have to meet a high degree of protection to reduce environmental damages in all of the EU's policy areas (Wysokinska, 2016). The precautionary rule and the concept that the polluter has to pay the cost for damages to the environment serve as the guiding principles of all EU decisions. If the member states would like to have more demanding requirements in a certain area, it is possible to implement even more demanding national environmental laws (Benson & Jordan, 2016). However, this environmental guarantee is only possible if it does not discriminate against other actors or goods and if it does not violate other important rules of the EU's common market policies. Because the EU nowadays has a set of common environmental policies, the issue of climate change is also very much an EU issue. Still, most of the member states also have their own agenda for how to implement policies to counter the challenges of GCC. This can be described as a system of "multilevel reinforcement" or Europeanization, by which the EU affects national legislation; internationalization, whereby the EU is the key actor in most aspects; and integration, through which the EU makes decisions that must later be implemented by the member states (Jordan et al., 2012; Böhringer, Keller, Bortolamedi, & Seyffarth, 2016). The climate change issue involves all these aspects and, for the EU, has become "an organizing focus for virtually all of its policies" (Jordan, Huitema, van Asselt, Rayner, & Berkhout, 2010, p. 58) and includes "varieties of market-based policy" (see Meckling & Jenner, 2016, p. 853).

Back in 1996, the EU accepted the goal of reducing the rise in the global temperature, setting the maximum at 2°C, and this has since been the guiding principle (Debeke & Vis, 2015). This was followed by the EU's first European Climate Change Programme (ECCP) in 2000 to avoid future climate change; it later became the main tool to achieve the goals ratified in the Kyoto Protocol (European Commission, 2016d). During the 2000s, the EU worked on various policies (i.e., related to mitigation, adaptation, and capacity building) in order to reduce the future risk of climate change, with all its possible ramifications for the Earth and human beings. Although there have been some critical remarks against the EU's climate policy, the EU has still been at the forefront of international efforts toward a new and more comprehensive global climate agreement (Bäckstrand & Elgström, 2013; Downie, 2013; Babonneau, Hauri, & Vielle, 2014). During 2016, the EU and its member states also ratified the Paris Agreement (2015), as well as establishing a new "Global Strategy." In this new Global Strategy, internal and external EU security is about to become more intertwined, and GCC is now seen as one of many potential security threats (European Commission, 2016h). Already, the EU has utilized many strategies and policies to deal with GCC, but what will eventually come out of this is, of course, still an open question (Strielkowski, Lisin, & Gryshova, 2016).

This chapter analyzes the EU's overall role in GCC. The first section describes how the EU views the nature and threat of GCC, followed by the second section, which deals with how the EU has approached the threat in terms of different strategies and policies in relation to the United Nations (UN) framework and to GCC as a threat to state and human security. In the subsequent, third section of the chapter, perhaps the most important issue is analyzed: what kinds of factors might limit the EU's capacities to truly achieve the organization's own objectives (i.e., capacities versus willingness and ability). Conclusions are presented in a final section of this chapter.

The incremental and anthropogenic nature: GCC as a human and state security threat

The European Commission, the EU's executive branch, recognizes in all of its official documents, publications, investigations, directives, and policies that greenhouse gases result from both natural processes and human activities. This recognition has been the case since GCC began to become an important issue within the old European Community (EC) in the late 1980s (Jordan et al., 2012). Through various activities, human beings are increasing the atmospheric concentrations of greenhouse gases and are thereby contributing to the warming of the climate (see European Commission, 2016a). In particular, the reduction of greenhouse gases, such as carbon dioxide, methane, nitrous oxide, and fluorinated gases, is important to avoid climate change. The European Commission recognizes these sources caused by human beings, particularly the burning of fossil fuels, such as oil and coal; the increase in livestock production; the deforestation across the world; land filling or waste generation; and, the use of industrial fluorinated gases.

As it is phrased in one of the EU-sponsored training workshops on mainstreaming climate change:

> Natural variability is an inherent feature of the climate, but there is no longer any reasonable doubt that the changes we are observing today are to a large extent driven by anthropogenic emissions of long-lived greenhouse gases. Indeed, human activities cause unprecedented emissions of such GHGs, and they have accumulated in the atmosphere at levels not observed over the past 650,000 years.
>
> (GCCA 2011, p. 2)

In another fact sheet from the European Commission (2015, p. 2), it is stated:

> Greenhouse gases emitted by human activities are warming the Earth and causing changes in the global climate. These changes are having increasingly severe human, economic and environmental impacts and will continue to do so over the coming decades.

Therefore, the European Commission, as the executive branch of the entire EU, understands that climate change is caused by humankind and that it already has and will continue to have a major impact on Europe as well as the entire world. The most obvious sign of this is that Europe's average land temperature in recent years has become 1.5°C higher compared with the preindustrial era (EEA, 2016b). In addition, the polar ice is melting, the sea is rising, and more extreme weather events are taking place around the world, including heavy rainfall, heat waves, and droughts. However, although all the member states are exposed to the impact of climate change, GCC affects Europe in different ways (Commission of the European Communities, 2007, 2009). Generally, the European Commission realizes that GCC will have a stronger impact on geographical areas such as the Mediterranean basin, the mountains, coastal and flood areas, and the Arctic.

The European Commission also projects different scenarios for various European regions (European Commission, 2013a, 2013b; EEA, 2015). In the Arctic, the temperature will rise much higher than average around the globe, which will lead to a decrease in the ice coverage, the Greenland ice sheet, and permafrost areas. According to the European Commission, it will also probably affect the biodiversity in the Arctic region. In Northern Europe, the temperature will also rise more than the global average, and this will increase river flows, winter storms, hydropower potential, and as a consequence of this most likely also the amount of summer tourists. It will also decrease snow, lake, and river ice cover and the demand for energy for heating. In Northwestern Europe, the winter precipitation will increase as well as river flows and coastal flooding. In the coastal zones and regional seas, the sea level will rise, and this will increase ocean acidity and surface temperatures. Also, it will affect fish and plankton species. In the mountainous regions, the temperature will rise more than average; as a result, glaciers will be diminished and permafrost areas will decrease. Furthermore, biodiversity will be affected, and there is greater risk of soil erosion. Finally, according to the European Commission, in the Mediterranean regions, the increasing temperature will affect mortality rates from heat, demand for water, and risk of forest fires, and it will cause the loss of entire systems of biodiversity. The European Commission also predicts that it will affect annual river flows and crop yields (European Commission, 2013a, 2013b; EEA, 2015).

In the end, the European Commission (Commission of the European Communities, 2007, 2009) believes that climate change will have a negative impact of economic losses, health problems, and deaths. In more concrete terms, this means there is an increased risk of damage to various property and infrastructure, with increasing costs to society. In particular, it will cause negative developments in sectors such as agriculture, forestry, energy, and tourism. But it will also affect the wildlife; plant and animal species will be affected by the higher temperature and will have to cope with the new conditions. Above all, it will also affect human health, in that both heat- and cold-related deaths will increase across different regions of Europe.

The European Commission's White Paper report from 2009 provides a clear picture and summary of the EU's view on the impact of climate change in Europe. Here, the Commission explicates a strong belief that climate change will also have major impacts on both state and human security:

> Climate change increases land and sea temperatures and alters precipitation quantity and patterns, resulting in the increase of global average sea level, risks of coastal erosion and an expected increase in the severity of weather-related natural disasters. Changing water levels, temperatures and flow will in turn affect food supply, health, industry, and transport and ecosystem integrity. Climate change will lead to significant economic and social impacts with some regions and sectors likely to bear greater adverse effects. Certain sections of society (the elderly, disabled, low-income households) are also expected to suffer more.
>
> (Commission of the European Communities 2009, p. 3)

While Europe generally has calmer weather systems than the hurricane-plagued Caribbean or the typhoon-haunted North Pacific, planning for weather-related disasters will become increasingly important. The EU's 2013 Adaptation Strategy (European Commission, 2013a, 2013b) is focused on "climate-proofing" activities, ensuring that Europe's infrastructure is made more resilient, promoting the use of disaster insurance, providing funding for cross-border water and flood management, and expanding the protection of areas with high drought, desertification, or fire risks.

In the EU, weather-related actions to prevent disasters across Europe are on the agenda and have so far not been seen as any major internal threat to state security. However, for almost a decade the EU has pointed out that the consequences of climate change could lead to several somewhat new conflicts

European Union and global climate change 135

around the world; one new issue that has occurred is migration due to the consequences of climate change, which is also seen as a rising challenge for the EU (Trombetta, 2014; Werz & Hoffman, 2016). Back in 2008, the High Representative of the European Commission and the Council of Europe (2008)—identified several possible state-and-human security threats around the world, including the following aspects:

- conflicts over resources such as water, food, and fish stocks;
- economic damage and risk to coastal cities and critical infrastructure due to rising sea levels, which will affect 20% of the world's population in places such as East China, India, and the Caribbean Sea;
- loss of territory and border disputes due to major changes in landmasses, for example, new and possible exploration in the polar zone;
- increased environmentally induced migration, for example, in Africa or the Middle East, which will put enormous pressure on transition and migration countries in Europe;
- a likely increase in fragility and radicalization in failed or weak states when governments are unable to handle all the consequences of climate change; more frequent tension over energy supply all around the world; and increased pressure on international governance to handle the appearance and consequences of various conflict dimensions, such as between the North and the South and between poorer countries such as India, China, and African countries.

As a consequence of this view of GCC as both an internal and external security threat, the EU has realized that it is not sufficient to deal with the issues as only internal security concerns among European countries; rather, they must be dealt with within the EU-system (Sonnsjö & Bremberg, 2016). As Richard Young (2014, p. 7) noticed: "Europe has been more successful at advancing internal climate objectives than at integrating climate security into its foreign policies." Therefore, for a long period of time, instead of securitizing GCC within the EU, the EU stressed the importance for dealing with its institutions on one hand, through its different "domestic" EU policy areas, such as with agriculture, the environment, industry, competition, and energy and, on the other hand, through international channels, which include the UN system and various multilateral and bilateral constellations around the world (Sonnsjö & Bremberg, 2016).

However, the EU has begun, at least in its own Global Strategy (European Commission, 2016h), to securitize GCC into its broader and soft power foreign policy. In light of this understanding there are three possible scenarios for strategies for the future that have been explored, where the EU now seems to lean more toward the first category (see Liberatore, 2013, pp. 91–92):

1) "Greening security," in which environmental, social, and economic aspects will be linked to a broader concept of human and comprehensive security;

2) "War on climate change," in which intelligence services will warn of the concrete effects of GCC, which will lead to border controls, restrictions on immigration, and border conflicts; and

3) "Much ado about nothing," in which GCC, after some years of attention, will fall back again into the hands of actors who have managed to underplay the consequences of GCC, and, thereby, the entire idea of solving GCC through multilateral cooperation with the United Nations and the EU will vanish.

To conclude, the EU mainly understands GCC as an issue caused by humankind. The EU also connects it to issues of both state and human security but had not until 2016 incorporated it into its official foreign and defense strategy to meet the external challenges, and, thereby, it is more linked to a broader concept of security (i.e., greening or environmental security).

EU policies and decisions and the EU's relation to the UN

In the past two decades, the EU's role in combatting GCC has paralleled both the general development of the EU and the framework established within the UN to handle GCC. The EU has also been the frontrunner in establishing and developing different global climate agreements. The EU is seen as a regional economic integration organization within the UN system on climate issues but can only act if the member states have agreed that the EU should represent them all (Pavese & Torney, 2012; Damro, Hardie, & MacKenzie, 2008). Today, the EU has a complex structure of strategies and a variety of somewhat market-based policies for addressing most areas of GCC, and since 2016 GCC is presently also a part of the EU's official foreign and security policy strategy (Meckling & Jenner, 2016, p. 853; European Commission, 2016h). Since the late 1990s, the EU has undertaken measures to uphold its climate policy that are regulatory (e.g., CO_2 emissions from cars), market-based (e.g., upper and lower limits for national fuel taxes), informational (e.g., ecolabels), and voluntary (e.g., the previous existing voluntary system for emission from cars) (see Jordan et al., 2012; Skjærseth, 2014). Since the Kyoto Protocol was ratified, parallel to the EU's own development of GCC policies, the EU has been participating in all major negotiations, agreements, and platforms, such as the Copenhagen Accord (2009), the Doha Amendment (2012), the Climate Summit in New York (2014), and the most recent agreement in Paris (2015) (see Bäckstrand & Elgström, 2013; Downie, 2013; Hustedt & Seyfried, 2016). Since the New York summit, the EU has also framed all eight action areas in accordance with the UN system: agriculture, cities, energy, financing, forests, industry, resilience, and transportation (see United Nations, 2014).

The background of the EU's climate policy is that, in 1990, the European Community (the forerunner of the EU) received its first mission to coordinate the member states' positions on the global discussions on climate change at one of the Environmental Council Ministers' meetings. However, it was still a somewhat controversial issue to put in the hands of the supranational level above that of the member states. Also, member states such as Great Britain under Thatcher's government (Harris, 2007) in the 1980s, had problems with taking a common stance developed by the European Community's member states. That same year, at a common Council meeting, the environmental and energy ministers agreed on the objective of stabilizing CO_2 emissions by 2000 at the same level as in 1990. These were the first few steps toward the upcoming common policies. When the European Community was transferred to the EU with the Maastricht Treaty, or the Reform Treaty as it is also known, the EU was enabled to make environmental decisions at the supranational level. In 2007, the European Commission launched a new strategy for environmental policy, which integrated clean energy, transportation, production and consumption, natural resources, public health, social cohesion, poverty, and other socioeconomic sustainability challenges into a climate change package (Wysokinska, 2016).

In the most recent treaty, the Treaty of Lisbon (2007), environmental issues were also upgraded to a so-called shared competence area between the EU and the member states. Basically, this means that the EU can set a minimum standard on most environmental issues, but the member states can take a harder stance through national legislation as long as it does not contradict the principles of the EU's common market polices. Therefore, during the last decade, the EU has implemented several policies and measures at the EU level to combat GCC in regard to both mitigation and adaptation. These policies include a wide range of actions, in accordance with the leading international communities on climate change, such as the United Nations Framework Convention on Climate Change (UNFCCC), including the Intergovernmental Panel on Climate Change (IPCC). The EU's policies also aim to strengthen the EU's own member states' resilience to GCC, which means that the organization includes actions to respectively strengthen state capacity building to address GCC.

In 2007, the EU adopted a climate and energy package to reduce greenhouse gas emissions by 20% by 2010 compared with 1990, including a 20% reduction of energy consumption and a 20% increase in the share of renewable energy (European Commission, 2016c). The long-term objective is to be 100% carbon free, and the target is to reduce greenhouse gas emissions by 80% by 2050. In order to achieve a 20% share of renewables in energy consumption and a 20% improvement by 2020, the EU began to implement a package of legislation, including the following aspects of climate change mitigation (EEA, 2016a; Skjærseth, 2014):

- strengthening the EU emissions trading system, with a linear reduction even beyond 2020 and expansion into new sectors;
- requiring sectors that so far have not been a part of the Emissions Trading System (ETS), such as housing, transportation, and agriculture, to have a binding target reduction of 10% by 2020 in each of the member states;
- developing binding national targets for renewable energy to bring down the greenhouse gas emissions; and
- creating legal requirements for the safe use of carbon capture and storage.

As a result, the EU has made several decisions to increase the use of renewable energy and combine heat and power installations, improve energy efficiency in buildings (private and public), reduce CO_2 emissions in new cars, and reduce emissions from landfills (European Commission, 2016b). Within the EU system, the Directorate-General for Climate Actions is taking the leading role to combat the challenges presented by climate change. It has taken several actions within its broader missions, such as formulating and implementing policies, leading international negotiations on climate change issues, implementing the EU's ETS, and monitoring them at the national level, as well as, in general, stimulating and promoting low-carbon adaptation measures.

Since the EU has taken early actions as a first mover to mitigate climate change, particularly related to clean energy technologies, most likely the EU will also benefit from this compared to other parts of the world (Karkatsoulis, Capros, Fragkos, Paroussos, & Tsani, 2016). However, several challenges remain to integrate some sectors, such as agriculture, into climate change mitigation policies (Fellmann et al., 2017).

In addition, the EU also has several mainstreaming adaptation measurements, including capacity building (see, Skjærseth, 2014). Back in 2007, the European Commission authored a "White Paper" report in 2009, "Adapting to Climate Change: Towards a European Framework for Action" (Commission of the European Communities, 2009). It focused on all the necessary actions to mainstream EU policies, develop common knowledge, and support developing countries and information sharing. The EU understands that adaptation efforts save lives and money, and therefore, the EU foresees the costs of adaptation reaching about 100 billion euro by 2020 (European Commission; Adaptation to Climate Change). In "The EU Strategy on Adaptation to Climate Change" (European Commission, 2013b), the EU tried to integrate adaptation into various EU policies, promoted member states to act, and recognized the need to make better-informed decisions at all levels. Besides this, the EU understands GCC as a vital issue at the international level, as climate change constitutes a global challenge.

In addition, by 2016, the European Commission launched its new strategy, "Shared Vision, Common Actions: A Stronger Europe" (European Commission, 2016h), in which climate change is a part of the EU's broader foreign and security policy agenda. However, in practice, every decision or foreign policy action to be accomplished from this strategy will need to be unanimously confirmed and implemented by the Council of Ministers before it becomes a viable security document, with real political implications. In this Global Strategy, besides seeing GCC as one of many threats and priorities, state and societal resilience for countries to the east and south of the EU is seen as a key for prosperity and democracy, and thereby security, both for these neighboring areas and for the EU itself. This approach entailing a linkage between internal and external security also includes the ambition to seek energy and environmental resilience for the EU. Since there has been doubt about the EU's ability to accomplish all its policies on GCC, the EU also confirms that "The EU will lead by example by implementing its commitments on sustainable development and climate change" (European Commission, 2016h, p. 40).

The EU's view on mainstreaming adaptation is framed within three major dimensions (European Commission, 2013b; Skjærseth, 2014).

The first dimension of the EU's stance is that the EU has integrated climate change into most of its own policies. First, the EU can have an influence on its regional policies through the European Regional Development Fund and the Cohesion Fund to adapt to future climate change. This financial influence includes infrastructure investments in transportation, power grids, water supply, sewage, buildings, and dykes. Second, the EU's common agricultural policy (CAP), to which most of the Union's budget goes, can play a decisive role in integrating climate change adaptation to ensure sustainability in all aspects of the agricultural and forestry sectors. In the most recent proposal for the CAP's long-term policies (2014–2020), adaptation is a significant objective, including sustainable uses of natural resources and climate actions. Third, the EU has also integrated a maritime action plan that aims to establish and develop sustainable sea-related activities, such as a common fishery policy and a good environmental status for all coastal areas. Fourth, the EU has also recognized the connections between climate change and water resources and management. Climate change might lead to scarcity and drought, particularly in Southern Europe. Fifth, the EU understands that climate change will have an effect on biodiversity and the entire ecosystem, and to combat this the EU is trying to implement climate regulation, carbon sequestrations, flood protection, and soil erosion mitigation. Sixth, climate change will affect human health, both directly via more extreme weather conditions and indirectly through new diseases. As a consequence, the EU adapted the "White Paper" (Commission of the European Communities, 2009) to respond to this future threat. Finally, the EU has identified that it needs to reduce weather-related disaster risks due to climate change, such as forest fires, floods, and droughts.

A second dimension of the EU's adaptation policy is to promote member states' actions (European Commission, 2013a, 2013b). The European Commission is promoting the idea of developing national strategies in each member state to adapt to climate change, mostly to support the building of national capacities such as funding, information, and various networking projects. However, by 2015, only 20 of the 28 member states had developed their own national adaptation strategies to implement mostly non-coercive policies in different sectors of society (European Commission, 2015, p. 14).

Finally, besides the EU's adaptation of policies and the member states' own strategies, the EU has also recognized the need for making better-informed decisions. To meet this need, the EU has established the EU program for research and innovation, Horizon 2020, in which climate actions are a cross-cutting issue. Therefore, the EU's policies to cope with GCC also aim to strengthen the member states' resilience to climate change. These policies include eight core actions (European Commission, 2013a, 2013b):

1) Guidelines for the member states in order to prepare them to formulate key indicators in their own adaptation strategies;
2) The LIFE-Work Program, which includes funding to build the capacity to increase the adaptation of actions between 2014 and 2020;
3) Support for the adaptation of local climate change actions in cities, based on the model of the Covenant of Mayors;
4) The Horizon Program (2020), which will bridge the knowledge gap on how to deal with climate change issues in terms of both methods and more overall knowledge;
5) Development of channels for information about global climate change through the European Environmental Agency;
6) Guidance to further facilitate and adapt the EU's strategy package into the agricultural and other cohesive policies (EU's largest budget);
7) Standardization of the energy, building, and industry sectors to establish a more resilient infrastructure; and
8) Increased insurance and other products on the market for when natural disasters and other similar events happen.

As a consequence of the EU's strategies on mitigation, adaptation, and capacity building, it is clear that the EU understands GCC mainly as an issue of human security, but also that it threatens state security around the world. Therefore, in addition, besides the EU having its own policies to combat GCC, the EU is also supporting less developed countries through various international and EU channels (European Commission, 2016c), mainly through facilitating capacity building in these countries. In the EU's Global Strategy (European Commission, 2016h) one can read:

> It is in the interests of our citizens to invest in the resilience of states and societies to the east stretching into Central Asia, and south down to Central Africa. A resilient society featuring democracy, trust in institutions, and sustainable development lies at the heart of a resilient state.
>
> (European Commission, 2016h, p. 23)

Thus, the EU will support and encourage sustainable development in the neighboring states to the east and south, as well as through all its multilateral channels promote democracy, human rights, anti-corruption efforts, and trust in public institutions. The idea is to prevent fragile states and build state capacity and resilience in the surrounding regions, and thereby avoid security threats to the European Union. In this approach, climate change is also seen as a threat, in which desertification, land degradation, and water and food scarcity are seen as challenges for the EU's ambition to enhance energy and environmental resilience (European Commission, 2016h).

When it comes to more general discussions on GCC, which have direct or indirect effects on United Nations activity, the EU is participating in the IPCC, the G8, the G20, the Major Economies Forum on Energy and Climate, the

Organisation for Economic Cooperation and Development, and the International Energy Agency. In addition, the EU supports the United Nations Framework Convention on Climate Change (UNFCCC) and thereby also supports the Cancun Adaptation Framework (2011) and the Nairobi Work Programme (2005), which provides much assistance to address issues and increase resilience against GCC in developing countries. There is also the Global Approach to Migration and Mobility, aiming to furnish a strategic framework to tackle migration policy and adaptation to climate change. The EU is also the major financial contributor to the Climate and Clean Air Coalition, which, for example, is dealing with issues to reduce emissions of methane and black carbon in agriculture, which ultimately relate to food security.

Above all, the EU also has its own Global Climate Change Alliance, which aims to provide financial and other support to handle and integrate global climate issues into developing countries' budgets and legislation. By 2016, the EU had 46 programs in 38 countries in Africa, Asia, the Caribbean, and the Pacific, mostly addressing agricultural issues dealing with GCC. In addition, the EU's Disaster Risk Reduction also links the risk of disasters and climate change assistance in a more effective way in the developing world, including the EU's overseas territories. Through the European Actions Service and Europe Aid, the European Commission also has the ambition to mainstream climate change in all its external actions and programs. It is mainly dealing with three geographical instruments to reach countries in the EU's neighborhood via enlargement, development, and cooperation funds (i.e., for both eastern and southern neighboring states, such as Ukraine, Georgia, Egypt and Tunisia, and other developing countries in Latin America, Africa, and Asia) (European Commission, 2016c).

The EU's willingness and ability to act on GCC

According to the EU's "Climate Actions Progress Report 2015" (European Commission, 2015), Europe is about to achieve its climate change targets for 2020 and thereby also those of the Kyoto Protocol. In 2014, the EU had reduced its emissions below its goal of the 20% reduction targeted for the year 2020 (compared to 1990); and achievement made in the context of economic growth (GDP of 46%) between 1990 and 2014. According to the EU, its "2020 Climate and Energy Package" (European Commission, 2016c) and the member states' national policies have been successful in creating new technology and innovations to reduce emissions in most sectors, such as renewable energy. At the same time, the European Commission (2016g) signaled that a few member states such as Malta, Ireland, Luxembourg, Belgium, Austria, Denmark, and Finland might need to take further actions to be able to reach their 2020 national targets.

Furthermore, the European Environmental Agency (EEA, 2016c) also came to the same kind of conclusion in its progressive report, "Trends and Projections in Europe 2016—Tracking Progress towards Europe's Climate and Energy Targets." In 2015, it was estimated that there was actually a minor decline in the greenhouse gas emissions. Still, the overall conclusion in the EEA's report is that the EU is about to reach its 2020 targets.

Therefore, it seems as though the EU, as a European organization with a somewhat supranational status in several policy areas, has the capacity, ability, and willingness to combat climate change in most of its aspects, including security issues. Still, there are some intervening challenges in this process. In order to reach the 2030 goal of a 40% reduction of emissions, the EU needs to accomplish more than it has so far, and new policies and strategies need to be implemented. In 2015, the projection by the EU itself was that the EU would only reach a 27% reduction of greenhouse gases (European Commission, 2015, p. 11). Another point here is also that although the EU is making all its efforts to respond to climate change, with broad strategies and policies covering most areas, sustainable development is still, to a large extent, associated with the member states' own decisions, capacities, abilities, and willingness to deal with future environmental challenges. The EU is an important global actor, but its position is based on the member states' preferences, and the member states also have to work individually as well as together. Though as an organization the EU has established how climate change needs to be addressed, there are still variations within the EU as well, both in terms of the contribution to global warming and financial capacity, as well as the real ability and willingness to act. Therefore, there are several remaining challenges.

First, although the EU is most often seen as taking a leading role in the world arena on the GCC issue, the European Commission cannot always act on behalf of the EU on all matters, mainly because climate issues or environmental policies are not an exclusive competence area of the EU; it is a shared competence between the EU and its member states (Pavese & Torney, 2012; Damro et al., 2008; the Treaty of Lisbon, 2007). This means that the position of the European Commission in all international negotiations and in its foreign and security agenda always relies on the member states' positions. This was also the case in the most recent Paris Agreement (2015), in which the EU played a significant role during the negotiations. This is also the case when it comes to implementing policies that connect external and internal security threats, including GCC, and to foster state and societal resilience in countries to the East and South of the European Union (European Commission, 2017). However, it is mostly the executive branch of the European Commission and one of the legislative branches, the European Parliament, that are in the position of leadership on climate change issues, together with some of the more climate-friendly member states' governments such the Nordic countries, Germany, and the Netherlands, which could change depending on separate elections in the member states' national elections (Jordan et al., 2012; Bäckstrand & Elgström, 2013; Downie, 2013). Generally, there are also other member states that are less climate-friendly actors, such as most former communist countries in Eastern Europe, that in the long run could decide the EU's common position, in particular with the ongoing nationalist conservative wave of electoral successes across Eastern Europe (and perhaps in Western Europe, too). Consequently, the EU must discuss issues internally first to reach a common position on common grounds, while non-European states could stay focused on external negotiations. As one official of the European Commission phrased it:

> [i]n the last hours, China, India, Russia, the US and Japan each spoke with one voice while Europe spoke with many different voices.... Sometimes we're almost unable to negotiate because we spend so much time talking to each other.
>
> (Haug & Berkhaut, 2010: 7)

Second, another challenge is the entire vehicle of integration among the member states of the EU, mainly in regard to economic integration. Economic integration means that the entire system is built on a free market of goods and services within the EU, without any trade barriers among the member states, resulting in one large economic market with a common commercial policy (Smith, 2016). This idea also includes a common trade policy with non-EU countries, by which the EU has the exclusive right to sign trade agreements around the world (i.e., the EU speaks with one in economic matters) (Pavese & Torney, 2012). Still, the EU climate policies are prioritizing many of these consequences, for trade and communications, but still there can be a contradiction here between the market-oriented EU and GCC. Here, the principle that goods and services should be obtained within the EU and between the EU and the rest of the world at the best affordable prices can contradict support of more local production, offering less transportation costs and more sustainable development (Smith, 2016).

Third, although the EU seems to be on a successful path for accomplishing its climate goals, roughly 20% of the EU budget can still be connected in many ways to mainstreaming climate policies. Because most of the budget covers agricultural, fishery, and structural and regional funds, which affect the environment heavily, it is still a relatively small proportion of the budget that is dealing with climate change actions, in particular in sectors such as agriculture. To the EU's defense, however, one has to admit that it definitely seems to be a question of progress, as by 2015 about 16.8% of the budget included GCC actions, and in 2016 it has increased to 20% (European Commission, 2015, p. 16). In particular, the sector of agriculture has a crucial and vital role in climate change and sustainability. Agriculture is both dependent on clean natural resources of soil, air, and water and on weather conditions, but it is also a part of the greenhouse gas effect. Therefore, the EU understands it as a twin challenge to produce enough environmentally sustainable food while at the same time reducing the emission of greenhouse gases. Besides this, the EU also has another problem in the mainstreaming approach with the aim of reducing the total greenhouse gas emissions throughout the entire Union. Here, the EU is not dealing with all issues that are affecting the greenhouse effect, and some policy areas fall between the EU and national legislation. Policy areas with shared competence include the common market, agriculture, fishery, transportation, environment, research, and innovation mainstreaming policies only affect the EU's decisions in these areas, but policies at the national level depend on whether or not certain areas are part of each of the member states' national climate action plan (see, the Treaty of Lisbon, 2007).

Fourth, because around 80% of the aggregated EU greenhouse gas emissions are linked to either energy production or energy used in transportation, one could further discuss what the EU is doing to handle this reality (Böhringer et al., 2016; Strambo, Nilsson, & Månsson, 2015; European Commission, 2015). Most of the EU's strategies and policies are of course dealing with these issues in terms of concrete actions, financial support, and, above all, research and innovation. The EU has an emission trading system and a regulatory system in the power and industry sectors, including aviation, for dealing with cutting most of these emissions. Still, the issue of, for example, transportation (as well as agriculture, housing, and waste) is mostly dealt with at the national level among the member states. Though these policies have binding annual domestic targets and are followed up by the European Commission, it is still left for the member states to accomplish the objectives (see, the Treaty of Lisbon, 2007).

Fifth, while the EU has clear objectives and a strategy for adaptation to climate change, which seems to be headed in the right direction, some member states have still failed to adopt their national agendas on climate change. So far, by 2016, most member states, but not all 28, had implemented their national agendas, but there is also variation in their objectives (European Commission, 2016c, 2016e, 2016f). Therefore, the entire system is built on differentiated burden sharing, by which some richer member states have to deliver more than others (Jordan et al., 2012). This also means that some states are more ambitious than others, which is reflected in the fact that eight member states still do not have their own national agendas. Also, almost half of the member states do not have a specific budget with which to implement their respective national agendas, which is an indication of whether or not they would prefer to prioritize climate change. In particular, the Visegrad countries (Hungary, Slovakia, and Poland), the Baltic States, Romania, and Bulgaria are slowing down the process for addressing climate change or seem always to be in favor of more burden sharing among the member states (Bocquillon & Maltby, 2017; Braun, 2014; Wysokinska, 2014; Marcinkiewicz & Tosun, 2015). Further, the richest countries such as the Nordic countries, Germany, and the Netherlands among others have to accomplish more than the poorer countries, relatively speaking. This perspective could in the long run slow down the entire process by the EU for combating GCC.

In addition, there is a challenge of implementation regarding GCC, as is the case in all EU policy areas (see Antimiani, Costantini, Kuik, & Paglialunga, 2016). The EU has a very ambitious target and a multitude of GCC policies but at the same time has a relatively weak capacity to implement or to manage everything that is appropriately initiated (Jordan et al., 2012); it is always up to the member states to decide the extent to which policies will be effectuated. The positive thing, though, is that the EU now in its own Global Strategy has committed that it will lead and implement necessary actions to deal with GCC.

European Union and global climate change   145

No matter these challenges, it seems that by 2016 the EU system had the willingness, capacity, and ability to meet all the challenges of GCC, including any potential security problems that will arise as a possible consequence. The EU also understands GCC as a potential problem of both state and human security and is taking steps to prevent it (Stang, 2014; European Commission, 2016h). However, the most recent crisis in the EU, with refugees coming from Syria and other countries, has also demonstrated the weakness of the EU, with a common internal market for people and goods without any state borders, where people can easily travel between the countries, but without any common external border or any common migration and asylum policies at the supranational level. Only recently has the EU begun to realize that a common market without any border between the member states requires a common external border, and also common migration and asylum policies, otherwise the entire EU system might collapse under a new wave of forced migration, caused by conditions due to or aggravated by GCC (Juncker, 2015). From a member state's perspective, therefore, there seems to be a demand for an internal EU securitization at the supranational level. The problem is, however, that the member states don't agree on what these policies might look like and, together with other challenging contemporary issues such as economic crises and right-wing nationalism, the issue of external security is exposing the weakness for the idea of European integration.

The EU is concerned about how the world must act to meet the global challenges of GCC, and at the supranational level the EU system seems to be ready to handle this to some extent, but not yet to securitize the issue into practice in its foreign and defense agenda. The EU has the same problems with more traditional security threats, which at the bottom line have to do with the fact that not all member states would like to give up their own sovereignty as nation-states. Still, too many member states seem to lack the willingness to deal with the situation, though most member states and the EU system both have the real capacity and ability to do so.

Concluding remarks

This chapter has explored the EU's role in global climate change and what type of challenges it might face in accomplishing the targets, which are fully in accordance with the UN, the Kyoto Protocol, and all other international global climate treaties including the 2015 Paris Agreement. The EU understands GCC as something that is affected greatly by human beings, and therefore, it is something the entire world must confront within the United Nations, and through many multilateral forums.

Up until 2017, the EU had set several long-term targets to reduce emissions by the years 2020, 2030, and 2050 and to finally, one day far ahead, succeeding in establishing a carbon-free world. To meet these objectives the EU has established several climate change mitigation and adaptation actions involving all types of policy areas. According to recent reports, the EU has been successful in reaching the target of reducing emissions by 20% by 2020, in comparison to

146 Martin Nilsson

1990, including an increase of 20% in renewable energy and decreasing the total energy consumption. In addition, the EU presently in its new Global Strategy also interprets the issue of GCC as a threat to state and human security, including all potential types of future conflicts and human disasters due to the negative consequences of GCC. In Europe, GCC might not affect state security per se, but it can affect the entire EU system at the supranational level. Moreover, the EU does not seem to be fully ready to securitize GCC into its foreign and defense policy agenda as one major issue, rather it is still mostly embedded into the EU's overall domestic policy areas and into international relations. However, the EU is already, and will continue to be, affected by threats to both state and human security in the Middle East and Africa, with migration waves to Europe as one of many possible consequences of GCC.

To conclude, although the EU is taking a leading role in the world in most questions of GCC, several challenges remain. These are mostly related to the construction of the EU system, including different opinions among the member states, a contradiction between the EU's system of a common commercial market and free trade versus GCC, and other challenges related to the budget, policies, and how they are implemented. In theory, the EU has the willingness, capacity, and ability to act, but to a large extent it depends on the will of the member states whether the EU can fulfill the future targets regarding GCC. This is particularly the case when it comes to dealing with the possible security consequences of GCC around the world due to weather conditions or wars over resources, leading to migration flows from the Middle East and Africa to Europe. As it is now, with the Syrian refugee crisis, the EU system does not yet seem to be ready for this security challenge.

References

Antimiani, A, Costantini, V., Kuik, O., & Paglialunga, E. (2016). Mitigation of adverse effects on competitiveness and leakage of unilateral EU climate policy: An assessment of policy instruments. *Ecological Economics*, 128: 246–259.

Babonneau, F., Hauri, A. & Vielle, M. (2014). Assessment of balanced burden-sharing in the 2050 EU climate/energy roadmap: a metamodeling approach. *Climatic Change* 134: 505–519.

Bäckstrand, K. & Elgström, O. (2013). The EU's role in climate change negotiations: from leader to 'leadiator'. *Journal of European Public Policy* 20(10): 1369–1386.

Benson, D. & A. Jordan (2016). Environmental policy. In M. Cini & N. Perez-Solorzano Borragan (Eds.), *European Union Politics* (2016, fifth edition) (pp. 333–346). Oxford: Oxford University Press.

Bocquillon, P. & Maltby, T. (2017). The more the merrier? Assessing the impact of enlargement on EU performance in energy and climate change policies. *East European Politics* 33(1): 88–105.

Braun, M. (2014). EU climate norms in East-Central Europe. *Journal of Common Market Studies* 52(3): 445–460.

Böhringer, C, Keller, A., Bortolamedi M., & Seyffarth, A.R. (2016). Good things do not always come in threes: On the excess cost of overlapping regulation in EU climate policy. *Energy Policy* 94: 502–508.

Commission of the European Communities (2007). *Green Paper. Adapting to climate change in Europe—options for EU action.* Brussels, June 29, 2007. COM (2007) 354 final.

Commission of the European Communities (2009). *White Paper. Adapting to climate change: Towards a European framework for action.* Brussels, April 4, 2009. COM (2009) 147 final.

Damro, C., Hardie, I., & MacKenzie, D. (2008). The EU and climate change policy: Law, politics and prominence at different levels. *Journal of Contemporary European Research* 4(3): 179–192.

Debeke, J. & Vis, P. (2015). (eds.). *EU climate policy explained.* London and New York: Routledge.

Downie, C. (2013). Shaping international negotiations from within the EU: Sub-state actors and climate change. *Journal of European Integration* 35(6): 705–721.

European Commission (2013a). An EU strategy on adaptation to climate change. Brussels, April 16, 2013. COM (2013) 216 final.

European Commission (2013b). *The EU strategy on adaptation to climate change.* Climate Action. Accessed November 10, 2016: https://ec.europa.eu/clima/publications/docs/eu_strategy_en.pdf

European Commission (2015). *Climate Actions progress report 2015.* Climate Action. Publication Office, November 2015. Accessed November 10, 2016: https://ec.europa.eu/clima/sites/clima/files/strategies/progress/docs/progress_report_2015_en.pdf

European Commission (2016a). *Climate Action. Causes of climate change.* Accessed November 10, 2016: http://ec.europa.eu/clima/change/causes_en

European Commission (2016b). *Climate Actions, What we do.* Accessed November 10, 2016: https://ec.europa.eu/clima/about-us/mission/index_en.htm

European Commission (2016c). *Climate Action. 2020 climate & energy package.* Accessed November 10, 2016: http://ec.europa.eu/clima/policies/strategies/2020_en

European Commission (2016d). First European climate change programme. Accessed November 10, 2016: https://ec.europa.eu/clima/policies/eccp/index_en.htm

European Commission (2016e). *Climate Action. International action on climate change. Fighting climate change requires action from all countries across the world.* Accessed November 10, 2016: http://ec.europa.eu/clima/policies/international_en

European Commission (2016f). The European climate adaptation platform. Website. Accessed November 10, 2016: http://climate-adapt.eea.europa.eu/

European Commission (2016g). *Implementing the Paris Agreement progress of the EU towards the at least -40% target.* Climate Action. November 2016. Accessed November 10, 2016: https://ec.europa.eu/clima/sites/clima/files/eu_progress_report_2016_en.pdf

European Commission (2016h). *Shared vision, common action: A stronger Europe. A global strategy for the European Union's foreign and security policy.* June, 2016. European Union Global Strategy. Accessed August 10, 2017: https://europa.eu/global-strategy/en/global-strategy-foreign-and-security-policy-european-union

European Commission (2017). *From shared vision to common action: Implementing the EU global strategy year 1.* June, 2017. European Union Global Strategy. Accessed August 10, 2017: https://europa.eu/globalstrategy/en/global-strategy-foreign-and-security-policy-european-union

European Environmental Agency (EEA) (2015). *Climate change impacts and adaptation.* Accessed November 10, 2016: www.eea.europa.eu/soer-2015/europe/climate-change-impacts-and-adaptation

148 Martin Nilsson

European Environment Agency (EEA), (2016a). *Climate change policies. Copenhagen.* Accessed November 10, 2016: www.eea.europa.eu/themes/climate/policy-context

European Environmental Agency (EEA), (2016b). *Global and European temperature.* Accessed November 10, 2016: www.eea.europa.eu/data-and-maps/indicators/global-and-european-temperature-3/assessment

European Environmental Agency (EEA), (2016c). *Trends and projections in Europe 2016—Tracking progress towards Europe's climate and energy.* EEA. Copenhagen. Accessed November 10, 2016: www.eea.europa.eu/publications/trends-and-projections-in-europe-2017

Fellmann, T., Witzke, P., Weiss, F., Van Doorslaer, B., Drabik, D., Huck, I., Salputra, G., Jansson, T., & Leip, A. (2017). Major challenges of integrating agriculture into climate change mitigation policy frameworks. *Mitigation and Adaptation Strategies for Global Change* 22(124): 1–18.

Global Climate Change Alliance (GCCA) (2011). *Training workshops on mainstreaming climate change in national development planning and budgeting. Handouts for participants.* Module 3: Understanding the basics of climate change science. Accessed November 10, 2016: www4.unfccc.int/nap/Country%20Documents/General/Module3_Handout_EN_2011-10-22.pdf

Harris, P. (Ed.). (2007). *Europe and global climate change: Politics, foreign policy and regional cooperation.* Cheltenham, UK: Edgar Elgar.

Haug, C. and Berkhout, F. (2010). Learning the hard way? European climate policy after Copenhagen. *Environment* 52(3): 20–27.

High Representative and the European Commission to the European Council (2008). *Climate change and international security.* S113/08. March 13, 2008. Accessed November 10, 2016: www.consilium.europa.eu/uedocs/cms_data/docs/pressdata/en/reports/99387.pd

Hustedt, T. & Seyfried, M. (2016). Co-ordination across internal organizational boundaries: How the EU Commission co-ordinates climate policies. *Journal of European Public Policy* 23(6): 888–905.

Jordan, A., Huitema, D., van Asselt, H., Rayner, T., & Berkhout, F. (2010). *Climate change policy in the European Union: Confronting the dilemmas of mitigation and adaptation?* Cambridge: Cambridge University Press.

Jordan, A., van Asselt, H., Berkhout, F., & Huitema, D. (2012). Understanding the paradoxes of multilevel governing: Climate change policy in the European Union. *Global Environmental Politics* 12(2): 43–66.

Juncker, J.C. (2015). *State of the Union 2015: Time for honesty, unity and solidarity.* President of the European Commission. Strasbourg, 9 September 2015. Accessed November 10, 2016: http://europa.eu/rapid/press-release_SPEECH-15-5614_en.htm

Karkatsoulis, P., Capros, P., Fragkos, P., Paroussos, L., & Tsani, S. (2016). First-mover advantages of the European Union's climate change mitigation strategy. *International Journal of Energy Research* 40(6): 814–830.

Liberatore, A. (2013). Climate change, security and peace: The role of the European Union. *Review of European Studies* 5(3): 83–94.

Marcinkiewicz, K. & Tosun, J. (2015). Contesting climate change: Mapping the political debate in Poland. *East European Politics* 31(2): 187–207.

Meckling, J. & Jenner, S. (2016). Varieties of market-based policy: Instrument choice in climate policy. *Environmental Politics* 25(5): 853–874.

Pavese, C.B. & Torney, D. (2012). The contribution of the European Union to global climate change governance: Explaining the conditions for EU actorness. *Revista Brasileira de Política Internacional* Vol. 55 (special Brasília): 125–143.

European Union and global climate change   149

Skjærseth, J.B. (2014). Linking EU climate and energy policies: Policy-making. *International Environment Agreements* 16: 509–523.

Smith, M. (2016). EU external relation. In M. Cini, & N. Perez-Solorzano Borragan (Eds.) *European Union politics* (2016, fifth edition) (pp. 214–226). Oxford: Oxford University Press.

Sonnsjö, H. & Bremberg, N. (2016). *Climate change in an EU security context—The case of the European external action service.* Stockholm: Stockholm University.

Stang, G. (2014). *Climate change and EU security: When and how they intersect.* European Union Institute for Security Studies, November, Brief SSUE, Nov. 2014.

Strambo, C, Nilsson, M., & Månsson, A. (2015). Coherent or inconsistent? Assessing energy security and climate policy interaction within the European Union. *Energy Research & Social Science* 8: 1–12.

Strielkowski, W., Lisin, E., & Gryshova, I. (2016). Climate policy of the European Union: What to expect from the Paris Agreement?. *Romanian Journal of European Affairs* 16 (4): 68–77.

The Maastricht Treaty (1992). The Treaty on European Union. Maastricht, 7 February 1992.

The Treaty of Lisbon (2007). Treaty on European Union, 2007. Part of the Treaty of Lisbon amending the Treaty on European Union and the Treaty establishing the European Community, signed at Lisbon, 13 December 2007 (2007/C 306/01). Lisbon, 17 December 2007.

Trombetta, M.J. (2014). Linking climate-induced migration and security within the EU: Insights from the securitization debate. *Critical Studies on Security* 2(2) (Special issue on Securitisation and Climate-induced Migration).

United Nations (2014). *Climate summit September 23 2014 in New York.* Action Areas/ Summit Announcement. Accessed November 10, 2016: www.un.org/climatechange/ summit/action-areas/

Young, Richard (2014). *Climate change and EU security policy—An unmet challenge.* Washington DC: Carnegie Endowment for International Peace.

Werz, M. & Hoffman, M. (2016). Europe's twenty first century challenge: Climate change, migration and security. *European View* 15: 145–154.

Wysokinska, Z. (2016). The "new" environmental policy of the European Union: A path to development of a circular economy and mitigation of the negative effects of climate change. *Comparative Economic Research* 19(2): 57–73.

7 China and global climate change

Daniel Silander and Martin Nilsson

China, as one of the top four emitting nations, is an important world actor in global climate change (GCC). Today, China accounts for about 30% of the total CO_2 emissions in the world, compared with the United States' (US) 15%, the European Union's (EU's) 19% and India's 6.5% (Olivier et al., 2015, pp. 3–4). With a growing population, economic development, and energy demand, Chinese greenhouse gas emissions (GHG) have increased significantly over the last decade (Hof et al., 2015). The Chinese economy has been based on high carbon intensity, twice as high as that of the US economy and three times higher than that of the 28 member states of the EU. Although it should be said that the level of GHG emissions per capita in China was equal to that of the EU-28 and only half that of the US (Olivier et al., 2015, p. 5), rapid economic developments in China since the 1980s have led to a growth of carbon emissions per capita by more than 2.5 times since early 2000 (Chadha, 2014).

Although China ratified the Kyoto Protocol, it did so as a non-Annex I country, leaving it without the requirement to limit GHG emissions. Up until about 2007/2008, the Chinese government did not acknowledge climate change and was a reluctant actor on the international scene on environmental protection. Over the last decade, however, China has shown increasing interest in the international debate on GCC and taken numerous domestic measures. China has not only become an important participant in the activities of the United Nations Framework Convention on Climate Change (UNFCCC) (see Chapter 2), its government has also made it the leading global producer on low-carbon technology (Gippner, 2014). The Chinese official objective is by 2020 to lower the carbon intensity by 40–45% compared with the level in 2005 (Wenying et al., 2016).

It is argued in this chapter that the new Chinese stand on GCC is surprising. It is further argued that the main causes for this change of policy are primarily due to national economic interests and the worries over slowing economic growth. In addition, the Chinese government has also acknowledged the human insecurity that has come with decades of industrialization and economic growth, which, if unsolved, may result in a challenge to the legitimacy of the Chinese Communist Party (CCP). As expressed by the Prime Minister Li Keqiang in his inaugural speech in March 2013, "It is no good having prosperity and wealth while the environment deteriorates," but it is also a problem to have "poverty and backwardness in the midst of clear waters and verdant mountains" (*The Economist*, 2013).

This chapter addresses the role of the Chinese government in global climate change and how China perceives and approaches the collateral challenges. The aim is to explore how the Chinese government acknowledges GCC in relation to state and human security and what measurements have been developed to mitigate and adapt to such changes both domestically as well as internationally through the UN. Following this introduction, the chapter is structured into four sections, including the conclusions. The first section addresses the official Chinese perceptions on GCC. The second section discusses China's existing policies on mitigation and adaptation to GCC and is followed by a third section highlighting the actual capacities of and hindrances to the Chinese government to promote a better environment. The main findings are finally set out in the fourth and concluding section.

China's perceptions on GCC—economic and human security as competing priorities?

Since the late 1980s, the official priority for the CCP has been modernization to limit poverty and economic inequality. Since Deng Xiao Ping's era, China has seen industrialization and economic growth rates exceeding those of any other nation. Previously, heavy industries required a large supply of energy, which greatly relied on coal. The call for economic growth for a population of about 1.3 billion people led to postponed worries and strategies on GCC both domestically and internationally (He et al., 2012; Richerzhagen & Scholtz, 2008).

Today, China is the largest GHG emitter in the world. Decades of economic growth, with around 8–10% GDP growth per year, have modernized large parts of Chinese society (in urban areas) and provided political legitimacy for the Communist regime, but has also led to environmental challenges (Albert & Xu, January 18, 2016; The World Bank, 2017). The CCP's main concern about economic growth has focused on energy demand and energy security. In order to continue its economic growth, Chinese authorities have traditionally used domestic supplies of carbon-based energy. With limited resources in oil, coal has accounted for about 70% of China's total energy supply demand, contributing about 80% of the total annual greenhouse gas emissions. It has been estimated that China has used as much coal to supply energy as the rest of the world combined, forcing China to import coal despite its own enormous coal supply (Climate Actions Tracker, 2016).

Today, China's economic growth continues, but at a slower path and based on: a growing service sector, which includes a lower demand for coal; a carbon trading market; a transformation of the auto industry, focusing on hybrids and electric vehicles and by strengthening regulations on fuel consumption; high-speed trains; and, promotion for various renewable capacities (Adler, 2016). The CCP worries over a future shortage of energy have led to a search for alternative means to secure national political and economic interests. The

Chinese government has looked for other energy sources as well as greater energy efficiencies. This search has been based on a growing official concern that economic decline could jeopardize the legitimacy of the CCP in the eyes of the population. In 2004, Premier Wen Jiabao stated that China would start to use an "iron hand" to become more energy efficient (Bradsher, 2010). This message signaled a policy change from the CCP. Since then, China has aggressively developed a strategy of ecological civilization, or green growth, based on high-technology, low-carbon industries. Such policy change has also included moving away from an isolated national approach on environmental policies, politically and scientifically, by becoming internationally oriented and active in debates and conferences on how to approach economic growth and climate change (Edmonds, 2011).

The new official concern over environmental pollution is twofold. First, a polluted environment is costly. The World Bank has estimated that environmental and natural resource degradation cost China about 9% of the total annual GDP and therefore jeopardizes economic growth. Different studies have pointed to different economic costs for environmental degradation, with estimates ranging from 3–10% of the annual gross national income (Kahn, 2016). These high costs establish expenses that come with degradation of water and farmland, limited manufacturing outcomes due to scarcity of necessary resources, premature deaths, health complications, and more. Second, a polluted environment, in jeopardizing health and welfare in China, could, in addition to a slowing economy, lead to widespread questioning of the political illegitimacy of the Chinese government. The decades of economic growth have led to serious environmental challenges that have been voiced by the media and the growing middle class in expanding Chinese cities and have resulted in serious political challenges to the Communist regime (Kahn, 2016; Ren, 2013; Wu & Gaubatz, 2013, parts 3–4).

However, China's economy is expected to continue providing for, on the one hand, necessary modernization to a growing population, but on the other hand, major challenges in further energy consumption and pollution. This leaves Chinese authorities in grave need, in a systematic and fundamental way, to transform the Chinese economy away from further carbon emissions based on fossil fuel consumption (Wang & Hao, 2012). As stated by Sternfeld in the comprehensive *Handbook of Environmental Policy in China*,

> During the last few decades, China has accomplished unprecedented economic growth and has emerged as the second largest economy in the world. The "economic miracle" has led hundreds of millions of people out of poverty, but has also come at a high cost. Environmental degradation and the impact of environmental pollution on health are nowadays issues of the greatest concern for the Chinese public and the government.
>
> (2017, p. 1)

The high levels of carbon emissions have come from coal to generate electricity for large-scale industrial plants (NDCR, 2007). At the same time as its industries facilitate employment and economic growth in urban China, recent years have shown alarming levels of air pollution in cities that have harmed human security for millions of people (see Shapiro, 2016). Such extreme levels of pollution have been stated to lead to high morbidity and mortality rates. Studies have also shown how the life expectancy north of the Huai River is about five to six years longer compared with the south with its high levels of air pollution (Albert & Xu, January 18, 2016). In recent years, estimates indicate that many Chinese cities have hazardous particulate matter in the air at about 40 times the level stated as safe by the World Health Organization (WHO), leading to closure of schools, halting of manufacturing and construction work, and imposition of traffic restrictions. About 80–90% of the air quality monitored in 367 cities exceeds the official limits on air pollution. Two major contributors to such health hazards have been the growing numbers of manufactured cars for the growing urban middle class and the emissions from coal-based power plants. In 2004, about 27 million people were car owners, a number that has increased to 154 million in 2014. The rapid urbanization in China, from about 36% in 2000 to an estimated 60% of the population in 2020, has also come with developments of urban industrial plants and manufacturing that all together have led to alarming levels of urban air pollution (Albert & Xu, January 18, 2016; see also Haidong et al., 2012). It has further been observed that 16 of the world's 20 most polluted major cities are located in China (Oculi, 2015; He et al., 2012, p. 1). In 2015, the Mayor of Beijing, Wang Anshun, officially announced the city to be "unliveable" due to permanent smog (in Sternfeld, 2017, p. 1).

With growing awareness among authorities, industrial workers, and environmental activists of the negative environmental consequences of economic growth (see Tilt, 2013; Zhang & Barr, 2013), Chinese cities have faced numerous protests stressing major concerns with alarming health challenges. Such demonstrations have at times turned into riots and social unrest in which the legitimacy of the CCP is questioned providing for potential state security challenges. This increasing number of urban demonstrations demanding governmental policies on mitigation and adaption has resulted in official action making amendments to the national Air Pollution Prevention and Control Law. From a human security perspective, the amended law explicitly addresses climate change and air pollution as threats to human security. The institutional mechanisms for control of air pollution were also implemented. It was decided that the Ministry of Environmental Protection (MEP) would work together with local governments and a governing body to set up strategies for the mitigation of air pollution. Failing provinces would have to produce annual reports on how to accomplish the objectives set out for air pollution and provincial local governments would be in charge of decreasing air pollution and staying in contact with the MEP for its monitoring procedures (Jingjing & Tang, November 25, 2015).

Besides air pollution, another alarming human security challenge for the Chinese government is increasing food and water scarcity (see Yong, 2009) due to pollution. The environmental degradation has come with water contamination and land deterioration, challenging the health of the people and their economic survival (Albert & Xu, January 18, 2016). Water scarcity has been increasing particularly in the northern parts of the country. Overall, the limited local water resources, increased water contamination, undeveloped spatial distribution of water resources, economic modernization, urbanization, and a fast-growing population are all factors that have resulted in jeopardized environmental and human security. The Chinese authorities face an urgent need to develop the water resource management and to safeguard water resources from further contamination (Yong, 2009).

Chinese officials have noted there to be a growing number of polluted agricultural areas. It has been argued that about 2% of China's arable land is polluted and a hazard to use. Polluted farmland has caused public unrest after announcements of Chinese rice having high levels of heavy metal, which local authorities had sought to prevent public disclosure (Tiezzi, January 1, 2014). In addition, China today has about 20% of the world's population but only about 7% of the global level of fresh water sources. Ongoing industrialization has led to substantial contamination of rivers, lakes, and groundwater, and in the overuse of water in the agriculture and coal industries, leaving hundreds of Chinese cities with a lack of fresh water and growing areas of desertification, impacting hundreds of millions of people (Haidong et al., 2012).

Climate change has also had implications for the Chinese coastal regions' erosion due to rising sea level, storms, and tides (NDRC, 2007). This has led to alarming environmental and economic challenges for many major cities along the long Chinese coastline (Caia et al., 2009). The Yangtze River Delta is one of the most populated and economically important areas in China and has become a symbol of the challenges of climate change confronting the Chinese economy and human security. With its densely populated metropolitan business and industrial areas, this delta is severely sensitive to climate change consequences in flooding, water pollution, and scarcity of energy. This area is subject to intense urbanization, due to existing social inequalities between urban and rural areas resulting in major migration flows within China (Gub et al., 2011). Rising sea levels along China's highly concentrated coastline with densely populated and economically important cities such as Guangzhou, Shanghai, and Tianjin present alarming concerns (Kahn, 2016).

Estimates of climate change-induced migration have noted that 30 million people have been displaced in China due to flooding, drought, desertification, water scarcity, and coastal erosion (Oculi, 2015). As argued by Matus et al. in their assessment of the impact of GCC on economic growth-related air pollution and public health:

As China continues a three decade-long trajectory of unprecedented growth and development, there has been increasing concern that its growth has come at substantial cost to its environment and public health. While there have been important quality of life improvements for the more than half a billion people who have been raised out of poverty, most traditional accounting has not fully considered the impacts of health and environmental externalities in analysis of China's development. China now faces severe challenges relating to its environment, including air pollution, the availability of clean water, and desertification. Issues such as these have the potential to create constraints on future growth. Those environmental problems that result in negative health outcomes, such as contaminated water and high levels of air pollution, also incur real costs on the individuals, the health system, and the economy as a whole.

(Matus et al., 2012, p. 1)

The many decades of prioritization of economic growth have led to serious challenges to human security. Although China has never officially pronounced a linkage between state security and climate change (Vorndick, 2015), clearly Chinese prioritization of economic growth has been a way to secure political stability. By providing modernization to a growing population, Chinese authorities have sought popular support to safeguard the communist monopoly of power. Although Chinese authorities have acknowledged climate change as a serious societal threat, it has never been explicitly referred to as a state security threat (Freeman, 2010). When the UK government initiated a UNSC debate on climate change and security in 2007, the Chinese regime argued that such debate was unnecessary. Although acknowledging that climate change could have security implications the Chinese position was that GCC is foremost an issue of sustainable development and should not be addressed by the UNSC, arguing that there is no clear link between climate change and national security, but rather that climate change may challenge economic security. There has been a scholarly and political debate in China on how to define state security. Some have argued that climate change causes threats that reduce living standards and creates social and political instability, and ultimately challenges state security. The official declaration has been that climate change threatens the economic foundation of China and must be mitigated through low-carbon technology and a green-way of living. In this way, China's official position has been that climate change poses limited risk to state security in terms of military and political security. The most severe challenge to China's security is the negative impact climate change has on economic growth and the impact this could provide for the legitimacy for the Communist political party (Freeman, 2010).

The Chinese government has also refused to accept a role for the UNSC to act on climate change. The Chinese-UN Ambassador Liu Zhimin, argued at the Security Council Meeting on Climate Change, on April 17, 2007, that "The developing countries believe that the Security Council neither has the expertise in handling climate change, nor is the right decision-making place for extensive participation" (in Freeman, 2010, p. 14). In addition, the Chinese position also stressed that "Climate change may have certain security implications, but generally speaking, it is in essence an issue of sustainable development" (in Freeman, 2010, p. 14). China has been unwilling to treat climate change as a state security issue. Climate change has been referred to as a development issue or a question of sustainable development rather than national security. There are two foremost reasons for this stand on climate change and state security. First, Chinese authorities are, as previously stated, deeply concerned over the negative implications climate change has for economic growth and secondly, the Chinese government has also been worried about the impact that UNSC decisions on the environment-security nexus could have on Chinese state sovereignty (Freeman, 2010).

Policies on GCC—mitigation, adaption, and capacity building

Over recent years, in preparation for the UN's Climate Change Conferences in Paris (2015) and Marrakech (2016), global attention grew significantly on the two largest GHG emitting nations (Song & Ye, 2015). China has, in particular, been a focus due to it having the highest level of emissions in the world and historically having few official strategies on how to manage GCC. Up until early 2000, the Chinese government had been highly reluctant to discuss climate change and pollution domestically as well as internationally. More recently, the Chinese President Xi Jinping has not only officially acknowledged climate change and the challenges of GHG emissions but also affirmed China's commitment to establish countermeasures. The main reason behind such affirmations has been the above-mentioned concern over human security-related concerns of future economic growth, economic costs with pollution and GCC, societal demands for a cleaner environment. But there has also been influence by the international community and discussions and reforms taken elsewhere (on the UN/EU and China, see Schroeder, 2017; Gippner, 2017). There are recent signs of worry within the CCP that economic decline and human insecurity could destabilize the popular support for the Party (Song & Ye, 2015; Hilton, 2016).

The beginning of Chinese environmental policies goes back to the 1972 United Nations Conference on the Human Environment in Stockholm, Sweden. This became the starting point for developing environmental institutions in China, although the following decades of Chinese policies stressed economic modernization in industrialization and urbanization. The economic transformation of China from the late 1970s and throughout the 1990s has been compared with the industrialization of the Western world in the early nineteenth century (Albert & Xu, January 18, 2016).

Until about a decade ago, few scholarly works acknowledged the growing Chinese interest in addressing climate change or environmental pollution. There was a scholarly agreement that Chinese officials would show limited interest in approaching environmental challenges and would instead continue to focus on economic growth based mostly on coal-based energy plants. Any international demands on reducing emissions were perceived as jeopardizing the energy supply for future economic growth (Heggelund, 2007). During the 1990s, China's climate policy was first administered by the Meteorological Institute (CMA), and it was transferred in 1998 to the National Committee on Climate Change (NC4), which became a rhetorical forum for politicians to impress the international community, rather than an effective administrative entity with objectives establishing concrete action (Barbi, da Costa Ferreira & Guo, 2016).

Between 1992 and 2006, some measures were taken to deal with GCC, mainly by introducing new laws, such as the Law on Prevention and Control of Air Pollution (1995), the Air Quality Standard (1996), the Law on Environmental Impact Assessment (2003), the Environmental Impact Assessment (2003), and the Renewable Energy Law (2005) (Barbi et al., 2016). However, China did not have any comprehensive climate change policy and the objectives were far away from meeting the targets of the UN's Kyoto Protocol system.

When the Kyoto Protocol was ratified in the late 1990s, China was a non-Annex B party without binding targets to limit green-house gases (GHG). The agreement between the richer developing nations, such as China, India, Brazil, and South Africa, and the rich Western world was that these countries were encouraged to take steps to deal with GCC but without any binding targets to reduce the level of GHG (Climate Home: News, February 16, 2015). When China finally officially announced its approval of the Kyoto Protocol at the World Summit on Sustainable Development in Johannesburg, in September 2002, the Chinese government made the following statement:

> The Chinese government believes that the United Nations Framework Convention on Climate Change and its Kyoto Protocol set forth the fundamental principles and provide an effective framework and a series of rules for international cooperation in combating climate change, and as such they deserve worldwide compliance.
>
> (The People's Republic of China, March 9, 2002)

However, despite China being one of the first states to ratify the first climate convention and going on to approve the Kyoto Protocol (thereby approving the entire UN policy on climate change policies), there were still no Chinese policies to halt GCC (Barbi et al., 2016; United Nations, 2017).

More recently, China has changed its position and has become more devoted to addressing GCC. In 2003, Chinese authorities introduced the first industry-specific regulatory agency, the State Electricity Regulatory Commission (SERC) as a capacity-building effort to assess and monitor this sector despite limited financial and administrative support due to the lack of a comprehensive reform package (Tsai, 2014). In 2004, the challenges presented by GCC were identified in the Initial National Communication on Climate Change and followed by a Second National Communication on Climate Change in 2008. These communications included data from the United Nations International Panel on Climate Change on the levels of emissions and their societal impact and were followed by official policies and strategies to handle climate change. In China's first National Climate Change Programme (2007), the government officially admitted that global warming is a serious problem and is being created by humankind. Furthermore, the Chinese government summarized GCC as a future challenge to human security. As stated, "The possibility of more frequent occurrence of extreme weather/ climate events would increase in China, which will have immense impacts on the socio-economic development and people's living" (NDRC 2007, p. 5).

China's journey toward a more comprehensive climate action plan, including mitigation policies, began with the 11th National Five-Year Plan (2006–2010) for economic and social development, in which some of the first Chinese climate targets was presented. One was to reduce the use of energy by 20% during the next five years, with a focus on the top 1,000 most energy-consuming Chinese factories (NDRC, 2006). The 11th Five-Year Plan symbolized a Chinese political understanding that economic growth had to be adjusted not to cause environmental degradation. The Chinese government declared a quantitative target to lower carbon-based energy use, with objectives to increase the use of non-fossil, renewable, and nuclear-based energy sources and to reduce pollutants. In 2007, China established its first comprehensive institution for GCC, launching the National Climate Change Program. For the first time, China adopted an advanced climate program, which was also in accordance with the UN's (particularly UNFCCC) view of GCC. As stated in the preamble:

> As it is mandated under the UNFCCC, the Government of China hereby formulates China's National Climate Change Programme (hereinafter referred to as the CNCCP), outlining objectives, basic principles, key areas of actions, as well as policies and measures to address climate change for the period up to 2010. Guided by the Scientific Approach of Development, China will sincerely carry out all the tasks in the CNCCP, strive to build a resource conservative and environmentally friendly society, enhance national capacity to mitigate and adapt to climate change, and make further contribution to the protection of the global climate system.
>
> (NDRC, 2007, p. 2)

In addition, the government officially admitted that global warming was a serious problem, stating:

> The Third Assessment Report of the Intergovernmental Panel on Climate Change (IPCC) has clearly indicated that most of the global warming observed over the past 50 years was likely induced by the increase in concentrations of greenhouse gases (GHGs), such as carbon dioxide (CO_2), methane (CH_4), and nitrous oxide (N_2O), due to human activities. In the context of global warming, climate in China has experienced noticeable changes over the past 100 years as well.
>
> (NDRC, 2007, p. 4)

In 2008 and for the years to come, the climate program was followed by a national carbon emissions trading plan focusing on making provinces invest in systems of carbon capture to lower the levels of carbon emissions. In addition, the Chinese government demanded that cities and provinces close inefficient factories, closing more than 1,000 coal-fired power plants. The government also launched a major strategy to invest in clean energy technology (such as wind turbines and solar plants) and clean coal technology, declared to expand nuclear power, established a Ministry of Environmental Affairs, signed numerous anti-pollution laws and thousands of decrees and decided on new tougher regulations on lighting and on automobile fuel consumption (Bradsher, 2010; *The Economist*, 2013). Around 2008 it was clear that "China is the world's worst polluter but largest investor in green energy. Its rise will have as big an impact on the environment as on the world economy or politics" (*The Economist*, 2013).

At the 2009 Copenhagen Summit, China made its first promise to reduce its GHG emissions by 40–45% per unit of GDP by 2020 (Lynas, 2009). It was a serious indication that GCC gradually had become an integrated political, economic and social issue handled at the top-level of the Chinese government (NDCR, 2016). In the 12th Five-Year Period ranging from 2011 to 2015, the Chinese government declared a new stand on climate change by pointing out the importance of reducing emissions and mitigating and adapting to climate change (CBI—The Voice of Business, 2011). Instead of traditional official statements of large-scale priorities and future objectives on climate change, a new clear-cut framework on how to halt emissions was presented. This framework was presented in a context on how to secure economic development and growth in China. It was argued that climate change and gas emissions called for developing new technologies, job creation, products, and services that would boost the future Chinese economy. Multiple policies and strategies were launched, such as objectives to increase forest coverage, lower energy intensity, decrease carbon dioxide emissions and increase the use of non-fossil fuels. These new policies from Chinese officials were a response to the challenges that ongoing industrialization had provided in pollution and in higher costs economically and societally. With shrinking economic growth, China was forced to make policy changes and to build a future economy based on the efficient use of energy and resources and new higher value technologies. To secure China's future economic growth, the Chinese government had to set out a new plan based on low-carbon development, a governmental approach of "ecological civilization" to halt climate change consequences in China (Hilton, 2016; Song & Ye, 2015).

Furthermore, the 12th Five-Year Plan (2011–2015) also established some key mitigation targets: a 17% reduction in carbon intensity, a 16% reduction in energy use and an increase of non-fossil energy to 11.4% of the total energy use (Chapter 3 in the 12th Five-Year Plan, 2011–2015 in CBI—The Voice of Business, 2011). The plan explicitly stressed the importance of a green governance approach by focusing on necessary reforms to be taken on institutional changes, decentralization of power, improved supervision, accountability and transparency to modernize the management and implementation of environmental reforms (He et al., 2012). China's entire policy of GCC was also restructured around the themes that the UN had established on mitigation, adaptation, and capacity building (see United Nations, 2017).

In 2015, the 13th Five-Year Plan was announced and stressed the new path of Chinese governance on climate change. The plan aimed to develop "a moderately prosperous society" and was organized around the five principles of innovation, openness, green development, coordination and inclusive development

(APCO, 2015). China's leadership provided support for innovating low-carbon technologies with greater expertise, expanded manufacturing and increased exporting. China's previous dependency on coal was stated to have decreased as it was replaced with renewable energy including half of the world's wind power and with hydro and nuclear power. The 13th Five-Year Plan also included mitigation policies to adjust China to a more durable and sustainable economy and was further developed in the National Plan on Climate Change (2014–2020) and in related documents such as the National Plan for Tackling Climate Change (2014–2020), the Energy Development Strategy Action Plan (2014–2020), and the National Strategy for Climate Adaption (2013). Besides the target of 6.5–7% annual growth, China also established targets for GCC, related to carbon emissions, energy and water consumption, efficiency of industries, energy production from renewables, and green infrastructure. The main targets for halting GCC were to reduce GHG emissions by 18% by 2020 (compared with 2015), peak the total carbon emissions by 2030, reduce energy intensity by 15% by 2020 (compared with 2015), increase non-fossil energy to 15% by 2020 (compared with 2015) and increase forest stock volume and coverage to 16.5 billion cubic meters (bcm) and 23.04% by 2020. In addition, the plan from 2016–2020 included $360 billion on renewable energy sources with the political objective to create 13 million new jobs in this area (NDRC, 2016; APCO, 2015; Wong, 2017; Hilton, 2016).

The change of policy on the economic–environmental nexus was obvious at the COP22 in Marrakech in 2016 where at first the US election process seemed to undermine the serious talks on global climate change, and where China stepped up to become a potential new global climate leader. The Chinese Vice-Foreign Minister Liu Zhenmin stated that China's national interests were to work toward a low-carbon future, with or without US collaboration. It seemed like China had decided to become a global leader on producing low-carbon goods by initiating new technological projects on already well-advanced areas of wind and solar power (Hilton, 2016). Over the last decade or even less, China has officially gone from being disinterested in international talks on global climate change to now presenting itself as the new global leader in the field. As stated,

> At the time, the US and China were locked into a toxic opposition created by the structure of the 1997 Kyoto Protocol, the international agreement that made climate action obligatory for rich countries, but only advisory for emerging economies, even those as large as China. The world's two biggest emitters of greenhouse gases seemed bound into a negative relationship in which the climate policy of one was conditioned by the willingness of the other to do as much, if not more. Since neither was willing, this dysfunctional pairing acted as dispiriting drag on global efforts. But between Copenhagen and Paris, China's global climate policy underwent a sea change....
>
> (Hilton, 2016)

On September 3, 2016, China ratified the Paris Agreement, which in contrast to previous international agreements had a less hierarchical approach. A month later, the NDRC's annual report, "China's Policies and Actions for Addressing Climate Change" (NDRC, 2016), addressed contemporary mitigation policies and how to optimize the industrial structure. Numerous policies addressed how to eliminate backward production capacity, upgrading traditional industries, supporting emerging industries, and developing the service industry. They went on to further stress how to optimize the energy structure by including strict control over coal consumption, using fossil fuels in a clean way, developing non-fossil energy, and accelerating overall energy reforms, such as an electricity pricing system and a power trading system, improving energy-saving accountabilities, including energy efficient standards, and labeling and boosting energy conservation in certain building projects, transportation plans and public areas.

Besides having an agenda on how to mitigate and adapt to GCC, the Chinese government declared a strategy to increase its capacity to address GCC, mainly to strengthen statistical tools for assessments and develop a GHG emissions reporting system, strengthen the scientific research and the technological support to GCC, and enhance information on GCC in the educational system and in personnel and team training in the government among public officials at the department level (NDRC, 2016). In addition, the Chinese authorities have also launched a comprehensive control policy targeting pollutants and emission sources throughout China to focus on the mitigation of increasing air pollution. Such a policy has embedded various mitigation and capacity-building measurements in investments in clean energy resources, promotion of clean and efficient coal use, regulations and control functions on vehicle pollution, new regulations and implementation of control of multiple pollutants emissions, and development of climate friendly air pollution control strategies (Wang & Hao, 2012). The new approach on climate change in China is drastically altered from the country's positions taken at previous summits. However, although it looks like China is willing to deal with GCC, the question is whether the government also has the necessary capacity to develop a climate friendly strategy Hilton, 2016; Adler, 2016) and whether the Chinese authorities are willing to accept that the transformation of the Chinese economy from fossil fuels to renewable energies most likely will have a negative impact on the Chinese economic growth, at least in the short-run (Li, 2014).

Capacities and remaining challenges to address GCC

In 2017, China was forecast to peak its emissions in 2025–2030 and thereby fulfil the Paris Agreement. However, there remain hindrances to overcome for becoming a global leader on GCC and developing a comprehensive climate-friendly strategy to protect and promote the environment. There are at least seven major challenges for Chinese authorities to address GCC.

The first fundamental challenge is that China (in contrast to previous policies) probably will have to reconsider the value of GCC in relation to economic growth (i.e., that there is a strong need to emphasize the values of a clean environment as a more important value than economic growth). Though there are indications in the most recent official plans and strategies on GCC that this is the case, still, it is up to the Chinese government to accomplish its targets for GCC, and most probably there will be some sort of a conflict of interest between targets of economic growth versus GCC in the future. The question is: What will happen then? Will China still consider economic growth less important than dealing with climate change? (see Barbi et al., 2016).

The second remaining challenge to Chinese leadership on climate change is the nation's authoritarian tradition of limited transparency regarding political decisions and official figures. Although China has taken numerous important measures on pollution and climate change and strongly declared its new vision of a Chinese economy based on low carbon emissions, the international community has continued to face challenges to conduct international monitoring of Chinese emission levels. The Chinese government has continued to lack the transparency and goodwill necessary to provide the international community with significant and trustworthy data about energy use and emissions. This jeopardizes the global efforts on climate change as set out in the Paris Agreement, which establishes monitoring and reporting to implement mitigation and adjustment policies for all states (Wong, 2017; Edmonds, 2011).

The third challenge stems from the complex and overlapping authorities that exist in the Chinese political system. The central government is the supreme authority of the overall objectives on environment issues with the National Leading Group for Addressing Climate Change, the National Leading Group on Energy Saving and Pollution Reduction and the National Development and Reform Commission (NDRC) being the most important actors for such work. The NDRC is the policy-making body of the government that is in charge of the five-year plans for meeting the economic and environmental objectives. Domestically, the NDRC has competed with the Ministry of Finance and the MEP for influence, where the former influenced environmental policies through national carbon tax-policies and the latter started to deal with climate change and not solely air and water pollution. On an international scene, the NDRC must also deal with the Ministry of Foreign Affairs as an influential international foreign policymaker. Studies have observed that the Chinese climate-change policy-making system is complex and with overlapping authorities (Tsang & Kolk, 2010).

A fourth challenge is the separation of power between centralized and provisional (local) authorities. The decisions made in the central government are meant to be accepted by the provisional level in a top-down model. However, provisional interests and needs have led to ongoing negotiations between the central and provisional levels over economic and environmental development issues. The provisional level is powerful and contains senior politicians empowered by the Party to implement decisions in the best way for provisional developments. Although the central authorities monitor and evaluate how the provisional level interprets and implements central decisions, the provisional

China and global climate change   163

authorities have substantial power to act on their own based on knowledge of and connections to the provisional interests and on central bureaucratic weakness. As stated by Tsai and Dean,

> the hierarchical interaction of central and local political elites, and in particular provincial secretaries, can explain the extent of reforms, whereas the type of reform is linked to distinct provincial economic conditions and the provincial secretary's interpretation of provincial priorities.
>
> (2014, p. 339)

Such local/provisional interests have primarily focused on local economic growth with signs of elite manipulation of environmental policies and growth statistics and with very limited transparency and participation by non-state actors. Another potential challenging factor to the implementation of environmental policies on the local level is the management structure of high turnover of local leaders on the provisional level. While the official policy of short-termed contracts for local leaders has aimed at promoting implementation of centralized environmental policies by avoiding individuals growing too strong by making them rotate every three to four years, this seems to result in decreased interest for implementing major reforms that might meet local resistance and in a rather selective focus on limited and more easily implemented projects. The overall consequences have been shortcomings in local implementation of policies on environmental issues (Zhang et al., 2014; Eaton & Kostka, 2014; Kostka & Mol, 2013; Edmonds, 2011).

The fifth challenge is the economic-structural imbalance of the political and economic powers between the urban east and the rural west, which has implications on overall Chinese mitigation and adjustment measures for climate change. The eastern provinces along the coastline have shown a great capacity to understand and follow through on central authority policies for economic growth and environmental protection. It is less clear whether the undeveloped rural areas in the west will do the same or whether these provinces will continue to focus on economic growth without an environmental perspective. This has previously led to local strategies of misinforming central authorities regarding environmental objectives, antipollution measures, and implementation of closing enforcement equipment and industries. Based on a tradition of constantly seeking economic growth, provisional authorities have lacked environmental awareness while continuing to initiate economic growth (Zhang et al., 2014).

The sixth challenge is with the large state-owned enterprises, and their core role in the energy sector and their contribution to GHG emissions by the Chinese economy (see Barbi et al., 2016; Zhang et al., 2014). These state-owned enterprises are often under the leadership of members of the CCP and the largest enterprises are run by members with equal power to ministers and provincial governors. At the same time as the CCP is providing these entities with supportive goods, policies, and means in the markets, the Party expects these enterprises to follow the central authorities' policies and guidelines on economic growth and environmental protection. The ties between the heads of the state-owned enterprises and the political party are often strong with leverage from both sides on influencing policy decisions and implementing strategies. Although these enterprises traditionally have played a crucial role for macroeconomic growth and stability (Li, 2008) more recently, the enterprises have become an obstacle to the reform programs on climate change and energy policy by halting the implementation of renewable energy in China. The coal-based state-owned enterprises have become challenged by the new central policies on non-fossil energy, which have created tension between the policy shift by the central authorities into renewable energy and the traditional coal-fueled plants. Although the state policies have included assistance for these enterprises to adjust to new technology and non-fossil energy, some of these enterprises have engaged in too many demanded reforms too quickly. This has led to reactions from the heads of enterprises against the pace of the central authorities' policies on renewable energy and energy efficiency.

Finally, the seventh issue is whether the Chinese government has the ability to enforce the new GCC laws and regulations and to adopt these under the principle of a more open and free economic market, in contrast to the previous more controlled market economy. This means that the government has both to establish market principles for the environment and to develop skills to supervise the market and the regulations on GCC; otherwise, it will be difficult to accomplish the GCC targets (Barbi et al., 2016). Substantial high-tech reforms need to be taken and financed to advance innovations and research to deploy new low-carbon technologies (Wenying et al., 2016), but such reforms also require political and judicial reforms to facilitate a market-oriented economy with improved conditions for investments, ownership, and entrepreneurship.

Conclusion

This chapter has addressed the Chinese position on global climate change. It has been argued that China was a highly reluctant actor on climate change until recently. The CCP's foremost interest in economic growth resulted in few policies on climate change and pollution. In early 2000, Chinese authorities showed a growing concern over its energy security for the promotion of further economic growth. The authorities became increasingly aware of the economic costs that came with climate change and pollution. Eventually, environmental degradation has also led to social and political unrest in Chinese society, due to human security challenges, leading to a questioning of the legitimacy of the CCP. In the more recent five-year economic plans, climate change and environmental pollution have been established in policies on economic growth. Today, China is in a major transformation to promote environmentally friendly technology for energy supplies. China is the global driving engine on low carbon technology and a leading actor in the debates and negotiations within UN structures. However, China has continued to refuse to link climate change and state security. Climate change has been perceived as a challenge only to economic growth and human security, with no references to state security. In addition, China has also refused to discuss such issues within the UNSC, being reluctant to foster international policies encompassing international and state security that could challenge Chinese sovereignty. Decades of economic growth and a traditional mindset that economic growth matters most has, however, had a devastating impact on the Chinese environment and society, delivering human health challenges, and food and water scarcity. Despite China's new role on environmental promotion and protection, there are the consequences of decades of rapid industrialization to address and much domestic political obstruction.

References

Adler, Ben (2016, September 29). The Magnificent Seven—7 signs that China is serious about combating climate change. *Grist*. Accessed January 29, 2017: http://grist.org/climate-energy/7-signs-that-china-is-serious-about-combatting-climate-change/

Albert, Eleanor & Xu, Beina (2016, January 18). *China's environmental crisis*. Council on Foreign Relations. Accessed January 10, 2017: www.cfr.org/china/chinas-environmental-crisis/p12608

APCO-Worldwide (2015). *The 13th Five-Year Plan: Xi Jinping reiterates his vision for China*. Accessed February 1, 2017: www.apcoworldwide.com/

Barbi, Fabiana, da Costa Ferreira, Leila & Guo, Sujian (2016). Climate change challenges and China's response: Mitigation and governance. *Journal of Chinese Governance*, 1(2): 324–339.

Bradsher, Keith (2010, July 4). China fears consumer impact on global warming. *New York Times*. Accessed February 4, 2017: www.nytimes.com/2010/07/05/business/global/05warm.html?ref=global-home

Caia, Feng, Xianze, Sua, Jianhui, Liub, Bing, Lib & Gang, Leia (2009). Coastal erosion in China under the condition of global climate change and measures for its prevention. *Progress in Natural Science*, 19(4): 415–426.

CBI—The Voice of Business, (2011, May 11). *China's 12th Five-Year Plan (2011–2015)*. Accessed February 1, 2017: http://cbi.typepad.com/china_direct/2011/05/chinas-twelfth-five-new-plan-the-full-english-version.html

Chadha, Mridul (2014, September 23). China's per capita emissions have exceeded those of Europe. *Clean Technica*. Accessed February 10, 2017: https://cleantechnica.com/2014/09/23/chinas-per-capita-emissions-exceeded-europe/

Climate Actions Tracker (2016). *Homepage*. November 2, 2016. Accessed February 1, 2017: http://climateactiontracker.org/countries/china.html

Climate Home: News. (2015, February 16). *Kyoto Protocol: 10 years of the world's first climate change treaty*. Accessed February 1, 2017: www.climatechangenews.com/2015/02/16/kyoto-protocol-10-years-of-the-worlds-first-climate-change-treaty/

Eaton, Sarah & Kostka, Genia (2014). Authoritarian environmentalism undermined? Local leaders' time horizons and environmental policy implementation in China. *The China Quarterly*, 218(2): 359–380.

Edmonds, Richard Louis (2011). The evolution of environmental policy in the People's Republic of China. *Journal of Current Chinese Affairs*, 40(3): 13–35.

Freeman, Duncan (2010). The missing link: China, climate change and national security. *Brussels Institute of Contemporary China Studies*, Asia Paper Series, Vol. 5(8): 1–36.

Gippner, Olivia (2014). Framing it right: China–EU relations and patterns of interaction on climate change. *Chinese Journal of Urban and Environmental Studies*, 2(1).

Gippner, Olivia (2017). China–EU relatations and patterns of interactions on emission trading. In Eva Sternfeld (Ed.) *Routledge handbook of environmental policy in China* (pp. 363–375). Abingdon & New York: Routledge.

Gub, Chaolin, Lingqian, Hua, Xiaoming, Zhangb, Xiaodan, Wangb, & Jing, Guob (2011). Climate change and urbanization in the Yangtze River Delta. *Habitat International*, 35(4): 544–552.

He, Guizhen, Lu, Yonglong, Mol, Arthur P.J., & Beckers, Theo (2012). Changes and challenges: China's environmental management in transition. *Environmental Development*, 3: 25–38.

Haidong Kana, Chena, Renjie, & Tongc, Shilu (2012). Emerging environmental health issues in modern China, ambient air pollution, climate change, and population health in China. *Environment International*, 42(July): 10–19.

Heggelund, Gørild (2007). China's climate change policy: Domestic and international developments. *Asian Perspective*, 31(2): 155–191.

Hilton, Isabel (2016, November 22). China emerges as global climate leader in wake of Trump's triumph—With the US president-elect threatening to withdraw from the Paris Agreement, Beijing is to ready to lead world's climate efforts, reports Environment 360. *Guardian*. Accessed January 18, 2017: www.theguardian.com/environment/2016/nov/22/donald-trump-success-helps-china-emerge-as-global-climate-leader

Hof, Andries F., Kumar, Atul, Deetman, Sebastiaan, Ghosh, Sambita, & van Vuuren, Detlef P. (2015). Disentangling the ranges: Climate policy scenarios for China and India. *Regional Environmental Change*, 15(6): 1025–1033.

Jingjing, Cai & Tang, Joyce (November 25, 2015). Will China's new air law solve its pollution crisis? *New Security Beat*. Accessed January 8, 2017: www.newsecuritybeat.org/2015/11/chinas-air-law-solve-pollution-crisis/

Kostka, Genia & Mol, Artrur P. (2013). Implementation and participation in China's local environmental politics: Challenges and innovations. *Journal of Environmental and Policy Planning*, 15(1): 3–16.

Li, Xing (2014). *Peak oil, climate change, and the limits to China's economic growth.* Abingdon & New York: Routledge.

Li, Xing (2008). *Three essays on China's state owned enterprises: Towards an alternative to privatization.* Saarbrücken: VDM Verlag.

Lynas, Mark (2009, December 22). How do I know China wrecked the Copenhagen deal? I was in the room. *Guardian*. Accessed on February 1, 2017: www.theguardian.com/environment/2009/dec/22/copenhagen-climate-change-mark-lynas

Matus, Kira, Kyung-Min, Nam, Noelle E. Selin, Lok N. Lamsal, John M. Reilly, & Sergey Paltsev (2012). Health damages from air pollution in China. *Global Environmental Change*, 22: 55–66.

NDRC—National Development and Reform Commission (2006). *The 11th Five-Year Plan: Targets, paths and policy orientation.* People's Republic of China. Accessed February 1, 2017: http://en.ndrc.gov.cn/newsrelease/200603/t20060323_63813.html—

NDRC—National Development and Reform Commission (2007). *China's national climate change programme.* People's Republic of China. Accessed February 1, 2017: www.china.org.cn/english/environment/213624.htm

NDRC—National Development and Reform Commission (2016). *China's policies and actions for addressing climate change.* People's Republic of China. Accessed February 1, 2017: http://en.ccchina.gov.cn/list.aspx?clmId=99

Oculi, Neil (2015. *Climate change as a security threat for the United States and China.* Humanity in Action. Accessed August 2, 2017: www.humanityinaction.org/knowledge base/739-climate-change-as-a-security-threat-for-the-united-states-and-china

Olivier, Jos G.J., Janssens-Maenhout, Greet, Muntean, Marilena, & Peters, Jeroen A.H.W. (2015). *Trends in global CO_2 emissions—2015 report.* The Hague: PBL Netherlands Environmental Assessment Agency.

People's Republic of China (2002, September 3). *China approves Kyoto Protocol* (March 9, 2002). Permanent Mission of the People's Republic of China to the United Nations Office at Geneva and Other International Organizations in Switzerland. Accessed February 1, 2017: www.chinaun.ch/eng/zmjg/jgjblc/t85571.htm

Ren, Xuefei (2013). *Urban China.* Cambridge & Malden: Polity Press.

Richerzhagen, Carmen & Scholz, Imme (2008). China's capacities for mitigating climate change. *World Development*, 36(2), February 2008: 308–324.

Schroeder, Patrick (2017). China's policy frameworks for sustainable consumption and production systems. In Eva Sternfeld (Ed.) *Routledge handbook of environmental policy in China* (pp. 346–362). Abingdon & New York: Routledge.

Shapiro, Judith (2016). *China's Environmental challenges.* Cambridge & Malden: Polity Press.

Song, Ranping & Qi Ye, (2015, September 29). *China's climate policies: How have they performed, and where do they need to go?* World Resources Institute. Accessed January 23, 2017: www.wri.org/blog/2015/09/china%E2%80%99s-climate-policies-how-have-they-performed-and-where-do-they-need-go

Sternfeld, Eva (2017). Introduction. In Eva Sternfeld (Ed.) *Routledge handbook of environmental policy in China* (pp. 1–4). Abingdon & New York: Routledge.

Tiezzi, Shannon (2014, January 1). Pollution threatens China's food security—China's soil and water pollution may seriously threaten food security in the coming years. *The Diplomat.* Accessed January 19, 2017: http://thediplomat.com/2014/01/pollution-threatens-chinas-food-security/

Kahn, Matthew (2016, December 7). For China, climate change is no hoax—it's a business and political opportunity. *The Conversation.* Accessed February 8, 2017: http://theconversation.com/for-china-climate-change-is-no-hoax-its-a-business-and-political-opportunity-69191

The Economist (2013, August 10). China and the environment—the East is grey. *The Economist.* Accessed February 10, 2017: www.economist.com/news/briefing/21583245-china-worlds-worst-polluter-largest-investor-green-energy-its-rise-will-have

The World Bank (2017). *Countries: China. Homepage.* Accessed February 1, 2017: www.worldbank.org/en/country/china/overview

Tilt, Bryan (2013). Industrial pollution and environmental health in rural China: Risk, uncertainty and individualization. *The China Quarterly*, 214.

Tsai, Wen-Hsuan (2014). Regulating China's power sector: Creating an independent regulator without autonomy. *The China Quarterly* 218(2): 452–473.

Tsai, Wen-Hsuan & Dean, Nicola (2014). Experimentation under hierarchy in local conditions: Cases of political reform in Guangdong and Sichuan, China. *The China Quarterly*, 218(June): 339–358.

Tsang, Stephen & Kolk, Ans (2010). The evolution of Chinese policies and governance structures on environment, energy and climate. *Environmental Policy and Governance*, 20(3).

United Nations (2017). *UN and climate change. Homepage.* Accessed February 1, 2017: www.un.org/climatechange/

Vorndick, Wilson (2015, August 14). Why climate change could be China's biggest security threat. Climate change may be a greater threat to China's long-term prosperity than its leaders recognize. *The Diplomat*. Accessed August 2, 2017: http://thediplomat.com/2015/08/why-climate-change-could-be-chinas-biggest-security-threat/

Wang, Shuxiao and Hao, Jiming (2012). Air quality management in China: Issues, challenges, and options. *Journal of Environmental Sciences*, 24(1): 2–13.

Wenying Chen, Xiang, Yin, & Hongjun, Zhang (2016). Towards low carbon development in China: A comparison of national and global models. *Climate Change*, 136(1): 95–108.

Wong, Edward, (2017, January 10). China wants to be a climate change watchdog, but can it lead by example? *New York Times*. Accessed January 17, 2017: www.nytimes.com/2017/01/10/world/asia/china-wants-to-be-a-climate-change-watchdog-but-cant-yet-lead-by-example.html?_r=0

Wu, Weiping & Gaubatz, Piper (2013). *The Chinese city*. Abingdon & New York: Routledge.

Yong, Jiang (2009). China's water scarcity. *Journal of Environmental Management* 90(11): 3185–3196.

Zhang, Da, Springmann, Marco, & Karplus, Valerie (2014). *Equity and emissions trading in China*. MIT Joint Program on the Science and Policy of Global Change. Accessed December 12, 2016: http://globalchange.mit.edu/files/document/MITJPSPGC_Rpt 257.pdf

Zhang, Joy Y. & Barr, Michael (2013). *Green politics in China: Environmental governance and state-society relations*. London: Pluto Press.

8 India and global climate change

John Janzekovic

India with its 1.3 billion citizens and a population density of 420 inhabitants per km² is on the cusp of an economic transformation. It has taken over 25 years to negotiate the difficult path through the maze of state and federal levies underpinned by an archaic mixed and socialist market structure. The new India has embraced the open market catchwords of growth and competitiveness in the structural transformation of its services sector with the industrial and agriculture sectors performing well but not to its full potential. There remains much to do to encourage public–private partnerships, to improve essential infrastructure and social services, provide greater access to education, and to manage effectively its bourgeoning tourism potential. With development come opportunities but also risk. India is facing two fundamental state and human security challenges. One is how to manage and sustain its level of economic growth; the other is how to deal with the many serious environmental challenges that confront India. Both challenges are formidable and they must be addressed together if sustainable development coupled with serious ecological consideration is to be realized.

The transition from a closed mixed economic base to an open market driven economy has India struggling to match its remarkable development growth and its power energy requirements. Higher incomes, rapid urbanization and industrialization, and ever-increasing development requirements have resulted in India rapidly moving towards being the prime engine of global energy demand. On the environment front for India, there is land degradation, river contamination, mass deforestation, disappearing water tables and toxic levels of air pollution. India has an archaic essential services infrastructure, poor waste management systems, a collapsing transport system, 300 million people without electricity, and further millions of people who only have sporadic supply on good days. The ecological concerns for India are not only the range and magnitude of its environmental problems but their level of criticality in regard to both state and human security. India is attempting to address many of these issues but the challenge to implement change and to maintain economic progress at the same time is formidable. This is not a problem just for India because the sheer scale and seriousness of its environmental problems have regional and global ramifications.

Poverty and inequality are rife with India, home to one-third of the world's extremely poor. Half of the world's 20 most polluted cities are in India and many

170 *John Janzekovic*

municipalities are burdened by political infighting, lack of finances, or just plain broke (Express News Service, 2016; Guruswamy, 2016; Nandi, 2016). Highly inefficient management systems are unable to cope with collapsing transport systems and with the relentless flood of people moving into cities to seek a better life (Tomer, 2016). Yet, India is also paradoxical because it has a youthful demographic with an attitude of enthusiastic entrepreneurship and resourceful resilience. India is more a civilization than a country with its diversity, beauty, and vitality; but such diversity is also the cause of debilitating social and environmental issues. India's caste-based discrimination and angry, radical Hindu nationalist sentiment are key factors that underlie a riven and often development-poor society (Agrawal, 2016; Mahapatra, 2015; Tharoor, 2016; Venkatachalam, 2016). The capacity to harness the significant potential of modern India lies with government, captains of industry, and the Indian people themselves. Responsible economic growth, a more harmonious social fabric, and seriously addressing its environmental issues are key factors for the development of modern India.

Access to and sustainable utilizations of energy are fundamental for India to redress past government inaction in these areas. By 2020, India will be poised to overtake China in its insatiable energy demands and by 2035 India is forecast to be the largest importer of coal and the second largest importer of oil globally (Barich, 2016; McHugh, 2015; Wang, 2016, pp. 114–115; WCA, 2016). By 2035, China will contribute to less than 30% of global energy growth compared with nearly 60% over the past decade but this is offset by India which has doubled its energy requirements over the past decade to account now for more than a quarter of the global energy demand growth (BP Energy Outlook Statistics, 2016, p. 13). This surge in demand is projected to be more than any other country over the next 25 years (IEA, 2016). India accounts for approximately 5% of global greenhouse gas (GHC) emissions and is one of the world's three largest emitters. China and the US are the other two.

The government's perception of the global climate change threat

Air, water, and land degradation and pollution are serious human security issues in India. India recognizes the anthropogenic nature of global climate change with frequent reference to the urgent need at both the domestic and international level for sustainable development and ecologically appropriate outcomes. As stated by India's Prime Minister:

> Climate change is not an issue of debate but a serious threat to existence. We must assume leadership in our region and call for a more concerted and fair global action to address the challenge of climate change.
>
> (Modi, 2015c)

India's earth sciences minister, Harsh Vardhan, blamed climate change for the heatwave that killed 2,500 people in mid-2015 and for deficient monsoon rains:

Let us not fool ourselves that there is no connection between the unusual number of deaths from the ongoing heat wave and the certainty of another failed monsoon.... It's not just an unusually hot summer, it is climate change.

(Vardhan, 2015)

The Government of India aims to reduce its emissions with a highly optimistic target of 40% renewables and non-fossil power generation capacity by 2030 (Jaishankar, 2016). In 2008, India developed its National Action Plan on Climate Change (NAPCC) as a policy direction initiative rather than an integrative legislative tool and, as a non-Annex I Kyoto Protocol country, it presented only relative not absolute targets. The 2008 NAPCC report made a number of references to the importance of co-joining development with climate change mitigation and adaptation.

In view of the large uncertainties concerning the spatial and temporal magnitude of climate change impacts it is not desirable to design strategies exclusively for responding to climate change.... It is imperative to identify measures that promote our development objectives, while also yielding co-benefits for addressing climate change objectives.

(Prime Minister's Council on Climate Change, 2008, p. 13)

India's former Prime Minister Manmohan Singh (2004–2014) established the Prime Minister's Council on Climate Change on June 6, 2007, to coordinate a national action plan for development and climate change assessment, mitigation, and adaptation. The Council was directed to produce an action plan to be institutionalized by the respective Ministries including Finance and Planning, Environment and Forests, Water Resources, Agriculture, Urban Development, Science and Technology Power, and Renewable Energy. Experts from industry, academics and civil society were invited to provide input in the development of the national action plan. The high-level ministerial and cabinet advisory group that constituted the Council was chaired by the Prime Minister. One year later NAPCC was released. The NAPCC presented eight National Missions complemented by a range of sub-national initiatives, all of which were and are today intended to simultaneously support development in India and to provide climate change related objectives and intentions (Prime Minister's Council on Climate Change, 2008, p. 2):

To protect the poor and vulnerable sections of society through an inclusive sustainable development strategy that takes climate change into account,

- To achieve national growth objectives with a distinct change in direction that enhances ecological sustainability, while reducing greenhouse gas emissions,
- To devise efficient and cost-effective strategies for end use demand side management,

- To deploy appropriate technologies for adaptation and mitigation of greenhouse gas emissions,
- To engineer new and innovative forms of market, regulatory and voluntary mechanisms to promote sustainable development,
- To implement programs through unique linkages as required with civil society, local governments and through public-private-partnership, and
- To welcome international cooperation for research, development, sharing and transfer of technologies supported by additional funding and a global Intellectual Property Rights regime that facilitates technology transfer to developing countries.

The NAPCC Missions have a wide range of aspiring intentions and targets (Javadekar & Lavasa, 2014, p. 3; Pandve, 2009; Prime Minister's Council on Climate Change, 2008, pp. 3–5; Sharma, 2008). The Sustainable Agriculture Mission aimed to develop climate-resilient crops and to improve agricultural practices with a focus on reducing methane, nitrous oxides and other emissions in agriculture. The intention was to make agriculture more productive, sustainable, and climate resilient and to conserve natural resources through soil and moisture conservation measures (Government of India (PIB), 2014; Jaiswal & Connolly, 2014, pp. 1–2).

The Enhanced Energy Efficiency Mission recommended energy consumption decreases in large energy-consuming industries and setting up public–private partnerships financing to reduce energy consumption through demand-side management. Anjali Jaiswal and Meredith Connolly (Jaiswal & Connolly, 2014, pp. 1–2) stated that the Indian government announced plans in 2014 to launch a National Wind Energy Mission and to restore an accelerated depreciation program for wind farms. Both the solar and wind sectors have significant opportunities to increase both local energy access and job creation.

The Green India Mission aimed to reforest six million hectares of degraded forest lands to expand forest cover from 23 to 33% throughout India. The Sustainable Habitat Mission promoted a core component of urban planning and the Energy Conservation Building Code to be based on energy efficiency, to mandate vehicle fuel economy standards, and to focus on waste management and recycling. The Sustainable Habitat Mission was set up with the objective of making cities more sustainable through a shift to public transport and improvements in energy efficiency in buildings (Digital Energy Solutions Consortium (DESC), 2010, p. 68). No specific targets for energy consumption have been set under the Sustainable Habitat Mission.

The Himalayan Eco-System Mission aimed to protect biodiversity in the Himalayan region by establishing an observational and monitoring network for the Himalayan ecosystem environment. The mission aims to assess climate impacts on the Himalayan glaciers and to foster community-based management of these ecosystems (Government of India Economic Survey 2011–12, 2012, p. 296). In 2009, Prime Minister Modi stated that the National Mission for Sustaining the Himalayan Eco-System:

India and global climate change 173

[i]mpacts directly on Water Security as well as Food Security and, therefore, involves the livelihood of hundreds of millions of our people. We all know that the entire Himalayan zone, including the high mountains, the foothills and the terai area, constitute an extremely fragile ecological zone. Over the years, there has been steady degradation of this sensitive zone as a result of deforestation, demographic pressures, rapid and often uncontrolled urbanization and road building and construction with only marginal attention being paid to environmental safeguards.

(Modi, 2009)

The Climate Change Knowledge Mission aimed to improve understanding of climate science financed by a new Climate Science Research Fund in order to improve climate modeling, and increase international collaboration. It also encouraged private sector initiatives to develop adaptation and mitigation technologies through venture capital funds. The Solar Mission attempted to make solar competitive with fossil-based energy, and to develop and use solar energy for power generation and other uses. The Water Mission determined pricing and other measures to set the goal of a 20% improvement in water use efficiency. The agriculture, water, and Himalayan eco-system missions targeted adaptation initiatives to ameliorate the effects of climate change. The habitat and strategic knowledge missions were mostly about complementing the knowledge base of responding to climate change, and only the solar, Green India (afforestation) and energy efficiency missions were focused on a reduction in the levels of emissions (Sinha, 2015). The PM's Council was reconstituted on November 2014 to again facilitate India's policy direction regarding how it will address both development and climate change through 2017.

India's Finance Minister Arun Jaitley tabled in Parliament the Macro-Economic Survey 2015–2016 prepared by the Chief Economic Advisor Arvind Subramanian. The Survey makes a number of important points regarding how India sees itself confronting the many challenges associated with global climate change both domestically and internationally (Subramanian & Jaitley, 2016b). Domestically, India has submitted relative targets for its renewable energy sector, particularly for solar and wind energy. The INDC policy referred to in the survey sets a target of 60 gigawatts of wind power as well as 100 gigawatts of solar power installed capacity by 2022. India's annual addition of 19 gigawatts between 2009 and 2014 was surpassed by a significant 26.5 gigawatts increase in 2014–2015. This was possible as a result of high power tariffs on industry firms that were shifting their purchasing power away from utilities and generating their own power (Agarwal et al., 2016).

Between FY2007 to FY2015 there was a 9.6% growth in industry self-generation compared with 4.6% electricity procurement from utilities. The industrial sector (mining, manufacturing, and electricity) achieved 3.1% growth during April–December 2015–2016 compared with 2.6% during the same period of 2014–2015 as a result of growth in the mining and manufacturing sectors (Subramanian & Jaitley, 2016c). India's goal was and is today to continue to reduce its overall emission intensity in conjunction with developing and protecting its economy. This approach mirrors the fundamentals underpinning the 2008 NAPCC and is based on India's base principle of equity and common but differentiated responsibilities (CBDR) approach.

Since his 2014 election, Prime Minister Narendra Modi has played an important role in redirecting India towards a much more environmentally aware stance to address global climate change (Chemnick, 2016; Mogul, 2016; PTI, 2016). Modi and his cabinet ministers have been active articulating India's mitigation and adaptation strategies by declaring highly ambitious targets for clean energy, urban and transport renewal, implementation of agricultural reforms, improving energy efficiency in industries, mass plantings of forests for carbon sinks, and a plethora of other initiatives both big and small. At the end of 2014, India's contributions and direct engagement during COP21 in Paris indicated a willingness to directly confront its own human and natural environmental challenges in dealing with climate change. However, neither state security nor human security as a result of climate change can be appropriately addressed unless indications of willingness are transposed to capacity and actuality.

Global climate change, India, and the UN

The climate change Conference of the Parties (COP) in Copenhagen 2009, Warsaw 2013 and in Lima 2014 provided significant impetus towards COP21 in Paris 2015. At the 2013 and 2014 conferences, states were invited to submit their Intended Nationally Determined Contributions (INDCs) towards reducing greenhouse gas emissions ahead of COP21. This resulted in a total of 147 countries (accounting for 86% of the global emissions) submitting their voluntary greenhouse gas (GHG) emission reduction pledges by 1 October 2015. The important Paris climate agreement adopted in December 2015 at the twenty-first session of UNFCCC was opened for signature on February 2016. India, along with 20 other states, signed the Agreement and declared that it would seek to join the climate deal "as soon as possible this year" and that it had started its domestic process to ratify it (Johnson, 2016; UNFCCC, 2016).

The Agreement entered into force after 55 Parties to the Convention have ratified the instrument. The 55 Parties collectively produce at least 55% of global greenhouse emissions. India's commitment to climate action was declared in a joint statement with the UK. PM Modi stated that India was committed to reducing its emissions intensity by 33 to 35% by 2030 compared with 2005 levels, and that it aimed to have 40% cumulative electric power installed capacity from non-fossil fuel based energy resources by 2030. India also made it clear that these initiatives were dependent upon nationally determined development measures and priorities (World Nuclear News, 2015). As the third largest greenhouse gas emitter after China and the United States, India's engagement at the UNFCCC was critical, as was India's proclaimed readiness to sign the Paris Agreement.

The Paris Agreement addresses all the important concerns and expectations of India.... The Union Cabinet chaired by the Prime Minister Shri Narendra Modi today gave its approval for signing the Paris Agreement adopted at the 21st Conference of Parties held in Paris in December 2015.

(Government of India (PIB), 2016a)

India's Ministry of Finance reported a range of domestic and international initiatives during 2015 leading up and subsequently to COP 21 on December 2015 (Government of India (PIB), 2016b). India submitted its INDCs to the UNFCCC on October 2, 2015. The INDCs are each country's commitments to reductions in greenhouse gas emissions. India's Environment Minister (Government of India (PIB), 2015) declared that India would reduce the emissions intensity of its GDP by 33 to 35% by 2030 from 2005 levels and that it would create a carbon sink of 2.5 to three billion tons of CO_2 equivalent through additional forest and tree cover plantings by 2030. Ambitious solar initiatives were declared including the intention to achieve a 40% electric installed capacity from non-fossil fuel-based energy resources by 2030 conditional on the support of technology transfer and low cost international finance.

India also declared that it aimed to significantly increase its solar power capacity and a "global solar alliance" led by the International Agency for Solar Policy & Application (INSPA) of all countries between the Tropic of Cancer and Tropic of Capricorn. India's stated mitigation strategies were focused on developing a clean energy system, improving energy efficiency in industries, developing an environmentally sensitive transport network and implementing a carbon sink and capture system. The Environment Minister listed intended adaptation strategies focused in the broad areas of agriculture, water, health, and disaster management. All these INDC strategies, the Minister said, were about protection of India's biodiversity and ecosystems by focusing around the key elements of emission reductions, capacity building, finance, and technology transfer.

Rajiv Chaturvedi (Chaturvedi, 2015, p. 1769) compared India's INDC pledges with other major economies and concluded that India's greenhouse gas emissions under its INDC scenarios would be about a third overall compared with China's. This was based on two well regarded but divergent approaches of emission reductions sharing between nations. He argued that approaches to the allocation of future emissions to different regions or geographies are generally being framed between two extremes. At one end is the "grandfathering" approach that allocates future emissions based on current shares of emissions. At the other end is the requirement for an abrupt transition to equal per capita emissions. The transition approach requires all regions of the world to be allocated a carbon budget equal to their share of the world population. Between these two extremes is the contractions and equities approach where national or regional per capita emissions are initially allowed to increase or decrease for a period of time until they converge to a point of equal per capita emissions across all regions in a given year. Chaturvedi concluded that the application of the contraction and convergence approach would result in India's INDC outcome projections having a "more than a 50% probability" of contributing meaningfully to limiting global warming below 2°C. This assumes that the other world regions also adhere to their proposed emission reductions.

To achieve its full potential to contribute to emissions reduction India will need genuine cooperation, assistance, and capacity building from developed countries and other advanced developing countries, which is currently not adequate (Chaturvedi, 2015, p. 1772).

India's overall strategy to curb its greenhouse gas emissions (GHG) and reduce its vulnerability to a changing climate is underpinned by a range of fundamental and serious, human security challenges. It has the third highest global GHG emissions and despite ambitious commitments including declarations to rapidly develop and deploy renewable energy such as solar, India's emissions are set to double by 2030. This will surpass both China and the United States (Davenport, 2014). India's major challenge is how to reconcile its rapid industrialization and development aims yet at the same time constrain its GHG emissions. According to the Environment Minister Prakash Javadekar:

> The government's first priority was to alleviate poverty and improve the nation's economy ... [This] would necessarily involve an increase in emissions through new coal-powered electricity and transportation....
>
> (Javadekar cited in Knappenberger, 2014)

> Twenty percent of our population doesn't have access to electricity, and that's our top priority. We will grow faster, and our emissions will rise.
>
> (Javadekar cited in Levine, 2015)

PM Modi declared, "India will fulfil expectations from it and its responsibilities... the country is working to take forward development and (protecting) environment together" (Modi, 2015b). Despite India's high overall GHG emissions its per capita emissions are one-third of the global average. This means that as its economy is expanding by over 7% each year and as its population continues to increase, India's emissions have a steep upward trajectory. External pressure for India to aggressively reduce its emissions profile is to Indian policymakers a threat to its economic development and its pursuit of affordable energy. This dichotomy is the key point why India is so focused, not unreasonably so, on the common but differentiated responsibilities (CBDR) approach. Discussion on the critical nature of CBDR to less developed countries in particular but also important ramifications for everyone else is presented later in this chapter.

PM Modi quickly increased India's various climate mitigation initiatives after he took office in 2014. In particular, he targeted 175 gigawatts (about 10% of India's overall electricity consumption) of total renewable energy capacity by 2022 by increasing five times his predecessor administration's targets. The global costs of support for energy transfer from the old polluting energy infrastructure to renewable or other less polluting technologies systems are daunting.

Less developed countries have set out actions in their INDCs that they say would, in total, cost over US$3.5 trillion to implement (Yeo & Evans, 2015). US$81 billion will come from domestic sources and US$407 billion has been requested from international donors. The remainder, including India's US$2.5 trillion estimate, is made up from costs that have not been specifically assigned to domestic or international funds. Basically, it is unknown from where these extra funds would come.

The majority of the INDCs cover the period 2015–2030 resulting in requests for international finance averaging out at US$27 billion per year. The UN-backed bank for climate-related projects, Green Climate Fund, is expected to channel most of the US$100 billion a year (determined in 2009) from the pledges of more developed nations to the recipient less developed nations. The Green Climate Fund is an outshoot of the Copenhagen climate agreement stipulating that 37 developed countries plus the European Union would mobilize (pledge and contribute) a combined $100 billion in public and private climate finance to developing countries by 2020. On July 2015, the Ad hoc Working Group on The Durban Platform for Enhanced Action (ADP) asked Parties to increase the goal of US$100 billion to US$200 billion (ADP, 2015, p. 34 Part II). However, up to June 2017 the Fund has only raised US$10.3 billion equivalent in pledges; a long way from US$100 billion and even further from the potential increased figure of US$200 billion (Cheikhrouhou, 2014, 2016; GCF Pledge Tracker, 2017). The Modi administration estimated that the price tag of India's entire INDC initiatives, (including public and private sector investment) would amount to "at least" US$2.5 trillion from 2015 through to 2030 (Upadhyay, 2015). Successfully achieving these INDC goals will require financial assistance and technology transfer from developed countries.

In total, 80% of India's projected INDC expenses are from the plan's mitigation commitments and by its ambitious deployment of renewable energy. The aggressive development of the solar industry hopes to lead the deployment pack at almost three quarters of renewable energy by 2030. India's Economic Survey 2015–2016 confirms the US$2.5 trillion costs estimates by PM Modi and again stresses the need for international funding to realize the final outcome.

While the maximum share of the country's current climate finance comes from budgetary sources, India is not relying solely on them and is experimenting with a careful mix of market mechanisms together with fiscal instruments and regulatory interventions. However, it needs to be emphasized that international finance is a critical enabler for the scaled-up climate action plans (Subramanian & Jaitley, 2016a, p. 184).

On January 4, 2016 India stated that it had the second highest number of projects registered under the Clean Development Mechanisms (CDMs) with 1,593 out of 7,685 projects registered by the UNFCCC. India has established the National Adaptation Fund for Climate Change (NAFCC) and the National Clean Energy Fund (NCEF) budgeted for US$64.8 billion for 2015–2016/2016–2017 (Chakravartty, 2016). This is paid for by a carbon tax on coal. Funding availability and capacity are as always criticalities that underpin ambitious climate mitigation schemes. There is a great deal that India must do to clean up its own

178 *John Janzekovic*

environmental back yard but it will struggle without considerable financial and development assistance from outsiders.

Common but differentiated responsibilities (CBDR)

India makes the firm point that efforts to respond to climate change and to foster sustainable development are closely associated with each country's economic capacity to deal with domestic and by extension global environmental challenges. Neither India nor any other country can go it alone. All must work together. This approach has culminated in formalizing the terms common but differentiated responsibilities (CBDR) in the wording of the Agreement during the Conference of the Parties to the United Nations Framework Convention on Climate Change (UNFCCC) COP21 in Paris, France. The principle of CBDR is firmly entrenched in all of India's declarations, proclaimed intentions about climate change, and its domestic and international policies (Desk, 2016; Mohnish, 2016). The more developed countries, particularly those that have contributed the most to global warming in the first place, have an obligation to financially support and help develop affordable, clean energy transfer technologies to less developed countries (Antholis, 2016). This is not an abrogation of responsibility by India who strongly advocated formal recognition of CBDR, rather it is a reality that less financially able economies simply cannot be expected to be the heavy lifters in attempting to address the world's or their own environmental problems.

In the lead up to the Paris Agreement, there were lengthy discussions and much dissent in an effort to address the concerns of various parties on the principle of common but differentiated responsibilities. CBDR means that all states are not equally responsible for global environmental problems but all states are equally responsible for the global environment. CBDR became part of international environmental law in 1992 in Rio de Janeiro at the United Nations Conference on Environment and Development.

In view of the different contributions to global environmental degradation, States have common but differentiated responsibilities. The developed countries acknowledge the responsibility that they bear in the international pursuit of sustainable development in view of the pressures their societies place on the global environment and of the technologies and financial resources they command (Rio Declaration, 1992, p. 2).

CBDR originated from the notion of the "common heritage of humankind" and it is a reflection of general principles of equity in international law. The equity principle acknowledges historical differences between less developed and more developed states regarding how each are able to contribute to global environmental problems, and the different economic and technical capacities each has to tackle the problem. The UNFCCC put it this way.

The Parties should protect the climate system for the benefit of present and future generations of humankind, on the basis of equity and in accordance with their common but differentiated responsibilities and respective capabilities.

Accordingly, the developed country Parties should take the lead in combating climate change and the adverse effects thereof.

(UNFCCC, 1992, p. 4)

The principle of CBDR is fundamental not only to India but also to global efforts to address climate change and it has found expression in numerous decisions of the UNFCCC Conference of the Parties (COP) (Cancun Agreements, 2011, p. 2; Copenhagen Accord, 2010, p. 1; Lima Call to Climate Action, 2011, p. 2). In the end, Parties mostly ended up agreeing on the critical relevance of the principle but there remain many differences of understanding regarding the relative weight of the common responsibility that states must share, the meaning of the terms "responsibilities" and "respective capabilities," and the relationship between responsibility and capability.

There are two fundamental elements underpinning the principle of common but differentiated responsibility as a response to climate change. The first needs to take into account the different circumstances and capacities of each state's contribution to addressing climate change, and each state's ability to control and reduce the threat. India and many less developed states are very clear where they stand on this issue. The second concerns the responsibility of all states to deal with the threat at the domestic, regional, and global levels. Again, India has firmly stated its position that the burden of addressing GCC must be shared by all. Less developed states are struggling under the combined burden of trying to modernize their economies for a better living standard for their citizens and at the same time developing mitigation and adaptation strategies to tackle serious, human security and state environmental issues.

From these requirements, there are at least two consequences. One relates to entitlements and requirements. That is, all states that are Parties to the Rio Declaration and the UNFCCC are obliged to participate at both the national and global levels to address climate change and environmental problems. The other is that even when states have identified their own environmental mitigation and adaptation strategies then the realization of such initiatives will still impose different obligations on states depending on their response capacities and capabilities.

CBDR remained a significant area of contention between states in 2014–2015 during negotiations over the wording for the Sustainable Development Goals (SDG) (IISD, 2015, 4; Meine van Noordwijk, 2016). Japan, Germany, Canada, the United Kingdom (UK), the European Union (EU), and the United States (US) asked to remove reference to CBDR arguing that it does not apply to a universal development agenda. South Africa, China, Saudi Arabia, the Maldives, Ecuador, Syria, India, Bolivia, Algeria for the Arab Group, Sri Lanka, Nigeria, Iraq, Uganda, and Tanzania called for retaining and even strengthening the draft's language on CBDR. On May 5–9, 2014, Counsellor Amit Narang from the Permanent Mission of India to the UN strongly dissented with the removal of CBDR from the 2014 Open Working Group (OWG) documents.

180   *John Janzekovic*

> Not only is the principle of common but differentiated responsibilities (CBDR) not reflected even in the context of climate change, but the very notion of differentiation, which speaks to the asymmetry between the developed and developing countries, has been eroded. This cannot be an acceptable basis going forward.
>
> (Narang, 2014, p. 1)

Narang argued that there were three crucial tests that the OWG must clear and the first draft document failed all three. The tests were differentiation, universality and multilateralism. That is, the notions of differentiation and universality were synonymous not in opposition.

The principle of universality demanded an equal and relevant agenda that was applicable to less developed and more developed countries alike. However, such an agenda must go beyond "mere policy prescriptions for developing countries" and must include concrete commitments for the more developed countries as well. This was particularly the case when addressing sustainability. Narang stated that the draft current document was primarily focused on actions expected by less developed countries and that such an approach was unacceptable (Narang, 2014, pp. 2–3). He again reiterated the importance of a multilateral approach. That is, the agenda must reflect a genuine intent for multilateral cooperation in order to meaningfully forge an international compact to address collective climate change challenges. The draft agenda, he said was primarily focused on national and domestic actions not on multilateral cooperation and international factors.

India argued that there were six myths associated with CBDR (ICTSD, 2015; IISD, 2015, pp. 3–5). These were: universality meant uniformity, CBDR is a historic relic and therefore is not relevant today (as argued by the US), CBDR is only applicable to the environmental dimension and it is simply a political principle with no technical relevance, the North–South divide has vanished, and that the CBDR approach implies inaction by some countries. India disagreed with all of these and stressed that the CBDR instead must be viewed as a call for action with equity being a fundamental principle that underpins the UN Charter and the Millennium Declaration. As a result of India's strong advocacy, the final Paris Agreement supported CBDR both in principle and in fact throughout the agreement (Paris Agreement, 2015, pp. 21–23).

Domestic mitigation and adaption approaches

In 2015, Modi claimed that what was needed was a paradigm shift in global attitudes towards climate change from carbon credit towards green credit. Instead of focusing on emissions and cuts alone, the focus, he argued, should shift to clean energy generation, energy conservation and energy efficiency initiatives (Modi, 2015a). India's domestic approach to its many climate change challenges is reflected to a significant extent by PM Modi's first year in office and his efforts to charting a different direction for India. That is, by redirecting investment policies toward climate change initiatives but linking these with domestic economic development. The notion of human security coupled with state development was critical. In an address to the Australian Parliament at the end of 2014, Modi outlined his intent.

> A roof over every head and electricity in every household...the next generation of infrastructure that does not take a toll on our environment.... Energy that does not cause our glaciers to melt—clean coal and gas, renewable energy or fuel for nuclear power; cities that are smart, sustainable and liveable; villages that offer opportunities; agriculture that yields more and farms that are better connected to markets; practices and technology that save water
>
> (Modi, 2014)

At the 2016 Economic Times Global Business Summit PM Modi reiterated his plans for India to mitigate the effects of climate change (ET Bureau, 2016; Modi, 2016). By 2030, reduction of India's emission intensity GDP by 33% and 40% of electric power capacity to come from non-fossil fuel, build an additional carbon sink of over 2.5 billion tons of carbon dioxide equivalent by creating additional forest cover, and take the lead in launching an international solar alliance involving 121 countries. In 2013–2014 India's solar power capacity was 974 megawatts. Modi planned to increase solar capacity from 2,500 megawatts in 2015–16 with a further increase to 12,000 megawatts in 2016–2017. By upscaling power and adding new electric power transmission lines over 22,000 kilometers (an increase of 32%) this has resulted in the cost of power declining 30% in the sector, overall.

India declared its intention to replace importing thermal coal within two to three years with solar power, wind farms, energy efficiency, grid efficiency, plus domestic coal and hydro as the preferred domestic solutions (Buckley, 2014). However, the attempt to diversify its power energy mix will face some steep challenges. Henry Wang argued that domestic energy production is expected to rise markedly by 95% by 2030 and that coal is likely to remain the dominant hydrocarbon fuel to account for 67% of total energy produced (Wang, 2016, pp. 114–115). Addressing India's very high air pollution levels is a linchpin of the government's human security, GHG mitigation strategies. The World Health Organisation (WHO) and pollution monitoring organisations estimate that every year 4.3 million deaths occur globally from indoor air pollution and 3.7 million deaths are from exposure to outdoor air pollution. (Piqueras & Vizenor, 2016; UNEP, 2016; WHO, 2015). That is, one out of eight global deaths are due to the effects of air pollution. Half of the world's population—over 3.5 billion people—live with unsafe air quality and more than half of premature deaths attributed to air pollution occurred in India and China. In India and Nepal, the percentage of people exposed to unsafe levels of fine particulate matter (PM) is almost 75% (Hsu, 2016). Sachin Ghude et al. (2016) conducted extensive geophysical research into premature mortality in India due to PM 2.5 and ozone exposure.

The WHO considers airborne particulate levels exceeding 10 micrograms/m³ measured at PM 2.5 levels to be unsafe. Their findings are that the high levels of PM 2.5 and ozone pollution levels considerably impact human mortalities and life expectancy in India (Ghude et al., 2016, pp. 4650–4658). Present-day premature mortalities due to PM 2.55 (~570,000) and ozone (31,000) exposure caused economic costs of approximately US$640 billion. This is a factor of 10 higher than India's total public and private health expenditure. Delhi is ranked by the WHO as the world's most polluted major city with PM 2.5 concentration recordings of Respirable Suspended Particulate Matter (RSPM) averaging from July to November 2015 to be double that of Beijing (*The Economist*, 2016). Beijing recorded 62 PM 2.5. 50.8 million people living in Lucknow, Faridabad, Ahmedabad, Kanpur, Varanasi, Hyderabad, and seven other cities breathe concentrations of particulates up to almost 125 PM 2.5s. Professor Chanda Venkataraman attributed India's high air pollution to coal, wood, and dung fires, which send enormous amounts of ash and toxic particles into the homes of poor families.

About 920,000 deaths there were attributed to outdoor pollution, such as the particulate matter spread by power plants and vehicle emissions. About 590,000 deaths were attributed to household pollution: the emissions from burning for heating and cooking (Yuhas, 2016).

India's pollution problems are exacerbated by its poorly maintained and obsolete coal-fired power stations but also by its use of poor quality domestic coal that has a very high pollution factor. India has the largest growth in coal consumption (435 Mtoe) overtaking the US as the world's second biggest consumer of coal after China. Michael McKenna and Joe Kelly (McKenna & Kelly, 2017) state that India's coal imports would rise 4.9 percent a year to 2021, and India was expected to overtake China as the world's largest coal importer over this period. India's demand for thermal coal is estimated to increase from 505 million tonnes in 2015 to 672 million tonnes in 2021. However, its domestic production will rise from 379 million tonnes to only 520 million tonnes. This leaves a shortfall in supply of 150 million tonnes. India's voracious power sector (44% of total energy demand) consumes over two-thirds of India's ever-increasing demand for coal. The Senior Fellow at India's Centre for Policy Research, Rajiv Kumar (Kumar, 2016) argued that despite India's stated commitments to mitigate its emissions, coal will continue to remain India's largest source of energy to power its economic growth over the next 25 years. India has low quality coal reserves of 301.56 billion tonnes and annually produces 500 million tonnes.

The majority of domestic coal output is produced by the public sector monopoly Coal India Ltd (CIL) with 88% of India's coal produced by opencast mining. This is by far the most ecologically degrading method of coal production. Then there are problems in coordinating coal supply and demand chains (Kearney, 2015; Sengupta, 2016). India's coal production grew by 4.7% each year to 600 million metric tons between 2005 and 2012 and coal-fired electric power capacity grew by 9.4% reaching 150 gigawatts. India set a coal production target of 1.5 billion metric tons by 2020 in order to address the shortfall in coal supply and to increase coal-fired power supply. However, by March 2016 state-owned CIL was forced to stop coal production at some mines and significantly reduce production at others because surplus coal stockpiles at most thermal power plants throughout the country were at overcapacity.

Despite the widespread coal oversupply problem there are still 57,000 megawatts of thermal units that do not have enough coal because those electricity providers have not signed up to a supply contract with CIL. They are therefore in breach of the National Coal Distribution Policy (NCDP). India has a coal fired installed capacity of 160 gigawatts out of the total 276 gigawatts, but only 10 percent uses clean coal-burning technologies. From 2017, India has declared that all new coal power plants will use clean technology with the intention to increase this to 24 percent by 2022. Kumar said coal is a necessary evil but that clean coal technology is better than the old polluting plants.

> India must make fundamental changes in energy policy. This includes the push in renewable energy. We are already talking about 175 GW of renewable energy. Even if 20 per cent (at current efficiencies) of renewable energy can be utilised, they can share the burden of the peak load, which is still met by coal-fired power plants.... Most of these technologies are available off the shelf. All India has to do is show political resolve.
>
> (Kumar, 2016)

Coal-fired power plants provide 70% of India's electricity, hydro power sourced from the northeast provides 17 percent, 10% comes from renewables such as wind farms, and 3.5% of electricity supply comes from nuclear power facilities. India's outdated, overburdened and poorly maintained electricity system is struggling to maintain supply for even part of the population of 1.3 billion people where a quarter-billion people have only sporadic electricity supply three to four hours a day and over 300 million people live without any electricity at all (Martin, 2015). India's Finance Minister Arun Jaitley declared that the government would allocate more funds to the power ministry in order to bring electricity to all of the country's villages with a deadline set as May 1, 2018 (Dua, 2016; *The Economic Times*, 2016).

The lack of access to electricity is a significant human security, socioeconomic, and development issue confronting India's population, particularly in the rural areas where there is a substantial and ever-increasing wealth gap. The burning of charcoal and wood for cooking is a significant contributor to carbon emissions and deforestation in India so replacing these highly polluting heat sources with electricity must be a first step to improved socio-economic development. However, unless there is an alternative to the antiquated coal-fired power stations then this would only shift the pollution problem elsewhere. India's approach to addressing its environmental challenges has been to tie

184 John Janzekovic

its mitigation and adaptation strategies to sustainable economic and social development. While many have questioned whether it is even possible that India's substantial environmental problems can be addressed meaningfully by this approach the problem is that a standstill or even a reduction of India's economic capacity would have serious human security outcomes for its 1.3 billion citizens. A deliberate decoupling of economic growth from environmental mitigation and adaptation efforts is not feasible either.

Conclusion

India has chosen a path to environmental sustainability without setting an absolute emissions cap and in doing so has promised only to limit the amount of carbon dioxide per unit of GDP. This is a relative target, not an absolute one. India is the fourth largest global polluter not only because of its inefficient power energy systems but because it has 1.3 billion people requiring access to its woefully inadequate power and energy infrastructure systems. Each Indian emits around one-tenth as much carbon dioxide as his or her Western European cousins. To expect India to put forward ambitious absolute emission reduction targets that will keep it poor because of a problem caused by rich, developed nations is not an approach that India has accepted.

India is a special case with its hugely ambitious claims of transitioning from coal fossil fuel and biomass (dung and wood) to solar and wind renewables with some further capacity for nuclear power expansion. India has made much of its desire to reduce its importation of coal but this will be offset by much larger increases in domestic coal production. On the environmental front this is a no-win scenario unless the overall use of coal fired power stations is significantly reduced or their efficiency is greatly increased. Neither looks likely and outside analysts are not optimistic of longer-term projections to 2030. India's nuclear power ambitions have not been addressed in this chapter and this is potentially another energy source that could help India's full load electrical energy requirements. Polls in India suggest that only recently has there been a gradual change of acceptance in a possible nuclear power future after recusal from the Non-Proliferation Treaty. It is highly possible that the change of public opinion towards the nuclear option will not be so gradual once it is realised that renewables have significant hurdles to overcome before they make any meaningful inroads into India's voracious energy demands.

The future of environmental mitigation and adaptation in India is intimately linked with its capacity to modernize and to develop its socio-economic capabilities. Improvement in the transportation and industry sectors, providing millions of Indians with wind and solar generated electricity, cleaning up or replacing obsolete waste management systems, agricultural reforms, plans to replant and reforest, and improving water management are all green initiatives but they are also development initiatives. Whether India advocates development as a driver for environmental change rather than the other way around is not what should be of primary concern. This is a reality particularly for less developed countries,

India and global climate change   185

and India is very clear that this is the path that it will take. What needs to concern everyone is how developed and financially able nations can practically support and directly help less developed nations such as India deal with their environmental and development challenges. India's domestic environmental problems transcend India's borders and the global impact is already very serious. The substantial ecological damage as a result of lamenting over who should pay for what and who should help whom reflects fiddling while India and the rest of the world choke.

References

ADP (2015, July 24). *Scenario note on the tenth part of the second session of the* ad hoc *working group on the Durban platform for enhanced action* (ADP), p. 34 Part II. Retrieved April 30, 2017 from: http://unfccc.int/resource/docs/2015/adp2/eng/4infnot.pdf

Agrawal, R. (2016, February 24). *India's caste system: Outlawed, but still omnipresent*, CNN. Retrieved from: http://edition.cnn.com/2016/02/23/asia/india-caste-system/ (Accessed May 2, 2017)

Agarwal, R., Jain, S., & Kothary, T. (2016, February 26). *Indian economic survey 2015–16*, AUM Capital. Retrieved April 24, 2017 from: www.indianotes.com/uploads/article_pdf/2016/AUM_EconomicSurvey_29Feb16.pdf

Antholis, W. (2016, June 23). *Climate change: An opportunity for India–U.S. cooperation.* Brookings. Retrieved March 15, 2017 from: www.brookings.edu/wp-content/uploads/2016/06/23-climate-change-india-us-cooperation-antholis.pdf

Barich, A. (2016, February 12). China coal demand set for decline. *International Coal News.* Retrieved March 6, 2017 from: www.internationalcoalnews.com/storyview.asp?storyID=826960585&section=News&sectionsource=s46&aspdsc=yes

BP Energy Outlook Statistics (2016). *BP energy outlook 2016 edition: Outlook to 2035*, British Petroleum Statistics, p. 13. Retrieved April 24, 2017 from: www.bp.com/content/dam/bp/pdf/energy-economics/energy-outlook-2016/bp-energy-outlook-2016.pdf

Buckley, T. (2014, November 13). *India's plan to stop importing coal deals another blow to Australia*, RenewEconomy.com.au. Retrieved March 15, 2017 from: https://web.archive.org/web/20150727185023/http://reneweconomy.com.au/2014/indias-plan-stop-importing-coal-deals-another-blow-australia-68894

Cancun Agreements (2011, March 15). *Report of the Conference of the Parties on its sixteenth session, held in Cancun from 29 November to 10 December 2010* United Nations Framework Convention on Climate Change p. 2. Retrieved April 24, 2017 from: http://unfccc.int/resource/docs/2010/cop16/eng/07a01.pdf

Chakravartty, A. (2016, February 26). *Economic survey tells government to utilise public finance to combat climate change* DownToEarth. Retrieved April 23, 2017 from: www.downtoearth.org.in/news/economic-survey-tells-government-to-utilise-public-finance-to-combat-climate-change-52964)

Chaturvedi, R. (2015, November 25). India's climate pledge and the global goal of limiting warming below 2 degrees C, *Current Science*, 109(10), 1769–1772.

Cheikhrouhou, H. (2014, December 9). *Towards an articulated vision for climate finance how can it support ongoing efforts to scale-up funding and investments?*, Green Climate Fund. Retrieved April 30, 2017 from: www.greenclimate.fund/documents/20182/44502/From_Signatures_to_Action___GCF_Funding_Proposals_Need_to_

186 *John Janzekovic*

Meet_the_Ambition_of_the_Paris_Agreement.pdf/dda4bbc2-a390-49b0-a098-214c70b8f1ab

Cheikhrouhou, H. (2016, April 22). *From signatures to action—GCF funding proposals need to meet the ambition of the Paris Agreement*, Green Climate Fund. Retrieved April 30, 2017 from: www.greenclimate.fund/documents/20182/44502/From_Signatures_to_Action___GCF_Funding_Proposals_Need_to_Meet_the_Ambition_of_the_Paris_Agreement.pdf/dda4bbc2-a390-49b0-a098-214c70b8f1ab

Chemnick, J. (2016, June 10), India's conservative prime minister proves unlikely climate ambassador, *Scientific American*. Retrieved March 16, 2017 from: www.scientificamerican.com/article/india-s-conservative-prime-minister-proves-unlikely-climate-ambassador/

Copenhagen Accord (2010, March 30). *Report of the Conference of the Parties on its fifteenth session, held in Copenhagen from 7 to 19 December 2009* UN Framework Convention on Climate Change, p. 1. Retrieved April 23, 2017 from: http://unfccc.int/resource/docs/2009/cop15/eng/11a01.pdf

Davenport, C. (2014, September 24). *Emissions from India will increase, official says*, *New York Times*. Retrieved April 30, 2017 from: www.nytimes.com/2014/09/25/world/asia/25climate.html?_r=1

Desk, N. (2016, April 22). *Prakash Javadekar: India shows the way to world on environmental issues*, Naradanews.com. Retrieved May 2, 2017 from: http://naradanews.com/2016/04/prakash-javadekar-india-shows-way-world-environmental-issues/

Digital Energy Solutions Consortium (DESC) (2010, July). *ICT's contribution to India's national action plan on climate change: National Mission on sustainable habitat*, CII-ITC Centre of Excellence for Sustainable Developmet, p. 68. Retrieved May 15, 2017 from: www.nicra-icar.in/nicrarevised/images/Mission%20Documents/Sustainable%20Habitat%20Mission%20CII-DESC.pdf

Dua, R. (2016, February 29). *Budget 2016: Power ministry gets Jaitley's thumbs-up over rural electrification*, IndiaToday.In. Retrieved April 23, 2017 from: http://indiatoday.intoday.in/story/budget-2016-power-ministry-gets-jaitley-thumbs-up-over-rural-electrification/1/608088.html

ET Bureau (2016, January 30). PM Narendra Modi's speech at The Economic Times global business summit: Full text, *The Economic Times: Politics and Nation*. Retrieved March 2, 2017 from: http://economictimes.indiatimes.com/news/politics-and-nation/pm-narendra-modis-speech-at-the-economic-times-global-business-summit-full-text/articleshow/50779147.cms

Express News Service (2016, February 7). *Wastelands of India: Here's how metros manage their trash* Indiaexpress. Retrieved May 2, 2017 from: http://indianexpress.com/article/india/india-news-india/wastelands-of-india-heres-how-metros-manage-their-trash/

GCF Pledge Tracker (2017, June 2, 2017). *Status of pledges and contributions made to the Green Climate Fund*, Green Climate Fund. Retrieved June 12, 2017 from: www.greenclimate.fund/documents/20182/24868/Status_of_Pledges.pdf/eef538d3-2987-4659-8c7c-5566ed6afd19

Ghude, S.D., Chate, D.M., Jena, C., Beig, G., Kumar, R., Barth, M.C., Pfister, G.G., Fadnavis, S. & Pithani, P. (2016, May 14). Premature mortality in India due to PM2.5 and ozone exposure. *Geophysical Research Letters*, 43(9), 4650–4658.

Government of India (PIB) (2014, July 15). *Schemes for development of agriculture and farmers' welfare*, Ministry of Environment and Forests—Press Information Bureau

(PIB). Retrieved May 12, 2017 from: http://pib.nic.in/newsite/PrintRelease.aspx?relid=106668

Government of India (PIB) (2015, October 2). *India's intended nationally determined contribution is balanced and comprehensive: Environment Minister.* Ministry of Environment and Forests—Press Information Bureau (PIB). Retrieved April 10, 2017 from: http://pib.nic.in/newsite/PrintRelease.aspx?relid=128403

Government of India (PIB) (2016a, April 20). *Cabinet approves signing the Paris Agreement.* India Government Cabinet. Retrieved April 28, 2017 from: http://pib.nic.in/newsite/PrintRelease.aspx?relid=139011

Government of India (PIB) (2016b, February 26). *India plays important role in adoption of Paris Agreement and launch of International Solar Alliance.* Ministry of Finance Government of India Press Information Bureau (PIB). Retrieved April 10, 2017 from: http://pib.nic.in/newsite/PrintRelease.aspx?relid=136873

Government of India Economic Survey 2011–12. (2012, January 6). *India Ministry of Finance, economic survey 2011–12*, Ministry of Finance, Government of India, p. 296. Retrieved May 15, 2017 from: http://indiabudget.nic.in/budget2012-2013/survey.asp and http://pib.nic.in/archieve/esurvey/esurvey2011/eng2011.pdf

Guruswamy, M. (2016, February 8). *Garbage crisis: Why Delhi's many municipal bodies must be merged,* Scroll.in. Retrieved March 16, 2017 from: http://scroll.in/bulletins/13/from-pioneering-businesses-to-conquering-us-television-four-indians-are-showing-us-that-all-is-within-reach

Hsu, A. (2016, January 23). *2016 report global metrics for the environment: The environmental performance index ranks countries' performance on high-priority environmental issues.* Yale Center for Environmental Law and Policy. Retrieved April 26, 2017from: https://issuu.com/2016yaleepi/docs/epi2016_final

ICTSD (2015, July 7). *UN talks review post-2015 development agenda "zero draft",* Switzerland International Centre for Trade and Sustainable Development. Retrieved April 29, 2017 from: www.ictsd.org/bridges-news/bridges-africa/news/un-talks-review-post-2015-development-agenda-%E2%80%9Czero-draft%E2%80%9D

IEA (2016, January 7). *IEA chief briefs Indian Prime Minister on energy outlook,* International Energy Agency. Retrieved March 12, 2017 from: www.iea.org/newsroomandevents/news/2016/january/iea-briefs-indian-prime-minister-on-energy-outlook.html

IISD (2015, June 28). *Summary of the sixth session of the intergovernmental negotiation process on the post-2015 development agenda, 22–25 June 2015.* UN Headquarters, New York, International Institute for Sustainable Development (IISD), pp. 3–5. Retrieved April 24, 2017 from: www.iisd.ca/vol. 32/enb3219e.html, www.iisd.ca/download/pdf/enb3219e.pdf

Jaishankar, S. (2016, June 13). *Speech by Foreign Secretary at the First Gateway of India dialogue (June 13, 2016),* Government of India: Ministry of Foreign Affairs. Retrieved March 5, 2017 from: www.mea.gov.in/Speeches-Statements.htm?dtl/26902

Jaiswal, A. & Connolly, M. (2014, September 19). *UN Climate Summit: A look at India's climate actions,* Natural Resources Defense Council (NRDC), pp. 1–2. Retrieved May 15, 2017 from: www.nrdc.org/experts/anjali-jaiswal/un-climate-summit-look-indias-climate-actions

Javadekar, P. & Lavasa, A. (2014, December). *India's progress in combating climate change: Briefing paper for UNFCCC COP 20 Lima, Peru*, Ministry of Environment, Forests and Climate Change: Government of India, p. 3. Retrieved April 29, 2017 from: http://envfor.nic.in/sites/default/files/press-releases/Indian_Country_Paper_Low_Res.pdf

188 *John Janzekovic*

Johnson, K. (2016, June 7). *India, one of the world's biggest polluters, will join climate change accord*, Foreign Policy. Retrieved April 24, 2017 from: http://foreignpolicy. com/2016/06/07/india-one-of-the-worlds-biggest-polluters-will-join-climate-change-accord/

Kearney, D. (2015, August 25). *India's coal industry in flux as government sets ambitious coal production targets*, Energy Information Administration (EIA). Retrieved April 28, 2017 from: www.eia.gov/todayinenergy/detail.cfm?id=22652

Knappenberger, P. (2014, September 26). *The world needs more energy, not less*, The CATO Institute. Retrieved April 30, 2017 from: www.cato.org/blog/world-needs-more-energy-not-less

Kumar, R. (2016, January 17). *The environment: Optimise utilisation of coal reserves*, BusinessToday.in. Retrieved March 6, 2017 from: www.businesstoday.in/magazine/cover-story/the-environment-optimise-utilisation-of-coal-reserves/story/227526.html

Levine, S. (2015, December 3). World's richest 10 percent responsible for about half of carbon emissions, *The Huffington Post*. Retrieved April 20, 2017 from: www.huffingtonpost.com.au/entry/climate-change-economic-distribution_us_565f0cede4b072e9d1c430e3

Lima Call to Climate Action (2011, February 2). *Report of the Conference of the Parties on its twentieth session, held in Lima from 1 to 14 December 2014*, United Nations Framework Convention on Climate Change p. 2. Retrieved April 24, 2017 from: http://unfccc.int/resource/docs/2014/cop20/eng/10a01.pdf

Mahapatra, D. (2015, November 16). Bihar election shows caste system still holds sway, *The Times of India*. Retrieved March 15, 2017 from: http://timesofindia.indiatimes.com/elections/bihar-elections-2015/Bihar-election-shows-caste-system-still-holds-sway/articleshow/49795824.cms

Martin, R. (2015, October 7). India's energy crisis, *MIT Technology Review*. Retrieved April 29, 2017 from: www.technologyreview.com/s/542091/indias-energy-crisis/

McHugh, B. (2015, December 21). *International energy agency report says Chinese coal demand to drop further but Australia to be world's largest exporter*, Australian Broadcasting Corporation (ABC) Rural. Retrieved March 6, 2017 from: www.abc.net.au/news/2015-12-21/iea-coal-report-says-china-demand-down-asian-demand-up/7045930

McKenna, M. & Kelly, J. (2017, May 27). *Adani collapse would hurt trading relationships: minerals council*, The Australian Newspaper. Retrieved June 12, 2017 from: www.theaustralian.com.au/national-affairs/state-politics/adani-collapse-would-hurt-trading-relationships-minerals-council/news-story/fb26e0ae3b453343d0e25b0638dbf36b

Modi, N. (2009, October 26). *Extracts from introductory remarks by prime minister at the meeting of PM's Council on climate change on the national mission on sustaining the himalayan eco-system*, Government of India: Prime Minister's Office. Retrieved May 12, 2017 from: www.moef.nic.in/downloads/public-information/PM_speech.pdf

Modi, N. (2014, November 18). Full text of Modi's address to the joint session of Australian Parliament, *The Hindu News*. Retrieved March 2, 2017 from: www.thehindu.com/news/resources/full-text-of-modis-address-to-joint-session-of-the-australian-parliament/article6610532.ece

Modi, N. (2015a, January 19). *PM calls for a paradigm shift in global attitudes towards climate change, from "carbon credit", towards "green credit"*, Government of India: Prime Minister's Office. Retrieved March 6, 2017 from: http://pib.nic.in/newsite/PrintRelease.aspx?relid=114787

Modi, N. (2015b, December). Prime Minister points to India's ambitious target of producing 175 GW of renewable energy, *The Hindu Times*. Retrieved March 12, 2017 from: www.thehindu.com/todays-paper/tp-national/india-will-fulfil-commitments-on-climate-change-says-modi/article7934917.ece

Modi, N. (2015c, March 20). *Raja Mohan: Modi and the Indian Ocean: Restoring India's sphere of influence*, Institute of South Asian Studies. Retrieved March 12, 2017 from: www.isas.nus.edu.sg/ISAS%20Reports/ISAS_Insights_No._277_-_Modi_and_the_Indian_Ocean_20032015163047.pdf

Modi, N. (2016, January 29). *Prime Minister's inaugural address, Airtel and the Economic Times: Global Business Summit (GBS) 2016*. Retrieved March 5, 2017 from: http://et-gbs.com/PostShowReport/GBS_Post_Show_Report_2016.pdf. See also, http://et-gbs.com/prime-minister-inaugural-address.php

Mogul, P. (2016, June 7). Modi in US: White House commends Indian prime minister on climate change leadership, *International Business Times*. Retrieved March 15, 2017 from: www.ibtimes.co.uk/modi-us-white-house-commends-indian-prime-minister-climate-change-leadership-1564033

Mohnish, M. (2016, June 27). *Outcome and Indian stance in COPs 1–21* Indian Council of World Affairs. Retrieved May 2, 2017 from: www.icwa.in/pdfs/VP/2014/Outcome andIndianstanceVP27062016.pdf

Nandi, J, (2016, May 13). 10 of world's 20 most polluted cities in India: List inside, *Times of India*. Retrieved May 2, 2017 from: http://timesofindia.indiatimes.com/life-style/health-fitness/health-news/10-of-worlds-20-most-polluted-cities-in-India-List-inside/articleshow/52249911.cms

Narang, A. (2014, May 5–9). *1th Session of the OWG on SDG, May 5–9, 2014 Statements delivered by Amit Narang, Counsellor, Permanent Mission of India to the UN General Comments on the Working Document and Focus Areas 1 and 2*, pp. 1–3. Retrieved March 2, 2017 from: www.pminewyork.org/pages.php?id=1922

Pandve, H. (2009, April). India's national action plan on climate change, *Indian Journal of Occupational Environmental Medicine* [serial online]. Retrieved April 29, 2017 from: www.ncbi.nlm.nih.gov/pmc/articles/PMC2822162/#CIT3

Paris Agreement (2015, December 12). *Conference of the Parties twenty-first session Paris, 30 November to 11 December 2015—Adoption of the Paris Agreement*, United Nations Framework Convention on Climate Change pp. 21–23. Retrieved April 26, 2017 from: https://unfccc.int/resource/docs/2015/cop21/eng/l09r01.pdf

Piqueras, P & Vizenor, A. (2016, April 26). *The rapidly growing death toll attributed to air pollution: A global responsibility*, Policy Brief for Global Sustainability Report—2016 Update Retrieved April 28, 2017 from: https://sustainabledevelopment.un.org/content/documents/1008357_Piqueras_The%20rapidly%20growing%20death%20toll%20attributed%20to%20air%20pollution-A%20global%20responsibility.pdf

Prime Minister's Council on Climate Change (2008, June 30). *National action plan on climate change*, Government of India, pp. 2–5, 13. Retrieved April 30, 2017 from: www.moef.nic.in/downloads/home/Pg01-52.pdf

PTI (2016, June 7). Modi demonstrated Indian leadership on climate change: White House, *The Times of India*. Retrieved March 16, 2017 from: http://timesofindia.india times.com/india/Modi-demonstrated-Indian-leadership-on-climate-change-White-House/articleshow/52634055.cms

Rio Declaration (1992). *Rio Declaration on Environment and Development 1992*, United Nations, p. 2. Retrieved April 26, 2017 from: www.jus.uio.no/lm/environmental. development.rio.declaration.1992/portrait.a4.pdf

Sengupta, D. (2016, March 4). CIL stops work at several mines, *The Economic Times: Metals and Mining.* Retrieved April 10, 2017 from: http://economictimes.indiatimes.com/industry/indl-goods/svs/metals-mining/cil-stops-work-at-several-mines/articleshow/51248175.cms

Sharma, S. (2008, July 24). *Missing the mountain for the snow.* Indiatogether.com. Retrieved April 26, 2017 from: http://indiatogether.org/napcc-environment

Sinha, A. (2015, January 3). Four new missions to boost response to climate change, *The Indian Express.* Retrieved April 30, 2017 from: http://indianexpress.com/article/india/india-others/four-new-missions-to-boost-response-to-climate-change/

Subramanian, A. & Jaitley, A. (2016a, February 26). *Government of India: Economic survey 2015–16—Vol. 2,* Ministry of Finance, p. 184. Retrieved April 10, 2017 from: www.unionbudget.nic.in/vol.2_survey.asp

Subramanian, A. & Jaitley, A. (2016b, February 26). *Government of India: Economic survey 2015–16—Vol 1,* Ministry of Finance. Retrieved April 10, 2017 from: www.unionbudget.nic.in/vol.1_survey.asp

Subramanian, A. & Jaitley, A. (2016c, February 26). *Government of India: Economic survey 2015–16, industrial, corporate, and infrastructure performance,* Ministry of Finance. Retrieved May 15, 2017 from: www.unionbudget.nic.in/es2015-16/echapvol.2–06.pdf

Tharoor, S. (2016, February 10). *How India's caste system survives,* The Daily Star: Project Syndicate. Retrieved March 6, 2017 from: www.thedailystar.net/op-ed/politics/how-indias-caste-system-survives-345505

The Economic Times (2016, January 19). About 25% of 18,452 unelectrified villages got power since August, *The Economic Times: Politics and Nation.* Retrieved April 28, 2017 from: http://economictimes.indiatimes.com/news/politics-and-nation/about-25-of-18452-unelectrified-villages-got-power-since-august/articleshow/50637804.cms

The Economist (2016, January 16). *Urban pollution in India: Particular about particulates,* Economist.com. Retrieved April 20, 2017 from: www.economist.com/news/asia/21688447-bold-experiment-has-improved-delhis-air-indians-want-more-particular-about-particulates

Tomer, A. (2016, January 14). *Poor municipalities are the biggest barrier to India's "smart cities,"* Brookings India. Retrieved March 6, 2017 from: www.thepoliticalindian.com/poor-municipalities-biggest-barrier-indias-smart-cities/

UNEP (2016, May 27). *Healthy environment, healthy people: Ministerial policy review session, second session of the United Nations Environment Assembly of the United Nations Environment Programme, Nairobi,* United Nations Environment Programme. Retrieved April 26, 2017 from: www.unep.org/about/sgb/Portals/50153/K1602727%20INF%205%20Eng.pdf

UNFCCC (1992). *United Nations Framework Convention on Climate Change* United Nations, p. 4. Retrieved April 20, 2017 from: https://unfccc.int/resource/docs/convkp/conveng.pdf

UNFCCC (2016, July 27). *United Nations Framework Convention on Climate Change—Paris Agreement,* United Nations. Retrieved April 30, 2017 from: http://unfccc.int/paris_agreement/items/9444.php

Upadhyay, A. (2015, October 2). *India seeks $2.5 trillion to curb fossil fuel pollution by 2030,* Bloomberg. Retrieved April 28, 2017 from: www.bloomberg.com/news/articles/2015-10-02/india-seeks-2-5-trillion-to-curb-fossil-fuel-pollution-by-2030

van Noordwijk, Meine (2016, January 4). *Tragedy of the common but differentiated responsibilities resolved, but is the principle applied consistently?,* Capri Collective

Action and Property Rights. Retrieved April 20, 2017 from: http://capri.cgiar. org/2016/01/04/blog-tragedy-of-the-common-but-differentiated-responsibilities-resolved-but-is-the-principle-applied-consistently/

Vardhan, H. (2015, June 2). *India minister blames climate change for deadly heatwave, weak monsoon*, Thomson Reuters—Africa. Retrieved April 30, 2017 from: http://af. reuters.com/article/commoditiesNews/idAFL3N0YO3UQ20150602

Venkatachalam, K.S. (2016, August 4). *Destroy India's caste system before it destroys India*, The Diplomat. Retrieved March 6, 2017 from: http://thediplomat.com/2016/08/ destroy-indias-caste-system-before-it-destroys-india/.

Wang, H. (2016). *Energy market in emerging economies: Strategies for growth*. New York: Routledge.

WCA (2016). *Energy in India: Key statistics*, World Coal Association. Retrieved March 12, 2017 from: www.worldcoal.org/file_validate.php?file=WCA_Energy%20factsheets _India.pdf

WHO (2015, May 2015). *World Health Assembly closes, passing resolutions on air pollution and epilepsy*, World Health Organisation. Retrieved April 28, 2017 from: www. who.int/mediacentre/news/releases/2015/wha-26-may-2015/en/

World Nuclear News (2015, November 13). *India and UK sign civil nuclear agreement, discuss climate change*, World-Nuclear-News.com. Retrieved April 23, 2017 from: www.world-nuclear-news.org/NP-India-and-UK-sign-civil-nuclear-agreement-discuss-climate-change-13111501.html)

Yeo, S. & Evans, S. (2015, October 2). *India's greenhouse gas emissions in 2030 would climb by around 90% compared to current levels, according to Carbon Brief analysis of its climate pledge to the UN*, Carbon Brief. Retrieved March 15, 2017 from: www. carbonbrief.org/indias-indc. See also www.carbonbrief.org/paris-2015-tracking-requests-for-climate-finance

Yuhas, A. (2016, February 2016). *Scientists: air pollution led to more than 5.5 million premature deaths in 2013* TheGuardian.com. Retrieved April 10, 2017 from: www.the guardian.com/environment/2016/feb/12/air-pollution-deaths-india-china

9   Japan and global climate change

Darlene Budd

Japan's economic industrialization "miracle" following World War II did not occur without a cost. The country's rapid economic growth resulted in numerous cases of extreme environmental degradation and caused much human suffering (Holroyd 2009: 77). By the 1970s, public opinion had become more critical of this growth at all costs post-war period and environmental interest groups formed and became quite active. This movement had implications not only for Japanese politics but also for Japanese environmental policy and regulation. Specifically, there was a pattern of the ruling Liberal Democratic Party (LDP) responding to protests in part due to increased support for environmentally focused politicians. Environmentally focused politicians were winning by large margins in local elections and displacing LDP incumbents and this threatened the power of the ruling party.

The LDP-controlled central government passed a number of policies designed to hold companies responsible for their actions that had negative environmental impacts. In the wake of the 1970s oil shocks, Japan adopted innovative manufacturing techniques that attracted international attention (Takahashi 2011: 5–6). A shift to clean energy, specifically nuclear energy, accompanied by additional environmental regulations, made Japan a world leader in environmental protection efforts (Takao 2012: 772). However, despite rapid progress, by 2000, Japan's commitment to global environmental protection had begun to wane and the country no longer stood out on the international stage (Hozinger et al. 2011). This pattern of inconsistent levels of attention to environmental protection is one of several characteristics that define Japan's environmental policy.

For example, one way that Japan responded to environmental impacts such as air pollution was to encourage the development of nuclear energy. Japanese citizens and government officials became less sure of the "nuclear solution" following the 1999 Tokaimura accident that resulted in the death of two reactor workers (Matsumura 2001: 353). This incident put the construction of more nuclear reactors on hold. Still, nuclear power produced 30% of the country's electricity by early 2011. As the salience of the hazards of nuclear energy faded, plans to increase capacity to supply 41% of the country's energy needs by 2017 and 50% of needs by 2030 were made part of Japan's energy security plan. Then, on March 9, 2011, the Tohoku 9.1 earthquake resulted in public outcry and demands to shut down all nuclear reactors in the wake of the Fukushima nuclear disaster. In September 2013, all of Japan's 54 nuclear reactors were shut down. In January 2016 Japan's Nuclear Regulation Authority (NRA) implemented new safety regulations, and three reactors were approved to resume operation (EIA 2017). As of March 2016, only one of the reactors was still operational (Soble 2016).

This experience of expanding and contracting the use of nuclear energy illustrates an important pattern with which to understand environmental policy in Japan. Throughout Japan's environmental history, civil society and public opinion on environmental issues related to consumer protection and safety have influenced domestic policy-making, often in response to environmental disasters. Public support for clean energy, clear water and clean air fluctuate depending on energy prices and the country's economic performance. This brief history of nuclear energy also illustrates that the Japanese government prioritizes domestic energy self-sufficiency over other environmental issues when large numbers of people are paying attention and the power of the ruling party is threatened.

This pattern of domestic politics generally plays out on the international stage. Four major factors that detract from prioritizing global climate change (GCC) domestically also, to an extent, detract from international commitment. These factors include: (1) energy security; (2) political party in power; (3) public opinion; and, (4) state of the economy. The politics of GCC policy in the international arena is notably different due to a fifth factor—the role of the United States. This chapter will address these issues in four sections that have been identified through the prominent concerns posed in the introduction to this book for major powers in addressing GCC and security. The first section considers how the problem of GCC is perceived by Japan. This is followed by a section that discusses the approach by Japan to the challenges of GCC in terms of the strategies of mitigation, adaptation, and capacity building. The third section presents the approach of Japan to the efforts of the UN in its attempts to address GCC. A fourth section delineates the capacities of Japan for addressing GCC from a security perspective. A final section concerning the impact of the US–Japan relationship concludes this chapter.

Perception of the threat of GCC

The challenges presented by GCC in Japan are best understood from a historical perspective. Japan's interest and action on environmental issues illustrates a number of paradoxes that characterize its response to GCC. In post-war Japan, manufacturing productivity was the highest priority and little consideration was given to the environment (Hachiya 2006). Productivity was made possible by the hard work, dedication, and sacrifice of Japanese workers and citizens. During this period, the citizenry shared a singular focus on recovery at any cost, even when these costs were borne by themselves or the environment. This sacrifice was reinforced by Japanese cultural norms for conformity and enabled rapid industrial growth to continue relatively unimpeded by environmental and social implications.

194 *Darlene Budd*

The birth of the modern environmental protection movement in the US began, according to many sources, with the publication of Rachel Carson's *Silent Spring* in 1962. In some ways, Japan's environmental movement began six years earlier. In 1956, 55 cases (17 of which resulted in death) of what would come to be known as "Minamata" disease were reported. Characterized by severe neurological damage, Minamata disease is caused by consuming fish or shellfish with high concentration levels of methyl mercury. The Chisso Minamata power plant was dumping mercury and other toxic waste into the Minamata Bay. Sickness, permanent neurological damage, and death forced citizens and government officials to come to terms with the environmental degradation and damage caused by decades of virtually unregulated economic growth. Bearing the brunt of industry neglect, Japanese citizens recognized the need to regulate industry to protect the environment long before government officials acknowledged the seriousness of the issue. After a second Minamata outbreak in 1965, public opinion leaders and government officials acknowledged that Japan's air and water pollution had become a public hazard (*kogai*) in need of attention (Hachiya 2006).

National attention to domestic environmental issues did *not* translate to acknowledging GCC as a potential threat that requires international attention and cooperation. While attention to domestic environmental problems increased, it took time, and international pressure, for Japan to acknowledge the relationship between human activity and depletion of the world's ozone layer caused by CFCs. In the late 1950s, scientists discovered that the ozone was significantly thinner than anyone had expected. In 1974, scientists realized that "CFCs would not only destroy the ozone layer; but that this would result in ultraviolet rays eventually causing severe damage to the biosphere" (Molina & Rowland 1974).

Interpreting this discovery as a serious threat to the global environment, Canada, Finland, Norway, Sweden, and Switzerland advocated "stringent control of CFCs within a legal framework" (Sato 2003: 170–171). Focusing on what was interpreted as a lack of scientific evidence, Japanese representatives (along with those of the European Community, and the Soviet Union) argued, "specific controls on CFC products should not precede a framework convention due to the absence of scientific consensus" (Sato 2003: 171). However, in 1984, Japanese scientist, Shigeru Chubachi "reported the existence of an ozone hole above the Antarctic" (Harris 2004: 171). This finding by a Japanese scientist, in part, changed the attitudes of Japanese members of the United Nations Environment Programme (UNEP) Working Group that later developed an international convention (the Vienna Convention) to address the CFC/ozone issue (Weiss 1998).

This pattern suggests that the Japanese governments' recognition of GCC has been incremental and, indeed, moving toward a sense that the challenge is a global problem. Initially, ozone layer depletion was not politically relevant to the Japanese government (Sato 2003: 172). However, the issue of GCC becomes more salient with Japan's international involvement on the issue over time, leading to the eventual recommendation to "implement concrete control on CFCs" (Sato 2003: 174). Japanese officials do commit to "strengthen[ing] scientific research on ozone and CFC issues" (Sato 2003: 174) suggesting that the Japanese government still needed additional evidence on GCC and possible approaches to addressing the issues.

Approach to GCC in terms of mitigation, adaptation, capacity building

Mitigation

Historically, domestic policy responses in Japan were influenced by direct evidence of human suffering and the ability of citizen groups and opposition political parties to use this suffering to threaten the dominance of the ruling LDP. The generally dominant LDP was usually more intent on protecting industry and encouraging rapid economic growth through lax environmental regulations. For example, the 1967 Basic Law for Environmental Pollution—the product of considerable political wrangling between the Ministry of Health and Welfare, and economic ministries and business organizations—proposed strict industrial liability for corporate misconduct. Continued objections from the economic ministries and business organizations following the passage of the 1967 Basic Law produced subsequent legislation that continued to prioritize development over the environment (McKean 1981: 19).

Angered by weakened liability and penalty clauses, citizens demanded more rigorous environmental standards and regulations and demonstrated their power by electing a resounding number of opposition party candidates during the next local elections for the National Diet (Takao 2012: 776). In response to the losses, the Liberal Democratic Party (LDP) reordered its policy agenda to prioritize the advancement of environmental protection policies. And, in 1970, the National Diet passed aggressive measures to achieve steep reductions in environmental pollutants. By the early 1970s, "Japan had some of the world's strongest environmental regulations" (Takao 2012: 772). Within a short time frame, Japan addressed urban air quality, cleaned up major waterways, and implemented industry regulations (Holroyd 2009: 79).

Throughout the 1970s, environmental mitigation followed a "pollution-and-response" approach that did not focus on broad governmental policy and far-reaching regulations (Sato 2003: 179). Generally, during this period, pollution mitigation in industrial and urban areas occurred as grassroots environmental groups used environmental litigation to address (and punish) specific polluters (Sato 2003: 180). Interestingly, an extensive study of *kogai* (public hazard) litigation observed that citizens:

> did not think about pollution as a threat to ... man's food sources and life-support system, ... about the effect of releasing high quantities of energy all over the surface of the globe (thermal pollution) on planetary weather or ... [about] the insulation of the earth from forces beyond our atmosphere.
>
> (McKean 1981: 140–141)

196 *Darlene Budd*

During this period, the environmental movement focused on reversing the negative effects of Japan's rapid industrialization process at specific point sources of pollution.

This mitigation approach was not without successes. As corporations were forced to adopt cleaner manufacturing processes or face substantial fines, Japan's air and water quality improved. Following these successes, the focus of the environmental movement shifted away from local water and waste management concerns to addressing the global environment. However, the approximately 3,000 environmental organizations registered in Japan in the mid-1970s did not share a cohesive strategy or agenda. As a result, by the mid-1970s, the LDP began to regain electoral momentum and public attention directed to environmental pollution began to wane. For example, one survey of Japanese citizens found that the percentage of individuals who felt adversely affected by air pollution had decreased from over 20% in 1973 to 9% in 1981 (Takao 2012: 777). The lack of focus by citizens and the absence of a coherent strategy from environmental groups led to setbacks in mitigation efforts.

During this period, a segment of environmental groups began to focus on global environmental issues and, because the focus was taken off domestic polluters, Japanese government officials were willing to follow this shift in priorities to a degree. For example, in 1977, the United States announced a timeline to phase out the use of CFCs in nonessential products leading to a wider belief that some environmental problems require a global solution unlike addressing point-source pollution of specific industrial emitters—the dominant perspective among Japanese government officials.

Following the announcement of the CFC phase-out in the US, the United Nations Environment Program (UNEP) began work on plans to coordinate efforts to protect the ozone layer and scheduled two international meetings on the topic in 1977 and 1978. Following the first meeting, the 13 nations and five international bodies in attendance agreed that

> possible regulatory actions should be discussed and harmonized to the extent possible in view of the need to approach international environment issues in a coordinated manner for maximum effectiveness and in view of the international economic and trade issues involved.
>
> (Stoel 1983: 45–74)

At the 1978 meeting scientists, universities, and international agencies comprising the Coordinating Committee on the Ozone Layer (CCOL) shared research results and findings with attendees that later were published as the *Assessment of Ozone Depletion and Its Impact* report (Sato 2003: 170). In response to the report, conference participants agreed that "there should be a global reduction in the release of CFCs" and called on "government, industry and other bodies" to work towards the goal of achieving a significant reduction in the release of CFCs in the next few years in relation to 1975 data (EEC 1978).

Some countries took affirmative steps to ban CFCs (Canada, Sweden, Norway, the Netherlands) and others either moved slowly (European Community nations) or were strongly opposed (Great Britain). Despite the fact that Japanese atmospheric scientists had participated in and made significant contributions to ozone depletion research, Japan followed the more conservative approach of the EC and Great Britain, arguing that "specific controls should not precede a framework convention due to the absence of scientific consensus" (Sato 2003: 171). Japan's more conservative approach to the ban on CFCs reflected a lack of agreement among domestic agencies and politicians. A lack of support for, or interest in, global climate change and in banning CFCs continued in Japan for most of the 1980s.

In 1988, the World Conference on Changing Atmosphere in Toronto, Canada called on all developed countries to "cut their Carbon dioxide (CO_2) emissions by 20% from 1987 levels by 2005" (Kameyama 2003: 137). Japan's Prime Minister Noboru Takeshita attended the conference, and was reportedly surprised to learn of the scope of the discussions taking place (Kameyama 2003: 137). The Japanese government believed that their domestic efforts to regulate business were successful due to the fact that Japan had become one of the most energy-efficient countries in the world. Further regulations were viewed as difficult and costly to business. Reflecting this sentiment, Japan, along with the United States and the Soviet Union, insisted that setting a "common numerical target for emission reduction was inappropriate at this stage" (Kameyama 2003: 138).

The alignment of the position of the Japanese government with the US and the USSR created front-page news in Japan. A large segment of the Japanese public viewed this response as inadequate and the ruling party again saw this as a potential threat to holding power. This domestic political context coupled with the realization that GCC *is* an international political issue, led some members of the Japanese Diet to propose Japan take the lead on addressing global environmental challenges (Ohta 2000: 104). However, as had occurred on other issues, there were tensions between domestic business interests that opposed further restrictions and regulations, and a growing national interest to play an international leadership role to address GCC. In 1988, Japanese policymakers recognized that climate change was not only a scientific debate but was also on the political agenda (Kawashima 2001: 168). This realization, along with pressure from the United States, eventually led to a Japanese commitment to work cooperatively with other nations to address GCC and devise a global environmental protection strategy.

GCC policy within Japan—mitigation

The response to the threat of GCC within Japan is influenced by the interaction of the national, prefecture, and local governments. The Japanese government's first response to GCC at the national level occurred in 1990 with the passage of the Action Plan to Arrest Global Warming (Sugiyama & Taekuchi 2011: 424).

The plan "aimed to stabilize CO_2 emissions at 1990 levels" by 2000 (Sugiyama & Takeuchi 2011: 424). To accomplish this goal, the Action Plan focused on reducing CO_2 emission levels through structural changes in urban and regional energy supply systems, reworking traffic systems and production processes, adjustments to the lifestyles of citizens (Takao 2012: 781). In 1993, Japan's Environmental Agency, (which would eventually become the Ministry of the Environment in 2001), distributed "Measures to Prevent Global Warming" guidelines (National Guideline 93) to assist local government efforts to meet the goals outlined in the Action Plan (Sugiyama & Takeuchi 2011: 425). There is evidence that by the 1990s many regional and local governments were prioritizing policies and programs to address the threat of global climate change (Sugiyama & Taekuchi 2011: 425). Mie Prefecture and the Tokyo Metropolitan Government (TMG) are two such sub-national examples.

The Global Warming Law passed in 1997 along with an amendment to the law in 2002 outlines expectations for Japan's 47 prefectural and 1,800 municipal governments. Sub-national government officials were expected to develop climate change countermeasures to address greenhouse gas emissions. And to this end, each prefectural government was made responsible for establishing a "center for climate change action" and appointing volunteers to help educate citizens and promote climate activities (Sugiyama & Takeuchi 2011: 426).

Following the passage (1997) and ratification (2002) of the Kyoto Protocol, the Japanese Diet issued a directive along with several incentive programs to guide and motivate prefectures and local governments. For example, the directive mandated that prefectures pass laws to promote energy conservation to attain a 6% reduction in emission levels from 1990 levels by 2005. In addition, the Conservation Law passed in 1998 mandated the "rational use" of energy that required "manufacturers to improve the energy efficiency of electrical appliances and cars by adopting, within a given time frame, the standards used by the most energy-efficient appliances" (Sugiyama & Takeuchi 2008: 426).

In an attempt to position itself as leader in the battle against GCC, Prime Minister Shinzo Abe of Japan announced the "Cool Earth 50" initiative at the 2007 G-8 summit meeting. Prime Minister Abe declared "a commitment to cut Japan's emission levels in half by 2050" as well as proposed steps to leverage the Cool Earth 50 initiative into a global initiative (Holroyd 2009: 75). In 2008, newly elected Prime Minister Yasuo Fukuda[1] announced to the G-8 Summit held in Toyako, Hokkaido, that "Japan would strive to reduce its GHG emissions by 60% to 80% from the existing levels, by 2050, and by 14% of present levels, by 2020" (Government of Japan, 2008 in Sugiyama & Takeuchi 2009: 427). While these goals were quite ambitious, each subsequent prime minister has faced the formidable challenge of balancing economic development and the energy security concerns of citizens at home with the need to address the dangers of global climate change.

In terms of domestic GCC policy in Japan, the first of two global warming countermeasures was passed in 1998 "to promote the control of greenhouse gas emissions due to social, economic, and other activities (Sabin Center for Climate

Change Law)." Another global warming counter measures bill was passed in 2010 to "promote global warming countermeasures while ensuring economic growth, stable employment and stable supply of energy" (Sabin Center for Climate Change Law). The second countermeasures law was accompanied by a clean-energy strategy that included the construction of 21 additional nuclear power plants (Sugiyama & Takeuchi 2008: 426).

Innovative technology such as advanced nuclear power plants, carbon capture and storage (CCS), emission standards for power stations and motor vehicles, and emissions trading schemes are common instruments to accomplish GCC goals (Compston & Bailey 2014: 148–149). These instruments have also been utilized in Japan. For example, to encourage the transition to low-carbon cities, the Japanese Diet passed the Tax Reform Act in March 2012, to introduce a carbon tax and the Low Carbon City Promotion Act in August 2012, "to establish a recognized system for low carbon buildings that contribute to the reduction of CO_2, and give preferential treatment to the buildings of high-performance evaluation through incentives such as tax reductions" (Sabin Center for Climate Change Law 2017). The government also launched a contest "to develop plans for the model environmental city" (Sugiyama & Takeuchi 2008: 427). The 12 selected cities proposed reductions in CO_2 emissions from 60% to 80% by 2050. This strategy of encouraging innovation at the subnational level eventually led other cities and prefectures to also develop plans to substantially lower carbon output by 2050 (Sugiyama & Takeuchi 2008: 427).

Experts generally agree that putting a price on carbon is essential to reducing carbon emissions (Compston & Bailey 2014: 140) because it provides incentives to invest in low-carbon energy production. A comparative study of China, the US, the EU, India, Russia, and Japan reviewed the progress made by each using a climate policy strength index and determined that "Europe is not the clear the frontrunner on climate stringency" (Compston & Bailey 2014: 160). Rather, Japan leads in as many categories as its European counterparts.[2] The index however, measures and compares the *policies* only, and does not measure the "extent to which the policies are implemented as intended" (Compston & Bailey 2014: 160). While the central government of Japan has adopted what some consider rigorous climate control policies to cut CO_2 emissions levels, Japan's 2006 CO_2 emission levels were 6.3% *above* the 1990-base line levels included in the Kyoto Protocol (Sugiyama & Takeuchi 2009: 424) suggesting problems with implementation. Subnational governments play an important role in the implementation of climate change efforts and, in some countries they are more aggressive addressing GCC than the national central governments (Roppongi et al. 2016: 2).

In Japan, prefecture and local governments provide policy innovations for consideration by other local governments countrywide. Mitigation efforts are encouraged by the local government Global Climate Change Centers that were created with the passage of the Global Warming Law in 1998. As mentioned above, one common mitigation approach—a carbon trading system—was first introduced in Mie Prefecture in 1995. Mie Prefecture experienced extreme air pollution during Japan's industrialization period in the 1960s and 1970s and, perhaps as a result, was more likely to embrace environmental regulations and conservation programs. (Puppim de Olivera 2009: 255). Other mitigation efforts instituted in Mie include the creation of a prefecture "eco-office" and "eco-point initiative" to reduce energy consumption by introducing programs to automate light switches, and reducing air-conditioning use by changing work dress codes in the summer (Puppim de Olivera 2009: 255). However, despite these efforts, 2003 emission levels in Mie Prefecture increased 9.3% from 1990 levels.

The case of Mie Prefecture is instructive and sheds light on the fact that despite considerable effort to adopt GCC policies, the results are not always as intended. Subsequent analysis revealed that in Mie prefecture, only large companies were involved in the implementation of climate change policies (Puppim de Olivera 2009: 255). Public officials in Mie Prefecture reported, "that Non-Governmental Organizations (NGOs) did not show much interest in contributing to the policy implementation" (Puppim de Oliveira 2009: 255). Also during this time period, data reveals a shift in consumer preferences. Consumers were increasingly purchasing larger cars and bigger homes. Air conditioning in houses and businesses became increasingly common; and, while the population in Mie remained stable, the number of households increased (Puppim de Oliveira 2009: 255). Ultimately, a lack of interest in the threat of global climate change among citizens and civil society groups in part, undermines the effectiveness of domestic mitigation efforts.

More recently, progressive-minded politicians at the local level with the help of environmental organizations and citizen groups have introduced GCC policies in their prefectures and cities. For example, the Tokyo Metropolitan Government (TMG) (2016) adopted the first mandatory policy in the world to link CO_2 emission control to a cap-and-trade system by setting binding targets for buildings (Roppongi et al. 2016: 2). Cities such New York and Paris have also set goals to reduce GHG emissions that are significantly lower than the national targeted levels (City of New York 2015; Mairie de Paris 2007). Maintaining the threat of global climate change as a top priority is an ongoing challenge. A recent study reveals that while 68% of Japanese citizens list global climate change as a major threat, cyber attacks (71%) and the threat of ISIS (69%) rank slightly higher. Those most worried about global warming are generally older Japanese (75% of those 50 and older), compared with younger Japanese (59% ages 18 to 34) (Stokes 2016).

Local government efforts, in some cases, seem to produce better results, especially when civil society and economic interests are included in the policy-making process. By 2013, total emissions in Tokyo were reduced by 23% on average from the base year. In total, 90% of the 1,281 regulated facilities achieved the first reduction target and 69% of them already met 2019 targets. The TMG has since been internationally recognized for its climate leadership and received several awards. This policy success is attributable to various factors that include leadership, capacity to implement and monitor the plan, stakeholder involvement in policy formulation, as well as gradual implementation and transparency (Roppongi et al. 2016: 13). Nonetheless, local government officials must consistently face the "difficulty associated with moving from the appreciation of the problem to the implementation of an effective and sustainable environmental regime" (Chasek et al. 2006: 230–231). To the extent that the effects of GCC significantly alter living conditions, citizens and government will be forced to modify lifestyle and adapt to the new conditions.

Adaptation efforts

Adaptation efforts are defined as adjustments in natural or human systems in response to the actual or expected effects of GCC. At the sub-national level of government there have been dramatic efforts at mitigation, but according to Puppim de Oliveira, there were "no actions of adaptation" so far (2009: 255). In Japan, at the sub-state level, "public officials mentioned the need for adaptation policies in the future" (Puppim de Oliveira 2009: 257). According to local level officials, if adaption efforts are to take shape in Japan, it is necessary to justify public and private infrastructure investments to address climate change with stronger evidence of the benefits and/or to have the national government provide resources to make adaption efforts more likely (Puppim de Oliveira 2009: 257).

Japanese researchers are, to a degree, conducting studies to determine possible adaptation strategies particular to environmental risks in Japan. For example, the effects of global climate change on rice paddy cultivation attract considerable attention from researchers. Some researchers have encouraged "*mitameshi*"—an adaptive management strategy for better human-nature relationships (Watanabe & Kume, 2009: 320–321). The "*mi*" of "*mitameshi*" means "to watch" or "to see" in Japanese, and "*tameshi*" means "to try," "trial" or "example." *Mitameshi* was first introduced during the Edo period (1603–1868) when "people carefully observed nature and the consequences of human actions on water development and management" (Watanabe & Kume 2009: 320–321). The *mitameshi* approach was used to build stakeholder consensus in developing solutions to water reclamation and irrigation issues. Once the current challenge is diagnosed, incremental development of a solution as well as implementation is emphasized. Local wisdom and experience is recognized as essential to the effort to adapt to changes in the environment (Watanabe & Kume 2009: 319).

Japan's adaptation efforts to date have focused on providing assistance on adaptation initiatives to developing countries. Japan has produced advances in innovative technology linked to mitigation efforts. In addition, overseas direct assistance (ODA) is a highly visible way Japan can establish its presence in the international community due to constitutional restrictions on its military spending and capabilities (Sunaga 2004). As a result, Japan's ODA "remains the cornerstone of Japanese foreign policy" (Thernstrom 2005). Examples of Japan's ODA efforts to facilitate GCC mitigation and adaption in developing countries abound.

For example, in 2014, Japan introduced drought tolerant genes to rice varieties in South Asia, Mexico and Africa. "Disaster Risk Reduction" workshops in

202 *Darlene Budd*

Vietnam, Indonesia, Myanmar, Turkey, and South Africa facilitated the development of evacuation and sanitation strategies for water-related disasters and led to the "Sendai Framework for Disaster Risk Reduction 2015–2030," which was incorporated into the United Nations Sustainable Development Goals (SDGs) issued in 2015. Japan has also provided "multifaceted assistance for infrastructure development and improvement in developing countries to strengthen resilience to climate change, utilizing Japan's knowledge and experience." Examples include:

- Construction and rehabilitation of irrigation systems in Myanmar, India, Pakistan, Afghanistan, Tanzania, Bhutan, and East Timor[;]
  - Construction of flood control facilities in Tunisia, Indonesia, Philippines, Peru
  - Installation and replacement of meteorological observation facilities in Myanmar, Bangladesh, Pakistan, Mauritius, Lao PDR

(Ministry of Foreign Affairs 2014)

Capacity building efforts

Poverty alleviation

Poorer countries and communities are more vulnerable to climate change than others. The degree of vulnerability is associated with the characteristics of a person or group that enable them to anticipate, cope, resist and recover from the impact of a natural disaster (Blaikie et al. 1994). At the national level, vulnerability manifests itself in poorer countries due to a lack of resources and capacity to respond (Warrick & Rahman 1992). Countries experiencing vulnerability benefit from Japanese assistance in the form of technology transfers, training, and loans. Japan provided $10.42 billion of Overseas Development Assistance (ODA) in 2015 making it the fifth largest donor of overseas development assistance. Only France ($10.92 billion), Germany ($20.86 billion), the United Kingdom ($19.92) and the United States ($30.77 billion) donate more (OECD 2017). Much of this aid is intended to address the issue of vulnerability due to poverty associated with lower levels of capacity to implement mitigation and adaption strategies in developing nations.

Japan's ODA includes bilateral aid given directly to developing countries; and, multilateral aid that is provided through international organizations. The Japanese International Cooperation Agency (JICA) provides bilateral aid in the form of Technical Cooperation, Japanese ODA Loans and Grant Aid (JICA 2012). The "Kyoto Initiative" is a policy framework written by the Japanese officials that would eventually become the Kyoto Protocol. The Initiative guides JICA's administration efforts. Emphasizing the importance of assisting developing countries in an effort to combat global warming, the ISD policy framework comprises three categories of assistance: (1) *Cooperation and Capacity Development* to address air pollution, waste disposal, energy saving technologies, forest conservation and afforestation; (2) *ODA Loans* to aid in this effort; (3) *Transfer of Technology* to develop global warming prevention measures in manufacturing plants, set up networks related to global warming prevention technology, and hold workshops on global warming prevention (JICA 2012).

Japan's ODA projects are numerous and coincide with Japan's emphasis on environmental assistance as part of their foreign policy. For example, bilateral assistance to Small Island Developing States (SIDS) in the Caribbean and the Pacific is provided to help these countries overcome vulnerabilities (Ministry of Foreign Affairs 2014: 4). The Japan–Caribbean Climate Change project involves eight Caribbean countries with aims to assist each country with development and implementation of climate change policies (Ministry of Foreign Affairs 2014: 4). Japanese officials and technicians have also provided the necessary technology and training to create a regional platform for information sharing on topics such as "how to manage and operate large dams in a flood situation" or "how to collect and share information following a disaster" (Ministry of Foreign Affairs 2014: 7). In the Pacific region, Japan has worked with government officials of small island nations such as Samoa and the Cook Islands to help develop water management programs (Ministry of Foreign Affairs 2014: 4). In Fiji, Japanese experts are working with weather service workers in to enhance the Fiji Meteorological Service's weather observation and forecasting abilities, and help facilitate the work of the organization to train workers in the region (Ministry of Foreign Affairs 2014: 4).

Developing a regional weather service will help decrease vulnerability to extreme weather events resulting from a lack of preparedness.

Technology transfer

Extreme weather events are more likely to leave residents in poor countries with extensive losses and little means to cope in the aftermath. Lack of insurance, savings, or credit make it almost impossible to replace possessions lost or destroyed by extreme weather such as homes, livestock, food reserves, household items and tools (Blaikie 1994). Japan's assistance in disaster reduction provides aid and support to vulnerable countries. For example, its Stand-by Emergency Credit for Urgent Recovery (SECURE) program provides expedited loans to countries in the disaster recovery stage (Ministry of Foreign Affairs 2014: 5). Along with loans, Japan extends technical cooperation to recipient countries for the implementation and/or reinforcement of disaster prevention measures. For example, the Philippines received technical and financial assistance following Typhoon Yolanda in 2013. Vietnam's central provinces experience frequent flooding and JICA is working with Vietnamese public officials to build "disaster resilient societies" in this region. Using Japanese technological know-how and experience, the project includes the development of integrated flood control plans as well as disaster evacuation systems that target Vietnamese provinces particularly vulnerable to disasters (Graham 2004).

204   *Darlene Budd*

Examples of Japanese technologies used to assist countries with adaptation measures involve the collection and calculations of data using global climate models. Climate change projection models are developed for vulnerable regions and the information is stored in a Data Integration and Analysis System (DIAS) that is available to developing countries. Japanese technicians provide instruction to local officials and workers on how to access, interpret and use the data for forecasting purposes. Additionally, Group on Earth Observations (GEO),[3] data and observation technologies are used to provide solutions to flood and other water-related disasters associated with climate change. Using this information, Japan provides support for the management of water resources in several African and Asian countries. In Pakistan, Cambodia and Tunisia, Japan has helped farmers better understand water cycles as well as agricultural and harvest statistics.

Good governance

Good governance is chiefly concerned with promoting government effectiveness (Grindle 2010: 2). Good governance is an essential foundation for the effectiveness to all government activities including development assistance. Thus, the promotion of good governance is itself one objective of development assistance. The concept of *mitameshi* [quotes above?]informs Japan's good governance philosophy. Specifically, JICA interprets governance as follows:

> The development and operation of all the institutions, including government organizations and systems, the synergetic relationship among government, civil society and the private sector, and the processes of decision making, in order to mobilize, allocate and manage the resources of the country efficiently and in a manner, that reflects the will of the people, with the aim of realizing the stability and development of the country.
>
> (Miyahara n.d.: 68)

As described earlier, the "*mitameshi*" approach was introduced during the Edo period to "build stakeholder consensus in developing solutions." Today, Japan's respect for state sovereignty and emphasis on individualized strategies for ODA projects prioritizes the role of local stakeholders throughout the policy development, administration, and evaluation process.

Approach within the efforts of the UN to the threats of GCC

There have been five major United Nations GCC agreements. The United Nations Framework Convention on Climate Change (UNFCCC) was the product of the COP3 meeting in Kyoto, Japan in 1997. Still in use today, the UNFCCC highlights awareness of GCC and the need for incremental efforts to address GCC. Japan's actions on climate change reflect a desire to participate, contribute, and at times, assume a leadership role to address GCC on a global scale

(Liefferlink et al. 2009 in Takao 2012: 773). Japan's motivations for taking a leadership role include international political standing. In addition, Japan's geographic location and exposure to natural disasters such as typhoons and earthquakes and a lack of natural resources require environmental sensitivity to avoid challenges that potentially compromise Japanese human security.

In terms of international relations, Japan has a tendency to side with the United States. After China (28.2%), the US (16.0%) emits the second highest level of greenhouse gases into the atmosphere (statista.com).[4] Thus, US support for any GCC global strategy is critical for success. The Japanese government and the US Environmental Protection Agency (EPA) have had a formal agreement to cooperate on environmental protection since 1975. Through this agreement, "the two governments exchange expertise; implement cooperative projects; and share information and data on research activities, policies, regulatory practices" (EPA 2017). This bilateral agreement between the two countries tends to extend to the international arena. In addition, Japan's approach within the UN is influenced by their ODA efforts as well as domestic politics. Japanese citizens and environmental groups have also influenced Japan's actions at UN environmental GCC conferences.

The United Nations Conference on Human Environment (UNCHE) held in Sweden in 1972 asserted the concept of a global environment and a global response to the negative effects of human activity. The focus of the conference was to give the international community the opportunity to comprehensively consider the "problems of the human environment" (Galizzi 2005: 953). The Stockholm Summit provided Japanese environmental activists an opportunity to share their stories of the Minamata mercury-poisoning disaster and ultimately influence global environmental activism (Avenell 2014). The 1972 meeting acknowledged environmental issues as a legitimate international concern. With the adoption of an action plan to address global environmental issues, a UN body was created to monitor and oversee future meetings and cooperative efforts. The body is the United Nations Environment Programme (UNEP), still in place today (source).

The next UN Conference on Environment and Development took place in Rio de Janeiro in 1992. Countries attending this conference focused on the relationship between environmental trends and development on the national and international levels (UN 1992). Participants at the Rio Convention or "Earth Summit" produced the Rio Declaration and Agenda 21 that outlined a plan of action for UN organizations and governments to address the negative effect of certain human activities on the environment. Countries also developed the Framework Convention on Climate Change (FCCC). Japan ratified the legally binding Convention in 1993 and became the 21st party to the Convention (Kawashima 2001: 170). Another 152 countries signed on to the Convention acknowledging the need to stabilize the level of greenhouse gases in the atmosphere, while ensuring that food production is not threatened, and allowing for continued economic development. Delegates agreed that developed countries should take the lead in reducing levels of greenhouse gas emissions. However, no specific emission

206 *Darlene Budd*

reduction targets were set, and time frames or penalties for violators were not determined. Participating countries agreed to meet regularly at COPs (Conferences of the Parties) to discuss implementation details of the UNFCCC objectives.

In terms of Japan's participation in the conference, Prime Minister, Kiichi Miyazawa, promised to increase foreign aid for environmental projects and acknowledged the scientific challenge presented by the need for serious pollution control. His speech was circulated among participants (Lewis 1992). Miyazawa did not attend the Summit due to debates taking place in the Japanese Diet over Japan's involvement in overseas military operations (Oka June 12, 1992). While Japanese participation in the 1972 and 1992 conferences was minimal, the political significance of the conferences resonated with Japanese officials who would not only attend future meetings but go on to host the next UN conference on GCC.

Following the two COPs meetings in Berlin and Geneva, Japan hosted the COP3 in Kyoto, Japan, in 1997. Japanese officials viewed the Kyoto meeting as an opportunity to capitalize on their experiences and research advancements in innovative technology and play a leadership role in the fight against GCC. Having addressed manufacturing waste and pollution in the 1960s and 1970s, Japan was "spending more of its gross national product on anti-pollution measures than any other country in the world" by the 1980s and "had the strictest pollution regulations in the world" (Fisher 2003: 188). However, Japan's high level of energy efficiency made it extremely difficult for Japan to make further improvements (Kawashima 2001: 167). Domestically, industry groups would challenge Japan's ambitious global strategy.

At the 1997 meeting in Kyoto, extensive negotiations over alternative formulas took place over the course of ten days. Ultimately, Japan agreed to accept the 6% emission reduction target based on 1990 levels during the 2008–2012 period. The meeting produced the Kyoto Protocol and included:

1 Emission-reduction targets of greenhouse gases for each of the member countries
2 A greenhouse gas emission-trading program
3 Agreement to hold future meetings to decide on penalties for countries who violate the agreement and to set regulation rules of the emission trading program.

The next step for Japan was to put policies in place to implement the Kyoto Protocol emission reductions. The Law Concerning the Promotion of the Measures to Cope with Global Warming was passed in 1998 and 'the Basic Guideline for Mitigation of Climate Change' was adopted in 1999 to deal with issues not included in the Global Warming law. The Law Concerning Rational use of Energy mentioned earlier was amended and in place in 1999. The law requires Japanese corporations to produce only the most energy efficient appliance models. At this particular time, the Japanese government is also considering a

Japan and global climate change 207

domestic emission trading and a carbon tax (Kawashima 2001: 178)[5] and is clearly motivated to achieve the 6% emissions reduction target (Fisher 2003: 190).

Despite the US withdrawal from the Kyoto Protocol during the Bush Administration in 2001, and some push back from Japanese industry, Japan ratified the Kyoto Protocol in 2002 (Kouchakji 2015: 1). In order for the Protocol to be implemented, at least 55 nations of the UN Framework Convention were needed to ratify the agreement. With developed countries representing a total of 55% of the greenhouse gas emissions in 1990, and the US responsible for 36% of the 55%, the US withdrawal decreases the likelihood that the Protocol will be ratified and jeopardizes the entire concept of addressing issues of GCC on a global level (Borger March 29, 2001). The Kyoto Protocol became a reality on February 16, 2005, seven years after it was first negotiated, and the goal of getting countries responsible for a total of 55% of the global emissions was achieved with the signature of Russia (Henry & Sundstrom 2007: 47).

In 2006, Japanese Prime Minister Shinzo Abe announced the "Cool Earth 50" initiative that included a pledge to cut Japan's emissions in half by 2050. He also hinted at the idea of expanding the initiative worldwide. The same year, Japan's ambassador to the UN, Tsuruoka Koji, presented Japan's plan as the foundation for a global strategy: "As a responsible member of the international community and the host country of the negotiations that led to the Kyoto Protocol, Japan is striving to take the lead in tackling global warming" (Japan Today August 2, 2007). Similar statements were reiterated at the Davos Forum in 2008 when Prime Minister Yasuo Fukuda pledged a five-year, $10 billion fund to help developing countries combat GCC. He also mentioned plans to cooperate with the US and EU to create a "Cool Earth Partnership" fund to work multilaterally on climate change mitigation (Holroyd 2009: 81). These statements and initiatives display Japan's ongoing commitment to addressing GCC on a global level in cooperation with UN members.

At the 2009 COP15 meeting in Copenhagen, Denmark, Japanese Prime Minister Hatoyama called on developed and developing countries to work together to further promote the initiatives begun under the Kyoto Protocol to reduce greenhouse gases. The "Hatoyama Initiative" included a pledge to reduce Japanese emissions by 25% by 2020, based on 1990 levels. Stating that Japan alone cannot halt global warming, Hatoyama called on developed countries to also pledge to set ambitious targets to not only reduce emission levels but to also assist developing countries by committing to offer additional public and private financing. Such assistance, he noted, should be recognized in a measurable, reportable and verifiable manner (Gatdula September 28, 2009). In monetary terms, Japan pledged $11 billion in 2010–2012, more than the EU combined ($10.6 billion) and the US ($3.6 billion) (Reuters 2009).

The Paris Agreement's central aim is to "strengthen the global response to the threat of climate change" by keeping a global temperature rise this century below 2°C above pre-industrial levels and to pursue efforts to limit the temperature increase even further to 1.5°C (UNFCCC 2017). The pledge to keep warming "well below" 2°C (3.6°F) was viewed as particularly ambitious but necessary to reverse the current trend in temperature increases (Upton March 17, 2016). Absent such a reversal, heat waves, floods and mosquito-borne epidemics are forecasted to become increasingly common and a threat to human security.

Japan signed the Paris Agreement on December 2015 and ratified the agreement on November 8, 2016. At the signing ceremony, Prime Minister Shinzo Abe stated, "We will play a leading role in the global community's efforts to deal with climate change and fulfill our responsibility to safely pass down this precious Earth to our children and their children." As a signatory Japan plans to cut greenhouse gas emissions by 26% from 2013 levels by 2030 by switching to more efficient power generation and promoting use of energy-saving light bulbs among other measures. It also aims for an 80% cut in emissions by 2050 (*Japan Times* November 9, 2016). Japan's delay in signing the Paris Agreement was, in part, due to the energy challenges it faces as it struggles to find alternative sources to replace the electricity once generated from Japan's 43 nuclear power plants that were shut down following the disastrous Fukushima meltdown five years ago (Upton March 17, 2016). In March 2017, the Abe government abandoned opposition to the construction of new coal power plants. Such a decision likely casts doubt on Japan's ability to meet targets to cut greenhouse gas emissions.

Because of the domestic context, Japan failed to ratify the agreement before November 4, 2016 and as a result was unable to participate in the COP22 meeting of the treaty signatories held in Marrakesh, Morocco. In order for Japan to have played a leadership role in this meeting ratification of the treaty had to have taken place before October 19. This was the date set for countries to attend the talks as formal members of the group. According to one Japanese news editorial, "the situation is threatening Japan's international stature and credibility, which have been built through strenuous diplomatic efforts over years, including those for winning support for the Kyoto Protocol, a climate agreement negotiated in the 1990s" (Brasor January 6, 2018). Some Japanese environmental activists also worry that the US withdrawal from the Paris Agreement may provide the pretext for Japan's coal and fossil fuel lobbies to pressure the Abe Administration to consider increased use of coal and oil instead of pursuing the goal of a low carbon society (Johnston June 2, 2017).

Limiting factors on the capacities to deal with GCC from a security perspective

As noted above, five factors influence Japanese GCC decisions and policy: (1) energy security; (2) political party in power; (3) state of the economy; (4) public opinion; and, (5) the United States. Of the factors that influence Japan's commitment to aggressively addressing GCC, energy security is most influential. On March 11, 2011, the 9.0-magnitude undersea earthquake originated just 50 miles off of Japan's eastern coastline. The most powerful earthquake in Japanese history produced a devastating tsunami with waves of over 130 feet. The tsunami hit the Fukushima Daiichi Nuclear Power Plant resulting in the meltdown of two nuclear reactors. Over 20,000 lives were lost, entire towns were destroyed and the terror of radioactivity brought Japan's nuclear energy program to a halt (Samuels 2013: ix). This triple catastrophe, referred to "3.11," directly influenced Japan's GCC policies and goals. In the wake of the disaster, Japanese public opinion polls found that a large percentage of citizens were demanding the shutdown of all nuclear plants. Shutting down nuclear power plants will result in renewed dependence on foreign oil and gas imports and other fossil fuels that contribute to CO_2 levels. This shift suggests that Japanese citizens have become more focused on the country's energy security and less concerned with GCC or they are not willing to endure the perceived risks of nuclear power for the sake of GCC.

Prior to the meltdown, 65% of Japanese citizens supported the expansion of nuclear power (Aldrich et al. July 20, 2015). By July 2015, the percentage of individuals in favor of pursuing a nuclear energy policy flipped and nearly 70% of respondents favored eliminating the use nuclear power in the country (Aldrich et al. July 20, 2015). Following this shift in public opinion, at least one major opposition party—the Democratic Party of Japan—proposed a phase out of nuclear power by the 2030s (Aldrich et al. July 20, 2015).

All 43 of Japan's operational nuclear reactors were shut down and remained so for two years. Nuclear power had provided nearly one-third of Japan's power while keeping energy costs low. With the introduction of strict safety standards and inspections three reactors were brought on line. After close monitoring, one and then two of the reactors were shut down again for safety reasons. By June 2017, five reactors have been restarted and are in use (Phys.org 2017) Japanese officials, including Yoiichi Miyazawa an LDP member of the House of Councillors acknowledge the tradeoffs of creating a low carbon society stating that, "It would be impossible to achieve all these three things simultaneously: Keep nuclear plants offline, while also trying to curb carbon dioxide, and maintain the same electricity costs" (Kurtenbach & Yamaguchi August 15, 2015).

Opposition to nuclear power has continued despite rising energy costs for both individual consumers and large corporations (Aldrich et al. July 20, 2015). Thus, political pressure and domestic politics, in the wake of the Fukashima disaster, limit the historically demonstrated capacity of Japan to address GCC. There have been several tangible examples of shifting voting patterns on environmental issues. For example, after four unsuccessful attempts running for office as an advocate of nuclear power, Ryuichi Yoneyama campaigned against the restart of Japan's largest nuclear power plant, and won the 2016 gubernatorial race in Niigata Prefecture. Backed by smaller, left-wing political parties Yoneyama beat former mayor Tamio Mori, the candidate supported by Prime Minister Shinzo Abe's pro-nuclear LDP. According to an exit poll conducted by NHK broadcasting, voters in Niigata voting for mayor opposed restarting the plant by 73% to 27% (Reuters October 17, 2016).

As noted above, domestic politics and the state of the Japanese economy also influence GCC policy. The Japanese economy has been sluggish for decades following the burst of Japan's "bubble economy" in 1992 (Fackler December 25,

210 *Darlene Budd*

2005). An upward trend in economic conditions during the early 2000s ended abruptly with the 2007–2008 global financial crisis. While Japan did not suffer from a housing collapse or toxic assets as occurred in the US, its economy suffered considerably due in large part to the steep decline in demand for products in the US and the EU (Fukao & Yuan June 8, 2009). Prime Minister Abe was elected to office in 2012 and promptly introduced "Abenomics" that used structural policies to increase competition, reform labor markets, and expand trade partnership, Abe's 2015 goal was to expand GDP by 20% (Aoki & Yoshida September 24, 2015). The start of 2017 marked the fifth consecutive quarter of recorded growth in Japan. This is the longest continuous growth period in more than a decade Analysts however, remain cautious as inflation levels and wages remain low (Ujikane May 17, 2017). Stable energy costs are critical to maintaining current growth levels. Whether Japanese citizens are willing to accept higher fuel and utility costs remains to be seen.

At this point in time, however, the policies of the Social Democratic Party along with left-leaning groups appear to be more in line with citizen views and values that reflect human security concerns and the LDP will likely need to take public opinion seriously.

Concluding remarks

The willingness of Japan to act on GCC is also influenced by the US–Japan relationship. Donald Trump's decision to withdraw the US from the Paris Agreement was a disappointment to many Japanese government officials, business leaders and environmental groups. "America's announcement that it is pulling out of the Paris climate change agreement is regrettable. We thought we could cooperate on climate change with the U.S. based on the agreement," was Chief Cabinet Secretary Yoshihide Suga's response. While, Foreign Minister Fumio Kishida stated that Japan would "work with other parties to the Paris agreement for its steady and full implementation" (Johnston June 2, 2017).

In addition to the withdrawal from the Paris Agreement, Trump has also vowed to discontinue funding for the UN Framework Convention on Climate Change and redirect climate programming funds to infrastructure projects (Chemnik 2016). However, President Obama's executive order ratifying the Paris Agreement may not be as easy to undo as some Republicans claim. Ultimately, isolationist moves by the United States may benefit Japan as it continues to strengthen its economy, enhance its military capabilities and play a key role in developing innovative technology to combat GCC.

Notes

1 Shinzo Abe is a member of the Liberal Democratic Party (LDP). His sudden resignation in 2007 resulted in the election of Yasuo Fakuda, member of the Social Democratic Party (SDP).
2 China, the US, and India each lead in one policy area and Russia is clearly behind.

3 GEO is a global network comprising government institutions, academic and research institutions, businesses, and scientists working together to create innovative solutions to global climate change that transcend national and disciplinary boundaries. www. earthobservations.org/geo_community.php

4 India (6.24%) and the Russian Federation (4.53%) are the next largest emitters of GHGs. Japan (3.67%) is in fifth place.

5 As of 2016, Japan's Environmental Ministry is still recommending such a tax (Jiji (1/31/2016).

References

Aldrich Daniel, Platte, James, & Sklarew, Jennifer F. (2015 July 20). Despite meltdowns, a tsunami and public opposition, Japan may soon restart a nuclear power plant—or several. *Washington Post.* Accessed March 4, 2017: www.washingtonpost. com/news/monkey-cage/wp/2015/07/20/despite-meltdowns-a-tsunami-and-public-opposition-japan-may-soon-restart-a-nuclear-power-plant-or-several/?utm_term=. 2a680daca5b6

Aoki, Mizuho & Yoshida, Reiji (2015 September 24). Abe aims arrows at new targets with three fresh goals for 'Abenomics,' 20% rise in GDP. *The Japan Times.* Accessed March 1, 2017: www.japantimes.co.jp/news/2015/09/24/national/politics-diplomacy/abe-outlines-new-goals-abenomics-20-rise-gdp/#.WMS0FGQrJPs

Avenell, Simon (2014 August 13). Japan's environmental nuggets, *Asian Currents*, Asian Studies Association of Australia. Accessed February 28, 2017: http://asaa.asn.au/japans-environmental-nuggets/

Blaikie, Piers, Cannon, Terry, Davis, Ian, & Wisner, Ben (1994). *At risk: Natural hazards, people's vulnerability and disasters.* London: Psychology Press.

Brasor, Philip (2018 January 6). Japan spends scant energy on renewable. *The Japan Times.* Accessed: www.japantimes.co.jp/news/2018/01/06/national/media-national/japan-spends-scant-energy-renewables/#.WnExPOg-d6w

Borger, Julian (2001 March 29). Bush kills global warming treaty, *Guardian.* Accessed February 22, 2017: www.theguardian.com/environment/2001/mar/29/globalwarming. usnews

Carson, Rachel, Darling, Lois, & Darling, Louis (1962) *Silent spring.* Boston, MA: Houghton Mifflin.

Chasek, Pamela, Downie, David & Welsh Brown, Janet (2006). *Global environmental politics*, 4th ed. Boulder, CO: Westview.

Chemnik, Jean (2016 November 10). Could Trump simply withdraw U.S. from Paris Climate Agreement?" *Scientific American.* Accessed January 30, 2018: www.scientific american.com/article/could-trump-simply-withdraw-u-s-from-paris-climate-agreement/

City of New York (2015). OneNYC. Accessed March 10, 2017: www.nyc.gov/html/planyc/html/home/home.shtml

Compston, Hugh & Bailey, Ian (2014). Climate policy strength compared: China, the US, the EU, India, Russia, and Japan. *Climate Policy*, 16(2), 145–164. Accessed March 10, 2017: www.tandfonline.com/doi/abs/10.1080/14693062.2014.991908?journalCode =tcpo20

EPA (2017). EPA collaboration with Japan. Accessed: www.epa.gov/international-cooperation/epa-collaboration-japan

European Economic Community (EEC) (1978). Concentration regarding international activities in the field of the environment (CRD III/REC, Topic III), paper presented at

212 *Darlene Budd*

the International Conference on Chlorofluoromethanes, Munich, December 6–8, Munich: EEC.

Fackler, Martin (2005 December 25). Take it from Japan: Bubbles hurt. *New York Times.* Accessed March 5, 2017: www.nytimes.com/2005/12/25/business/yourmoney/take-it-from-japan-bubbles-hurt.html

Fisher, Dana R. (2003). Beyond Kyoto: The formation of a Japanese climate change regime, in Paul G. Harris (Ed.), *Global warming and East Asia: The domestic and international politics of climate* (pp. 187–206). New York, NY: Routledge.

Fukao, Kyoji & Yuan, Tangjun (2009 June 8). Why is Japan so heavily affected by the global economic crisis? An analysis based on the Asian international input-output tables. VOX Centre for Economic Policy Research. Accessed March 7, 2017: http://voxeu.org/article/why-has-japan-been-so-hard-hit-global-crisis

Galizzi, Paolo (2005). From Stockholm to New York, via Rio and Johannesburg: Has the environment lost its way on the global agenda? *Fordham International Law Journal,* 29, 952–1008.

Gatdula, Donnabelle L. (2009 September 28) Japan seeks unified stance on climate change, *The Philippine Star.* Accessed March 8, 2017: www.philstar.com/business/508799/japan-seeks-unified-stance-climate-change

Government of Japan (2008). *Fukuda vision.* Accessed February 28, 2017: www.kantei.go.jp/jp/hukudaspeech/2008/06/09speech.html

Graham, Jeff (2004). Japan's regional environmental leadership. *Asian Studies Review* 28(3), 283–302.

Grindle, Merilee (2010 June). Good governance: The inflation of an idea. Harvard Kennedy School Faculty Research Working Paper Series, RWO 10–023:2. Accessed March 10, 2017: https://research.hks.harvard.edu/publications/getFile.aspx?Id=562

Hachiya, Noriyuki (2006). The history of minamata disease: Entering the second half century, JIMAJ Energy Services. Accessed March 10, 2017: www.med.or.jp/english/pdf/2006_03/112_118.pdf

Harris, Paul G. (Ed.) (2004) *Global warming and East Asia: The domestic and international politics of climate change.* London: Routledge.

Henry, L.A. & Sundstrom, L.M. (2007). Russia and the Kyoto Protocol: Seeking an alignment of interests and image. *Global Environmental Politics,* 7(4), 47–69. The MIT Press. Retrieved March 8, 2017, from Project MUSE database.

Holroyd, Carin. (2009) National mobilization and global engagement: Understanding Japan's response to global climate change initiatives. *Asian Perspective,* 33(2), 73–96.

Holzinger, Kathirina, Knill, Christopher, & Sommerer, Thomas (2011). Is there convergence of national environmental policies? An analysis of policy outputs in 24 OECD countries. *Environmental Politics,* 20(1), 22–41.

Japan Times (2016 November 9). Japan ratifies Paris climate pact, will become signatory in 30 days. Accessed March 2, 2017: www.japantimes.co.jp/news/2016/11/09/national/japan-ratifies-paris-climate-pact-will-become-signatory-30-days/#.WDENi7wrLrk

Japan Today. (2007 August 2). Japan recommends removing ties, jackets, turning AC down at U.N. Accessed: www.japantoday.com/jp/news/414010.

JICA (2012). JICA assistance for climate compatible development in Small Island Developing States (SIDS. Accessed February 28, 2017: www.jica.go.jp/english/our_work/climate_change/pdf/policy_sids_03.pdfJiji. (2016 January 31) Carbon tax proposed by environment panel to achieve Japan's lofty emissions cut goal. Accessed March 8, 2017: www.japantimes.co.jp/news/2016/01/31/national/carbon-tax-proposed-environment-panel-achieve-japans-lofty-emissions-cut-goal/#.WMRg5GQrJPs

Johnston, Eric. (2017 June 2). Japan disappointed by Trump's decision to quit Paris agreement. *Japan Times*. Accessed July 31, 2017: www.japantimes.co.jp/news/2017/06/02/national/japan-disappointed-trumps-decision-quit-paris-agreement/#.WYCm7fryur8.

Kameyama, Yasuko (2003). Japan's foreign policy: From reactive to proactive, in Paul G. Harris (Ed.), *Global warming and East Asia: The domestic and international politics of climate* (pp. 135–151). New York, NY: Routledge.

Kawashima, Yasuko. (2001). Japan and climate change: Responses and explanations. *Energy and Environment*, 12(2), 167–179.

Kouchakji, Katie. (2015). Japan: An emissions trading case study. IETA Climate Challenges Market Solutions. Accessed February 27, 2017: www.edf.org/sites/default/files/japan-case-study-may2015.pdf

Kurtenbach, Elaine & Mari Yamaguchi. (2015 August 15). Japan restarts reactor, committed to nuclear power despite Fukushima fiasco. 89.3 KPCC. Accessed March 2, 2017: www.scpr.org/news/2015/08/11/53715/japan-committed-to-nuclear-power-despite-fukushima/

Lewis, Paul. (1992 June 14). The Earth Summit; Negotiators in Rio agree to increase aid to Third World. Accessed March 10, 2017: www.nytimes.com/1992/06/14/world/the-earth-summit-negotiators-in-rio-agree-to-increase-aid-to-third-world.html

Mairie de Paris (2007). *Paris climate and energy action plan*. Paris: Mairie de Paris. Accessed March 10, 2017: www.energy-cities.eu/IMG/pdf/Paris_climate_protection_plan_2007.pdf

Matsumura, Hiroshi. (2001). Japanese ratification of the Kyoto Protocol. *Climate Policy*, 1(3), 343–362.

McKean, Margaret. (1981). *Environmental protest and citizen politics in Japan*. Berkeley, CA: University of California Press.

Ministry of Foreign Affairs (2014 November). Japan's adaptation initiatives. The Government of Japan. Accessed February 21, 2017: www.mofa.go.jp/files/000062532.pdf

Miyahara, Chie. (n.d.) *JICA's approach to good governance and anti-corruption*. Accessed January 30, 2018: www.unafei.or.jp/english/pdf/PDF_GG5_Seminar/GG5_Adviser1.pdf

Molina, Mario J. & Rowland, F.S. (1974). Stratospheric sink for chlorofluoromethanes: Chlorine atom-catalyzed destruction of ozone, *Nature*, 249, 810–812. Accessed March 10, 2017: www.nature.com/nature/journal/v249/n5460/abs/249810a0.html

OECD (2017) *Development aid rises again in 2016*. Accessed: www.oecd.org/dac/financing-sustainable-development/development-finance-data/ODA-2016-detailed-summary.pdf.

Ohta, Hiroshi (2000) Japanese environmental foreign policy. In T. Inoguchi and J. Purnendra (Eds.), *Japanese foreign policy today* (pp. 96–121). New York: Palgrave.

Oka, Takashi. (1992 June 12). Japan debates peacekeeping 'til the cows come. *Christian Science Monitor*. Accessed February 28, 2017: www.csmonitor.com/1992/0612/12182.html

Phys.org. (2017 June 6). Nuclear-wary Japan restarts another atomic reactor. Accessed August 1, 2017: https://phys.org/news/2017-06-nuclear-wary-japan-restarts-atomic-reactor.html

Puppim de Oliveira, Jose Antonio (2009). The implementation of climate change related policies at the subnational level: An analysis of three countries. *Habitat International*, 33: 253–259.

Reuters (2009 December 18). Factbox: Main points on the Copenhagen Accord. Online Japan's Oil imports. Accessed August 1, 2017: www.reuters.com/article/us-copenhagen-climate-accord-factbox-idUSTRE5BI00M20091219

Reuters (2016 October 17). Japanese anti-nuclear candidate wins election at site of world's biggest atomic power station. Accessed March 10, 2017: www.theguardian.com/world/2016/oct/17/japanese-anti-nuclear-candidate-wins-election-at-site-of-worlds-biggest-atomic-power-station

Roppongi, Hitomi, Aki Suwa & Jose A. Puppim DeOliveira (2016 March). *Innovating in sub-national climate policy: the mandatory emissions reduction scheme in Tokyo.* Climate Policy. Accessed March 10, 2017: www.tandfonline.com/doi/abs/10.1080/146 93062.2015.1124749?journalCode=tcpo20

Sabin Center for Climate Change Law (2017). *Japan.* Columbia Law School. Accessed February 22, 2017: http://columbiaclimatelaw.com/resources/climate-change-laws-of-the-world-2/climate-change-laws-of-the-world-database/japan/

Samuels, Richard J. (2013). *3.11: Disaster and change in Japan.* Ithaca, NY: Cornell University Press.

Sato, Atsuko (2003). Knowledge in the global atmospheric policy process: The case of Japan. In Paul G. Harris (Ed.), *Global warming and East Asia: The domestic and international politics of climate* (pp. 167–186). New York, NY: Routledge.

Soble, Jonathan. (2016 March 10). Court orders one of Japan's two operating nuclear plants to shut down. *New York Times.* Accessed February 28, 2017: www.nytimes.com/2016/03/10/world/asia/japan-nuclear-plant.html?ref=asia&_r=0

Statista.com (2017). *The largest producers of CO₂ emissions worldwide in 2016, based on their share of global CO₂ emissions.* Accessed March 10, 2017: www.statista.com/statistics/271748/the-largest-emitters-of-co2-in-the-world/)

Stoel, Jr., Thomas B. (1983). Fluorocarbons: Mobilizing concern and action. In David A. Kay & Harold K. Jacobson (Eds.) *Environmental protection: The international dimension* (pp. 53–71). Allanheld, NJ: Osmun.

Stokes, Bruce (2016). Japanese back global engagement despite concern about domestic economy, Pew Research Center, 2016. Accessed July 31, 2017.

Sugiyama, Noriko & Takeuchi, Tsuneo (2011). Local policies for climate change in Japan. *The Journal of Environment & Development,* 17(4), 424–441.

Sunaga, Kazuo. (2004) *The reshaping of Japan's Official Development Assistance (ODA) charter.* APEC Study Center Columbia University, 2004. Accessed March 10, 2017: https://pdfs.semanticscholar.org/ed1f/110055e1376dc8d072e6a82e27b0ca16dd03.pdf

Takahashi, Wataru (2011 October 24). *The Japanese financial sector's transition from high growth to the 'lost decades': A market economy perspective.* Discussion Paper Series RIEB, Kobe University. Accessed March 10, 2017: www.rieb.kobe-u.ac.jp/academic/ra/dp/English/DP2011-29.pdf

Takao, Yasuo (2012). The transformation of Japan's environmental policy. *Environmental Politics,* 21(5), 772–790.

Thernstrom, Amy. (2005) Japanese ODA at 50: An assessment. *Woodrow Wilson International Center for Scholars,* 2005. 1–5. Accessed March 9, 2017: www.wilsoncenter.org/sites/default/files/AsiaReport128.pdf

Tokyo Metropolitan Government (2016). Tokyo cap-and-trade program. *Current Topics.* Accessed March 9, 2017: www.metro.tokyo.jp/ENGLISH/TOPICS/2016/161116_01.htm

Ujikane, Keiko. (2017 May 17). *Japan is set for its longest run of economic growth in a decade,* Bloomberg.org. Accessed August 1, 2017: www.bloomberg.com/news/articles/2017-05-16/japan-is-set-for-its-longest-run-of-economic-growth-in-a-decade

UN (1992). *UN conference on environment and development.* Accessed March 9, 2017: www.un.org/geninfo/bp/enviro.html

UNFCCC (2017). *The Paris Agreement.* Accessed: January 30, 2018: http://unfccc.int/paris_agreement/items/9485.php

Upton, John (2016 March 17). How the world has changed since the Paris Agreement on global warming, *Scientific American.* Accessed March 9, 2017: www.scientific american.com/article/how-the-world-has-changed-since-the-paris-agreement-on-global-warming/

Warrick, R. and Rahman, A.A. (1992). Environmental and Socio-political Aspects of Sea-Level Rise. In I. Mintzer (Ed.) *Confronting climate change: Risks, implications, and responses.* Cambridge: Stockholm Environment Institute and Cambridge University Press.

Watanabe, Tsugihiro & Kume Takashi (2009). A general adaptation strategy for climate change impacts on paddy cultivation: Special reference to the Japanese context. *Paddy Water Environ*, 7, 313–320.

Weiss, Edith Brown (1998). Vienna convention for the protection of the ozone layer. Accessed March 10, 2017: http://legal.un.org/avl/ha/vcpol/vcpol.html

10 Russia and global climate change

Ana Karaman

Russia is the largest country in the world by its landmass and ninth largest by its population size. It spans 11 time zones and covers a variety of environments including permafrost covering 60% of the country's landmass—an area in excess of ten million square kilometers (approx. 3.9 M square miles). Over the last decade, air temperatures in Russia have been rising 2.5 times faster than the average globally with an average annual increase in temperature in Russia of 0.42°C compared with the global annual average 0.17°C for the same period of time (Lazare, 2015). Russian scientists attribute this increase in air temperatures and recent unprecedented increase in average annual precipitation rates and permafrost degradation to global climate change (GCC) (Fedorov & Konstantinov, 2009). Several recent natural disasters and catastrophic events have especially heightened the severity of the impact of GCC throughout the Russian Federation on its human and state security.

This chapter examines the effects of GCC on human and state security in the Russian Federation. Following this introduction, the next part of this chapter discusses the impact of GCC on the Russian population, its economy, and its indigenous communities. Following this, an overview of the response on the domestic level to the impacts of GCC is presented; this material will cover the Russian Climate Doctrine, mitigation and adaptation measures and strategies, and specific Russian regions particularly affected by climate change. The Russian response to GCC impact on the international level is delineated in the next part. Here, the nation's dependency on oil and gas exports and the potential in the development of the Russian Arctic and the concomitant security concerns are shown to have a large impact on the evolving international approach to the politics of GCC. The final part of the chapter provides some conclusions.

Climate change and impact on the Russian population

The August 2013 catastrophic flood in the Amur region (river on the Russian–Chinese border) was recorded as the worst flood in Russia in the last 120 years. It impacted Amur Oblast, Jewish Autonomous Oblast, and Khabarovsk Krai. The total territory under the flood reached more than eight million square kilometers, encompassing 37 municipal regions and 235 localities and more than

400,000 people were impacted with about 100,000 being evacuated from the flood-impacted areas (RT News, 2015).[1] Russia's anomalous heat during the summer of 2010 led to 56,000 deaths as a result of overheating, droughts, forest fires, and smog (Kondratenko, 2016).[2] In summer 2016, thawing permafrost led to an outbreak of anthrax in the Yamal Peninsula, Siberia, where 90 people were hospitalized and more than 2,000 reindeer died (Interfax/Ведомости, 2016).[3]

Climate change impact on Lake Baikal has become a major concern from the perspective of freshwater supply. Situated in southeast Siberia, the 3.15-million-ha Lake Baikal is the oldest (25 million years) and deepest (1,700 m) lake in the world and a UNESCO world heritage site. It contains 20% of the world's total unfrozen freshwater reserve. Known as the 'Galapagos of Russia', its age and isolation have produced one of the world's richest and most unusual freshwater faunas, which is of exceptional value to evolutionary science. Of its 2,500 known animal species, 75% are endemic. Of particular note are the 350 species of amphipod shrimps, most of them endemic and gigantic in size, and its iconic freshwater seal (nerpa). The lake has experienced a rapid warming and the average water temperature increased by 1.2°C in the period from 1946 to 2004. In addition, since 2014 Lake Baikal has experienced unusually low water. In February 2015, the Russian government had to issue an administrative order permitting continued usage of the lake water to support the functions of the economic and social spheres of the region during the autumn and winter period when the lake level was below the set minimum (Kondratenko, 2016).

According to the Russian Ministry of Natural Resources, direct and indirect consequences of climate changes will lead to an average 1 to 2% drop in the country's gross domestic product (GDP) by 2030 with some regions losing as much as 4 to 5% of their GDP during the same period (Davidova, 2017). For example, the economic impact of the 2013 Amur flood was estimated at approximately $32 M (RIA, 2013). In addition, the thawing of the permafrost has led to soil instability and, consequently, damage to the foundation of the infrastructure including oil and gas pipelines. According to Russian sources, damage to oil and gas pipelines in Western Siberia costs Russia up to 55 billion rubles annually (Kondratenko, 2016).

The effects of global warming especially impact the indigenous communities of the Russian North and Far East whose livelihood is directly tied to the ecosystem because fluctuations in air temperature have significant implications for permafrost. Permafrost degradation and increasing air temperatures lead to shorter periods of extreme winter cold and much warmer summers triggering altered seasonal timings (phenology) and ranges of animals and plants (Roshydromet, 2008). One example of the direct impacts of increased temperatures in the northern regions is the significantly reduced usability of the winter roads built over frozen rivers and lakes—*зимники (zimniki)*—used to deliver goods during winter months to the regions that are otherwise accessible only by air, train, or barges (Makarov, 2014). As a result, prices on goods and services increase, leading to lower standards of living. On the geological level, thawed permafrost leaks methane gas that is at least ten times more potent as a GHG than CO_2.

Russia's response to the GCC impacts on domestic level

The climate doctrine

While environmental concerns historically have been of low interest to the Russian general public, recent high publicity events related to rapid deterioration of permafrost and other climate changes heightened the importance of climate politics. To address the issues of climate change, the Russian government has developed the Climate Doctrine of the Russian Federation (adopted December 17, 2009). The Doctrine is a compilation of goals, principles, measures, and implementations of consolidated domestic and international politics of the Russian Federation with respect to climate change and its consequences. The scientific basis for the Doctrine includes the acknowledgment of the anthropogenic nature of climate change that leads to unfavorable and dangerous consequences for human beings and the environment. The Doctrine underscores that one of the primary characteristics of climate change is that it is always lagging behind anthropogenic factors as well as the efforts to mitigate them. From the perspective of climate politics, such a delay presents a critical factor for the adaptation to the unavoidable climate change consequences in the future. Specifically, it stresses that Russia is experiencing critical climate changes that have negative impacts on the socio-economic development of the country, in general, but also on the lives and health of the population, in particular. The Doctrine lists the following climate changes as the most critical: (1) increased heath risk and mortality rates for some social groups of the population; (2) increased repeated droughts in some regions and extreme levels of precipitation and floods leading to soil deterioration in other regions; (3) increased risk of forest fires; (4) thaw of permafrost in Siberia leading to deterioration of infrastructure; (5) shifts in ecological balance; (6) spread of infectious diseases; and finally, (7) increased use of electricity for air-conditioning during summer seasons for most localities (Kremlin, 2009).

While being based on scientific studies, the Doctrine is first and foremost a political document that stresses the necessity of finding a balance between the need to address the problems of climate change, including those in its most extreme manifestations (heat waves, floods, droughts, etc.) and the need for effective economic development and social justice. In this realization, the search for an appropriate balance is subject to political decision-making rather than a scientific solution. The Doctrine specifies that the strategic goal of Russian climate politics is a provision of secure and stable development of the Russian Federation including institutional, economic, ecologic, and social aspects of development in the conditions of climate change and resulting threats. As such, the Doctrine lists the following major principles of Russian climate politics: (1) global character of the Russian interests in the area of climate change and its consequences; (2) superiority of national interest in the articulation and implementation of climate politics; (3) clarity and transparency of the climate politics; (4) acknowledgement for the need of domestic actions as well as Russia's equal partnership in international research programs and projects in the area of climate; comprehensive accounting for potential losses and gains associated with climate change; and, (5) precautions during planning and implementation of measures to protect the humans, economy, and the state from the unfavorable consequences of climate change (Kremlin, 2009).

The Doctrine stresses that expected climate changes cause a threat to Russian state security and hence it is critical for Russia to develop an independent ability to evaluate the climate change data and to draw conclusions about their impact on the Russian Federation. At the same time, the Doctrine acknowledges the need for a clear and transparent exchange of ideas and data on all levels of cooperation including international. The Doctrine notes the unique characteristics of the Russian Federation in solving the problems of climate change (Kremlin, 2009). On the other hand, the Doctrine notes that climate change has positive implications for industrial and economic development of the Russian Federation. Among the positive consequences are the following: reduced use of energy for heating during the cold seasons; improved condition for marine transportation in the Arctic seas as well as simplified access to Arctic oil and its development; improvement of structure and increased variety of crops and livestock; and, increased productivity of the boreal forest (Taiga).

The Doctrine highlights the uniqueness of the Russian Federation as manifested by its favorable position to adapt to climate changes compared with other countries and regions. Specifically, the Doctrine states that Russia's large landmass, significant water resources, and low population density in the areas especially impacted by climate changes, provide a high potential for the country to adapt. As a result, the Doctrine states that while forming Russian climate politics, including the country's position on the international level, it is important to take into consideration the size of the landmass, the relatively low population density, the need for increased transportation, and the cold climate that as well leads to additional energy expenditures (Kremlin, 2009).

To summarize, the Doctrine states that GCC is one of the most serious international problems of the twenty-first century that poses a threat to state and human security and cannot be resolved exclusively via scientific methods but is, indeed, subject to political choices. It stresses the need to develop a balanced approach to resolving climate change problems that accounts for the need of economic development and takes into consideration a comprehensive analysis of negative as well as positive implications that climate change has for the Russian Federation. In developing its position at the international level, the Doctrine identifies Russia's domestic interest of economic development as the foundation. Therefore, for the Russian Federation, the question of climate politics is, first and foremost, a question of the state security in relation to the country's economic development and hence, Russia's position with respect to GCC cannot be separated from its plans, goals, and circumstances of economic development.

Mitigation and adaptation measures

Russia has been taking steps to develop measures to reduce the losses and damage from natural disasters. The 2014 Progress Report on the Implementation of Climate Doctrine identifies adaptation measures to prevent growth in the frequency of forest and peat fires; mitigation of production loss risks in agriculture; limiting negative impacts caused by more frequent floods due to higher rainfall and rising sea levels; and, mitigation of mountain glaciation degradation, dangerous mudflow, and avalanches (CDP, 2014). The local government of Saint Petersburg plans to incorporate the measures into the city's plan of economic and social development until 2030.

Early in 2017, Russia started to work on a national climate change adaptation strategy. The adaption plans for all regions, including Siberia and Far East, are intended to minimize the negative impacts of climate change and expected to be completed by the end of 2018. This initiative comes on the tail of the recent changes to the Russian Climate Doctrine that prescribed several ministries, including the Ministry of Economics, the Ministry of Energy, and the Ministry of Construction, as well regional governments should develop methodology of calculating risks and losses from climate change and to develop potential adaptation measures and scenarios. In his interview to *Kommersant*, Sergey Donskoy, head of the Ministry of Nature, stated that at the moment only six regions out of 85, including Moscow and Saint Petersburg, are working on regional adaptation plans. Donskoy attributed the lack of action in other regions to the lack of necessary resources to develop such plans and a clear need for a federal legislation that would require the regional governments to develop adaptation plans and that would allocate resources from the federal budget on development and implementation of adaptation plans (Davydova, 2017).

The complexity of the Russia's efforts to address GCC on domestic level could be seen in relation to the nation's agricultural politics including grain production. Despite being among the world's top five wheat producers and exporters from 2000, Russia's position in grain trade has significantly fluctuated due to severe droughts. For example, in 2010 severe droughts led to the drastic measure of a grain export ban, while in 2012 severe droughts called for significant export reduction. In both cases, these measures sent grain prices soaring worldwide (Ukhova, 2013). However, in other years, Russia's grain production has been very high due to favorable weather conditions. In 2016, Russia became the lead wheat exporter by exporting 35 million tons, well ahead of the EU and US (Medetsky, 2016). Russia's long-term agricultural strategy is to achieve self-sufficiency by 2023–2024 and to increase grain production to 130 million tons per year by 2030. While the impact of global warming on agriculture is widely debated among scientists, with some suggesting that increasing temperatures coupled with longer growing seasons and higher atmospheric concentration of CO_2 will lead to increased grain production (Pegov, Khomyakov, & Khomyakov, 2000; Fischer, Shah, Tubiello, & van Velhuizen, 2005), others argue that grain production will be significantly reduced due to more severe and frequent droughts (Dronin & Kirilenko, 2008). According to the Russian Ministry of Agriculture, agricultural self-sufficiency can be achieved by higher productivity and, in particular, by increasing the amount of land under grain by 10–12 million hectares and by injecting additional funds for agrarian credits. In relation to the GCC, Russia's agrarian politics incorporate adaptation measures to respond not only to increasing temperatures but also to drastically changing precipitation patterns. The report on human development in the Russian Federation (Grigoriev & Bobylev, 2015) predicts that the most significant impact of the GCC on the central part of Russian Federation and the Volga region (Povolzhye)—the large region of Russia in the Volga Basin centered along the Volga River and a historical breadbasket of Russia—will be in the form of reduced precipitation and increased land aridity (Grigoriev & Bobylev, 2015). The report expects that the region's spring grains production will decrease due to the limited precipitation; however, the conditions will favor the winter grains production. In response to these changing conditions, Russian farmers increased the lands under winter grains in the fall of 2016 by approximately 6% to 17.35 million hectares (Devitt, 2016).

Specific Russian regions

The human development report identifies Siberia and the Far East as the two Russian regions most negatively impacted by GCC. Specifically, both Siberia and the Far East are expected to have the highest number of floods and forest fires compared with other regions. In addition, the report predicts that in the next ten years the temperatures in the Far East would rise much faster than in other regions of Russia. Analyzing the regions' potential for climate adaptation, the report states that both Siberia and the Far East have the lowest potential for adaptation due to a very low level of population real wealth, high proportion of the population in poverty, and a low level of health care. At the same time, the report notes that the Far East's agrarian conditions will significantly improve due to increasing temperatures (Grigoriev & Bobylev, 2015). In May 2012, the Russian government established the Ministry for Development of the Far East to coordinate federal programs in the region. One of the most ambitious goals of the Ministry is to repopulate the Far East. By the initiative of the Ministry, starting in February 2017, any Russian citizen can apply for a free hectare of land in the remote areas of the Far East. The only condition is to develop the land within five years. However, the program does not account for expected climate change in the region and does not explain how repopulating the Far East would impact the region's potential for adaptation to the climate change. From this perspective, the recent ambitious plan by the Russian government to repopulate the Far East serves as another illustration of subordinating climate concerns to economic needs.

The Arctic is another area that has been experiencing dramatic climate change with temperatures warming at double global averages. This results in a significant negative impact on the infrastructure and livelihood of the indigenous

222 *Ana Karaman*

population of Arctic. In 2008, the Russian Ministry of Natural Resources and Ecology developed a "Strategic Program of Action to the Protection of Marine Environment against Pollution in the Russian Federation's Arctic Zone." The program calls for establishing protected areas, helping the native populations, and adopting stricter ecological norms and work rules in the Arctic (Ministry of Economic Development of Russia, 2008).

Russia's response to GCC impact on the international level

Oil and gas dependency

On the international level, Russia has significantly changed its approach to the politics of GCC. While Russia was among the first nations to sign the United Nations Framework Convention on Climate Change (UNFCCC) in June 1992 (ratified in December 1994), it remained a relatively minor player in international climate change politics until 2001. While a member of the Annex I countries, Russia has also been classified by the Convention as an Economy in Transition (EIT) and, hence, was not required at the time to cut its level of emission (Oberthur & Ott, 1995). When Russia signed the Kyoto Protocol in March 1999, the country was required to maintain its emissions at 1990s levels. At the time of signing, this requirement was not problematic due to a significant decline in Russian economic production following the collapse of the Soviet Union. Even with an increase in economic production, Russia faced a very low risk of exceeding the 1990s emission levels. At the same time, Russia's potential gain from emission trading was estimated at approximately $10 to 20 billion per year particularly due to the US participation in emissions trade. The withdrawal of the US from the Kyoto Protocol in 2001 left Russia without the main potential purchaser of its emissions surplus and reduced the potential value from emissions trade to no more than $1–2 billion per year (Chandler & Popov, 2003). At the same time, the US withdrawal created an opportunity for Russia to emerge as a key player in GCC politics and to leverage this new position to advance its other political and economic interests. Equally important, however, it transformed the international climate change politics into Russia's levers to bolster its negotiating power in other arenas of international politics (Henry & Sundstrom, 2007; Kotov, 2004; Tipton, 2008).

Russia's decision to ratify the Kyoto Protocol in 2004 and to basically save it from collapse has been widely attributed to the EU's backing of Russia's membership of the World Trade Organisation (WTO). In his official comment, Putin linked the two issues stating, "The EU has met us halfway in talks over the WTO and that cannot but affect positively our position vis-a-vis the Kyoto Protocol" (Walsh, 2004). Clearly, Russia successfully used its strategic position in GCC politics as a bargaining chip to support its long-standing attempt to enter the WTO. As a result, some authors (Falkner, Stephan, & Vogler, 2010) pointed out that once Russia achieved that goal and ratified the Kyoto Protocol, its position on the international arena of GCC became reduced, once again, to a minor player. Indeed, Russia has shown little interest in GCC politics since the Kyoto Protocol. However, that apparent lack of interest does not signify Russia's losing its key position in international climate change politics. It seems rather to indicate that given the complexities of international and domestic politics, Russia will carefully weigh when and how to use its GCC politics chip to gain advances to its other international interests while, at the same time, taking necessary steps to strengthen its legitimacy as a key party to any GCC negotiations.

The Russian position on the Paris Climate Agreement (2015) clearly illustrates the caution with which the Kremlin will use its position. The ongoing need to rebalance oil production and, hence, stabilize oil prices, puts an additional pressure on Russia to work together with the Organization of the Petroleum Exporting Countries (OPEC) and non-OPEC oil producers. In this context, Russia tries to position itself as an intermediary between OPEC members who are riven by internal rifts and to negotiate future oil production freezes. Siding with Venezuela, whose economy lost 5.7% in 2015 due to the dramatic fall in oil prices, Russia attempted to persuade Saudi Arabia to reduce oil production. However, the Saudi's primary interest was in keeping oil prices low due to their concern over demand erosion (Henderson, 2016). As such, any public commitments to reduce future reliance on fossil fuels, including ratification of the Paris Agreement, would have weakened the Russian position in its negotiations with OPEC. As Van de Graaf (2017, p. 184) points out, "despite the fact that the Agreement does not specifically refer to 'oil', 'gas', 'energy', 'fossil fuels' or even carbon …, its clear objective is to phase out fossil fuels entirely before the end of the century."

Russia's dependency on oil and gas exports plays a significant role in the caution with which Russia approaches the politics of GCC. Despite signing the UNFCCC in 1992, Russia has understood that any further binding commitments could negatively impact its revenues from energy exports. Starting with the first Conference of the Parties (COP) in Berlin in 1995 and at the following COP-2 in Geneva in 1996, Russia has openly sided with OPEC (Oberthur & Ott, 1995, p. 146). During the Kyoto negotiations, Russia coalesced with the JUSCANZ (Japan, United States, Canada, and New Zealand) group advocating for emissions trading and a multi-gas approach (Korppoo, Karas, & Grubb, 2006, p. 7). Following Kyoto, Russia together with the US (US) opposed the EU's proposal to impose limits on the use of the 'flexibility mechanisms' that would call for greater domestic emissions reductions. In additional to multinational agreements, oil exports play an important role in Russia's bilateral and regional politics. For example, in 2015 Russia started the oil-for-goods program with Iran allowing Iran to supply Russia with 500,000 barrels per day (b/d) crude oil in exchange for cash that then is used to buy Russian commodities such as grain, equipment, and construction materials (Baczynska & Devitt, 2015).

Arctic development

Northern sea route and exports

The development of the Russian Arctic is another area of Russia's significance in the international arena of GCC. The decreasing surface of Arctic ice directly correlates with a decrease in ice cover of the seas of Siberia (Kara, Laptev, Eastern Siberian, and Chukchi) and has significant implications for Arctic marine transportation and shelf exploration. From the marine transport system perspective, this creates a potential for the Northern Sea Route (NSR) to become a valid alternative to the southern navigation routes through the Suez or Panama Canals since the NSR shortens the transport distance from northern Europe to northeast Asia and northwest North America by up to 50% (Khon, Mokhov, & Semenov, 2017). As such, commercializing the NSR carries significant economic benefits for both Russia via passage fees and for the countries engaged in intercontinental navigation between Atlantic and Pacific oceans. For example, Lee and Song (2014) concluded that utilizing the NSR instead of the traditional Suez Canal route carries significant economic benefits for China, Korea, Japan, Thailand, and the Philippines by significantly shortening the shipping distance and time between Asia and Europe.

Khon et al. (2017) estimate that by the end of the twenty-first century the NSR's annual ice-free navigation period with only a minor icebreaker support might be from from to 6.5 months. Should this estimate hold then the Russian government has clear prospects of raising the NSR's role in the intercontinental marine transport system from a seasonal supplemental route to an alternative commercial navigation route. However, as Moe and Brigham (2017) point out, internationalization of the NSR remains a long-term goal of the Russian Federation with many unknown factors such as the changing climatic conditions, impacting the predictability of reliable navigation seasons, and adequate tariffs, accounting for the need to hire an icebreaker and to pay a pilotage fee.

While internationalization and commercialization of the NSR carries significant long-term economic benefits for Russia, the most immediate benefit is tied to the utilization of the NSR for maritime export of natural resources from the Russian Arctic. By some estimates, the Russian Arctic has 30% of the untapped natural gas and 13% of oil worldwide (Johnston, 2010). In June 2015, the Russian Federation adopted the Integrated Development Plan for the Northern Sea Route 2015–2030. According to the Plan, Russia will invest in continuing development of the Arctic infrastructure projects including the construction of the Yamal Liquefied Natural Gas (LNG) plant and the port of Sebetta on the Yamal Peninsula. Other projects include Novatek's Arctic LNG-2 on Yamal and Gydan, development of an offshore loading terminal for crude oil in the Sabetta Port as part of the Transneft-Arctic Project, and expansion of the VOSTOKcoal Project to transport coal from the Taymyr Peninsula, from the port of Dikson. The overall impact of all these projects will be an increase in transport volumes on the NSR to 100 million tons per year by 2030 (Information Agency of Russia, 2015).

The information bureau of the NSR Administration, the governmental agency created in 2013 to oversee all aspects of the NSR, has reported that traffic volume on the Northern Sea Route in 2016 has increased by 35% in comparison with 2015. The agency reported that traffic volume of oil and oil products increased four times and LNG transportation slightly rose while volume of coal transportation reduced by 38% (NSR, 2016).

These data correlate with Russia's rapid development of the Arctic offshore oil fields. The exploration of oil in the Russian Arctic has a long history and goes back to the pre-World War I era. During the Soviet era, the world's first oil field in the Arctic—Chibyuskoe—was discovered in the Republic of Komi in 1930. Two years later, geologists discovered the large Yarega oil field. Both fields were developed in the 1930s. Exploration of oil and gas in the Arctic region has continued throughout the Soviet era and after the collapse of the Soviet Union. But unlike the historical efforts that were focused mainly on the onshore exploration and development, the current efforts center around offshore fields. In 2014, Russia's fourth largest oil company Gazprom Neft started oil extraction from the Prirazlomnoye field, an offshore oilfield located in the Pechora Sea, south of Novaya Zemlya, Russia. In the summer of 2016, the company had four wells in production at the northern Prirazlomnoye field and started two more (Gazprom Neft, 2017). By 2020 the annual production from the field is projected to reach six million tons. Further offshore plans of the company include a continuing exploration and development of Dolginskoye field located on the Arctic shelf of the Pechora Sea approximately 75 kilometers off the coast.

Sanctions' impact

A unique characteristic of the offshore Arctic oil exploration is that Russia needs to rely on international partnership due to the lack of adequate domestic equipment and modern offshore energy technology. For example, the Prirazlomnoye field was discovered in 1989. However, it took about 15 years before production began in 2014 due to technical difficulties. According to Staalesen (2014), half of the drilling equipment, services, and technology on the platform is Western and half of that is Norwegian. This dependency on Western technology and equipment was highlighted by the impact of the US and European sanctions imposed in 2014 on Arctic and deep-water offshore oil equipment. Thus, Gazprom Neft-Sakhalin started drilling in Dolginskoe field with a forecasted production start in 2020. However, the development was stalled when Western European suppliers could not deliver technology due to the sanctions. Consequently, Gazprom Neft signed a joint venture agreement with PetroVietnam to develop the Dolginskoe field, including exploration, development, and sales of oil eventually to be produced (Gazprom Neft, 2013). Another significant impact of the sanctions was on Rosneft's projects in the Kara Sea when Rosneft's partner—Exxon—withdrew from all projects in fall 2014. As another consequence of the sanctions, Rosneft had to freeze an ambitious project in Murmansk region that planned to outfit the existing Roslyakovo shipyard to accommodate Arctic operations as well as develop supporting the infrastructure with an estimated 2,000 additional jobs in the region. Interestingly, because the shipyard in Roslyakovo used to service the Northern Navy, the Roslyakovo had a status as a closed military territory and was inaccessible to the foreigners. However, in order to accommodate the cooperation plans on Arctic offshore development, Roslyakovo was released from its status as a closed military territory and annexed by the city of Murmansk as an industrial area (Kelly, 2016). In summary, the economic sanctions of 2014 clearly demonstrated dependency of Russian Arctic offshore projects on Western technologies and equipment (Aalto, 2016).

In response, the Russian government took steps to "Russify" the technologies and to proceed without its Western partners. In addition to Exxon, Eni of Italy and Statoil of Norway had joint ventures to work with Rosneft in the Kara, Laptev, and Chukchi seas of Russia. To add to its in-house capabilities, in the spring of 2014, Rosneft bought the Russian and Venezuelan well-drilling business of Weatherford. In October 2014, Putin approved the creation of a state-owned oil exploration drilling corporation to replace Western oil service companies such as Halliburton, Baker Hughes, and Schlumberger. If successful, these efforts will allow Russia to pivot from imported to domestic technologies and equipment to accommodate the entire offshore field lifecycle from exploration to production not only to deal with the sanctions but for the overall approach to Arctic oil development (Kramer, 2014).

Another challenging aspect of the sanctions is the availability of credit for Arctic oil development. Prior to the sanctions, Western companies had committed significant investments to Arctic oil exploration and extraction. For example, Exxon paid $700 million to drill the Universitetskaya-1 well in the Kara Sea. Overall, Exxon agreed to finance most of its joint operations with Rosneft in the Kara Sea and Black Sea, estimated at $3.2 billion, and to fund the $200 million initial cost of the two companies' Arctic Research Center, even though Exxon only controls 33.33% of these projects (Aalto, 2016). Jointly, the three companies—Exxon, Eni, and Statoil—planned to invest $20 billion in oil exploration projects with Rosneft (Kramer, 2014). Hence, from the financial perspective, the sanctions caused a serious threat to the viability of the Russian Arctic projects.

To deal with the issue of Western credit withdrawal, Russia turned to Asia and especially China. In 2016, when the Russian government announced its plans to privatize a portion of its majority shares of Rosneft, the China National Petroleum Corporation (CNPC) expressed a great interest to buy. However, Wang Yilin, the chairman of the CNPC, in his interview for a Russian TV station emphasized that in return for its investment, CNPC would seek a membership on Rosneft's board of directors (Reuters, 2016). In response, Alexei Ulyukayev, Minister of Economic Development of Russia, told the press that the Russian government would consider this request based on the size of CNPC's holding. As the Russian media reported, a membership on Rosneft's nine-member board of directors would represent CNPC's "deepest penetration into Russia's energy sector, which has gradually opened to Chinese investment after keeping it at arm's length for years" (Lelyveld, 2016).

Russia and global climate change   227

Militarization of the Arctic

Russia's intensified efforts to extract oil from the offshore fields are directly interlinked with the country's efforts to expand the NSR. The NSR provides a direct way to deliver natural resources, including the oil from offshore fields to the rest of the country without the necessity to build pipelines. From that perspective, melting of the Arctic ice will clearly be beneficial to the Russian economy and will turn the Arctic, which is estimated to hold more hydrocarbon reserves than Saudi Arabia, into a territory of critical strategic importance. This, in its turn, has led the Russian government to strengthen its military presence in the Arctic in a clear attempt to dominate the region over the traditional rivals—Canada, Norway, Denmark, and the US, as well as a new contender—China.

The impact of militarization of the Arctic on global security and the escalation of disputes in the Arctic Circle are widely discussed topics. One of the questions is whether the UN provides a sufficient and adequate framework to address disputes and claims of the circumpolar states—Russian, Canada, the US, Denmark via Greenland, Norway, Finland, Iceland, and Sweden. Except for the US, all these states have ratified the United Nations Convention on the Law of the Sea (UNCLO) that provides a legal framework to address disputes and territorial claims. While many territorial claims have been submitted to the UN, it remains to be seen whether the current institutional framework will allow for a resolution of the most significant of those claims including the Russia's 2015 claim to 463,000 square miles of the Arctic sea shelf (Isachenkov, 2015). For example, Ebinger and Zambetakis (2009) believe that despite the recent escalation, most relationships between the circumpolar states are characterized by the spirit of cooperation. In contrast, Borgerson (2008) believes that the current institutional structure of the Arctic is inadequate for orderly development of the region.

Despite the low oil prices and Western sanctions, the Russian government puts significant resources into building three new nuclear icebreakers, re-opening the Soviet era military bases and establishing new ones, as well as enhancing Russia's Northern Fleet, based near Murmansk. The Fleet is expected to get its own icebreaker and two ice-capable corvettes armed with cruise missiles. While no other country has a breaker fleet, Russia presently has a fleet of 40 icebreakers, including six that are nuclear. The build-up did not go unnoticed by the US, Norway, and Canada and led to some recent counteractions. In March 2012, North Atlantic Treaty Organization (NATO) carried out its Cold Response exercise that involved more than 16,000 military personnel on the stretch from Sweden to Canada. The Russian military responded with its own maneuvers that included testing of the Arctic-suited T-80 tanks, which have gas turbine engines and are much easier to start in the cold weather than the traditional diesel ones. The exercise also included the Russian Northern Fleet and Air Defense planes, and marine aviation (Kramnik, 2012).

In early spring 2014, NATO led the Cold Response exercise in the High North designed to train together militaries of 16 countries in the conditions of the Arctic Circle. On December 1, 2014, Russia created the new Arctic Joint Strategic Command. The new command fully incorporates the Northern Fleet and based on the Northern Fleet and substantial elements of the 1st Air Force and Air Defense. The new command became an addition to the previously existing four military districts. The creation of the new command has followed by a five-day military exercise that involved about 80,000 troops, 220 aircraft, 41 ships, and 15 submarines.

In May and June 2015, NATO and Russia engaged in the Cold War era rival war games. On May 25, Norway led a nine-country exercise named "Arctic Challenge" that involved over 4,000 personnel and close to 100 fighter jets. In response, the same day NATO launched its exercise in the Arctic, Russia launched its own combat readiness drill that involved about 250 aircraft and 12,000 military personnel and took place over the Ural Mountains and Siberia while the Russian Northern Fleet was put on a full combat alert. Arctic Challenge Exercises 2017 have been scheduled for May 2017 under the lead of the Finnish Air Force. Overall, more than 100 aircraft from 12 nations will participate in the air exercise carried out in the airspace over the northern areas of Finland, Sweden, and Norway.

While NATO has been reluctant to define a specific Arctic strategy, the alliance feels the pressure from its Nordic non-member partners. At the 2016, US-Nordic Leaders' Summit, the Arctic was one of the main points of discussion. The joint statement stressed the necessity of collaboration with Russia and the goal of keeping the region's peace and stability. However, the same statement also condemned "Russia's illegal occupation and attempted annexation of Crimea, … its aggression in Donbas, and its attempts to destabilize Ukraine" (Office of the Press Secretary, White House, 2016). The Warsaw NATO Summit of 2016 did not mention the Arctic, but it put a further emphasis on counteracting Russia. This creates a significant challenge for sustainable Arctic cooperation between Russia and the Nordic nations not only with respect to security and defense but also for the rest of region's issues including climate change.

Perhaps, no other region demonstrates the complexity of the GCC issues for Russia like the Arctic. On one hand, the Russian government is conscious of the problem of the rapidly rising temperatures in the region and the resulting impediments to the environment, infrastructure, and the conditions of human life of the local population. On the other hand, the changing climate conditions have transformed the Arctic into a strategic geo-political region and Russia is determined to retain its dominance in the region and capitalize on the benefits from rich oil and gas deposits as well as the expanded use of the NSR. This, in turn, calls for revival and expansion of military presence. Several scholars argue that Russian militarization of the region is primarily explained by Russia's efforts to protect its economic interests in the region (Brutschin & Schubert, 2016; Konyshev & Sergunin, 2014). As such, the environmental concerns while not being ignored are clearly subordinated to the broader political and economic interests. The Western sanctions in response to the Ukrainian events have pushed Russia to seek a greater self-reliance and to pivot its international position towards non-Western alliances (Konyshev, Sergunin, & Subbotin, 2017). From this perspective, the future cooperation with the West on the issues of GCC will remain linked to Russia's long-term plans for the country's economic development and, hence, its national security interests. It is unlikely that Russia will be willing to separate these interlinked issues on the international arena. At the same time, the Russian government is acutely aware that as the international attitudes towards GCC swing with changing Western governments, the recent US election as one example, any significant progress on the issues of GCC will require a partnership with Russia. Consequently, Russia sees a clear benefit in taking time to assess the situation in its full complexity and to design an approach that is the most beneficial for the country's more immediate goals of economic development and preserving its bargaining strength for an appropriate moment.

Leveraging international framework

Baikal is one example of Russia's successful use of the international framework to address domestic problems of GCC. In May 2016, Russia reached a bilateral agreement with Mongolia that put on hold Mongolia's plans to build a cascade of hydropower plants, including one on the Selenga (Shuren) River, and two on Selenga tributaries—the Orkhon and Egyin Gol. These plans were widely viewed by Russian scientists as well as the Russian general public as posing a serious ecological threat to Lake Baikal since up to 50% of its annual water inflow is from the Selenga River. By the results of negotiations with the Russian Ministry of Natural Resources, the Mongolian government promised to not take any steps that will harm the ecosystem of Baikal and to freeze the project until additional research analyzing a potential negative impact of hydroelectric plants on Baikal is conducted (Gazeta.Ru, 2017). Prior to negotiations with Mongolia, Russia successfully engaged Greenpeace and other activists to put pressure on the World Bank to freeze financing of two out of three major dams, one on the Selenga and one on the Orkhon River. At the end of 2016, Russia entered into a bilateral agreement with a group of Chinese investors to develop hospitality and tourism on the lake. The project amounts to $11 billion and is sited at the former Baykalsk pulp and paper mill that has been the major polluter in the area and was closed down in December 2013. While the overall goal of the initiative is to boost economic development of the region, the agreement states that the development will take place in strict compliance with ecological standards and environmental laws (RBC, 2016).

Conclusion

Despite a historically low priority for climate change issues, the current significant environmental events have led the Russian government to reprioritize the importance and urgency of addressing the impacts of GCC. The Russian government officially acknowledged anthropogenic factors of climate change as well as

230 *Ana Karaman*

lagging efforts to mitigate those. Hence, concluding that adaptation is essential for the unavoidable climate change consequences in the future. Presently, Russia has taken steps, described in this chapter, to mitigate and adapt to GCC's negative impacts on the socio-economic development of the country, in general, and on the lives and health of the population, in particular. However, those steps are always subordinated to the country' goals of continuing economic development. The unique geographical location of the Russian Federation allows the country to reap immediate economic benefits from the impacts of GCC and necessitates a more complex political solution to adaptation at the domestic level. On the international arena, it is unlikely that Russia will yield its ability to leverage GCC politics to advance its other political agenda and shift to considering GCC politics in isolation from other international objectives. The complexity of relationships between the major players and the swinging position of the US opens the doors for Russia to wait for an opportune moment to leverage its GCC bargaining chip.

Notes

1 In their report "We and the Amur Floods: Lessons (Un)Learned" Simonov, Nikitina, Osipov, Egidarev and Shalikovsky (2016) stated:

> In Russia, losses resulting from floods are aggravated ... by the following circumstances:—Sharp reduction in the number of hydrometric stations on Russian rivers during the last 25 years;—Lack of an efficient information system capable of notifying the population about flood threats, along with certain ill-preparedness of local residents to take adequate action;—Inadequate legislation on property insurance and flood-damage compensation in flood-prone areas that creates incentives for inappropriate floodplain development.
>
> (p. 3)

2 On July 11, 2010, the temperatures reached 44.0°C (111.2°F) in the southern republic of Kalmykia. Anomalous summer temperatures made an unfortunate note in the *Guinness Book of World Records* as the deadliest summer ever in Russia.
3 The previous outbreak of anthrax in this area was 75 years ago, since then carcasses of infected animals have been frozen in permafrost. Due to the recent increase in temperature leading to a permafrost thaw, infected carcasses rose to the surface spreading infectious spores across the tundra. The Russian media broadly publicized the event by showing military units cleaning the quarantined area.

References

Aalto, P. (2016). Modernization of the Russian energy sector: Constraints on utilizing Arctic offshore oil resources. *Europa-Asia Studies*, 68(1), 38–63.

Baczynska, G. & Devitt, P. (2015, April 13). *Russia and Iran begin massive oil-for-goods deal*. Reuters. Retrieved from www.businessinsider.com/russia-and-iran-begin-massive-oil-for-goods-deal-2015-4. Date retrieved 3/11/17.

Borgerson, S. (2008) Arctic meltdown: The economic and security implications of global warming. *Foreign Affairs*. Retrieved from www.foreignaffairs.com/articles/arctic-antarctic/2008-03-02/arctic-meltdown. Date retrieved 12/17/16.

Brutschin, E. & Schubert, S.R. (2016). Icy waters, hot tempers, and high stakes: Geopolitics and geoeconomics of the Arctic. *Energy Research and Social Science*, 16, 147–159.

CDP (2014). *Russia climate change report.* Retrieved from https://b8f65cb373b1b7b 15feb-c70d8ead6ced550b4d987d7c03fcdd1d.ssl.cf3.rackcdn.com/cms/reports/documents/ 000/000/863/original/CDP-Russia-climate-change-report-2014.pdf?1472042732. Date retrieved 3/12/17.

Chandler, W., & Popov, I. (2003). *Russia's decisive role in the Kyoto Protocol.* Joint Global Change Research Institute, PNNL-14302, Retrieved from www.globalchange. umd.edu/data/aisu/publications/PNNL-14302.pdf.

Davidova, A. (2017, February 7). *В России оценят ущерб от будущей непогоды (In Russia estimates of the future climate change).* Kommersant. Retrieved from www. kommersant.ru/doc/3212233. Date retrieved 8/26/17.

Devitt, P. (2016, November 10). Russia's 2017 grain crop prospects brighter due to larger sowing areas. Reuter. Retrieved from www.agriculture.com/markets/newswire/russias-2017-grain-crop-prospects-brighter-due-to-large-sowing-area. Date retrieved 8/15/17.

Dronin, N. & Kirilenko, A. (2008). Climate change and food stress in Russia: What if the market transforms as it did during the past century? *Climatic Change*, 86(1), 123–150.

Ebinger, C. & Zambetakis, E. (2009) The geopolitics of Arctic melt. *International Affairs*, 85(6), 1215–1232.

Falkner, R., Stephan, H., & Vogler, J. (2010). International climate policy after Copenhagen: Towards a 'building blocks' approach. *Global Policy*, 1(3), 252–262.

Fedorov, A.N. & Konstantinov, P.Y. (2009). Response of permafrost landscapes of Central Yakutia to current changes of climate, and anthropogenic impacts. *Geography and Natural Resources*, 30(2), 146–150.

Fischer, G., Shah, M., Tubiello, F.N., & van Velhuizen, H. (2005). Socio-economic and climate change impacts on agriculture: An integrated assessment, 1990–2080. *Phil Trans Royal Soc B*, 360, 2067–2073.

Gazeta.Ru (2017, January 25). *Лавров заявил о стремлении не допустить строительства ГЭС Монголии близ Байкала (Lavrov stated the goal of not allowing a construction of Mongolian HPP near Baikal).* Retrieved from www.gazeta.ru/social/ news/2017/01/25/n_9605405.shtml. Date retrieved 3/12/17.

Gazprom Neft (2013, November 12). *«Газпром нефть» и PetroVietnam заключили соглашение об инвестициях в модернизацию завода Dung Quat (Gazprom Neft and PetroVietnam reached an agreement about investments into modernization of Dung Quat plant).* Retrieved from www.gazprom-neft.ru/press-center/news/1095866/. Date retrieved 3/12/17.

Gazprom Neft (2017). *Приразломное (Prirazlomnoe).* Retrieved from www.gazprom-neft.ru/company/business/exploration-and-production/new-projects/prirazlomnoe/. Date retrieved 3/12/17.

Grigoriev, L.M. & Bobylev, S. H. (2015) (Eds.) *Доклад о человеческом развитии в Российской Федерации за 2015 год (Human development report Russian Federation 2015).* Retrieved from http://ac.gov.ru/files/publication/a/7198.pdf. Date retrieved 3/12/17.

Henderson, J. (2016, December). *Room for cynicism and hope in Russia's deal with OPEC.* Oxford Energy Comment. Retrieved from www.oxfordenergy.org/wpcms/wp-content/uploads/2016/12/Room-for-cynicism-and-hope-in-Russias-deal-with-OPEC. pdf. Date retrieved 3/11/17.

Henry, L.A., & Sundstrom, L.M. (2007). Russia and the Kyoto Protocol: Seeking an alignment of interests and image. *Global Environmental Politics*, 7(4), 47–69.

Information Agency of Russia (2015, June 8). *Премьер-министр РФ Дмитрий Медведев подписал комплексный проект развития Северного морского пути. (Prime Minister of Russia Dmitriy Medvedev signed a comprehensive development plan of the Northern Sea Route).* Retrieved from http://tass.ru/ekonomika/2027639. Date retrieved 3/12/17.

Interfax/Ведомости. (2016, August 4). *Минобороны направило модуль «Орлан» на борьбу с сибирской язвой в ЯНАО (Ministry of Defense sends modul "Orlan" to fight anthrax in Yamolo Nenezkoi Autonomous Okrug).* Retrieved from www.vedomosti.ru/politics/news/2016/08/04/651714-minoboroni-orlan-yazvoi. Date retrieved 2/3/17.

Isachenkov, V. (2015). *Russia to UN: We are claiming 463,000 square miles of the Arctic.* Retrieved from www.businessinsider.com/russia-to-un-we-are-claiming-463000-square-miles-of-the-arctic-2015-8?r=UK&IR=T. Date retrieved 3/11/17.

Johnston, P.F. (2010). Arctic energy resources and global energy security. *Journal of Military and Strategic Studies*, 12 (2). Retrieved from http://oceans.mit.edu/wp-content/uploads/arctic_energy_security.pdf. Date retrieved 1/12/17.

Kelly, M.L. (2016, August 3). *A once-closed Russian military town in the Arctic opens to the world.* National Public Radio. Retrieved from www.npr.org/sections/parallels/2016/08/03/488356877/a-once-closed-russian-military-town-in-the-arctic-opens-to-the-world

Khon, V.C., Mokhov, I.I., & Semenov, V.A. (2017). Transit navigation through Northern sea route from satellite data and CMIP5 simulations. *Environmental Research Letters*, 12 (2). Retrieved from http://iopscience.iop.org/article/10.1088/1748-9326/aa5841/meta

Kondratenko, T (2016, October 25). *Изменение климата в России (Climate Change in Russia).* Russian Climate. Retrieved from http://climaterussia.ru/klimat/izmenenie-klimata-v-rossii. Date retrieved 3/11/17.

Konyshev, V., & Sergunin, A. (2014). Is Russia a revisionist military power in the Arctic? *Defense Security Analysis* 30(4), 323–335.

Konyshev, V., Sergunin, A., & Subbotin, S. (2017). Russia's Arctic strategies in the context of the Ukrainian crisis. *The Polar Journal*, June 9, 1–21.

Korppoo, A, Karas, J., & Grubb, M. (Eds.) (2006). *Russia and the Kyoto Protocol: Opportunities and challenges.* London: Chatham House.

Kotov, V. (2004). The EU-Russia ratification deal: The risks and advantages of an informal agreement. *International Review for Environmental Strategies*, 5(1), 157–168.

Kramer, A. (2014, October 29). The 'Russification" of oil exploration. *New York Times.* Retrieved from www.nytimes.com/2014/10/30/business/energy-environment/russia-oil-exploration-sanctions.html?_r=0. Date retrieved 12/17/16.

Kramnik, I. (2012, April 25). NATO, Russia stage Arctic war games. Space War. Retrieved from www.spacewar.com/reports/NATO_Russia_stage_Arctic_war_games_999.html. Date retrieved 12/20/17.

Kremlin (2009). *Климатическая доктрина Российской Федерации (Climate Doctrine of the Russian Federation).* Retrieved from http://kremlin.ru/events/president/news/6365. Date retrieved 2/11/17.

Lazare, S. (2015, December 25). *Russia warming over two times faster than rest of planet.* Common Dreams. Retrieved from www.commondreams.org/news/2015/12/25/russia-warming-over-two-times-faster-rest-planet. Date retrieved 1/14/17.

Lee, S. W. & Song, J.M. (2014). Economic possibilities of shipping though (sic) Northern Sea Route. *The Asian Journal of Shipping and Logistics*, 30(3), 415–430.

Russia and global climate change   233

Lelyveld, M. (2016, June 20). *China boosts role in Russian oil sector.* Radio Free Asia. Retrieved from www.rfa.org/english/commentaries/energy_watch/china-boosts-role-in-russian-oil-sector-06202016111458.html. Date retrieved 3/12/17.

Makarov, D. (2014, April 14). *Якутия закрывает зимники: ледовые дороги стали опасными (Yakutiya shuts down zimniki: ice roads become dangerous).* Vesti.Ru Retrieved from www.vesti.ru/videos/show/vid/590781/. Date retrieved 12/15/17.

Medetsky, A. (2016, October 7). *Russia becomes a grain superpower as wheat exports explode.* Bloomberg. Retrieved from www.bloomberg.com/news/articles/2016-10-06/russia-upends-world-wheat-market-with-record-harvest-exports. Date retrieved 2/15/17.

Ministry of Economic Development of Russia (2008). *Strategic action program for protection of the Russian Arctic environment.* Retrieved from https://oaarchive.arctic-council.org/bitstream/handle/11374/1029/ACSAO-DK03_7_1a_SAP_Arctic.pdf?sequence=1&isAllowed=y. Date retrieved 12/7/17.

Moe, A. & Brigham, L. (2017). Organization and management challenges of Russia's icebreaker fleet. *Geographical Review,* 107(1), 48–68.

NSR (2016) *The traffic volume on the NSR has increased in 2016.* Retrieved from: www.arctic-lio.com/node/264. Date retrieved 2/14/17.

Oberthur, S., & Ott, H.E. (1995). UN convention on climate change: The first conference of the parties. *Environmental Policy and Law,* 25 (4–5), 144–156

Office of the Press Secretary, White House (2016, May 13). *U.S.–Nordic leaders' summit joint statement.* Retrieved from https://obamawhitehouse.archives.gov/the-press-office/2016/05/13/us-nordic-leaders-summit-joint-statement. Date retrieved 3/1/17.

Pegov, S.A., Khomyakov, D.M., & Khomyakov, P.M. (2000). Global change impacts on the socio-economic situation in Russia. In Kotlyakov, V.M. (Ed.) *Global and regional climate change and its environmental and socio-economic impacts* (pp. 60–69). Moscow: Geos (in Russian).

RBC (2016, October 24). *Китай вложит $11 млрд в развитие туризма на Байкале (China will invest $11billion into development of tourism in Baikal).* Retrieved from www.rbc.ru/rbcfreenews/580d8ce39a79477b7b62e6f7. Date retrieved 3/3/17.

Reuters (2016, May 30). *China's CNPC says could consider raising rosneft stake.* Retrieved from www.reuters.com/article/us-russia-china-oil-co-rosneft-cnpc/chinas-cnpc-says-could-consider-raising-rosneft-stake-idUSKCN0YM061. Date retrieved 3/11/17

RIA (2013, August 11). *Gone with the water: Floods in Russia's east cause over $30 mn in damages.* Retrieved from https://on.rt.com/chnv2y. Date retrieved 12/20/16.

Roshydromet: Federal service for hydrometeorology and environmental monitoring. (2008). *Assessment report on climate change and its consequences in Russian Federation.* Retrieved from http://climate2008.igce.ru/v2008/pdf/resume_ob_eng.pdf. Date retrieved 12/17/16.

Simonov, E., Nikitina, O., Osipov, P., Egidarev, E., & Shalikovsky, A. (2016). *We and the Amur floods: Lessons (un)learned?* Retrieved from www.wwf.ru/data/amur/we-and-the-amur-floods_eng.pdf. Date retrieved 1/12/17.

Staalesen, A. (2014, September 16). In times of sanctions, Prirazlomnaya goes Russian. *Barents Observer.* Retrieved from http://barentsobserver.com/en/energy/2014/09/times-sanctions-prirazlomnaya-goes-russian-16-09. Date retrieved 1/15/17.

Tipton, J. (2008). Why did Russia ratify the Kyoto Protocol? Why the wait? An analysis of the environmental, economic, and political debates. *Slovo,* 20(2), 67–96.

Ukhova, D. (2013). *After the drought: The 2012 drought, Russian farmers, and the challenges of adapting to extreme weather events.* Oxfam. Retrieved from www.oxfam.org/

sites/www.oxfam.org/files/cs-russia-drought-adaptation-270913-en.pdf. Date retrieved 12/14/16.

Van de Graaf, T. (2017). Is OPEC dead? Oil exporters, the Paris Agreement and the transition to a post-carbon world. *Energy Research & Social Science*, 23, 182–188.

Walsh, N.P. (2004, February 22). Russian vote saves Kyoto Protocol. *Guardian.* Retrieved from www.theguardian.com/world/2004/oct/23/society.russia. Date retrieved 12/12/16.

11 Conclusion

State powers on global climate change—lessons learned

Daniel Silander and Don Wallace

The examination in this book, *Global Climate Change, Policy and Security: State and Human Impacts*, departs from the contemporary international debate on global climate change (GCC) by its examination of this serious phenomenon as a human-caused challenge to both state and human security. The challenges arising from GCC have in different ways presented threats to the human society. Desertification, droughts and scarcity of basic human resources have already resulted in ecological refugees or forced migration and have contributed to social, economic, and at times political destabilization and conflicts (state insecurity) in societies with less potential to initiate adaptation and capacity building strategies. GCC requires local, domestic, and international responses. To this, the international community of major state powers has reluctantly, but lately developed a comprehensive process to address GCC that will seek a common platform for confronting environmental challenges and for protecting and promoting state and human security.

This study has a focus on major states powers on the GCC (including the EU) in its examination of how these states have domestically and internationally, through the United Nation-system (UN), perceived GCC and its consequences for security, and promoted the policies and strategies (mitigation, adaptation, and capacity building) that have or need to be instituted. From the start of this study it has been argued that GCC is a shared and complex problem and that collective actions are required to cope with the security challenges—both human and state—presented by this phenomenon. This collective action requires cooperation among major state powers, between major and minor state powers, and throughout the developed and the less developed world. Successfully addressing the challenges of GCC will require a collective action among all these actors that overrides concerns over state sovereignty, state security, and possibly economic growth.

This book has explored multiple GCC strategies proposed by the major state powers in the international community. In Chapter 1, *Introduction: security and global climate change*, an overview was presented of the recognition by the international community of the phenomenon of climate change and its environmental impact. Additionally, this chapter discussed state and human security and conceptualized these concepts in relation to the ongoing global debate on climate change. It is argued that the traditional notion of state security with its focus on state sovereignty presents a major hindrance to global collective strategies on GCC and for the enhancement of human security. Today, GCC poses major and complex challenges to human society and consequently a grave danger to human security in many parts of the world. It is also illustrated in this book how such grave dangers are challenging state security as well and how many parts of the world face an alarming security-environmental nexus where climate change challenges both state and human security. As stated in this study, human security challenges caused by climate change may very well lead to state insecurity in political tension, violence and forced migration due to scarcity of basic human resources. This is especially so in weak states with fragile and dysfunctional political institutions.

The discussion in Chapter 1 provided two frameworks that are used to address concerns facing the major national powers in their efforts to address the challenges of GCC. The first framework is a categorization of the three strategies that have been considered under the United Nations Framework Convention on Climate Change (UNFCCC) regime by the international community for addressing the threats emanating from global climate change. Described are the efforts being made to achieve these strategies of mitigation, adaptation, and capacity building (this third strategy involves alleviation of poverty, transferring technologies and good governance). A second framework for assessing the efforts of major national powers is the impact of the differentiation of the framing of the impacts of GCC in terms of security, with human security and state security as alternative, if not competing, routes. The examination in this chapter observes that GCC strategies are enhanced when state security is not prioritized over human security. Further, as the perceptions of the challenges of GCC get more securitized in terms of state security, there will be an increased tendency to invoke exceptional measures that are not part of normal democratic processes. Effective GCC policies, which would enhance human security, will likely be thwarted by a shift to a predominant focus on concerns of state security. This chapter identifies several prominent concerns facing major national powers in this competition of strategies for addressing GCC. These concerns, which are considered in subsequent chapters, include a nation's perception of GCC, its approach to meet the challenges of GCC both domestically and internationally (in the framework being developed by the UN), and factors that portend limitation on the readiness for addressing GCC.

Chapter 2 addressed *The UN regime on global climate cchange* by examining the activities of the two primary UN entities that address the underlying security challenges arising from GCC: (1) the regime of the UN Framework Convention on Climate Change (UNFCCC), and (2) the UN Security Council (UNSC). There is recognition of the efforts the UNFCCC regime has made in developing the GCC strategies of mitigation, adaptation, and capacity building. While initially the threat of GCC was seen in terms of challenges to development, the regime has more recently expressed increased alarm with the existential threat posed by the phenomenon. With the 2015 Paris Agreement, a reinvigoration of the multilateral approach was instilled for addressing GCC that discarded the mandatory strategy of common, but differentiated responsibilities that had divided industrialized and developing nations. Much remains to be developed to fulfil the goals of the Paris Agreement at subsequent COP meetings and at national and local levels. A continued lack of unanimity in the international community (as seen in the subsequent move of the US to withdraw from the Paris Agreement) on the urgency to take concerted action presents the largest challenge to fulfilling the promise of the 2015 Paris Agreement.

The UNSC's perspective on dealing with threats to international peace and security has been expanding in recent years, and observers have noted that the UNSC could rely upon recent precedent to securitize GCC and require states to initiate mitigation and adaptation strategies. However, in the two formal sessions undertaken on the explicit issue of GCC, there was pronounced opposition, by developing nations along with China and Russia, for the UNSC to consider GCC as such a threat. Both China and Russia argued that the UNSC had limited expertise on climate change, but expressed concern that a UNSC policy on GCC and international peace and security could be a threat to state sovereignty. Yet, in its otherwise expanding role for addressing threats to international peace and security, the UNSC has formally securitized issues, such as pandemics, that could relate to discrete environmental challenges arising from GCC. There is the possibility that this securitization however, will be done at the expense of the resources that support traditional human security needs. These two entities, the UNFCCC regime and the UNSC, correspond respectively with the two themes of security under discussion in this book, human and state security.

Chapter 3 on *Geography of GCC: Asia-Pacific Region—human and state security* by Patrick D. Nunn and Carola Betzold dealt with the Asia–Pacific region (about one fourth of the Earth's surface), and addressed how this geographically diverse region shares in the challenges presented by GCC. First, it is observed that the Asia–Pacific region has seen major economic and population growth over the last few decades with a remarkable increase of gross domestic product (GDP). Second, it is argued that the largest proportion of these people live in Low Elevation Coastal Zones (LECZ), which have the highest concentration of coastal megacities in the world and with ongoing urbanization taking place. The Asia-Pacific region faces dramatic strains due to GCC and rising sea levels; GCC challenges economic growth and state and human security in the region. It is further noted that the region contains states with different levels of capacities to mitigate and adapt to GCC. While 11 states are classified as developed states, nine as least-developed and 18 as developing states, there are estimations that the region lacks a common readiness to address GCC. With ongoing urbanization and population growth in the coastal regions, GCC provides additional pressure on security in terms of, *inter alia*, increasing temperatures, eroding soil, decreasing coastal areas, declining food and water resources due to shifting weather and forced migration, within and among states. Within the next few decades many coastal communities in this region will be involuntarily displaced by rising sea level. Besides obvious human security challenges, the authors argued that state security is also under pressure in terms of loss of livelihoods, due to water scarcity and/or disease outbreaks, requiring state intervention, forced displacement of people leading to migration flows, and concentration of people in areas already under pressure from the scarcity of resources that could result in social tension and/or civil unrest. The Pacific Island countries have acknowledged the security risks provided by GCC, calling for immediate strategies to protect and promote security. Since climate-driven conflicts resulting from the socioeconomic marginalization of migrants can cross national boundaries, adaptation efforts at both national and regional levels are necessitated. While some major member states of the Association of Southeast Asian Nations (ASEAN) have been somewhat more reluctant to address GCC and instead have focused on economic growth, the vast majority of states in the Asia-Pacific region today share a great concern over GCC consequences, with 28 out of 31 states in the Asia-Pacific having ratified the 2015 Paris Agreement.

Chapter 4, *Geography of GCC: The climate-security nexus in Africa*, adds another geographical perspective by focusing on climate change consequences in Africa. Although Africa is a major continent with various types of states and regime capacities to handle climate change, this chapter stressed that while Africa is the lowest carbon emitter in the world, it is highly vulnerable to climate change. This is due to the fact that many African states have limited resources for adaptation, apart from mitigation. This chapter addressed climate change consequences in African societies due to rising temperature, escalation of droughts, storms, and floods across the continent creating a scarcity of resources, climate refugees, and social and political tensions. It is argued that climate change poses great dangers to state and human security in many African societies. It is observed that already fragile states with minimal political and economic capacities are those that come under great challenges with climate change. Climate change should be understood as a factor that further contributes to destabilization and stress in already struggling societies. In short, climate change and political fragility pose grave challenges to human and consequently state security in Africa. Although this chapter presents an in-depth discussion on the environmental–security nexus in Sudan's Darfur regional, state and human security face challenges in many more African societies. This common challenge has left Africa to seek international responses, and it has led to regional efforts to speak with one voice on proposals for mitigation and adaptation. There are signs of an improved regional stand on climate change in international forums, but differences exist among states on how to perceive economic growth and environmental protections and how to agree on political, economic, and technical strategies for efficient countermeasures to GCC challenges.

The subsequent chapters examine how major powerful states have domestically and internationally, through the UN system, perceived GCC and its consequences for security. As indicated in Annex I to the report of the 21st COP held in 2015 in Paris, the US, EU, China, India, Japan, and Russia represent the top sources of current GHG emissions. These chapters also discuss how these major states promote the policies and strategies (mitigation, adaptation, and capacity building) that have been or need to be taken. This examination indicates that the answers to the concerns of how these states are addressing climate change hinge to a great extent on how the relative perspectives of human and state security are prioritized for these GCC challenges.

Chapter 5, written by Niall Michelsen, provides the first analysis for the book of a major state power's policies on GCC by focusing on *The United States and global climate change*. It is stated that the American political stand on climate change has shifted over time with different dominating perspectives on the reality of climate change and ties to human activities. At the 1992 Earth Summit, President George H.W. Bush agreed on the responsibility of the developed world to address rising temperature and pollution based on the capacity and responsibility to mitigate gas emissions. Subsequently, President Clinton negotiated and signed onto the Kyoto Protocol, formally embracing the responsibility of the developed world for addressing GCC. The succeeding George W. Bush Administration questioned the scientific findings on anthropogenic climate change and raised concerns regarding the economic costs that mitigation efforts would place on the US economy and did not pursue getting the Kyoto Protocol ratified. The Obama presidency, by contrast, was in concert with the growing global consensus on the human causes of climate change and its negative consequences on state and human security and the pivotal role for the US to play internationally. The efforts to securitize GCC by the Obama Administration were unsuccessful in garnering broad public support in the US for addressing these issues; yet, they did succeed in engaging the US military into adopting a GCC state security-related agenda. The new Trump Administration has ardently questioned the international consensus on climate change. By pointing out climate change as a Chinese problem, Trump questioned the UN framework on climate change and existing international climate agreements and has subsequently moved to have the US withdraw from the 2015 Paris Agreement that Obama had signed. However, the Trump Administration has already been met with challenges in existing regulations, programs, and initiatives among authorities at both state and federal levels. It is also argued in the chapter that although the current Administration does not see climate change as a major security threat to the US there is a growing concern over the costs that come with climate change. The US has the capacity to be the global leader on climate change. Its wide range of capacities—political, technological, and economic—could be used to establish meaningful mitigation efforts internationally to alleviate the ongoing negative environmental process. Though the economics might favor a US position that prioritizes domestic adaptation policies over mitigation efforts, the chapter observes that adopting such a position would represent an abdication by the US of its international leadership. As one of the largest emitters in the world, there is a responsibility for using such capacities for a better world, but it would require a multilateral approach from a unilateralist Trump Administration and at minimum a recognition that climate change is human-made and a serious security challenge that extends beyond more parochial national economic and energy issues.

240 *Daniel Silander and Don Wallace*

Martin Nilsson in Chapter 6 on *The European Union and global climate change* discusses the shared competence between individual member states and the EU on environmental issues and how the organization of its present 28 member states has over the last two decades developed policies on climate change. It is observed that most EU member states have a long history of progressive state environmental policies and that the EU has taken a leading role in global talks on environmental protection and global climate change. While each member state pursues its own regulations and laws, the EU has developed binding standards for member states. Further, as embedded in the 2007 Treaty of Lisbon, all EU policies and decisions must consider negative environmental impacts. Both the precautionary principle and the concept that the polluter must pay the costs for environmental damage serve as the guiding principles of EU decisions. Today, the EU sets out common standards for environmental protection, but each member state is allowed to implement more restrictive environmental standards as long as they do not violate EU common market policies. Based on member state interests, in promoting a European green policy on climate change, the EU introduced its first European Climate Change Programme (ECCP) in 2000, which became the most important mechanism to meet the Kyoto Protocol objectives. Since then, the EU has developed numerous policies on mitigation, adaptation, and capacity building to climate change challenges. These demonstrate that the EU is addressing GCC largely from a human security perspective. The European Commission has acknowledged, in its public statements and reports, that climate change and greenhouse gases are a consequence of human activities that must be urgently confronted in order to save the environment and human and state security in Europe and globally. In 2015, the EU's Climate Actions Progress Report affirmed that some progress has been achieved on climate change objectives for 2020 in accordance with the Kyoto Protocol. In 2016 the EU developed a Global Strategy that portrays GCC as one of many potential security threats to the region. The recent migration waves from the Middle East and Africa, areas prone to the debilitating effects of GCC, present challenges to the external security of the EU and to integration and collaboration among member states. In the future, it will be necessary to find shared agreements among member states and between member states and the EU Commission on how to mitigate and adapt to climate change and how to continue to support both the free market and a sustainable environment, but also how to handle migration flows often exacerbated by climate change in weak states. Thus, while the EU has generally been a leader in international efforts to address GCC, stressing a concern of human security needs, there is a developing securitization in the EU of the challenges of human migration. This phenomenon, likely exacerbated by weather-related events, could lead to a prioritization of state security over human security in the developing EU policies on GCC.

Chapter 7, *China and global climate change*, co-authored by Daniel Silander and Martin Nilsson, addressed the transformation of China's stand on climate change over the last two decades. The authors argued that China has been a reluctant actor domestically and internationally in talks on mitigation and

Conclusion 241

adaptation to climate change. The Chinese authorities have for decades promoted economic growth that has resulted in China becoming one of the top emitting states in the world, with about 30% of the total CO_2 emissions. Decades of growing population and economic growth has resulted in greater energy demand and devastating environmental impact. Over the last decade, China has transformed its economic policy to encompass sustainable energy supplies and human security as its main priorities. Based on its first Climate Change Program of 2007, China has continued to address pollution and global warming in terms of an economic growth-environmental nexus that requires strong governmental control. Worries about future economic decline, due to scarcity of energy and increasing costs for pollution and human insecurity, have led the Chinese Communist Party (CCCP) to stress the necessity of low-carbon technology for economic growth and improved human security. China is today an important actor within the UNFCCC and has stated an interest in becoming a leading global actor regarding clean technology. Domestically, Chinese authorities have developed a strategy of ecological civilization or green growth that promotes high-technology in clean coal production (wind turbines, solar plants, and nuclear power), low-carbon industries, and closure of inefficient factories and coal-fired power plants, introducing national carbon emissions trading schemes and amending existing environmental laws as well as signing numerous new anti-pollution laws and decrees on electricity use and gas consumption. It is still too soon to tell whether the Chinese authorities will succeed in this new approach to improve its devastated environment and transform the country into a green-actor on economic growth. But, compared with previous decades, the political will is now present, although many obstacles remain. As discussed in Chapter 2, China has sought to prevent consideration by the UNSC as an international security dilemma, preferring the more human security-oriented perspective of viewing GCC as a challenge to economic development. This prioritization of human over state security perspectives matches its recent domestic policies for addressing mitigation of GHG emissions.

Chapter 8 on *India and global climate change*, by John Janzekovic, addressed the dual challenges of sustaining economic growth and in mitigating and adapting to numerous environmental challenges in the country. As in many states around the world, India strives for economic development, but with economic growth comes further environmental challenges. The environmental challenges are many. India is today facing a wide range of human insecurities both from the undeveloped socioeconomic structures in the country and the environmental degradation as one of the world's largest emitters. It is seen that decades of economic modernization, including industrialization, urbanization, and growing incomes, have come with a lack of diversity in energy resources and a degraded environment. A large population, widespread poverty, income inequality, a lack of a coherent source of electricity, and a dysfunctional transportation system are all factors that compound a coherent GCC strategy for India. However, Indian authorities acknowledge the anthropogenic nature of climate change and have called for domestic, regional, and global measures to protect human security.

The government has developed ambitious objectives to reduce substantially gas-emissions and to implement renewable and non-fossil power capacities. The objective has been to develop mitigation strategies to develop clean energy systems, restructure industries to become energy efficient and to improve its transportation network, but also to develop adaptation strategies to improve food and water-supply and health and disaster management. However, the government has openly and intensively argued that the developed world, with its wide range of capacities, must contribute with resources to allow a global transformation. The Indian call for common, but differentiated responsibilities has stressed the importance of global initiatives on climate change and that states with greater capacities must assist less developed states to find a path of sustainable development in both economic growth to fight poverty and to enhance green growth. The Indian government has shown great commitment to address the challenges of climate change and environmental degradation, but economic growth is a keystone to battle poverty and underdevelopment. Further economic modernization and a growing population will provide serious challenges to the objective of curbing greenhouse gas emissions, especially where India has the largest growth in coal consumption and is presently the second largest consumer after China. Chapter 2 had noted that India has been one of the leading proponents in the UN system for taking a human security, as opposed to a state security, perspective with GCC. A position that coincides with its concern for economic development.

Four major factors confront Japan's efforts to prioritize GCC as an international commitment in its domestic politics. Darlene Budd in Chapter 9 on *Japan and global climate change* identified these factors as: energy security, political party in power, domestic public opinion and state of the economy. This chapter also addressed the influence of the US on Japan's GCC policy. Japan's GCC policies have been shaped by its post-World War II history of economic modernization and the environmental challenges these developments presented, where domestic politics had to respond to public demands over profound water and air pollution concerns. In recent years Japan has taken on a robust role in advocating for acknowledging and addressing the challenges of GCC in its foreign policy and for providing development assistance. The contributions it has made to the ongoing formation of the UNFCCC regime have been significant, for example hosting the important conference leading to the Kyoto Protocol. Yet, Japan has not been able to escape its long struggle with its geography and its exposure to natural disasters. The consequences of recent nuclear energy disasters have undercut Japan's inclination to provide a leading role in the global community's efforts to deal with climate change. This form of international leadership in the past had resonated in domestic politics. But, Japan's efforts to pursue an international agenda centered on human security for addressing GCC may be undercut by the more state security attributes that stem from a lack of non-carbon-based alternatives to nuclear energy and its continuing concerns over its economic growth. Turning towards concerns of state security may diminish this country's once robust efforts in the UNFCCC regime for addressing GCC.

Chapter 10 by Ana Karaman on *Russia and global climate change*, explored the multinational agreements of this country that have focused on political and economic concerns with GCC including Russia's hesitancy regarding the Paris Agreement. Russia's economic dependency on fossil fuels exports plays a significant role in the caution with which the country approaches the international politics of GCC. The issue of climate politics is, first and foremost, a question of Russia's economic development and this chapter shows that Russia's position with respect to GCC cannot be separated from its state security concerns oriented for economic development. Plans for repopulating regions in its eastern areas illustrate the subordination of climate concerns to national economic needs. The chapter's discussion on the environmental impact of GCC on the Russian natural environment as well as the approach taken by the Climate Doctrine of the Russian Federation shows an equivocation with the needs of economic development attributes of human security. As a result, environmental concerns, though not ignored, are manifestly subordinated to broader political and economic interests of state security. There are profound opportunities as well as challenges to the climate that arise in the development of the warming Arctic region. The complexity of the GCC issues for Russia become paramount in this part of the world, creating a significant challenge for sustainable Arctic cooperation between Russia and adjacent nations not only with respect to state security and defense, but also the rest of region's concerns for climate change. The future cooperation with the West on the issues of GCC will remain linked to Russia's long-term plans for its economic development as well as its state security interests. The challenge for addressing GCC is the unlikely willingness for Russia to separate these interlinked issues.

Based on the different analyses on the efforts of major state powers addressing the challenges of GCC, what are the lessons learned? The last decade or so of international debate has resulted in a larger consensus among state powers that GCC is real, but there are divergent positions on the extent of the global threat to both state and human security. Based on the different analyses presented in this book there are several instructive facets presented as a conclusion for this study.

Observations could begin with the lessons that are more aspirational. This would be the starting point for a hopeful international community that is largely dependent on the actions that need to be taken by the major GHG contributors to the dilemma of GCC. The discussions and negotiations within the UN framework have over the last several years have yielded an important tool for the search for a common set of strategies on GCC among the major and minor powers and the developed and the less developed world. The international community would want to have these major contributing states develop a realization and a commensurate set of measures that will fulfill the paramount needs of a coherent international strategy for addressing GCC. These chapters do indicate that major state powers have increasingly acknowledged the anthropogenic nature of GCC and its challenging consequences on state and human security and have made an urgent call for mitigation and adaptation strategies. A further aspirational lesson is that it appears that most major states have realized, particularly with the strides made by the international community in 2015 and 2016, that collective action is an imperative to deal with climate change and not an alternative. An individual approach to GCC without international collaboration is not only inefficient, but also counter-productive.

Though the notion of state sovereignty is still a hindrance to global efforts on GCC, there are major states that have over the last few years been willing to modify this perspective in order to engage in international efforts that result in speaking with one voice on GCC. The EU and Japan have, in many ways, led international cooperative efforts in addressing GCC through creating the UNFCCC framework and EU member states have fostered attempts to enlarge the agenda of the UNSC. These aspirational lessons are tempered by some practical realities of concerns for state security. Because of its geographic proximity, the EU member states have become the destination of migratory populations and a unified strategy is being developed for addressing the security challenges raised by this phenomenon. Japan is facing the prospect of limited alternatives to providing for energy security, while wanting to escape decades of economic stagnation.

As indicated in several of these chapters, despite growing concerns for environmental degradation caused by human activities, some developing states in the world have seen rapid economic growth in recent decades, creating alarming challenges for the goal of successfully addressing GCC. There is today environmental degradation in these states that might never be restorable, and there are some (the Asia-Pacific region) for which GCC presents a real threat to their very existence. Adapting to these realities, let alone preventing them, will require substantial resources. In this regard, some of the top carbon-emitters in the world have recently come to the conclusion that energy efficiency and clean-energy systems and reduced oil and coal consumption are needed for a strategy to halt the rising levels of emissions in the world. The highly populated nations of China and India have both called for a transformation of their economies seeking a new, more amenable development policy based on concerns for human security. However, the challenge for these states is to continue to alleviate massive societal poverty through modernization at the same time as protecting and promoting the environment. India, without the resources of a China, is more dependent on the industrialized nations for assistance in this transition. Both GCC and poverty need to be addressed through human security strategies on sustainable development.

The very label of "aspiration" connotes an ongoing dilemma that frames the background for these lessons. This is reflective of an unequal sharing of political power between developed and developing countries that has provided initial barriers to a cohesive international strategy, such as the formalized approach of the UNFCCC's Common but Differentiated Responsibilities (CBDR) for determining the various responsibilities and prescribed undertakings for states. Though continued in the mandated goals in the Kyoto Protocol, these have been alleviated by the less hierarchical, self-determined obligations in the Paris Agreement. Major powers that were not subject to the mandates of Kyoto, either by choice (the US) or by design (China), are now parties to the Paris Agreement (though the US has given notice of its intent to leave the Paris Agreement). Yet, less developed states will continue to struggle under the chronic human security demands of trying to improve their economies for their citizens that are being compounded with costly measures of implementing mitigation and adaptation strategies to GCC issues. With the recognition that the challenges of GCC are not limited to concerns of human security, there is presented the concern that just as major powers begin to see the need to take concerted action to address GCC, their attention will be shifted to state and international security. Various military assessments openly view the challenges of GCC as "threat multipliers" by exacerbating the social and environmental conditions that can lead to political instability in already fragile states and thus threaten human security in these developing countries and the state security of these major powers. This focus on state security could deprive necessary resources from needed programs for human security, as well as undercut the strategies based in needs for human security (those of mitigation, adaptation, and capacity building) that will be needed to address GCC.

Each of the major powers seems attuned to their domestic concerns of ensuring national security through their economic development and growth. The perspective is that these concerns, as well as those of national security, are necessarily inversely linked to efforts at addressing GCC (e.gs. Russia and the US). Concern will likely increase as to whether these unilateralist US policies for addressing the challenges of GCC will be adopted by other major powers, such as Russia. Russia has historically been using its position in GCC politics to advance its national and international interests and will unlikely address GCC challenges in isolation from these other political objectives.

The impacts of GCC present challenges to underlying conditions that are required to ensure the quality of livelihood needed for human security. Originated as a concept to complement that of state security, human security was seen as a necessary component for the success of efforts made to ensure state security. The quest for preserving state security in the face of the many challenges arising from the phenomenon of GCC can likely upend the international agenda for preserving human security. The focus of state security is on post hoc events rather than preventive policies for addressing the threats posed by disintegrating societies.

Additionally, GCC is reframing various state and international institutions' understandings of human security. The focus in these chapters has been on the efforts of major powers for addressing GCC. As suggested above in the recapping portion of this chapter, there is some identifiable emphasis in GCC policies of these major powers in relation to human and state security and that in recent years there is observed for some a shift in these policies in this emphasis. Table 11.1 summarizes several of the points made in this concluding chapter to underscore this reframing.

Table 11.1 observes that state security concerns stemming from GCC have contributed to US national defense policy statements. The EU is concerned with the impact of climate migration from neighboring areas. Russia and the US seem

Table 11.1 Trends in human/state security emphasis in GCC policies for major powers

	Emphasis on human security	Direction of any recent shift in emphasis	Emphasis on state security	Comments
US		>> Increased emphasis on state security	X	Current Trump Administration policies that have a connection to GCC will be in the form of defense measures for adaptation. Prior US Administrations have promoted GCC policies in terms of national defense (including Obama) and have generally voiced concern about the trade-off between the economy and environmental protection (with the possible exception of Obama).
EU	X	>> Some Increased emphasis on state security		The EU has long been a promoter of the human security aspects of GCC, though in recent years it is facing a state security concern stemming from forced migration arising from effects of GCC.
China	X	<< Increased emphasis on human security		China has until recently limited its environmental policies due to a presumption of a trade-off between the economy and the environment, it has consistently seen the effects of GCC as raising development issues, though not along the broad terms of sustainable development. Recently, it has voiced support for taking a strong position on combating GCC.
India	X	Continuing emphasis on human security		India has long expressed the position that human security needs should be met as it sees GCC as a challenge to development goals. Policies regarding GCC are limited where India sees a tradeoff between the economy and the environment.
Japan	X	>> Some increased emphasis on state security:		Japan has also been a promoter of the human security aspects of GCC. However, in recent years due to catastrophic events in its nuclear power network, it has seen itself more vulnerable at the international level as it seeks to broaden energy resources to increased levels of fossil fuels.
Russia		Continuing emphasis on state security	X	Russia has voiced support for international GCC initiatives, however it has steadily seen a need to develop fossil fuel resources to support its economic needs that in turn enhance its state security.

Conclusion 247

to consistently emphasize state security, while Japan and the EU are seeing some shift in this direction. The US, Russia, and Japan have in common state security concerns that are oriented for economic development. China appears to have shifted to human security concerns that are focused on economic development, joining India in this emphasis, and demonstrating a new perception of human security in the challenges of GCC. The shifts to emphasis on state security reflect the GCC challenges that have broadened this national security agenda and its consequent discourse of international relations (Hassan et al., 2017).

A reframing of the understandings of human security could draw lessons from the concept of sustainable development. Though its focus is on essential needs of the world's poor, the underlying tenets of sustainable development can be applied to the GCC policies of both developed and developing states for a further reframing of the balance of human and state security. Both the Agenda for Development (UNGA, 1997a, p. 1) and the Programme for the Further Implementation of Agenda 21 (UNGA, 1997b, p. 23) assert: "Economic development, social development and environmental protection are interdependent and mutually reinforcing components of sustainable development." These multiple benefits of sustainable development provide a wider range of benefits than conventional economic development efforts. Sustainable development clearly enhances the prospects of human security as both concepts are based on similar concerns. In its broadest sense, *human security* includes a variety of security-related aspects: economic, nutrition, health, environmental, personal, community, and political (Vajpeyi, 2013). The concept of human security has evolved as a "holistic development-oriented acuity" (Nef, 1999).

A frequently cited definition for sustainable development is from *Our Common Future*, also known as the Brundtland Report, which states in part: "Sustainable development is development that meets the needs of the present without compromising the ability of future generations to meet their own needs" (WCED, 1987). As noted in Chapter 1, the Brundtland Report provided the impetus for the convening of the Earth Summit in Rio de Janeiro five years later, which provided the first international agreement made on climate change (UN Commission on Sustainable Development, 2007). Some observers (e.g., Schenck, 2008; Ruhl, 1998) give voice to a need of not predefining means to achieve the goals of sustainable development (Eisen, 1999). But, others have argued that sustainable development is not about development in the tradition sense; it is about pursuing social, economic, environmental, and security objectives in ways that are mutually reinforcing (Gauna, 2012). Two decades ago Professor Dernbach observed:

> These seemingly disparate issues have been brought together in international efforts at sustainable development in a recognition that countries can neither coherently nor effectively address the environmental impacts of a problem, such as climate change, unless the international community also address its economic and social dimensions.
>
> (Dernbach, 1998, p. 283)

The concerns identified in Chapter 1 regarding the GCC strategy of developing capacity for developing nations evoke this similar breadth of goals. An underlying message in these chapters is that attaining a truly *sustainable* transition that succeeds with the challenges of GCC will necessitate progress across multiple strategies beyond mitigation goals (von Stechow, 2015). Toward this broader reframing a fundamental reformulation of governance at national and international levels is necessitated beyond developing countries. A reframing of human security for the challenges of GCC in the context of sustainable development goals will require integrated decision-making that requires all levels of governments to engage in long-range planning, and to systematize the assessment of economic, environmental, social, and security impacts. The concern for a state security focus for GCC strategy is that it results in fragmented decision-making where these categories are compartmentalized and policy choices are made according to the salient security issue at the time (Tsosie, 2009).

Under a sustainable development perspective there is no essential tradeoff between economic development and environmental protection. Human security should be seen more than security from violent conflict:

> [P]rotecting and improving environmental quality should go hand in hand with economic development and can produce more growth together with social development, peace, and security.
>
> (Halvorssen, 2011, p. 408)

There is a semblance of recognition of the mutually reinforcing components of climate protection and economic development in the 2016 Marrakech Action Proclamation, which asserted that the transition in the economies of party-states needed to fulfil the Paris Agreement's objectives actually provides an opportunity for increased prosperity. This assertion, harkening to the recognition of the components for sustainable development, clearly challenges the perception of a fundamental trade-off between economic development and climate protection held by several of the major powers that success at GCC efforts will only be accomplished with the subordination of their nations' economies.

As 2016 was coming to an end it was becoming clear that the new Presidency in the US would become a critical question mark regarding the ability of state powers to confront the challenges of GCC. Any activity taken by the US, under this Administration, will likely address the effects of GCC from a posture of state security, where adaptation strategies will be enhanced to address perceived threats to its sovereign interests. The evolving unilateralist posture in this government's foreign policy will likely discount the need for capacity building in the developing world. Despite the many promising developments in 2016, the US national elections, which brought into power the Trump Administration, raise anew the need to understand the struggle within the conflicting roles of state and human security for facilitating a successful set of GCC strategies. The state security mindset of the present Trump Administration does not bode well for GCC strategies based on human security that rely upon democratic processes.

With over two decades passing since the UNFCCC entered into force, the science of GCC has not changed. It remains to be seen whether the continuing struggle between the poles of state and human security that underlie the political agendas of major national powers and the efforts by the international community to address GCC will lead to a level of success. The chapters in this book that have examined the GCC agendas of these major nation powers indicate that the resolution of this struggle will largely determine the scope of the success for confronting the challenges of GCC. The efforts of the international community have been frustratingly slow to realize the challenges of GCC and to act on this realization. For almost three decades, the UNFCCC regime has struggled to find consensus for addressing these challenges. With the Paris Agreement entering into force in 2016, it seemed that an important moment had been reached and that an arrangement that emphasized human security could address the strategies of mitigation, adaptation, and capacity building, strategies that the international community must undertake. The details in these efforts will need to be developed by the year 2020 when the Kyoto Protocol expires, albeit in a framework of the conflicting goals between human and state security.

References

Dernbach, John C. (1998). Legal structure and sustainable development: Reflections on comparative law, environmental law, and sustainability. *Widener Law Symposium Journal*, 3, 279–286.

Eisen, Joel B. (1999). Brownfields policies for sustainable cities. *Duke Environmental Law & Policy Forum*, 9, 187–228.

Gauna, Eileen (2012). Environmental law, civil rights and sustainability: Three frameworks for environmental justice. *Journal of Environmental and Sustainability Law*, 19, 34–59.

Halvorssen, Anita M. (2011). International law and sustainable development—Tools for addressing climate change. *Denver Journal of International Law & Policy*, 39, 397–421.

Hassan, Mabroor, Manzoor Khan, Afridi, & Khan, Muhammad Irfan (2017, June). Environmental diplomacy in South Asia: Considering the environmental security, conflict and development nexus. *Geoforum*, 82, 127–130.

Nef, Jorge (1999). *Human security and mutual vulnerability: The global political economy of development and underdevelopment* (2nd edition). Canada: International Research Development Centre.

Ruhl, J.B. (1998). The seven degrees of relevance: Why should real-world environmental attorneys care now about sustainable development policy? *Duke Environmental Law & Policy Forum*, 8, 273–294.

Schenck, Lisa (2008). Climate change "crisis"—Struggling for worldwide collective action. *Colorado Journal of International Environmental Law and Policy*, 19, 319–379.

Tsosie, R. (2009). Climate change, sustainability and globalization: Charting the future of indigenous environmental self-determination. *Environmental & Energy Law & Policy Journal*, 4, 188–255.

UN Commission on Sustainable Development (2007). *Framing sustainable development—The Brundtland Report—20 years on.* Accessed October 7, 2017: www.un.org/esa/sustdev/csd/csd15/media/backgrounder_brundtland.pdf

UNGA (1997a). *Agenda for development, ad hoc open-ended working group of the General Assembly on an agenda for development*, U.N. Doc. *A/RES/51/240*, Accessed October 7, 2017: www.un.org/documents/ga/res/51/ares51-240.htm

UNGA (1997b). *Programme for the further implementation of Agenda 21*, U.N. GAOR, 19th Special Sess., Annex, U.N. Doc. A/RES/S-19/2. P 23 (1997). Accessed October 7, 2017: www.un.org/documents/ga/res/spec/aress19-2.htm

Vajpeyi, Dhirendra K. (2013). Introduction. In Vajpeyi, Dhirendra K. (Ed.) *Climate change, sustainable development, and human security: A comparative analysis*, (pp. 1–25). Lexington Books: Plymouth, UK.

Von Stechow, Christoph (2015). Integrating global *climate change* mitigation goals with other sustainability objectives: A synthesis. *Annual Review of Environment & Resources*, 40, 363–394.

WCED (1987). *Report of the World Commission on environment and development: our common future*. Accessed October 7, 2017: www.un-documents.net/wced-ocf.htm

Index

Action Plan to Arrest Global Warming (Japan 1990) 197–8
adaptation, to the impacts of GCC 16–18, 24–5, 73; in China 156–61; in European Union 134, 140; in India 180–4; in Japan 201–2; in Russia 220–1; in United States 110, 120
adaptive management, strategy for 201
Ad hoc Group on the Berlin Mandate 45
Ad hoc Working Group on The Durban Platform for Enhanced Action (ADP) 177
African Group of Negotiators (AGN) 89
African Union (AU): Commission 89; peace agreement 97; Summit (2007) 89
Agenda 21 action plan 3, 41, 205, 247
air pollution 169, 181, 192, 194, 203; ash and toxic particles 182; in China 153–4; deaths caused by 181–2; due to power plants 182; due to vehicle emissions 182; household 182; impact of GCC on economic growth-related 154; indoor and outdoor 181–2; institutional mechanisms for control of 153; Ministry of Environmental Protection (MEP) 153; ozone pollution 182; particulate matter (PM) 181; sources of 182
air quality 153, 181, 195, 196
Alliance of Small Island States (AOSIS) 88
Annan, Kofi 13
anthrax, outbreak of 59, 217, 230n3
aquaculture 70
Arctic region: ice, melting of 224; marine transportation in 224; militarization of 227–9; oil fields 219, 225; shelf exploration 224; US-Nordic Leaders' Summit 228; war games 227–8
Arrhenius, Svante 1

Asia-Pacific Partnership on Clean Development and Climate (APP) 50–1, 116
Asia-Pacific region, impact of GCC in 67; aquaculture 70; climate-driven conflict 75–6; climatic diversity 69; disaster-prone area 69; displacement and migration 74–5; emissions of greenhouse gases 69; fisheries management 70; food production 68; human health issues 70; human security 71–3; linking to security 70–1; loss of livelihoods, water scarcity, disease 73–4; potable-water availability 68; ratification of Paris Agreement (2015) 79; recent and future human impacts 68–76; regional and national awareness on 76–8; socio-economic challenges related to 76; state security 68, 73; University of Notre Dame Global Adaptation Index (ND-GAIN) on 76; water scarcity 69
Association of Southeast Asian Nations (ASEAN) 238

Baikal Lake 217, 229
Ban, Ki-moon 13, 56, 93, 96; on climate change conflict 98
Al-Bashir, Omar Hassan 97–8
Basic Law for Environmental Pollution (Japan 1967) 195
biomass 184
Brown, Lester 27, 120
bubble economy 209
building human resilience, strategy of 19
Bush, George H.W. 106, 108, 239
Bush, George W. 106, 112–13
Byrd-Hagel Resolution on Climate Change (1997) 110–11

252 Index

Cancun Adaptation Framework (2011) 141
capacity building, for dealing with climate
  change 18–20; alleviation of poverty
  18–19; Chinese policies on 156–61; of
  developing nations 47; in European
  Union 140; good governance 19–20;
  strategy of 21; transferring technologies
  19
cap-and-trade system 200
carbon-based energy, supplies of 151, 158
carbon capture and storage (CCS) 137,
  158, 199
carbon dioxide (CO_2) emissions 69, 158,
  200; in China 150; in European Union
  150; in India 150; objective of
  stabilizing 137; in United States 150
carbon emissions 1, 28, 88, 152, 241; in
  China 150, 158, 160; in India 183; in
  Japan 199; problem of 56; reduction of
  1; trading-system schemes in 16; in
  United States 119
carbon sinks 111, 174, 175, 181
carbon tax 162, 177, 199, 207
carbon trading market 151
Carson, Rachel 194
cash cropping 73
caste-based discrimination 170
challenges of GCC 2, 22, 41
changing weather patterns, adverse effects
  of 13
Chaturvedi, Rajiv 175
chikungunya 70
China National Petroleum Corporation
  (CNPC) 226
China's GCC policies: Air Pollution
  Prevention and Control Law 153; Air
  Quality Standard (1996) 157; carbon
  emissions per capita 150; on challenges
  to address GCC 161–4; CO_2 emissions
  150; on economic and human security
  151–6; on energy demand and energy
  security 151; Energy Development
  Strategy Action Plan 160; on energy
  efficiency 151–2; Environmental Impact
  Assessment (2003) 157; on
  environmental promotion and protection
  165; greenhouse gas emissions 150,
  157; on implementation of renewable
  energy 164; on industrialization and
  economic growth 151; Kyoto Protocol,
  ratification of 150, 157; Law on
  Environmental Impact Assessment
  (2003) 157; Law on Prevention and
  Control of Air Pollution (1995) 157; to

lower carbon-based energy use 158; on
  mitigation, adaption, and capacity
  building 156–61; National Climate
  Change Programme 157–8, 160;
  National Development and Reform
  Commission (NDRC) 162; National
  Five-Year Plan on 158–9; National
  Leading Group for Addressing Climate
  Change 162; National Leading Group
  on Energy Saving and Pollution
  Reduction 162; National Plan for
  Tackling Climate Change 160; National
  Strategy for Climate Adaption 160; and
  as one of the top four emitting nations
  150; and perceptions on GCC 151–6;
  Renewable Energy Law (2005) 157;
  State Electricity Regulatory
  Commission (SERC) 157
China–US climate change agreement
  (2015) 118
Chinese Communist Party (CCCP) 150–1,
  163, 241
Chisso Minamata power plant (Japan) 194
chlorofluorocarbons (CFCs) 194, 196–7
Churkin, Vitaly 55
civil society organizations 94
Clean Development Mechanisms (CDMs)
  177
clean energy 161, 192, 244; generation of
  180; investments in 114; technologies
  for 109, 114, 158
clean technology 183, 241
Climate Actions Progress Report (EU
  2015) 141, 240
Climate and Clean Air Coalition 141
climate change 13, 15; human-caused 29
Climate Change Knowledge Mission
  (India) 173
"climate-proofing" activities 134
climate-resilient crops, development of
  172
Climate Science Research Fund (India)
  173
climate security 28, 135
climate-security nexus, in Africa: African
  Union (AU) Summit (2007) 89; armed
  conflicts and 87; changes and challenges
  associated with 87–92; Darfur conflict
  96–9; desertification of Sahara and
  Sahel regions 86; Earth Summit (1992)
  88; economic growth and 88; First
  Regional African Ministerial
  Preparatory Conference (1991) 88; food
  shortages 90; impact on African

Index   253

societies 90; melting of snow on Mt. Kenya and Mt. Kilimanjaro 86; "One Continent, One Voice" strategy 89; political rights and civil liberties 94; in poorly functional states 92–6; in Sub-Saharan Africa 87, 91

Climate Summit in New York (2014) 136

climatic shift, consequences of 9

Clinton, Bill 106, 110, 113

Clinton, Hillary 112

coal-burning technologies 183

coal consumption 161, 182, 242, 244

coal-fired power stations 153, 158, 182–3

Coal India Ltd (CIL) 182, 183

coal mines 182; open-cast mining 182

coal power plants 183, 208

coal production, method of 182, 184, 241

coal supply and demand chains 182

coastal flooding 73, 133

coastal megacities 67, 237

coastal regions, impact of GCC on 154

Cohesion Fund 139

Cold War 53, 228

common agricultural policy (CAP), European Union 139

common but differentiated responsibilities (CBDR) 176, 178–80

common heritage of humankind, notion of 178

Conference of the Parties (COP) 43, 45, 110, 179, 206; 22nd session of 51; Ad hoc Group on the Berlin Mandate 45; in Berlin 223; in Copenhagen 46–7, 118, 174; in Doha 47; human rights obligations 50; in Lima 174; in Nairobi 90; in Paris 51; in Warsaw 174

conflicts, climate-driven: in Africa 87, 92; in Asia-Pacific region 75–6; Ban Ki-Moon's statement on 98; Darfur civil war 96–9; due to increase in temperature 93; inter-state 92; pastoralists–farmers conflict 93; Syrian conflict 9–10

Conservation Law (Japan 1998) 198

Convention on Biological Diversity 3

Convention to Combat Desertification 91

"Cool Earth 50" initiative (Japan) 198, 207

Cool Earth Partnership 207

Coordinating Committee on the Ozone Layer (CCOL) 196

COP15 meeting 207

Copenhagen Accord (2009) 136

Copenhagen School of Security Studies 6, 27

Council of Europe 135

crime against humanity 58, 98

crop yields, impact of climate change on 134

cross-border water, funding of 134

cyber attacks 200

cyclone 4, 69, 72; Nargis 57, 74

dams 229; to control floods 203; cross-border 71

Darfur civil war 96–9; Arabs and other non-Arab tribes 99; causes of 98–9; diplomatic mediated talks 97; discovery of gold 98; Doha Document for Peace (2011) 97; due to climate change 98; Fur and Zaghawa tribes 99; Justice and Equality Movement (JEM) 97, 99; Liberation and Justice Movement (LJM) 97; referendum for independence of South Sudan 98; Sudan Liberation Movement (SLM) 97, 99; UN/AU (UNAMID) peacekeeping forces 98; use of chemical weapons against civilians 98

Data Integration and Analysis System (DIAS) 204

deforestation 169, 173; in India 183

dengue fever 70

Deng, Xiao Ping 151

de Oliveira, Puppim 201

desertification 90–1, 93–4, 134, 154–5, 235

Directorate-General for Climate Actions (European Union) 138

disaster evacuation systems 203

disaster insurance, use of 134

disaster management 175, 242

disaster resilient societies 203

Disaster Risk Reduction policy (European Union) 141, 201–2

disease outbreaks: anthrax 59, 230n3; in Asia-Pacific countries 73; chikungunya 70; dengue fever 70; Ebola 59–60; Minamata disease 194

Doha Amendment (2012) 46–7, 136

Doha Document for Peace (2011) 97

Donskoy, Sergey 220

Downie, C. 111

droughts 4, 9, 13, 69, 90–1, 98, 110, 114, 116, 133, 154, 201, 218, 220, 235, 238

Earth Day 50, 110

Earth Summit (1992), Rio de Janeiro 3, 41, 45, 88, 108, 121, 205, 239, 247

Ebola outbreak, in West Africa 59–60

254   Index

ecological civilization 152, 159, 241;
  strategy of 241
economic–environmental nexus 160
economic inequality 151
economic security: in China 151–6; and
  climate change 155; for developed
  countries 8
Economic Support Fund 117
Economy in Transition (EIT) 222
"eco-office" prefecture 200
eco-point initiative 200
electricity generation 183; by using nuclear
  power 183
electric power transmission 181
electric vehicles 151
emission standards: for motor vehicles
  199; for power stations 199
Emissions Trading System (ETS) 137,
  144, 199
energy conservation 161, 180, 198
Energy Conservation Building Code 172
energy-consuming industries 172
energy consumption 88, 137, 146, 152,
  172, 200
energy demand 170, 182, 184, 241; in
  China 150–1; in India 169
energy efficiency 152, 172, 174, 180–1,
  198, 206, 244; in buildings 138
energy-saving innovations 109
energy security 77, 113, 122–3, 151, 164,
  192–3, 198, 208, 209, 242, 244
environmental degradation 10–11, 14, 96,
  99, 153, 158, 164, 178, 192, 194, 241,
  242, 244; economic costs for 152;
  impact on well-being of humans 5
environmental destruction 58
environmental hazards, consequences of
  58
Environmental Modification Convention
  58
environmental pollution 152; air pollution
  192, 194; Basic Law for Environmental
  Pollution (Japan 1967) 195; impact on
  health 152; water pollution 194
environmental protection 13, 41, 52, 88,
  108, 120–1, 150, 163–4, 192, 194–5,
  197, 205, 238, 240, 247–8
Environmental Protection Agency (EPA),
  US 29, 108, 110–11, 116, 119–21, 205
environmental security 28, 136; concept of
  13, 20; definition of 14; management of
  26; threats to 14
environment-society interactions 113
Europe Aid 141

European Actions Service 141
European Climate Change Programme
  (ECCP) 132, 240
European Commission (EC) 132, 134, 141,
  142, 240; discussions on climate change
  with member states 136; Environmental
  Council Ministers' meetings 136; High
  Representative of 135; objective of
  stabilizing CO_2 emissions 137; "Shared
  Vision, Common Actions: A Stronger
  Europe" strategy 138; White Paper
  report 134, 138
European Council 10
European Environmental Agency (EEA)
  140, 141
European Parliament 142
European Regional Development Fund 139
European Security Strategy 10
European Union (EU) 26, 177, 179;
  adaptation strategy to climate change
  134; Climate Actions Progress Report
  (2015) 141, 240; climate and energy
  package to reduce greenhouse gas
  emissions 137; "climate-proofing"
  activities 134; common agricultural
  policy (CAP) 139; common fishery
  policy 139; common market policies
  131, 137; differentiated burden sharing
  144; dimensions of mainstreaming
  adaptation 139; Directorate-General for
  Climate Actions 138; Disaster Risk
  Reduction 141; emission trading system
  144; European Climate Change
  Programme (ECCP) 132, 240; on GCC
  as a human and state security threat
  132–6; Global Strategy on GCC 132,
  135, 140, 240; Horizon Program 140; on
  impact of climate change 134; Kyoto
  Protocol, ratification of 132, 136; LIFE-
  Work Program 140; maritime action
  plan 139; official foreign and security
  policy strategy 136; Paris Agreement,
  ratification of 132; planning for weather-
  related disasters 134; policies and
  decisions 136–41; program for research
  and innovation 139; on reduction of
  GHG emissions 111; relation to the UN
  136–41; role in combatting GCC 136;
  shared competence area with member
  states 137; strategies on mitigation,
  adaptation, and capacity building 140;
  Strategy on Adaptation to Climate
  Change 138; sustainable sea-related
  activities 139; use of renewable energy

Index   255

138; on weather-related actions to prevent disasters 134; willingness and ability to act on GCC 141–5
export-oriented economies 111
extinction, risk of 4
Exxon Mobil 24, 225–6

farmlands, pollution of 154
fear, freedom of 21
Federal Emergency Management Agency (FEMA), US 109, 122
fisheries management 70
floods 69; management of 134; in Russia 216–17
food: poverty 90; production 1, 7–8, 68, 93, 205; security 13, 52, 74, 77, 91, 93, 141, 173; shortages 9, 90
forest fires, risk of 134, 139, 217, 218, 221
Forest Principles 41
fossil-based energy 173
fossil fuels 16, 88, 184; consumption of 24; production of 223; reserves 25
Fragile State Index 95
Freedom House 94, 100n1
fuel consumption 152, 159; regulations on 151
Fukushima Daiichi Nuclear Power Plant, Japan 208
Fukushima nuclear disaster 193, 208
Fund for Peace 100n2

Ganges–Brahmaputra–Meghna delta 71, 75
Gazprom 225
Geneva Convention 58
genocide 9, 96–8
geo-engineering 24
Ghude, Sachin 181
Global Approach to Migration and Mobility 141
Global Change Research Program, US 120–1
global climate change (GCC): challenges to human society 236; consequences of 4–5, 15; cost-benefit analysis of 7; environmental impacts of 4, 12; human impacts of 1–2; human security and 12–15; integrated decision-making 248; international recognition of 2–4; international strategies to counter *see* strategies to counter GCC; relationship with conflict 21; and return to state security 27–8; securitization of *see* securitization of GCC; validity of 4
Global Climate Change Alliance 141

Global Climate Change Initiative (GCCI) 117; Congressional Research Service's (CRS) report on 118
global efforts on GCC 244
Global Environment Facility 117
global financial crisis (2007–2008) 210
global inequality, politics of 47
global solar alliance 175
global warming 4, 15, 98, 113, 158, 178, 200, 202, 220; countermeasures for 198–9; Global Warming Law (Japan 1997) 198–9, 206; impact on indigenous communities 217; prevention measures 203
Global Warming Law (Japan 1998) 198–9, 206
Global Water Partnership 8
good governance policies, for combating climate change 19–20
Great Recession 117
Green Climate Fund 17, 117, 118, 177
green energy 159
green growth 152, 241, 242
greenhouse gas (GHG) emission 13, 15, 43, 69, 142, 170, 174, 205, 239; in China 150, 157; climate and energy package to reduce 137; contribution of oil and coal in 151; control of 198; emission-trading program 206; European Union (EU) goal of reducing 111, 137; India's strategy to curb 176; Kyoto Protocol for reduction of 207; mitigation strategies for 181; reduction of 205, 206; targets to limit 157; US's plan to curb 110
Green India Mission 172, 173
greening security 135
Greenpeace 229
gross domestic product (GDP) 67, 217, 237
ground-water salinization 69
Group of 77 and China (G77/China) 88–9
Group on Earth Observations (GEO) 204

Hamilton, Clive 24
Hansen, James 48
Hatoyama Initiative 207
hazard impacts, freedom from 21
health expenditure, public and private 182
health management 242
high-speed trains 151
Himalaya-Hindu Kush (HKH) glaciers: human vulnerability due to loss of 72; melting of 71; shrinkage and loss of 72

256 Index

Himalayan Eco-System Mission (India) 172, 173
Horizon Program 140
Huai River 153
humanitarian intervention, concept of 56
human-nature relationships 201
human security 31, 52, 145, 247; in Asia-Pacific region 71–3; challenges caused by climate change 236; in China 151–6; concept of 12, 45, 55; definition of 13; deprivation of immediate basic needs 72; and economic development 243; and erosion of livelihood assets 72; and global climate change (GCC) 12–15; IPCC report on 93; and sustainable development 49; threats to 58; UNFCCC concerns on 44–5
hybrid vehicles 151
hydro power 160, 183
hydropower plants 229

ice-free navigation 224
India's GCC policies: on air pollution 181–2; Climate Change Knowledge Mission 173; Climate Science Research Fund 173; on coal consumption 182; commitment to climate action 174; common but differentiated responsibilities (CBDR) 178–80; on community-based management of ecosystems 172; demand for thermal coal and 182; on domestic mitigation and adaption approaches 180–4; Energy Conservation Building Code 172; engagement at the UNFCCC 174; Enhanced Energy Efficiency Mission 172; on environmental mitigation and adaptation 184; on global climate change threat 170–4; Green India Mission 172, 173; Himalayan Eco-System Mission 172, 173; INDC initiatives 177; Ministry of Finance 175; mitigation and adaptation strategies 174; National Action Plan on Climate Change (NAPCC) 171; National Adaptation Fund for Climate Change (NAFCC) 177; National Coal Distribution Policy (NCDP) 183; National Wind Energy Mission 172; on nuclear power 183; Prime Minister's Council on Climate Change 171–2, 173; public and private health expenditure 182; public–private partnerships 169; on reforestation 172; renewable energy

capacity 176; Solar Mission 173; strategy to curb greenhouse gas emissions (GHG) 176; Sustainable Agriculture Mission 172; Sustainable Habitat Mission 172; and United Nations 174–8; Water Mission 173
industrial fluorinated gases, use of 132
information technology 114
Intended Nationally Determined Contributions (INDCs) 16, 47, 174, 177
Intergovernmental Panel on Climate Change (IPCC) 3, 93, 117, 137; Fourth Assessment Report (2007) 7; on levels of emissions and their societal impact 157; Third Assessment Report 158; UNGA endorsement of 3
International Agency for Solar Policy & Application (INSPA) 175
International Centre for Environmental Management (ICEM) 18
International Civil Aviation Organization 51
international climate governance 42
International Criminal Court (ICC) 97, 98
International Energy Agency 141
International Law Commission (ILC) 57
inter-state conflicts 92
inter-state relations 68
Irrawaddy Delta (Myanmar) 74
ISIS 200

Jaitley, Arun 173, 183
Japan–Caribbean Climate Change project 203
Japanese International Cooperation Agency (JICA) 202, 203
Japan's GCC policies 242; Action Plan to Arrest Global Warming (1990) 197–8; actions at UN environmental GCC conferences 205; actions on climate change 204; adaptation efforts 201–2; air and water pollution 194; air and water quality 196; approach to the ban on CFCs 197; approach within the efforts of UN to the threats of GCC 204–8; Basic Guideline for Mitigation of Climate Change (1999) 206; Basic Law for Environmental Pollution (1967) 195; capacity building efforts 202–4; carbon tax 207; CFC/ozone issue 194–5; Chisso Minamata power plant 194; coal and fossil fuel lobbies 208; Conservation Law (1998) 198; "Cool Earth 50" initiative 198, 207;

countermeasures for global warming 198–9; "Disaster Risk Reduction" workshops 201–2; economic industrialization "miracle" and 192; Edo period (1603–1868) 201; emission trading 207; energy security plan 192; environmental policy and regulation 192; environmental protection efforts 192; Fukushima Daiichi Nuclear Power Plant 208; Fukushima nuclear disaster 193, 208; Global Warming Law 198–9, 206; good governance 204; Hatoyama Initiative 207; ISD policy framework 202; *kogai* (public hazard) litigation 195; Kyoto Initiative 202; Liberal Democratic Party (LDP) 192, 195; limiting factors on capacities to deal with GCC 208–10; Low Carbon City Promotion Act (2012) 199; Mie Prefecture 199; Minamata disease 194, 205; Ministry of Health and Welfare 195; *mitameshi* (adaptive management strategy) 201, 204; mitigation strategy 195–7; nuclear power plants 208; Nuclear Regulation Authority (NRA) 193; opposition to nuclear power 209; overseas direct assistance (ODA) 201–3; and perception of the threat of GCC 193–5; politics of 193; "pollution-andresponse" approach 195; poverty alleviation efforts 202–3; on rational use of energy 198; response to the threat of GCC 197–201; rice varieties 201; Sendai Framework for Disaster Risk Reduction 2015–2030 202; signing of Paris Agreement 208; Tax Reform Act (2012) 199; on technology transfer 203–4; Tokaimura accident (1999) 192; water reclamation and irrigation issues 201

Javadekar, Prakash 176
JUSCANZ group 223
Justice and Equality Movement (JEM) 97

Kerry, John 51, 115
Kigali Amendment (2016) 51
Kiichi, Miyazawa 206
King, David 10
kogai (public hazard) litigation 194–5
Kosi River 72
Kumar, Rajiv 182
Kyoto Protocol (1997) 15, 42, 45–6, 48, 54, 108, 110–11, 117, 121, 141, 145, 160, 199, 202, 207–8, 222, 239–40, 249; Chinese ratification of 150, 157; Doha Amendment (2012) 46–7; European Union ratification of 132, 136; First Commitment Period (2008–2012) 46; goal of 45, 111, 244; implementation of 46; Russian ratification of 222; Second Commitment Period (2012–2020) 46; withdrawal of the US from 207, 222

land degradation 13, 90–1, 140, 169, 170
land filling 132
land management 111
land temperature, rise in 134
Least Developed Countries (LDCs) 67, 76, 88
life expectancy 23, 153, 182
LIFE-Work Program 140
Li, Keqiang 150
Lisbon Treaty (2007) 137, 142
Liu, Zhenmin 54, 155, 160
livelihoods, loss of 73–4
Low Carbon City Promotion Act (Japan 2012) 199
Low Elevation Coastal Zone (LECZ) 67, 69, 70, 78, 237

Maastricht Treaty 137
Major Economies Forum on Energy and Climate 140
malnutrition 9, 90
marine protected areas, establishment of 70
Marrakech Action Proclamation (2016) 52, 60, 248
mass atrocity crimes, risk of 56–9, 61
Mekong Delta (Vietnam) 17, 74
methane (CH_4) gas 132, 141, 158, 217
migrations and displacement, climate-induced 245; in Asia-Pacific region 74–5; in China 154; in Sub-Saharan Africa 92; Syrian refugee crisis 146
militarization: of GCC challenges 27; of society 11
military insurgencies 95
military operations, for disaster relief 26
Millennium Development Goals (MDGs) 49
Millennium Summit of the UN (2000) 49
Minamata mercury-poisoning disaster 194, 205
mitameshi, concept of 201, 204
mitigation strategies, for combating climate change 15–16, 24–5; in China 156–61; commitments of UNFCCC on

258   *Index*

mitigation strategies *continued*
44; EU Commission on 240; European
Union on 140; in India 175, 180–4; in
Japan 195–7; in Russia 220–1; in United
States 110–13; UNSC resolution on 54
Modi, Narendra 174–6, 181
Montreal Protocol 51, 106
mosquito-borne viral disease 70, 208
much ado about nothing, notion of 136

Nairobi Work Programme (2005) 141
Narang, Amit 179–80
National Adaptation Fund for Climate
Change (NAFCC), India 177
National Clean Energy Fund (NCEF),
India 177
National Climate Change Programme
(2007), China 157–8
National Coal Distribution Policy (NCDP),
India 183
National Wind Energy Mission (India) 172
natural disasters 57; preparedness for 118;
in Russia 220; strategies to reduce loss
due to 220; weather-related 21–2
natural resource degradation 94, 152
nitrous oxide (N_2O) 132, 158, 172
Noboru, Takeshita 197
non-fossil energy, policies on 159–61, 164
Non-Governmental Organizations (NGOs)
87, 200
North Atlantic Treaty Organization
(NATO): Arctic Challenge 228; Arctic
strategy 228; Cold Response exercise
227; Warsaw NATO Summit (2016)
228
Northern Sea Route (NSR):
commercialization of 224; economic
benefits for Russia 224;
internationalization of 224; utilization
for maritime export 224
North–South divide 180
nuclear energy 160, 183, 192–3, 242
nuclear power plants 199, 208; Fukushima
Daiichi Nuclear Power Plant 208–9;
Japanese opposition to 209

Obama, Barack 108, 113–14, 116–20
ocean acidification, risk of 4, 69
ocean temperature, rise of 4
offshore energy technology 225
oil consumption 244
oil-for-goods program 223
oil shocks of 1970s 192
"One Continent, One Voice" strategy 89

Organization for Economic Co-operation
and Development (OECD) 22, 141
Organization of Petroleum Exporting
Countries (OPEC) 88, 223
Orkhon River 229
Ovalau Island (Fiji) 72
overseas direct assistance (ODA) 201, 202
Oxfam 17
ozone layer, depletion of 194
ozone pollution 182

Pacific Island countries 53, 238
Panama canal 224
pandemics: GCC-induced 59; HIV/AIDS
59; risk to stability and security 59;
threats of 58–60; as threat to
international peace and security 59
Paris Climate Agreement (2015) 1, 3,
15–16, 18, 42, 47, 54, 118, 142, 178,
207, 236–7; adaptation policies 48–9;
Article 4(2) of 47; Article 28 of 52;
capacity building policies 48–9;
consensus before and after 50–2;
contribution of China in 77; European
Union ratification of 132; on GHG
mitigation 47–8; goal of 3, 48; human
rights obligations 50; Japanese
ratification of 208; Kigali Amendment
(2016) 51; loss and damage policies
48–9; mitigation policies 48–9;
objectives of 52; ratification by Asia-
Pacific countries 79; recent
developments in 19; Russian position on
223; US decision to exit from 119
particulate matter (PM) 181; hazardous
particulate matter 153; Respirable
Suspended Particulate Matter (RSPM)
182
pastoral nomadism 98
permafrost, degradation of 59, 133–4,
216–18, 230n3
potable-water availability 68
poverty: alleviation of 18, 176, 202–3,
236, 244; in Asia-Pacific region 76;
food poverty 90; poverty-environment
trap 73; reduction 88; societal 244; in
Sub-Saharan Africa 92; urban poverty
92
power energy mix, diversification of 181
power plants: coal-fired 158, 182–3, 241;
pollution caused by 182
Progress Report on the Implementation of
Climate Doctrine (2014) 220
Pruitt, Scott 108

Index 259

public awareness, of GCC 25
public–private partnerships 169, 172

Quadrennial Defense Review (2014), US 10, 12
quality of life 88, 154, 245

R2P principles: applicability of 57; and GCC strategies 56–7; limitations of 58; obligations of 56; of response 57–8; scope of 57
rainfall: limited 91; rainstorms 91
reforestation 172
Reform Treaty 137
renewable energy: deployment of 164, 177; European Union use of 138; hydro power 160; national targets for 137; nuclear power 160; for reducing greenhouse gas emissions 137; solar energy 160; technologies 29, 176; wind power 160
Respirable Suspended Particulate Matter (RSPM) 182
Rio Declaration on Environment and Development (1992) 41, 178–9, 205
river contamination 169
river flows, impact of climate change on 134
Russia's GCC policies: access to Arctic oil 219; annexation of Crimea 228; Arctic development 224–9; Arctic infrastructure projects 224; Arctic Joint Strategic Command 228; Arctic offshore oil fields 225; Baikal Lake 217; Climate Doctrine and 216, 218–20, 243; death due to summer heat 217; direct and indirect consequences 217; economic dependency on fossil fuels 243; floods 216–17; freshwater supply 217; global warming 217; grain trade 220; impact of sanctions 225–6; Integrated Development Plan for the Northern Sea Route 224; leveraging of international framework 229; militarization of the Arctic 227–9; mitigation and adaptation measures 220–1; Northern Fleet 227–8; Northern sea route and exports 224–5; oil and gas dependency 222–3; oil and gas exports 216, 223; oil-for-goods program with Iran 223; Paris Climate Agreement (2015) 223; permafrost covering 216, 217; Progress Report on the Implementation of Climate Doctrine (2014) 220; ratification of UNFCCC 222; response to impacts on domestic level 218–22; response to impacts on international level 222–9; rise in temperature 216; on Russian population 216–17; specific Russian regions 221–2; Transneft-Arctic Project 224; VOSTOKcoal Project 224; Yamal Liquefied Natural Gas (LNG) plant 224
Ryuichi, Yoneyama 209

Sahara and Sahel regions, desertification of 86
Schelling, Thomas C. 18
sea levels, rise in 9, 68–9, 71–2, 116, 154, 237; displacement and migration due to 74–5
sea temperature, rise in 134
securitization of GCC 6–7, 21; militarization issues 25–7; mitigation/adaptation 24–5; state-centric 5–6, 8–12; threats to 2–4, 7–15
security-environmental nexus 236
security risks, climate-related 116, 238
Selenga (Shuren) River 229
Sendai Framework for Disaster Risk Reduction 2015–2030 (Japan) 202
Serageldin, Ismail 8
"Shared Vision, Common Actions: A Stronger Europe" strategy 138
Shigeru, Chubachi 194
Shinzo, Abe 198, 207–9
Singh, Manmohan 171
Small Island Developing States (SIDS) 203
social inequalities 154
soil degradation 91
solar energy 160, 173, 181
solar industry, development of 177
Solar Mission (India) 173
Stand-by Emergency Credit for Urgent Recovery (SECURE) program 203
State Electricity Regulatory Commission (SERC), China 157
state powers, on global climate change 235, 236
state security 58; in Asia-Pacific region 68, 73; concept of 12, 236; GCC and the return to 27–8; and sustainable development 49; UNFCCC concerns on 44–5
state sovereignty, notion of 5, 89, 156, 204, 235–7, 244
Stern Review on the Economics of Climate Change 7

260 *Index*

Stockholm Declaration (1972) 2, 41, 205
storm surges 71
Strategic Climate Fund 117
strategies to counter GCC 15–20;
  effectiveness of 25; first strategy
  (mitigation) 15–16; impact of
  securitization 20–2; implementation of
  20–8; and major powers 22–7; second
  strategy (adaptation) 16–18; third
  strategy (capacity building) 18–20
Subramanian, Arvind 173
Sub-Saharan Africa 87, 91; agricultural
  economies in 93; conflicts between
  pastoralists and farmers 93; Darfur civil
  war 96–9
Sudan conflict 11
Sudan Liberation Movement (SLM) 97
Suez canal 224
Sundarbans mangrove forest 71
sustainable development 19, 41, 52, 142,
  247–8; in China 77; human security and
  49; state security and 49
Sustainable Development Goals (SDGs)
  49, 179, 202
Syrian conflict, impact of climate change
  on 9–10
Syrian refugee crisis 146

Tax Reform Act (Japan 2012) 199
technology transfers 202, 203–4; for
  combating climate change 19
tectonic subsidence 72
Tillerson, Rex 24, 119
Tokaimura accident (Japan 1999) 192
Tokyo Metropolitan Government (TMG)
  198, 200
Transneft-Arctic Project (Russia) 224
Trump, Donald 116–20, 210
Tsuruoka, Koji 207

ultraviolet rays 194
UN Charter 53, 61, 180
UN Commission on Sustainable
  Development 41, 247
UNESCO world heritage site 217
United Nations Conference on Climate
  Change 156
United Nations Conference on
  Environment and Development
  (UNCED) 205; First Regional African
  Ministerial Preparatory Conference
  (1991) 88
United Nations Conference on Human
  Environment (UNCHE) 2, 156, 205

United Nations Convention on the Law of
  the Sea (UNCLO) 227
United Nations Development Programme
  (UNDP) 2, 45; Human Development
  Report 12
United Nations Environment Programme
  (UNEP) 2, 205; Adaptation Gap report
  17; Emission Gap Report 4; Working
  Group 194
United Nations Framework Convention on
  Climate Change (UNFCCC) 3, 15–17,
  41, 106, 121, 137, 141, 157, 178, 204,
  205, 210, 236, 249; China's engagement
  at 150, 158; Common but Differentiated
  Responsibilities (CBDR) 244;
  Conference of the Parties (COP) 179;
  India's engagement at 174; Marrakech
  Action Proclamation (2016) 52;
  mitigation, adaptation, and capacity
  building 44–5; objectives and
  obligations of 43–4; ratification by
  Russia 222; security and accession
  49–50; on security and GCC 42–52;
  subsequent developments in reducing
  GHG emissions 45–50; Technology
  Mechanism of 19
United Nations General Assembly
  (UNGA) 2, 41; adoption of the SDGs by
  50; endorsement of IPCC 3
United Nations High Commissioner for
  Refugees (UNHCR) 74
United States Agency for International
  Development (USAID) 117
United States (US), GCC policies of 106;
  administrations on GCC and security
  113–16; Byrd-Hagel Resolution on
  Climate Change (1997) 110–11; Clean
  Power Act 121; Clean Power Plan 116,
  119; on clean technologies 109; Climate
  Change Action Plan 110; Climate
  Change Adaptation Plans 120; on
  climate-related security risks 116;
  Council of Economic Advisors (CEA)
  111; Department of Homeland Security
  109; Economic Support Fund 117; effort
  to cut GHG emissions 112;
  Environmental Protection Agency
  (EPA) 29, 108, 110–11, 116, 119–21,
  205; Federal Clean Air Act 120; Federal
  Emergency Management Agency
  (FEMA) 109; on fossil fuel production
  123; Global Change Research Program
  120; on International Leadership 118;
  mitigation strategies 110–13; on

National Security 118; on Natural Disaster Preparedness 118; presidential administrations' perceptions on climate change 107–10; as second largest emitter 106; transition from Barack Obama to Donald Trump 116–20; Waxman–Markey Bill (2009) 116
universality, principle of 180
University of Notre Dame Global Adaptation Index (ND-GAIN) 68, 76
UN Millennium Declaration 180
UN Security Council (UNSC) 7, 30, 77, 93; Arria-Formula meetings 54; Chapter VII of 53–4, 58–9; Charter to maintain international peace and security 53–5; conflict prevention capacities 55; on Darfur civil war 97; GCC and pandemics 58–60; GCC and R2P principles 55–8; on GCC and security 52–60; Meeting on Climate Change (2007) 155; Presidential Statement on adverse effects of GCC 55; Resolution 794, 58; Resolution 1373 53; Resolution 1540 53, 54; Resolution 1625 55; Resolution 2177 59; resolution on climate change mitigation 54; on risk of armed conflict 56; role in dealing with GCC 59; on specific effects of a GCC-induced threat 60
UN World Summit Report (2005) 56
urban planning 172
urban poverty 92
US Global Change Research Program (USGCRP 2016) 120–1
US Institute of Peace 11
US–Japan relationship 193, 210

Vardhan, Harsh 170
vector-borne diseases 4, 59
vehicle emissions, pollution caused by 120, 182
vehicle fuel economy 172
Venkataraman, Chanda 182
venture capital funds 173
Vienna Convention 194
VOSTOKcoal Project (Russia) 224

Wang, Henry 181

want, freedom from 21
war crimes 58, 97, 98
war on climate change 136
Warsaw International Mechanism for Loss and Damage Associated with Climate Change Impacts 49
Warsaw NATO Summit (2016) 228
waste generation 132
waste management systems 169, 184
water-borne diseases 4
water cycles 204
Water Mission (India) 173
water pollution 154, 162, 194
water quality 196
water-related disasters: associated with climate change 204; evacuation and sanitation strategies for 202; floods 69; in Russia 216–17; Sendai Framework for Disaster Risk Reduction 2015–2030 202
water resource management 154, 204
water scarcity 69, 73–4, 93; in China 154
water security 173
water tables 169
Waxman–Markey Bill (2009) 116
weather-related disasters, planning for 22, 57, 134, 139
Wen, Jiabao 152
wind farms 172, 181, 183
wind power 160, 173
Working Group on Climate Change 41
World Bank 8, 17, 23, 41, 60, 86, 95, 117, 152
World Conference on Changing Atmosphere (1988) 197
World Health Organization (WHO) 60, 153, 181
World Meteorological Organization 2, 41
World Summit on Sustainable Development 157
World Trade Organization (WTO) 222

Xi, Jinping 156

Yamal Liquefied Natural Gas (LNG) plant (Russia) 224
Yangtze River Delta 154
Yasuo, Fukuda 198, 207, 210n1

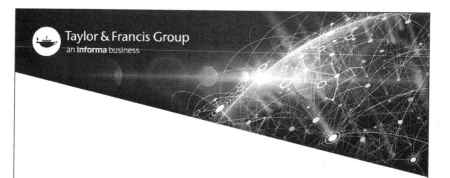

Taylor & Francis eBooks

www.taylorfrancis.com

A single destination for eBooks from Taylor & Francis with increased functionality and an improved user experience to meet the needs of our customers.

90,000+ eBooks of award-winning academic content in Humanities, Social Science, Science, Technology, Engineering, and Medical written by a global network of editors and authors.

TAYLOR & FRANCIS EBOOKS OFFERS:

A streamlined experience for our library customers

A single point of discovery for all of our eBook content

Improved search and discovery of content at both book and chapter level

REQUEST A FREE TRIAL
support@taylorfrancis.com